Economic Transformation for Poverty Reduction in Africa

This book is an edited volume which contains empirical studies on determinants of poverty and its reduction in Africa. It looks at multidimensional measures of poverty, production and productivity-related factors, policies influencing poverty and random, hazardous but preventive factors influencing poverty levels and their reduction.

The book argues that we need to account for different dimensions of poverty, when it is measured and classified, and for identifying the determinants of poverty and factors reducing poverty.

The studies in the volume provide readers with a comprehensive picture of the state of poverty, its measurement, causal factors and efficient policies and practices in poverty reduction on the African continent as a whole and also in selected countries.

Almas Heshmati is Professor of Economics at Sogang University, South Korea and at Jönköping International Business School, Jönköping University.

Routledge Studies in Development Economics

For a complete list of titles in this series, please visit www.routledge.com/series/SE0266

129 **Structural Transformation and Economic Development**
Cross regional analysis of industrialization and urbanization
Banji Oyelaran-Oyeyinka and Kaushalesh Lal

130 **The Theory and Practice of Microcredit**
Wahiduddin Mahmud and S. R. Osmani

131 **The Economics of Child Labour in the Era of Globalization**
Policy issues
Sarbajit Chaudhuri and Jayanta Kumar Dwibedi

130 **International Taxation and the Extractive Industries**
Resources without Borders
Edited by Philip Daniel, Michael Keen, Artur Świstak and Victor Thuronyi

131 **Fiscal Policy and the Natural Resources Curse**
How to Escape from the Poverty Trap
Paul Mosley

132 **Sustainable Growth in the African Economy**
How Durable Is Africa's Recent Performance?
Jeffrey James

133 **Fair Trade and Organic Initiatives in Asian Agriculture**
The Hidden Realities
Rie Makita and Tadasu Tsuruta

134 **Economic Transformation for Poverty Reduction in Africa**
A Multidimensional Approach
Edited by Almas Heshmati

Economic Transformation for Poverty Reduction in Africa

A Multidimensional Approach

Edited by Almas Heshmati

LONDON AND NEW YORK

First published 2017
by Routledge
2 Park Square, Milton Park, Abingdon, Oxon OX14 4RN

and by Routledge
711 Third Avenue, New York, NY 10017

Routledge is an imprint of the Taylor & Francis Group, an informa business

British Library Cataloguing-in-Publication Data
A catalogue record for this book is available from the British Library

Library of Congress Cataloging-in-Publication Data
Names: Heshmati, Almas, editor.
Title: Economic transformation for poverty reduction in Africa : a multidimensional approach / edited by Almas Heshmati.
Description: First Edition. | New York : Routledge, 2017. | Series: Routledge studies in development economics ; 134 | Includes bibliographical references and index.
Identifiers: LCCN 2016057928 | ISBN 9781138635197 (hardback) | ISBN 9781315206516 (ebook)
Subjects: LCSH: Poverty—Government policy—Africa. | Africa—Economic policy. | Economic development—Africa. | Agriculture—Economic aspects—Africa. | Entrepreneurship—Africa.
Classification: LCC HC800.Z9 E26 2017 | DDC 338.96—dc23
LC record available at https://lccn.loc.gov/2016057928

ISBN: 978-1-138-63519-7 (hbk)
ISBN: 978-1-315-20651-6 (ebk)

Typeset in Galliard
by Apex CoVantage, LLC

Contents

Figures

Tables

Contributors

Dan Ayebale, Faculty of Business and Administration, Uganda Christian University.

Justin Bem, Banque des États de l'Afrique Centrale, Yaoundé, Cameroon.

Kahsay Berhane, Department of Economics, Addis Ababa University, Addis Ababa, Ethiopia.

Oumer Berisso Metaksa, Department of Economics, College of Business and Economics, Addis Ababa University, Ethiopia.

Mekonnen Bersisa, Department of Economics, College of Business and Economics, Addis Ababa University, Ethiopia.

Alemayehu Geda, Department of Economics, Addis Ababa University, Ethiopia.

Almas Heshmati, Sogang University, Seoul, South Korea, and Jönköping International Business School, Jönköping University.

Chinasa I. Ikelu, African School of Economics, Cotonou.

Messarck Katusiimeh, Faculty of Social Sciences, Uganda Christian University.

Vincent Kisenyi, Faculty of Business and Administration, Uganda Christian University.

Sunyoung Lee, University of Colorado Denver, USA, and Better World, Seoul, Korea.

Fred Matovu, School of Economics, Makerere University, Uganda.

Martha Kibru Melese, Addis Ababa University, Ethiopia.

Francis Menjo-Baye, Faculty of Economics and Management, University of Yaounde II, Yaounde, Cameroon.

Richard Kerongo Mose, Department of Tourism and Hospitality, School of Business and Economics, Kisii University, Kisii, Kenya.

Joseph Ndagijimana, College of Business and Economics, Department of Economics, University of Rwanda, Rwanda.

Etienne Ndemezo, College of Business and Economics, Department of Economics, University of Rwanda, Kigali, Rwanda.

Pierre M. Nguetse-Tegoum, Ministry of Economy and Planning, Yaoundé, Cameroon.

Tharcisse Nzasingizimana, College of Business and Economics, Department of Economics, University of Rwanda, Rwanda.

Masoomeh Rashidghalam, Department of Agricultural Economics, Tabriz University, Tabriz, Azerbaijan.

Richard Sebaggala, Faculty of Business and Administration, Uganda Christian University.

Addis Yimer, Department of Economics, Addis Ababa University, Addis Ababa, Ethiopia.

Abbreviations

AA Max-Temp	Average annual maximum temperature
AA Min-Temp	Average annual minimum temperature
AA Temp	Average annual temperature
AARF	Average annual rain fall
AAU	Addis Ababa University
AC	Adaptive capacity
ACLED	Armed Conflict Location and Events Data
ACZ	Agro-climatic zone
ADF	Augmented Dickey-Fuller
AEZ	Agro-ecological zone
AfDB	African Development Bank
AMG	Augmented mean group
BNR	National Bank of Rwanda
CCEMG	Common correlated effects mean group
CDF	Cumulative distribution function
CEDAW	Convention on the Elimination of All Forms of Discrimination against Women
CSA	Central Statistical Authority
CV	Contingent valuation
CZ	Climate zone
DHS	Demographic and Health Survey
ECAM	Cameroonian Households Survey
ECCU	Eastern Caribbean Currency Union
EDI	Energy Development Index
EESI	Employment and the Informal Sector Survey
EIVC	Living Standards of Rwandan Households
EPDC	Education Policy and Data Center
EPRDF	Ethiopian People Revolutionary Democratic Force
ETB	Ethiopian trade point
FA	Farmers association
FAO	Food and Agriculture Organization
FDI	Foreign direct investment
FDRE	Ethiopia: Green Economy Strategy

FE	Fixed effects
FeMSEDA	Federal Micro and Small Enterprises Development Agency
FGLS	Feasible Generalized Least Squares
FGT	Foster, Greer, and Thorbecke
GBA	Gender-based analysis
GDP	Gross Domestic Product
GHG	Greenhouse gas
GNI	Gross National Income
GTP	Growth and Transformation Plan
HDI	Human Development Index
HDR	Human Development Report
HICES	Household Income Consumption and Expenditure Survey
HIPC	Heavily Indebted Poor Countries
HIV/AIDS	Human Immunodeficiency Virus/Acquired Immune Deficiency Syndrome
ICOR	Incremental capital output ratio
IEA	International Energy Association
IFPRI	International Food Policy Research Institute
IGS	Integrated Household Survey
IMF	International Monetary Fund
INS	Institut National de la Statistique, République du Cameroun
IPCC	Intergovernmental Panel on Climate Change
IRR	Investment return rate
JIBS	Jönköping International Business School
KCCA	Kampala Capital City Authority
KNBS	Kenya National Bureau of Statistics
LDC	Least developed countries
LES	Linear Expenditure System
LFS	Labor force survey
LHCEPP	Household consumption expenditure per capita
LM	Lagrange Multiplier test
LSME	Living Standard Measurement Survey
LSMS-ISA	Living Standards Measurement Study–Integrated Surveys on Agriculture
MDU	Man-day equivalent unit
MENR	Ministry of Environment and Natural Resources
MEPI	Multidimensional Energy Poverty Index
MoA	Ministry of Agriculture
MoFED	Ministry of Finance and Economic Development
MoT	Ministry of Tourism
MRS	Marginal rate of substitution
MVS	Marginal value of safety
NGO	Non-governmental organization
NISR	National Institute of Statistics of Rwanda
NMA	National Meteorological Agency

NPV	Net present value
OECD	Organization for Economic Cooperation and Development
OFID	OPEC Fund for International Development
OLS	Ordinary least squares
OPHI	Oxford Poverty and Human Development Initiative
ORG	Office of Registrar General
PASDEP	Accelerated and Sustainable Development to End Poverty
POLS	Pooled ordinary least squares
PPP	Purchasing power parity
PSLCE	Primary School Leaving Certificate Examination
R&D	Research and Development
RDB	Rwanda Development Board
RE	Random effects
RTA	Road traffic accidents
RUI	Rural–urban inequality
RWF	Rwandan francs
SDG	Sustainable development goals
SDPRP	Sustainable Development and Poverty Reduction Program
SIDA	Swedish International Development Cooperation Agency
SME	Small and medium enterprises
SSA	Sub-Saharan Africa
TLU	Tropical livestock units
TVET	Technical and vocational education
UEUS	Urban Employment/Unemployment Survey
UNESCO	United Nations Educational, Scientific and Cultural Organization
UNFCCC	United Nations Framework Convention on Climate Change
UNCTAD	United Nations Conference on Trade and Development
UNDP	United Nations Development Programme
UN-OHRLLS	United Nations Office of the High Representative for the Least Developed Countries
UNWTO	United Nations World Tourism Organization
USAID	United States Agency for International Development
USD	United States dollar
VA	Vulnerability assessment
VAT	Value added tax
VOSL	Value of statistical life
WAEMU	West African Economic and Monetary Union
WB	World Bank
WDI	World Development Indicators
WEO	World Energy Outlook
WHO	World Health Organization
WIDER	World Institute for Development Economics Research
WTP	Willingness to pay
WTTC	World Travel and Tourism Council

1 Introduction to economic transformation for poverty reduction in Africa

Almas Heshmati

1. Background and motivation

The major policy challenges facing Africa are how to sustain a high rate of economic growth that reduces multidimensional poverty and is both socially inclusive and environmentally sustainable at the same time. Population ageing and growth, rapid urbanization, increasing need for provision of services, the need to reverse economic growth which declined after the 2008 global financial crisis, corruption and inefficiency and responding to climate change are among the other challenges facing Africa. Against this background, the Jönköping International Business School (JIBS) and the University of Rwanda organize a conference on economic development in the region every year. This volume is a collection of selected empirical studies on determinants of poverty and its reduction in Africa. The papers were selected from a set of more than 90 papers presented at the conference on '*Recent Trends in Economic Development, Finance and Management Research in Eastern Africa*', Kigali, Rwanda, on 20–22 June 2016. Following the review process and revisions, 13 papers were accepted for publication in this edited volume.

The studies are grouped into domains that influence the level and development of poverty in Africa. The core argument for using a multidimensional perspective on poverty is the need to account for different dimensions of poverty when it is measured and classified and for identifying the determinants of poverty and the factors that reduce it. The studies in the volume provide a comprehensive picture of the state of poverty, its measurement and causal factors. They investigate heterogeneity by household characteristics and efficient policies and practices in poverty reduction on the African continent as a whole and also in selected countries in Eastern Africa. In these countries poverty rates are high and multifaceted, which pose major challenges for governments and organizations whose aim is alleviating poverty.

The volume contains a collection of empirical studies on the levels, variations and determinants of poverty and its reduction in Africa. The first chapter is an introduction/summary written by the volume's editor. The remaining 13 inter-related studies are grouped into four domains which influence the levels, variations and development of poverty on the African continent as a whole and also in individual countries. The objectives are to account for different dimensions of poverty in its measurement and to identify the determinants and factors reducing its levels. The studies provide a comprehensive picture of the state of poverty, its measurement, causal factors and efficient policies and practices for reducing poverty in Africa. The results can have strong implications for poverty reduction policies.

2. Brief summary of individual studies

The 13 chapters are grouped into 4 research areas: multidimensional measures of poverty and its incidence, gap and severity (5 chapters); production and productivity-related factors (3 chapters); policies influencing poverty (3 chapters); and random and hazardous but preventive factors influencing poverty levels and their reduction (2 chapters). A brief summary of individual chapters is now provided.

Part I: Climate, energy and food security

Part I of the edited volume contains four chapters on climate, energy and food security issues and their relationship with poverty and its determinants.

Oumer Berisso Metaksa in Chapter 2, '*Impact of weather variations on cereal productivity and the influence of agro-ecological differences in Ethiopian cereal production*', investigates the impacts of weather and agro-ecological variations on cereal productivity in Ethiopia. This study confirms the importance and strong influence of rainfall and temperatures on cereal production. There is evidence that agro-ecological differences and crop productivity regress over time. Increases in crop productivity are not uniform in the different agro-ecological zones. It suggests some policy options for the government in planning climate change adaptation strategies and agricultural policies to reduce poverty.

Richard Kerongo Mose's study in Chapter 3, '*Vulnerability and impact assessment of climate change on East African wildlife tourism: a study of Maasai Mara ecosystem*', assesses the vulnerability and impact of climate change on wildlife-based tourism in Maasai Mara in Kenya. The area is a unique biodiversity hotspot where wildebeest migration forms the cornerstone of tourism flows. Their results show that changing climate is exacerbating conflicts affecting the migration patterns of wildlife, damaging infrastructure and increasing overhead costs for tourism businesses. The chapter concludes that there is a need to have place-specific climate change vulnerability indicators so as to counter the impact of climate change on wildlife tourism and poverty in Kenya.

The second study by Mekonnen Bersisa in Chapter 4, '*Multidimensional measure of household energy poverty and its determinants in Ethiopia*', uses a multidimensional measure of household energy poverty and its determinants. It investigates the importance of access to and affordability of energy for the well-being of society. The objective of the paper is analyzing the extent and determinants of energy poverty. The paper shows that the extent of energy poverty in rural and small towns in Ethiopia is very severe. A larger family size, living in a rural area and having a male head increase the probability of a household being multi-dimensionally energy poor. It recommends that interventions for reducing energy poverty should be coupled with poverty reduction policies.

The third study by Sunyoung Lee in Chapter 5, '*Household food security and school enrollment: evidence from Malawi*', explores the association between subjective household food consumption levels as a proxy of subsistence income levels and school enrollments in Malawi. The results suggest that having 'enough food' plays a key role in lowering school dropout rates. However, complicated dynamics exist around the level of perceived subsistence levels. In general, parents need two conditions to be fulfilled for sending their children to school: sufficient resources for basic needs and higher utility from educating their children for their futures. The results point to measurement errors in capturing household financial resources in poor rural areas. The chapter suggests policy measures for promoting school enrollments and lowering dropout rates.

Masoomeh Rashidghalam in Chapter 6, '*Analysis of poverty and its determinants in Rwanda*', provides an understanding of the socioeconomic characteristics that influence households' poverty status in different provinces and districts in Rwanda. It identifies the poverty line at the province and district levels and then computes the incidence, intensity and severity of poverty at individual household levels. It also estimates the effects of different household characteristics on poverty and its variations. The estimation results show that living in a rural area, distance to the market, family size, marital status and age of household head, female-headed household, high population density and population growth increase the probability of being poor and its depth, while literate household heads and ownership of property and assets reduce the incidence and intensity of poverty.

Part II: Taxes, trade openness and capital

The chapters in Part II discuss the association between tax reforms, trade openness and capital flight with poverty.

Etienne Ndemezo and Francis Menjo-Baye in Chapter 7, '*Assessing the revenue implications of indirect tax reforms in Rwanda*', discuss the revenue implications of the value added tax rate reform in Rwanda. They estimate the elasticity of the taxable base with respect to the tax rate. Their analysis leads to two main outcomes: the tax reform slightly raised household consumption expenditures and the increase in tax revenue was significant. The behavioral component was lower and mainly borne by the poorest households. They find consumption spending by poor households to be relatively insensitive to changes in relative prices after the tax reform.

Chapter 8, '*Differential impact of trade liberalization and rural–urban income inequalities on poverty in African countries*', by Kahsay Berhane investigates the differential impact of trade liberalization and rural–urban income inequalities on poverty reduction in 42 Africa economies. It uses low household consumption expenditure per capita as a proxy for poverty. The differential impacts are captured through the country heterogeneity effect. Both the trade openness and rural–urban income inequality variables have a higher significant negative impact on poverty. Moreover, their impact on poverty is not uniform for all African countries.

The research by Alemayehu Geda and Addis Yimer in Chapter 9, '*Effects of capital flight on growth and poverty Reduction in Ethiopia: evidence from a simulation-based analysis*', estimates the volume and negative effects of capital flight on growth and poverty reduction in Ethiopia. It finds the average growth lost owing to capital flight to be about 2.2 per cent per annum. Using elasticity of poverty with respect to income and inequalities the paper also finds the effect of capital flight on total poverty. Growth in Ethiopia was accompanied by rising inequalities that wiped out the positive effect of growth on poverty reduction. A simulation exercise for the elasticity of poverty with respect to income and inequality shows that poverty would have reduced in the absence of capital flight.

Part III: Employment, gender wage differentials and start-ups

Part III analyzes the relationship between employment, gender wage differentials and business start-ups.

Martha Kibru Melese's study presented in Chapter 10, '*Employment and incidence of poverty in urban Ethiopia*', employs two different techniques to explore poverty in urban Ethiopia to explain the probability of being poor. The results from the analysis show that a household head and other members' characteristics matter to the household's poverty position. The results from logistic and quintile regressions are used to explain expenditure per capita, which specifically show that occupation characteristics are important determinants of poverty status in urban Ethiopia. The study finds that households with more own-account workers and unpaid family workers are more prone to poverty. This result confirms the important role of employment in poverty reduction.

Pierre M. Nguetse-Tegoum and Justin Bem in Chapter 11, '*Impact of gender wage differentials on poverty and inequalities in Cameroon*', analyze the distributional impacts of gender wage differentials on poverty and income inequalities in Cameroon. Their results show that females' returns to education off-set the gap. The impact of the gender wage gap on poverty shows that the eradication of gender segregation in the formal sector will help improve living conditions and reduce the incidence of poverty but increase income inequalities. The impact of the gender wage gap on poverty shows that the eradication of gender segregation in the formal sector will help improve the living conditions of people from households in which at least one woman is working in the formal sector. At the national level, it will also reduce the incidence of poverty.

The study by Joseph Ndagijimana, Tharcisse Nzasingizimana and Almas Heshmati in Chapter 12, '*Econometric analysis of business start-ups in Rwanda*', investigates the effects of interest rate spread, inflation, exchange rate and taxation on business start-ups in Rwanda. Their econometric analysis reveals how starting a business in Rwanda is affected by these determinant factors and their relationship with banks' market operations. The chapter also provides policy recommendations on how to promote business start-ups, thereby reducing poverty at different levels and locations.

Part IV: Diversity, conflicts and hazardous factors

Part IV covers the prevalence of diversity, various forms of conflicts and hazardous factors affecting poverty.

Chapter 13, '*A within-country study of conflict and poverty in Nigeria*', by Chinasa I. Ikelu is a within-country study of conflict and poverty in Nigeria. It conducts an econometric analysis of the economic and relative development factors that contribute to an increase in conflicts and terrorism in Nigeria. The poorer areas, particularly those with higher rates of illiteracy and mortality, are more exposed and prone to conflicts. The results show strong evidence that ethnic, linguistic and religious diversity in Nigeria is correlated with the intensity of conflict and poverty. This evidence implies that poverty causes conflict. The chapter proposes suitable policy measures aimed at reducing poverty.

The last study in Chapter 14, '*The cost of commercial motorcycle accidents in Uganda*', by Richard Sebaggala, Fred Matovu, Dan Ayebale, Vincent Kisenyi and Messarck Katusiimeh explores the private and social costs of motorcycle accidents in Uganda. It enhances our understanding of the direct and indirect costs of road traffic accidents. In addition to the human capital cost estimation approach, this study also applies the willingness-to-pay approach to estimate the amount that riders will have to pay for reducing risks of loss of life based on a contingent valuation method. Their estimates show that motorcycle accidents are associated with huge economic and non-economic burdens borne by the poor victims and society as a whole which aggravate the state of poverty.

3. Final words

The primary audience for this edited book includes undergraduate and graduate students, lecturers, researchers, public and private institutions, NGOs, international aid agencies and decision makers. The book can serve as complementary reading to texts on economic development, welfare and poverty in Africa. The organizers of the annual conference on economic development in East Africa will market the book in their annual East Africa conferences. There are many books on poverty in Africa but they rarely discuss multidimensional measures of poverty, a subject which has been at the forefront of poverty and well-being research in recent years.

This edited book is authored by African experts in the field who employ diverse up-to-date data and methods to provide robust empirical results based on representative household surveys, covering individuals or multiple countries on the continent. It contains a wealth of empirical evidence, deep analyses and sound recommendations for policymakers and researchers to design and implement effective social policies and strategies to prevent and to reduce poverty and its negative effects on poor households. As such the book is a useful resource for policymakers and researchers involved in fighting poverty. It will also appeal to a broader audience interested in economic development, resources, policies, economic welfare and inclusive growth.

The editor is grateful to a host of dedicated authors and rigorous referees who helped in assessing the submitted papers. Many were presenters at the 2016 conference at the University of Rwanda. Special thanks go to Bideri Ishuheri Nyamulinda, Rama Rao and Lars Hartvigson and the remaining members of the Organization Committee for their efforts in organizing the conference. The editor would also like to thank Yong Ling LAM for guidance and for assessing assess this manuscript for publication by Routledge. Financial support by the Swedish International Development Cooperation Agency (SIDA) to organize the conference is gratefully acknowledged.

Part I

Climate, energy and food security

2 Impact of weather variations on cereal productivity and the influence of agro-ecological differences in Ethiopian cereal production

Oumer Berisso Metaksa

1. Introduction

While climate change is a global phenomenon, its potential effects are not uniform; rather they are unevenly distributed both between and within countries (O'Brien and Leichenko, 2008). The extent to which these impacts will be felt depends in large part on agro-climatic/ecological characteristics and the extent of local and national adaptations and adaptive capacities. However, there is consensus that over the coming decades, anthropogenic climate changes will cause dramatic transformations in the biophysical systems that will affect human settlements, the ecosystem, water resources and food production, all of which are closely linked to human livelihoods (IPCC, 2012). These transformations are likely to have widespread implications for individuals, communities, regions and nations. In particular, poor and natural resource-dependent rural households will bear a disproportionate burden of the adverse impacts. Research findings reveal that weather variability due to climate change has a significant impact on global and regional food production systems, which in turn increases uncertainty about future incomes, thus having serious impacts on agriculture and poverty in developing countries, particularly in sub-Saharan Africa (SSA) (UN-OHRLLS, 2009). Climate change effects poverty and food insecurity and it becomes a fuel in rising prices for staple grains that may result in a substantial reduction in real incomes – and thus an increase in poverty – especially for households spending a large share of their incomes on staple grains. In particular, the effect of poverty is enormous in SSA, where yield impacts of climate change are severe (characterized by low productivity) and no stratum has any experience of significant poverty reduction.

Ethiopia's agricultural production is dominated by subsistent farmers who make the country one of the most vulnerable to weather variability and climate change in the continent. The sector contributes about 40 per cent to the Ethiopian GDP, directly provides employment and livelihood to more than 83 per cent of the population and contributes about 85 per cent to its total export earnings (AfDB, 2011). However, the country's agricultural production is characterized by high dependency on rainfall, traditional technology, high population pressure and severe land degradation. This is compounded by one of the lowest productivity levels in the world and is largely dominated by subsistence and smallholders, who have less capacity to adapt to climate change and who usually cultivate areas which on average are less than 1.5 hectares (FAO, 2009). Ethiopia's ecological system is fragile and vulnerable to climate change and is characterized by diverse topographic features that have led to the existence of a range of agro-ecological zones (AEZs), each with distinctly varied climatic conditions.

Cereals as Ethiopia's major food crop are especially vulnerable to the adversities of weather variability and climate change. Cereal production is also characterized by poor productivity. Cereals are particularly important to the country's food security, as it is a principal dietary staple for most of the population. Cereal production also comprises about two-thirds of the agricultural GDP and one-third of the national GDP and is a source of income for a majority of the people. It is the most vital crop in the country's crop production in terms of production volume, planted area and farm households. According to CSA (2015) cereals had a share of more than 79 per cent of the total crop area and 85 per cent of grain crop production for the Meher season in the 2014 production year. Moreover, 81 per cent of the farmers – particularly those concentrated in central Ethiopia – practice mixed farming and are primary cereal producers.

Cereal production was marked by remarkable growth in Ethiopian crop production during the last decade. Several CSA publications (Table 2.1) indicate that total cereal production grew consistently from 2004 to 2014, from an average of 16 million metric tons in 2004–08 to 21.6 million metric tons in 2009–14, averaging 18.8 million metric tons during the last decade. This shows that cereal crop production grew by 27.4 per cent from 2004 to 2014 at a rate of 2.74 per cent per annum.

However, productivity of the sector has steadily declined in the last two decades (Aberra, 2011), thanks largely to the effect of climate change. According to GTP (2010), Ethiopia annually loses 2 to 6 per cent of its total production due to the climate effect. In sum, because of significant dependence on the agricultural sector for production, employment and farm households' revenue, Ethiopia is seriously threatened by climate change, which contributes to weather variations

Table 2.1 Cereal production, planted-area and yield trends for the Meher season (2004–14)

Years	*2004–08*	*2009*	*2010*	*2011*	*2012*	*2013*	*2014*
Hectare (million ha.)	9.3	9.2	9.7	9.6	9.6	9.8	10.1
Output (million Qt.)	16.0	155.3	177.6	188.1	196.5	215.8	360.1
Yield (Qt./ha)	14.6	16.9	18.3	19.6	20.5	22.0	23.3

Source: CSA publications

and frequent (sometimes prolonged) droughts and flooding, which have compromised production of food crops and led to poverty and food insecurity.

In a conventional rain-fed farming system such as Ethiopia, farmers use direct factors of production to produce several outputs. However, farmers' abilities to operate efficiently often depend on production risks such as weather factors, agro-ecological characteristics, operational conditions and practices such as the production environment and farm-specific characteristics such as technology selection or/and managerial practices. Hence, production is influenced by the weather and agro-ecological and farm household characteristics, which by extension affect farmers' efficiency and productivity. Several empirical works have been undertaken to investigate the impact of climate change on Ethiopian agriculture using different methodologies (see Bamlaku et al., 2009; Kassahun, 2011; Mintewab et al., 2014). Several of the works assess long-term climate change patterns rather than weather variability that captures short-term patterns; some conduct their investigations based on a single crop and others do so at the national level. Climate change may have short-term pattern effects due to weather variations or/and area-specific effects and hence, agro-ecology based analyses, for example, may provide better insights. Consequently, there is dearth of literature linking short-term weather effects to influences of agro-ecological factors for farm-level cereal productivity. Accordingly, this research is designed to bridge this gap by providing an analysis of the impacts of weather variations on cereal productivity and the influence of agro-ecological differences on cereal producers. It aims to answer the question: how do production risks – weather factors, agro-ecological and farm households' demographic and socioeconomic characteristics – influence cereal production and productivity in the main cereal crop-producing regions in Ethiopia?

This study makes significant contributions to existing literature regarding the impact of climate change on crop productivity. First, while the effects of annual and seasonal weather variations capturing short-term patterns are likely to differ from the long-term patterns of climate change, these possible differentials have not been thoroughly assessed in previous related studies in Ethiopia. To the extent that the pattern of climate change mimics weather uncertainty, policy measures aimed at mitigating the impacts of climate change could also be used for assessing weather uncertainty. This distinction is relevant in a setting like Ethiopia, where both seasonal and yearly variations in rainfall are huge and the rainfall is also very erratic. Second, the study makes an important contribution to the existing methodologies in its approach. It introduces a methodological innovation on the impact of climate change literature employing a combination of standard production function and the production risk and damage control framework approach as a model. We analyzed unbalanced panel data typically applying a fixed effects model that enables keeping the time-variant effects of annual and seasonal weather while at the same time controlling for unobserved time-invariant effects at a farm household level that potentially leads to omitted variable biases in cross-sectional Ricardian studies. Finally, the study incorporates agro-ecological factors, other exogenous factors and weather factors over a shorter period of time as opposed to long-term average climate variables normally used in a Ricardian analysis. It bases the AEZ analysis considering cereal cropping activities on a farm and is therefore replicable elsewhere in the country, between regions and within AEZs. The study provides valuable information which is needed for developing agro-ecologically adaptive strategies in response to the impact of climate change on crop production with growth, poverty and food-security implications.

The rest of the chapter is organized as follows. Section 2 presents a review of empirical literature and an overview of climatic conditions in Ethiopia. Section 3 gives the method and the data used for the study. Section 4 discusses the empirical findings and Section 5 provides a conclusion.

2. Review of empirical literature

2.1 Impact of climate/weather variations on crop productivity

Studies on the impact of climate change on crop productivity have increased over the decades, with a more recent focus on developing countries in general and a specific focus on Africa in particular. Most of the studies assess the extent to which adaptation options can lessen the expected impact of climate change. In what follows, we review the studies that focus on the impact of climate change on crop productivity in developing countries in general. This is followed by a review of studies on Ethiopia.

Liangzhi et al. (2005) investigated climate impact on Chinese wheat yields using time series and cross-section data from 1979–2000 for major wheat-producing provinces and corresponding climate data such as temperature, rainfall and solar radiation. They found that a 1 per cent increase in temperature in the wheat-growing season reduced wheat yields. They also reported that rising temperatures over the two decades prior to their study accounted for a 2.4 per cent decline in wheat yields, while a major growth in wheat yields came from increased use of physical inputs. Guiteras (2009) estimated the impact of climate change on Indian agriculture using the FGLS estimation method. His results suggest that climate change is likely to impose significant costs on the economy unless farmers can quickly recognize and adapt to increasing temperatures. The study further reported that such rapid adaptation may be less plausible in a developing country where access to information and capital for adjustment is limited.

Lee et al. (2012) analyzed the impact of climate change on agricultural production in 13 Asian countries. Their study used the agricultural production model and estimated a fixed effect panel model for agricultural production using seasonal climate variables and other input variables. Their result showed that higher temperatures and more precipitation in summer increased agricultural production while higher fall in temperatures was harmful in South and South East Asia. They reported that an overall increase in annual temperature decreased agricultural production. Addai and Owusu (2014) analyzed the sources of technical efficiency of maize farmers across AEZs in Ghana, using a stochastic production frontier panel data model. They reported that extension, mono cropping, land ownership and access to credit positively influenced technical efficiency. High input prices, inadequate capital and irregularity of rainfall were the most pressing problems facing maize producers in the forest, transitional and savannah zones, respectively.

In the Ethiopian context, several empirical works have been undertaken to investigate the impact of climate variations on agriculture at different levels using different methodologies. Bamlaku et al. (2009) investigated efficiency variations and factors causing inefficiencies across AEZs in Ethiopia using a stochastic frontier analysis. They showed that seasonal climate conditions and agro-ecological settings had a significant impact on technical efficiency. Their study also observed that education, proximity to markets and access to credit contributed to a significant reduction in farm inefficiencies. Kassahun (2011), in his analysis of climate variability and its economic impact on agricultural crops using the Ricardian approach, analyzed the marginal effects of temperature and rainfall on crop productivity based on farm data generated from 174 farmers. Regressing net revenue, he reported that climate, socioeconomic and soil variables had a significant impact on farmers' net revenue per hectare. His results from a marginal analysis show that a 1°C increase in temperature during the main rainy and dry seasons reduced net revenues. He also reported that a 1°C increase in temperature during the short rainy and autumn seasons marginally increased net revenue per hectare. His study also reported that an increase in precipitation by 1mm during the main rainy and dry seasons reduced net revenue per hectare. Mintewab et al. (2014) assessed the impact of weather/climate change measures on agricultural productivity of households, measured in terms of crop revenue in Ethiopia. They used four waves of survey data, combined with interpolated daily temperature and monthly rainfall data from meteorological stations. Their findings showed that temperature effects were distinctly non-linear, but only when the weather measures were combined with the extreme ends of the distribution of climate measures. In addition, they reported that contrary to expectations for rain-fed agriculture, rainfall generally had a less important role to play as compared to temperature.

2.2 *Overview of climatic conditions in Ethiopia*

Ethiopia is characterized by diverse climatic conditions. The country's climatic system is largely determined by the seasonal migration of the inter-tropical convergence zone and a complex topography (NMA, 2001). One can identify three distinct rainfall regimes in Ethiopia classified according to annual distributional patterns. The southwest and western areas of the country are characterized by a uni-modal rainfall pattern; the central, eastern and north-eastern parts exhibit a quasi bi-modal rainfall pattern; and the south and south-eastern areas a distinct bi-modal rainfall pattern (The World Bank, 2006). Mean annual rainfall ranges from about 2,000mm over some areas in the southwest to less than 250mm over the Afar lowlands in the northeast and Ogaden in the southeast while the mean annual temperature varies from about 10°C over the highlands of the northwest, central and southeast areas to about 35°C on the north-eastern edges. The country's climate is characterized by a history of climate extremes such as droughts and floods, increasing trends in temperature and a decreasing trend in rainfall with increasing variability (Demeke et al., 2011). Annual average minimum temperature has been increasing by about 0.25°C every 10 years and the maximum by 0.1°C every decade. Despite ample groundwater and surface water resources, agriculture in Ethiopia is largely rain-fed. As a result, rainfall is considered as the most important climatic element determining the performance of Ethiopian agriculture and hence its broad economy. Moreover, the rain-fed nature of agriculture underlines the importance of the timing and amount of rainfall that occurs in the country.

2.3 *Agro-ecological classification in Ethiopia*

Ethiopia is characterized by a diverse topography and various atmospheric systems that result in varying climatic conditions in the country. According to NMA (1996) the climatic conditions of the country can be divided into 11 climatic zones (CZs), broadly categorized as dry climate, tropical rainy climate and temperate rainy climate. These climatic conditions are directly related to ecological conditions in the country. Most importantly, the varying topography across the country and the different atmospheric circulation patterns observed determine rainfall and temperature patterns across CZs. Average temperature, distribution of annual rainfall and the length of the crop growing period substantially vary across the different CZs. Hence, based on the favorability of climatic and ecological conditions for agricultural production activities, MoA (2000) broadly classified the country into five major AEZs – desert, lowland, midland, highland and upper highland (Table 2.2). Further, based on homogeneity in terms of basic ecological elements of climate, physiography, soil, vegetation, land use,

Table 2.2 Classification of AEZs in Ethiopia

AEZs	*Average-annual rainfall (mm)*	*Altitude (meters)*	*Average-annual temperature (°C)*	*Length of growing period (days)*
Upper-highland	1,200–2,200	>3,200	<11.5	211–365
Highland	900–1,200	2,300–3,200	11.5–17.5	121–210
Midland	800–900	1,500–2,300	17.5–20.0	91–120
Lowland	200–800	500–1,500	20.0–27.5	46–90
Desert	<200	<500	>27.5	0–45

Source: MoA (2000)

farming system and animal production, MoA (2000) classified the major AEZs into 18 agro-ecological sub-zones.

Farmers associations (FAs) selected for this study also experienced a range of agro-climatic conditions which enabled us to classify them into three AEZs (Table 2.3). Accordingly, one FA was categorized as lowland AEZ, three FAs were categorized as midland AEZs and four FAs were classified as highland AEZs.

Accordingly, in the study area the midland AEZ covered the largest percentage (45.87 per cent), followed by the highland AEZ (31.55 per cent), while the lowland AEZ covered the lowest percentage at 22.57 per cent. This AEZ classification of the study area may allow inter-regional comparisons of our results. Moreover, the central and most of the eastern half of the country that includes our study area have two rainy periods and one dry period. The two rainy periods are locally known as the Meher season (the long rainy season extends from June to September) and Belg (the short rainy season extends from February to May). The annual rainfall distribution over this region shows two peaks corresponding to the two rainy seasons separated by a relatively short 'dry' period, which covers the rest of the year (October–January). In Ethiopia crop production in the Meher season is usually harvested in September–December and this accounts for 90–95 per cent of the production while the Belg season accounts for only 5–10 per cent of the total annual production (CSA, 2007). The failure of seasonal rains poses a risk of drought that reduces households' farm production by up to 90 per cent (The World Bank, 2003), though severity, occurrence and frequency of drought vary across the country. Thus, understanding annual and seasonal weather factors in different parts of the country or in different AEZs helps in assessing its impact on cereal productivity in different seasons, which also enables us to associate the weather effect and yield data to appropriate seasons.

Table 2.3 Classification of the study area into AEZs

FAs/survey sites	*Average-annual rainfall (mm)*	*Altitude (m)*	*Average-annual temperature (°C)*	*AEZs*
Faji	77.80	2,750	13.24	Highland
Kara-Fino	77.80	2,750	13.24	
Milki	77.80	2,750	13.24	
Oda-Dhawata	70.16	2,211	17.23	
Sirba-Godeti	92.40	1,763	20.16	Midland
Turufe	65.26	1,937	17.51	
Somodo	139.63	1,718	20.00	
Koro-Degaga	62.65	1,351	22.93	Lowland

Source: Author's classification

3. The method and data

3.1 Theoretical approach

Agricultural crop production requires farmers to produce the maximum output for a given level of possible input use. However, farmers' ability to produce efficiently often depends on production risks (variations in weather conditions), the production environment (operational conditions and practices) and farm-specific characteristics (technology selection or managerial practices) that could in turn lead agricultural production and productivity trends to fluctuate over time. Modeling the effect of agricultural inputs on crop production is not as straightforward as the standard production function (for example, CDPF) suggests. The manner in which certain inputs such as damage control inputs, contextual variables (that characterize operational conditions and practices) and production risk factors enter the production function has led people to question the conventional Cobb-Douglas specification. In some studies, inputs are presumed to directly increase potential yields as in CDPF. However, several studies reveal that inputs (for example, damage-control inputs) do not directly increase potential yield but rather reduce damage to potential yields. Thus, productivity assessment using such different conditioned production factors/inputs is not as straightforward as that from direct (yield enhancing) inputs.

Lichtenberg and Zilberman (1986) were the first to propose a model to discuss the special nature of damage control inputs as damage-abating inputs (such as pesticides) rather than as crop yield-increasing inputs (such as fertilizers) using a built-in damage control function. Subsequently, there has been some debate about the appropriate way to model productivity assessment in agriculture under different operational risk conditions and practices. Consequently many studies adapted this study by using a different functional form for the production function and using other unique estimation procedures. These studies noted the importance of such factors including weather variables in both the production and damage abatement functions, in impact and in productivity assessments.

Their arguments can be used to assess the impact of weather variations and agro-ecological and households' characteristics on crop productivity. For example, a strategy such as increased irrigation or considering weather factors such as changing temperatures or even agro-ecological characteristics, such as altitude, and a household's characteristics, such as the age or educational level of the household head, cannot enter the production function directly, though they have a bearing on the level of production. In a weather/climate change setting, there is a need for specifying weather factors and agro-ecological factors alongside the usual production function.

Lichtenberg and Zilberman (1986) modeled the damage control function with a separable structure as:

$$y = F\left\{x^D, g(x^P, Z)\right\} \tag{1}$$

where x^D is a vector of direct inputs, x^P is a vector of damage control inputs and Z is a vector of damage factors.

For this study, assuming the same argument in a climate change setting and using the formulations of Kuosmanen et al. (2006) and Lichtenberg and Zilberman (1986), we assumed that weather factors, farm household characteristics and agro-ecological factors influenced cereal yields but not in the same manner as direct inputs. Hence, we hypothesized that cereal productivity is subjected to factors such as direct factors of production, weather factors, farm household demographic and/or socioeconomic characteristics and agro-ecological factors and can be modeled as a composed function of a conventional production function and a function of non-conventional factors of production with a separable structure.

For this assume that $i = (1, \ldots, N)$ farm households operating in time periods denoted by $t = (1, \ldots, T)$ using a technology sub-set Γ denoted by $X^D = (x_1^D, \ldots, x) \in \Re^{N+}$ vector of direct inputs, used to produce a non-negative vector of farm outputs denoted by $Y = (y_1, \ldots, y_m) \in \Re^{M+}$. In changing climate with variable weather patterns, agricultural households with heterogeneous household demographic and/or socioeconomic characteristics is denoted by the vector $Z = (z_1, \ldots, z_r) \in \Re^{R+}$ and the production risk facing farmers due to extreme conditions of variability in weather factors is denoted by the vector $W = (w_1, \ldots, w_s) \in \Re^{S+}$. These farmers also operate in certain agro-ecological zones that have a range of climatic conditions (rainfall, temperature and elevation) denoted by the vector $E = (e_1, \ldots, e_m) \in \Re^{D+}$.

Hence, under our assumption, cereal crop productivity can be modeled as:

$$Y = F\{X^D, g(Z, W, E)\} \tag{2}$$

Assuming multiplicative separability of the weather factors, farm household characteristics and agro-ecological factors from production activities (Kuosmanen et al., 2006), the function F can be equivalently expressed as:

$$Y = f(X^D) \times g(Z, W, E) \tag{3}$$

where f is a function of vector $\boldsymbol{X}$ and consists of conventional, directly yield-enhancing inputs and g is a function of vectors Z, W and E and consists of indirect factors of production. In this formulation the function $f(.)$, will have a CDPF functional form. However, it may lack an appropriate functional form for the $g(.)$ function in literature, though several cumulative distribution functions such as logistics, Weibull and exponential functions are available. In this paper, we employ the exponential functional form for the $g(.)$ function, as has been used in most empirical works, and it generally represents weather factors well and tends to be more flexible (Shankar and Thirtle, 2005).

Further, as Carpentier and Weaver (1997) have pointed out, for the requirements of multiplicative separability we assumed that: (1) function $f(.)$ so as to exhibit constant returns to scale; and (2) the influence of function $g(.)$ are independent of the mixture of direct inputs *f*(.). But Kuosmanen et al. (2006) were able to demonstrate that this condition does not imply that *f*(.) and *g*(.) have no interdependencies or have no substitution possibilities or their marginal products will be independent. Extending this to the climate change setting, multiplicative separability does not imply that direct inputs, weather factors and agro-ecological characteristics have no interdependencies. Hence, based on these theoretical and conceptual approaches defining *f*(.) and *g*(.) functions as:

$$f(.) = \beta_0 \prod X_{it}^{\beta} \ \ and \ \ g(.) = \exp\left(\sum W_{it}^{\delta} + \sum Z_{it}^{\eta} + \sum E_i^{\alpha}\right); \tag{4}$$

We reformulate Eq. 3, in a panel data context as:

$$Y_{it} = \beta_0 \Pi X_{it}^{\beta} \times \left[\exp\left(\sum W_{it}^{\delta} + \sum Z_{it}^{\eta} + \sum E_i^{\alpha}\right)\right] \times \exp^{\varepsilon_{it}} \tag{5}$$

where β, δ, α and η represent the regression coefficient for respective variables to be estimated and ε_{it} is the composite error term. All other variables maintain their previous definitions.

3.2 *Empirical model specification*

For empirical applications after including major variables (weather and production factors) and non-climatic factors (farm households' demographic and socioeconomic characteristics and agro-ecological factors and the trend) in Eq. 5, we specify the farm household-specific cereal productivity model as:

$$Y_{it} = \beta_0 \Pi X_{it}^{\beta} \times \left[\exp\left(\sum W_{i(t-1)}^{\delta} + \sum Z_{it}^{\eta} + \sum E_i^{\alpha} + T_t^{\mu}\right)\right] \times \exp^{\varepsilon_{it}} \tag{6}$$

Eq. 6 can be transformed into a logarithmic form to obtain the following log-linear equation:

$$\begin{aligned} \ln Y_{it} = \beta_0 + \sum_{j=1}^{7} \beta_j \ln X_{it} + \sum_{h=1}^{16} \delta_h W_{i(t-1)} + \sum_{n=1}^{6} \eta_n Z_{it} \\ + \sum_{k=1}^{2} \alpha_k E_i + \mu_t T_t + \mu_{tt} T_t^2 + \varepsilon_{it} \end{aligned} \tag{7}$$

where *ln* is the natural logarithm; $i \in (1,2, \ldots ,N)$ is an index for farm household *I*; and $t \in (1, 2, \ldots ,T)$ represents time period *t*. *y* is farm household-level total cereal production in monetary value per unit land; *X* includes the jth direct input quantity for the ith farmer at time period *t*; and *Z* includes the household's demographic and socioeconomic characteristics. *W* includes annual and seasonal weather factors at time (*t–1*); *E* includes a set of regional dummy variables; *T* is a trend – the production years. Finally ε_{it} is the composite error term decomposed into $\varepsilon_{it} = \alpha_i + u_{it}$; a normally distributed is a time-varying random shock $u_{it} \sim N(0, \sigma_u^2)$ and an unobserved time-invariant farm household-specific effect, (α_i). β, δ, α, η and μ represent regression coefficients for the respective variables to be estimated.

3.3 Estimation methods

The model in Eq. 7 is similar to standard panel data models. It utilizes the panel feature of the data via α_i, which is a time-invariant household-specific effect. This time-invariant attribute of farm households may include some unobservable household-specific heterogeneity such as a farmer's instinctive ability, unrelated to the production process but that affects the output. This model can be estimated assuming that either α_i is a fixed parameter that influences directly the dependent variable (the fixed effects [FE] model) or a random variable that has a correlation with the independent variables (the random effects [RE] model). Hence, for this study we estimated the FE model using the fixed effects (within) estimator, which allows us to address the issue of an endogeneity and time-invariant individual heterogeneity, which is important in a farm productivity analysis. We also estimated the RE model, though this model tends to be avoided by economists and other social scientists due to its strong, often unrealistic assumption and issues of bias and uncertainty (Hausmann and Taylor, 1981).

In our model the dependent variable and direct input variables have been included in their logarithmic values to provide convenient interpretations and to reduce heterogeneity of the variance of production. Other explanatory variables entered the equation in a linear fashion. Hence, we made the interpretation for the variables using elasticities as we used the log-linear functional form of the model specification. The coefficients reflect percentage change in cereal productivity in response to percentage changes in respective inputs. However, the calculation of elasticities depended on the way in which the explanatory variables were specified (Nisrane et al., 2011). For those specified in the logarithmic form, their coefficients themselves were the elasticities and as such were directly interpretable. For those that entered the equation in a linear fashion, their coefficient estimates did not represent elasticity; instead they represented change in the logarithm of the dependent variable for a unit change in the respective inputs. Hence, for these variables, $\beta_j = \partial \ln Y_{it} / \partial X_j$, and the elasticity of value of the dependent variable with respect to these inputs is calculated as $E_{YX} = (\partial \ln Y_{it} / \partial X_{it}) \times X_{it}$ where Y_{it} is cereal productivity and X_{it} is mean value of input X, which entered the equation linearly. For the dummy variables, $\beta_j = \partial \ln Y_{it} / \partial X_j$ is not defined because it is discontinuous. However, Nisrane et al. (2011) show that elasticity with respect to those dummy variables is given by $E_{YX_{DV}} = Exp(\beta_{DV}) - 1$, where X_{DV} represents the dummy variable and β_{DV} is its estimated coefficient.

3.4 Data and variables

Our study employed a four-round panel dataset commonly called the Ethiopian Rural Household Survey (ERHS) collected from randomly selected farm households in rural Ethiopia in 1994, 1999, 2004, 2009 and 2015. Originally, the first four waves were conducted in collaboration with the Department of Economics, Addis Ababa University (AAU) and the International Food Policy Research Institute. Data collection started in 1989 on seven study sites. The

1989 survey was expanded in 1994 by incorporating other survey sites in different regions in the country. From 1994 onwards data collection has been done in a panel framework. The number of study sites has increased to 15 with the resulting sample size totaling 1,477 farm households. The newly included study villages were selected in order to represent the country's diverse farming systems. Before a household was chosen, a numbered list of all households was developed with the help of local FA authorities. Once the list had been constructed, stratified random sampling was used to select sample households in each village, whereby in each study site the sample size was proportionate to the population, resulting in a self-weighing sample.

The last round was extended from the original sample, forming a sub-sample of the original sample covering eight FAs following a similar strategy, comprising 503 farm households by the researcher in 2015. This was implemented in collaboration with the Department of Economics, AAU and the Department of Environment for Development at the University of Gothenburg, Sweden. The survey sites included FAs in Amhara and Oromia regional states or regions that represented the largest proportion of the predominantly settled farmers in the country. The eight FAs were selected carefully in order to represent the major cereal-producing areas that may represent different AEZs in the country. These FAs were characterized by a mixed-farming system. The content of the questionnaire was extracted from ERHS and it focused only on those parts that were required for the intended study.

The dataset was comprehensive and addressed farm households' demographic and socioeconomic characteristics; production inputs and outputs; and access to institutions. Moreover, important secondary data needed for the study such as geographical location, elevation and metrological data on weather variables of FAs were obtained from the Ethiopian Meteorology Authority. The metrological dataset included daily observations of rainfall and maximum and minimum temperatures, data that was collected in stations close to the study villages in 1999–2015. Consequently, this study utilized four (1999, 2004, 2009 and 2015) rounds of data, forming 446 panel households consisting of 1,648 observations that were surveyed from 1999 onwards. The four rounds were selected to allow for even time spacing and covering approximately similar time frames. The 1994 survey was excluded as it misses most of the important variables for the analysis.

Variables used in the analysis

We used monetary measures of some inputs and outputs and made their weighted aggregations at the farm household level in order to avoid the problem of indivisibility of input and output variables. The dependent variable used in the analysis was total cereal production value per unit land for each farm household. In our model, we hypothesized that direct factors of production, weather factors, farm households and agro-ecological characteristics affected cereal productivity. Accordingly, we included as explanatory variables the *direct factors of production*. These included area planted; total cereal-sown area (measured in hectares); labor employed (measured in man-day units); the amount of fertilizers used (measured in kilograms); machinery implements used (measured in monetary equivalents); livestock ownership (measured in tropical livestock units, TLUs) as a proxy for wealth and livestock asset endowments; agro-chemicals (measured in monetary equivalents) that include different agro-chemicals (pesticides, herbicides and insecticides); and oxen as animal draft power (measured in the number of oxen owned). Oxen are mainly used in traditional farming during land preparation and the harvesting period. *Farm household demographic and socioeconomic characteristics* included age of the household head; education of the household head (measured in years of schooling); household's family size; the number of plots that the farmers were cultivating, which was used as a proxy to measure farm-land fragmentation; and agricultural advisory services as public support to farmers represented by the participation of farmers in governmental agricultural extension services (1 = if household participated and 0 = otherwise).

Weather variables included lagged annual and seasonal weather measures, averages of rainfall and temperature observations for a year prior to the corresponding survey years and their squared terms. Inclusion of seasonal weather variables matched the production cycle with rainfall and temperature fairly well within the pre-planting, planting, growing and maturing/harvesting periods of cereal production. Accordingly, *annual weather variables* included annual precipitation (the mean annual rainfall of a year prior to the corresponding survey years); annual temperature (the mean annual temperature of a year prior to the corresponding survey years) and their squared terms. *Seasonal weather variables* included summer precipitation (summer rainfall average prior to the corresponding survey years), fall precipitation (fall rainfall average prior to the corresponding survey years) and spring precipitation (average spring rainfall prior to the corresponding survey years); as well as summer temperature (average summer temperature prior to the corresponding survey years), fall temperature (average fall temperature average prior to the corresponding survey years) and spring temperature (average spring temperature prior to the corresponding survey years); and their squared terms. The *AEZs' dummy variables* included AEZs' characteristics to represent location-specific time-invariant factors to account for productivity differences that could result from the overall agro-ecological factors that could not be captured by other variables in the model. Finally, *the trend* – time trend and its square – was used as a proxy for technical changes in crop production due to technological changes over time. The linear term captures the direction of the change and those effects that we cannot measure but that nonetheless had an effect on farm output (for example, input prices), while the squared term captures the non-linear shift in the production function over time.

3.5 *Descriptive analysis*

Table 2.4 presents a descriptive summary and evolution of cereal production, inputs and farm households' characteristics. On average, the farmers were able to produce 19.5 quintals of cereals during 1999–2014.

Table 2.4 Summary statistics of input-output data and farm household characteristics (466 farmers, 1,648 observations) (1999–2014)

Variables/years	*1999*		*2004*		*2009*		*2014*		*All*	
	Mean	*SD*	*Mean*	*SD*	*Mean*	*SD*	*Mean*	*SD*	*Mean*	*SD*
Output (Q)	12.6	13.2	12.5	13.0	20.7	23.9	30.2	40	19.5	27
Yield (Q/ha)	9.6	7.3	7.8	9.0	19.5	55.6	21.2	29.8	15.1	34
Value ('000'ETB)	5.1	5.6	5.5	7.1	32.7	75.2	21.0	26.1	17.0	43
Direct inputs										
Fertilizers (kg)	107.8	115.1	88.0	140.9	81.0	104.3	179.0	166.2	116.1	139
Agro-chemicals (ETB)	26.9	71.5	23.7	77.0	114.7	461.5	336.7	675.5	133.9	447
Labor (MDU)	316.3	423.9	266.2	290.7	170.8	241.4	593.9	1222.2	342.6	714
Machinery (ETB)	0.6	4.6	41.3	301.4	836.8	3216.4	376.4	915.5	336.3	1776
Livestock (TLUs)	5.7	4.3	4.5	4.0	7.2	6.3	7.9	7.4	6.5	5.9
Farm-size (ha)	1.5	1.1	4.9	22.6	2.8	14.2	1.8	1.4	2.6	12.4
Number of oxen	1.8	1.2	1.4	1.3	1.9	1.5	1.9	1.4	1.8	1.4
Household characteristics										
Number of plots	3.4	2.3	3.0	1.8	4.2	2.9	3.7	2.4	3.6	2.4
Head's age	51.1	15.5	52.8	15.8	51.5	15.5	49.7	14.7	51.2	15.4
Household's size	6.2	2.9	4.6	2.3	5.6	2.7	6.1	2.8	5.7	2.7
Head's Educ. (years)	4.3	6.0	4.5	6.4	6.3	7.1	4.6	5.5	5.0	6.3
Agri. Ext. service	42.60		23.55		43.50		39.01		38.29	

Source: Author's calculations

Observing the summary statistics year by year in Table 2.4 and Figure 2.1a, mean of cereal output and productivity increased over time during the study period. Mean of output was about 12.6 quintals in 1999, which rose steadily to 30.2 quintals in 2014. In terms of yield captured in quintals per acreage, farm households had a mean of 9.6 units in 1999, which increased to 21.2 units in 2014. Average yields in terms of monetary value at constant prices was 17,000 for the four waves, which grew consistently from the lowest value of 5,100 ETB in 1999 to the highest value of 21,000 ETB in 2014; this was an annual growth rate of about 5 per cent. For such production, farmers on average used 342.7 man-day equivalent units (MDUs) of labor, 116.1 kilograms of fertilizers and spent 133.9 ETB for agro-chemicals to cultivate 2.6 hectares of cereals per farm household.

The number of plots cultivated by farmers, which is also used as a proxy to measure land fragmentation among subsistent smallholders, averaged 3.6 plots. Average livestock ownership was 6.5 TLUs, while oxen ownership was 1.8, that is, almost two oxen per household. A majority of the farmers were male (76.58 per cent). On average, the household heads were 51.2 years old and had an average of five schooling years. The households' family size averaged six. In addition, on average, 38.29 per cent of the farmers were reported to be in contact with agricultural extension agents but had very little contact per month.

As shown in Figure 2.1b, average annual rainfall was 81.77mm and average annual temperature was 18.53°C, with a maximum of 26.13°C and a minimum of 10.92°C. When we see the weather variable annual trends, we notice that

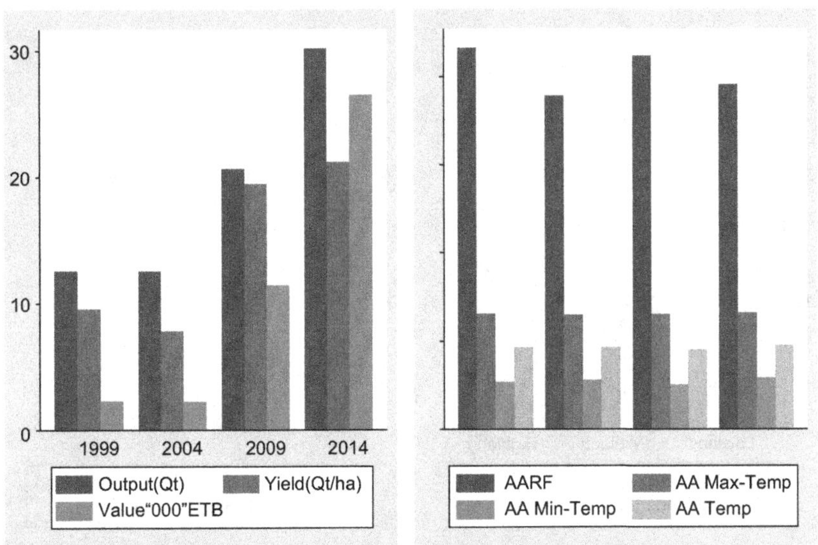

Figure 2.1 Average output, yield and weather variables by years

Source: Author's computation

average annual rainfall distribution declined over time as the mean annual rainfall in 1998 was 86.5mm, which showed a slight decline in 2014 to 78.32mm. In contrast distribution of annual average temperature increased over time – mean average annual temperature in 1998 was 18.46°C, which showed a slight increase to almost 19.02°C in 2014. This descriptive summary shows that in general there were significant weather variations during the study period. On average it shows a decline in annual rainfall by almost 8.18mm and an increase in annual temperature by 0.56°C; that is, rainfall declined by 2.73mm and the temperature increased by 0.19°C per year.

A comparison of the AEZs

As shown in Figure 2.2a, as one moves from lowland to highland AEZs, we find that both cereal outputs and yields increase. Observing weather variables across AEZs in Figure 2.2b, one can see that the mean average annual rainfall and the maximum and minimum temperature in the lowland AEZ was 62.65mm, 31.44°C and 14.43°C, respectively. Similarly, mean average annual rainfall and maximum and minimum temperature in the midland ACZ was 95.73mm, 26.82°C and 11.28°C, respectively, while it was 78.7mm, 20.0°C and 6.1°C, respectively, in the highland AEZ.

On the other hand, when we look at cereal production, yield and weather variables over the panel years in each AEZ, we find that average outputs and yields rose steadily per panel year in each AEZ. This shows that outputs and yields

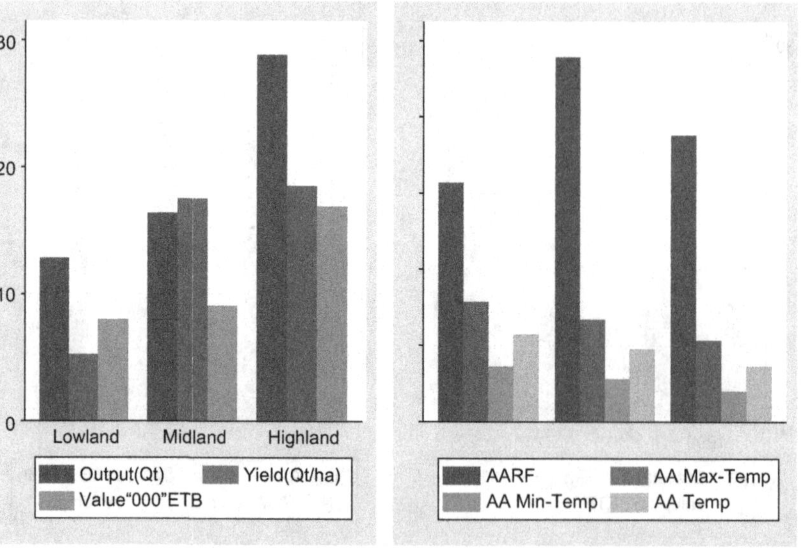

Figure 2.2 Average output, yield and weather variables by AEZs

Source: Author's computation

increased over time in all AEZs. However, average annual weather variables per year in each AEZ were not uniform; for example, it seems that rainfall declined in midland and highland AEZs, while their temperatures tended to rise. In the case of the lowland AEZ it seems to be the opposite.

4. Empirical results and discussion

4.1 Estimations and econometric diagnoses

Table 2.5 presents parameter estimates from FE and RE models. The FE model was used to capture any time-invariant unobserved farm household-specific heterogeneity effects and the RE model was used to capture the influence of the agro-ecological effect. Several estimation diagnoses were also performed. In order to check for multicollinearity and confounded effects among the explanatory variables, pair-wise correlation coefficients among variables were estimated. These correlation coefficients verified the explanatory variables. Fertilizers, agro-chemicals, livestock, machinery and oxen were positively and highly correlated with cereal productivity, while it was negatively correlated with labor, planted area, age and temperature. The remaining variables were positively correlated with cereal productivity. Only a pair of weather variables showed a correlation higher than 0.50, indicating serious multicollinearity and possible confounded effects. The remaining pairs had low pair-wise correlations with each other. This shows that there was very weak collinearity between them, implying almost the non-existence of the multicollinearity problem. The Ramsey (1969) regression specification error test revealed that (prob>F = 0.1136), indicating there were no omitted variables; the Breusch-Pagan LM test for random effects revealed that there was no unobserved household-heterogeneity as the *p*-value was greater than 0.05. We also performed the Hausmann-test (Wooldridge, 2002) to check the appropriateness of the FE model or the RE model's estimates. The result revealed fixed effects estimation as more efficient as compared to random effects. Accordingly, our report is primarily based on results from fixed effects. We used the robust standard errors to diminish the heteroskedasticity problem.

4.2 An analysis of estimation results

Table 2.5 presents the regression results on the panel dataset. In general it can be seen from the table that almost all parameter estimates from either of the models have the expected signs and are significantly different from zero at the 5 per cent level or below. The fixed effect estimates differ slightly from the random effect estimates with some improvements and the parameters are still significant. Hence, after assessing the models' estimates, we chose to refer to the fixed effects results, except for the agro-climatic dummy variables that were used to identify the impact of agro-ecological differences for interpretation. As expected, most of the direct production inputs and household characteristics impacted cereal productivity in the right way and were significant

Table 2.5 Parameter estimates: impact of climatic and non-climatic variables on cereal productivity (466 farmers and 1,648 observations)

Explanatory variables	*Dependent-variable: aggregate cereal yields*				
	Random effect		*Fixed effect*		
	Coefficients	*Std.Err. (Robust)*	*Coefficients*	*Std.Err. (Robust)*	*Elasticities*
Fertilizers	0.044***	0.015	0.020	0.017	0.020
Agro-chemicals	0.039***	0.012	0.037***	0.013	0.037
Labor	0.042**	0.023	0.024	0.025	0.024
Machinery	0.025*	0.015	0.019	0.017	0.019
Livestock	0.191***	0.029	0.125***	0.037	0.125
Land-size	-0.284***	0.059	-0.303***	0.062	-0.303
Oxen	0.157***	0.053	0.091	0.063	0.091
Number of plots	0.069***	0.010	0.054***	0.012	0.023
Head's age	-0.020**	0.010	-0.025**	0.011	-0.149
Age-squared	0.016*	0.009	0.019*	0.010	0.065
Family size	0.008	0.009	0.015	0.011	0.010
Head's Education	0.002	0.004	0.007*	0.004	0.004
Agricultural Ext. Services	0.113**	0.047	0.099*	0.057	0.406
Annual precipitation	0.043	0.039	0.281***	0.054	2.501
Annual precipitation^2	-0.015	0.013	-0.076***	0.017	-0.541
Summer precipitation	-0.031***	0.008	-0.017	0.013	-0.323
Summer precipitation^2	0.008***	0.002	-0.002	0.003	-0.077
Fall precipitation	-0.106***	0.021	-0.016	0.028	-0.125
Fall precipitation^2	0.06***	0.012	0.009	0.016	0.061
Spring precipitation	0.017*	0.009	-0.052***	0.012	-0.313
Spring precipitation^2	-0.009*	0.004	-0.003	0.007	-0.012
Annual temperature	-2.468	1.832	-12.700***	2.830	-27.764
Annual temperature^2	2.574	4.790	28.950***	6.907	12.029
Summer temperature	1.011	0.912	-4.800***	1.091	-11.045
Summer temperature^2	-1.412	2.209	11.800***	2.606	5.412
Fall temperature	-5.218***	1.482	9.700***	2.273	20.142
Fall temperature^2	13.300***	3.437	-22.2***	5.358	-8.605
Spring temperature	8.343***	1.814	7.673***	2.370	17.772
Spring temperature^2	-15.400***	3.944	-18.100***	5.066	-8.419
Highland	5.136***	0.857	..	..	62.579
Midland	2.665***	0.487	..	..	5.284
Time	0.129***	0.010	0.078***	0.011	18.428
Time^2	-0.476***	0.109	-0.831***	0.210	

Constants	−281.800***	24.532	−152.80***	23.337
F-statistic	Wald chi²(32) = 3151.26***		F(30, 445) = 77.01***	
R-squared	Within = 0.5931		Within = 0.6121	
	Between = 0.6026		Between = 0.0096	
	Overall = 0.5968		Overall = 0.1174	

Note: * = $p < 0.05$; ** = $p < 0.01$; *** = $p < 0.001$

in the model. As shown in Table 2.5 inputs such as agro-chemicals, livestock ownership, number of plots, education and agricultural extension services significantly enhanced cereal productivity. On the other hand, cereal-sown land size and head's age negatively influenced cereal productivity.

The estimated coefficient of agro-chemicals showed a positive and significant enhancement of cereal productivity at 1 per cent. Its elasticity implies that an increase in agro-chemical use by one unit increased cereal productivity by 0.037 per cent. Consistent with our expectations, livestock ownership was positively and significantly associated with cereal productivity at 1 per cent, implying that the more livestock a household had the better its cereal productivity. This result is in line with the findings of several other empirical works (Nisrane et al., 2011). The elasticity of this variable indicates that an increase in livestock ownership by 1 per cent increased productivity by 0.125 per cent. The positive sign indicates that the availability of this asset was essential in several respects. For instance, farmers with more livestock units, which can readily be converted to money, could more easily buy modern farm inputs such as seeds, fertilizers and other chemicals, than those who owned fewer livestock units. Moreover, apart from smoothing their incomes, families with more animals were also more likely to have larger protein intakes than those with fewer animals, which helped improve their working efficiency. They also used dung cakes to fertilize homesteads. Besides, pack animals were used for timely transportation of the crops to a threshing point. Since threshing is conducted using animal power, the availability of livestock, especially during peak periods, is vital for reducing post-harvest losses.

The number of plots that the farmers cultivated was included in the analysis to assess the effect of dissected plots for a given size of cultivated land on farming productivity; this was positively and significantly associated with cereal productivity at the 1 per cent level. The result implies that for a given amount of land for crop cultivation, an increase in the number of plots for cultivation led to increased cereal productivity. The positive sign of this coefficient may also represent the reduced risks that different plots provided if the plots were sufficiently disbursed, such that farmers faced different degrees of weather-induced variations and mineral content. Moreover, the result can be explained in terms of access to farmland and that farmers with more plots were likely to adopt innovations because they may be willing and able to bear more risks than their counterparts and may have preferential access to farm inputs, and this enabled them to improve the level of their crop production and productivity. Its elasticity indicates that an increase in the number of plots that farmers cultivate by 1 per cent will increase cereal output and hence increase productivity by more than 0.023 per cent.

Regression results further indicate that the land area on which cereals were cultivated had a negative and significant impact at the 1 per cent level, which conforms to the inverse farm size productivity relationship found in other studies (Tesfay et al., 2005). Its estimated elasticity shows that an increase in cultivated land by 1 per cent will decrease cereal productivity by 0.303 per cent.

Estimates of the educational levels of household heads show that education affected cereal productivity positively at the 5 per cent significance level. Its elasticity indicates that an increase in educational level by 1 per cent will increase cereal productivity by 0.004 per cent. This result is in line with Battese's and Coelli's (1995) result; they hypothesized education to increase a household's ability to use existing technologies and efficient management of production systems and hence to attain higher productivity levels. Among the socioeconomic variables, access to agricultural extension services as public support to farmers turned out to have a significantly positive impact at the 10 per cent level. The result reveals that increased access to extension services and more contacts with extension agents were associated with improved farming information, which is important for crop productivity. Thus, ceteris paribus, the corresponding elasticity, shows that an increase in participation and number of contacts with extension agents could lead to an increase in cereal productivity by 0.406 per cent.

Age had a significant negative impact on cereal productivity at the 5 per cent level while its square affected positively at the 10 per cent significance level, indicating that age had a non-linear relationship with crop productivity. This further indicates that older household heads were less productive as compared to younger ones. Moreover, the result can be explained in terms of crop production practices. The negative sign for the coefficient could be attributed to the unwillingness of older and more experienced farmers to use new techniques and modern inputs, whereas younger farmers by virtue of greater opportunities to formal education may be more skillful in their search for information and the application of new techniques (Hussain, 1989). This result may be supported by the result from the descriptive summary, as the age of the farmers ranged between 17 and 103 years with a mean of 51 years, implying that farmers were relatively old – a condition that might have affected productivity negatively. In sum, its elasticity indicates that as a farmer gets older by 1 per cent, cereal productivity will decline by 0.004 per cent until a turning point is reached beyond which getting older by 1 per cent will increase productivity by 0.065 per cent.

Weather variations' effects on yield

The effect of weather variables' variability specified in the study is anticipated, as climate-related variables significantly affected cereal productivity. Linear and squared term coefficients from both the models revealed that cereal productivity was generally sensitive to weather variables. The results reveal that most of the squared terms of weather variables were significant annually and seasonally at the 1 per cent level, implying that weather variations had a non-linear effect on cereal productivity. When the coefficients of quadratic terms were positive, the crop productivity function had a U-shape; it will have an inverted U-shape when the quadratic term is negative. This shows that there is a known amount and time range of temperature and precipitation in which a crop grows best across the seasons and/or annually, although optimal weather factors vary from crop to crop (Mendelsohn et al., 1994). For example, in this study, it was hypothesized that peak mean rainfall influenced crop productivity positively; that is, more rainfall increased the productivity of cereal crops. Expectedly, the results show that an increase in precipitation, particularly for annual mean rainfall, had a positive effect on crop productivity. However, this was up to a point and then production and hence productively started declining, as shown by the coefficient of the squared term of annual rainfall. Similar explanations hold for other weather variables' results.

The results show that annual rainfall affected crop productivity positively, while its squared term had a significant negative effect at the 1 per cent level. This means that annual rainfall had a negative effect on cereal crops until a turning point was reached, but beyond that rainfall had a positive impact. Its coefficient suggests that if annual rainfall was favorable (in terms of timeliness, amount and distribution), then households experienced a relatively better crop productivity condition. This result may be due to the fact that rainfall enhances crop productivity as it improves the soil's capacity and enables it to use the fertilizers and other inputs effectively (Tchale and Suaer, 2007). Analyzing seasonally, the results show that precipitation during the spring season affected cereal productivity negatively at the 1 per cent significance level. Similarly, summer and fall seasons' precipitation affected cereal productivity negatively. The decrease in crop productivity with increasing summer precipitation indicates that the existing current level of precipitation was enough for planting. The reduction in crop productivity with an increase in precipitation during the fall season – the period commonly known as the harvesting season in the study area – was due to crops' reduced water requirements and consequently more precipitation damaged the crops (Deressa et al., 2009) during the harvesting season.

Contrary to annual precipitation, annual and summer season temperatures associated negatively with cereal productivity. Moreover, coefficients for temperature variables were found to have large values, implying that temperature variations had a large impact on cereal productivity. The results show that annual and summer season temperatures affected cereal productivity negatively while their square terms had a positive effect, all significantly at 1 per cent. This may be due to an increase (downward move) in average minimum temperature or (upward move) in average maximum temperature measured annually or during the crop growing season, which in turn led to a decline in crop productivity. The result is in line with that of Schlenker et al. (2006), who showed that the extreme end in average temperature distribution was always harmful for crop growth, irrespective of the type of crop. Regression results also show that average temperature during fall and spring affected cereal productivity positively, while their squared terms had a negative effect at 1 per cent. The results suggest that an increase in temperatures enhanced cereal productivity during these seasons. During the fall season, a higher temperature was beneficial for harvesting. It is important to note that most crops have finished their growing period by autumn, and a higher temperature quickly dries up the crops and facilitates harvesting so it has a positive effect on crop productivity (Mendelsohn and Dinar, 2003). In general these findings confirm that weather variability is one of the critical 'drivers of crop productivity' in many African agrarian households (The World Bank, 2006).

Marginal-impact analysis of weather variables

Further, considering linear and squared terms, the weather coefficients reveal that cereal productivity was generally sensitive to weather variations. However, their effect was not obviously determined simply by looking at the coefficients. This is due to the fact that the linear and the squared terms play a role; rather their effect can be interpreted based on their marginal-effects or elasticities (Kurukulasuriya and Mendelsohn, 2008). This is important in order to observe the overall effect of an infinitesimal change in weather variables on cereal productivity and for avoiding complexity in the analysis and interpretations due to squared terms.

Following Lee et al. (2012), denoting weather variables as W, one can derive the marginal-impacts (elasticities in our case) of weather variables (W_i) on cereal productivity evaluated at the mean of that variable:

$$E\left[\frac{dY}{dW_i}\right] = E\left(\beta_{1i} + 2\beta_{2i}W_i\right) * E\left(W_i\right) = \left(\beta_{1i} + 2\beta_{2i}E(W_i)\right) * E\left(W_i\right) \\ = \left(\beta_{1i} + 2\beta_{2i}\bar{W}_i\right) * \bar{W}_i \tag{8}$$

where E is the expectations operator and β_{1i} and β_{2i} are the semi-elasticities of the linear and quadratic terms, respectively. $E(W_i) = \bar{W}_i$, are mean values of the corresponding weather variable.

Table 2.6 shows elasticities of annual and seasonal weather variables, which show effects of increases in temperature by 1°C and precipitation by 1mm per annual/season on cereal productivity. The sign of the calculated elasticities of precipitation variables indicates that a 1mm increase in annual precipitation has a positive effect, while seasonal precipitation has a negative effect on cereal productivity. On the other hand, an increase in annual and summer temperature

Table 2.6 Calculated elasticities of weather variables on cereal productivity

Variable	*Annual*	*Summer*	*Fall*	*Spring*
Precipitation	1.686*	-0.576	-0.041	-0.326*
Temperature	-23.330*	-8.953*	17.098*	14.476*

Note: * = $p < 0.001$.

decreases cereal productivity, while an increase in temperatures during fall and spring increases cereal productivity. Hence, as shown in Table 2.6, their elasticities suggest that any increase in average annual precipitation by 1mm will increase cereal productivity levels by 1.686 per cent. Interpreting the result the other way around, a decrease in precipitation by 1mm annually will lead to a decrease in cereal productivity by 1.686 per cent while a 1mm increase during the spring will lead to a decline in crop productivity by 0.326 per cent, both at 1 per cent. The elasticities of temperature variables indicate that a 1°C increase in annual and summer temperatures could lead to a decrease in cereal productivity by 23.330 and 8.953 per cent, respectively, while a 1°C increase in fall and spring temperatures will lead to an increase in cereal production and thus an increase in productivity by 17.098 and 14.476 per cent, respectively, all at 1 per cent.

As expected, geographical differences affected cereal productivity positively at the 1 per cent level. It appears that farming in midland or highland areas as compared to lowland areas contributed to increase in productivity. This points to the importance of location-specific determinants of cereal productivity, with households in the highland demonstrating higher productivity compared to those in the lowland. Hence, in line with the descriptive result, the corresponding computed coefficients show that cereal productivity increased in highland AEZs by 62.579 per cent and also increased in midland AEZs by 5.284 per cent. Therefore, more production with better productivity was likely to be at higher altitudes where rainfall and temperature are favorable for farm production.

Lastly, the results for the time trend variable – a proxy variable for technical change in cereal production – positively impacted cereal productivity at the 1 per cent level. The linear term suggests that there is technological regress or upward shift in production between these time periods and the squared term indicates technical regress at a decreasing rate. Its calculated elasticity shows that there has been an increase in cereal productivity by 18.428 per cent over the past 15 years, implying that there were technical improvements among Ethiopian cereal farmers during 1999–2014.

5. Conclusion and recommendations

A large body of literature demonstrates negative impacts of climate change and weather variations on crop production and productivity. In particular, as climate change is likely to intensify high temperatures and low precipitation, its most dramatic impacts will be felt by smallholder and subsistence farmers. Considering Ethiopian cereal production, it is observed that while a major part of the productivity increase was due to increased use of physical inputs and governmental support, the gradual increase in annual and seasonal weather factors in the last few decades had a measurable effect on production and productivity. In this paper we evaluated the impacts of climatic/weather and non-climatic factors on cereal productivity and provided a descriptive and econometrics analysis of their impacts on cereal productivity, using four-round panel data from randomly selected rural farm households covering the period 1999–2014. Consistent with previous findings of productivity studies in SSA, which primarily considered conventional agricultural production inputs and climate factors, our results confirm the importance and statistically strong dependence between most of the explanatory variables and cereal productivity.

Our descriptive results showed that cereal crop production and productivity increased over the period and in each ACZ. The average annual rainfall distribution trend declined, while the average annual temperature increased through the study period. However, the trend was not uniform in AEZs. Econometrics results indicate inputs such as use of agro-chemicals, livestock, number of plots and participation in agricultural extension services significantly enhanced cereal productivity. On the other hand, cereal planted area, household head's age and educational level influenced cereal productivity negatively. Linear and squared weather variables' coefficients revealed that cereal productivity is generally sensitive to weather variations. Further, linear and squared estimates of weather variables – annually and seasonally – were found to be significant determinants of productivity, implying that climate had a non-linear effect on cereal productivity.

Average annual rainfall affected cereal productivity positively while its square term had a negative effect. Its marginal effect suggests that an increase in average annual precipitation by 1mm will increase productivity by more than 1.686 per cent. Spring precipitation affected cereal productivity negatively while summer and fall precipitation affected it positively. On the other hand, annual temperature affected cereal productivity negatively while its square term had a positive effect. Its marginal effect suggests that a 1°C increase in annual temperature could reduce productivity by 23.33 per cent. This may be due to an increase in average annual minimum or maximum temperature during the crop growing season, which in turn will lead to a decline in cereal productivity. Further, fall and spring temperatures affected cereal productivity positively while the summer season temperature affected it negatively.

Moreover, in line with the descriptive results, our results show that geographical differences – a set of regional dummy variables – considerably affected cereal productivity. Its statistical significance points to the importance of location-specific determinants of cereal productivity with households in the highland demonstrating a higher position compared to those in the lowland. Therefore, more productive production is likely to be in higher altitudes where rainfall and temperature are favorable for cereal production. Lastly, an estimate of the time trend variables showed a technological regress but at decreasing rates in cereal productivity over the period. These outcomes are important and can be used to inform the government on possible policy decisions, such as where to emphasize when planning climate change adaptation strategies to be promoted and ways to envisage better provision of extension services that are tailored to the peculiarities of the ACZs across the country. Thus, the study's results confirm that weather effects contribute to less performance in cereal productivity in Ethiopia. Having poverty and food security implications, the study therefore recommends public policies which are geared at improving agricultural extension services, farmers' education, supply of agricultural inputs and climate change adaptation strategies and policies that could meet the needs of farmers and which are suitable to AEZs.

References

Aberra K., (2011). "The Impact of Climate Variability on Crop Production in Ethiopia: Which Crop Is More Vulnerable to Rainfall Variability?" Paper presented at the 9th International Conference of EEA, Addis Ababa, Ethiopia.

Addai, K.N. and V. Owusu (2014). "Technical efficiency of maize farmers across various agro ecological zones of Ghana", *Journal of Agriculture and Environmental Sciences*, 3(1), 149–172.

African Development Bank (AfDB) (April 2011). *Federal Democratic Republic of Ethiopia: Country Strategy Paper 2011–15.* Available at: www.afdb.org/en/.../afdb/Documents/.../Ethiopia-2011-2015.

Bamlaku, B.A., E.A Nuppenau, and H. Boland (2009). *Technical Efficiency of Farming Systems Across Agro-Ecological Zones in Ethiopia: An Application of Stochastic Frontier Analysis.* Germany: Justus-Liebig University of Giessen.

Battese, G.E. and T.J. Coelli (1995). "A model for technical inefficiency in a stochastic frontier production function for panel data", *Empirical Economics*, 20, 325–332.

Carpentier, A. and R.D. Weaver (1997). "Damage control productivity: Why econometrics matters", *American Journal of Agricultural Economics*, 79, 47–61.

Central Statistical Agency (CSA) (2007). *Statistical Abstract 2007.* Ethiopia: CSA.

Central Statistical Agency (CSA) (2015). "Report on area and production of major crops: Private peasant holdings, Meher season", Agricultural Sample Survey 2014/15, Addis Ababa, Ethiopia.

Demeke, A.B., K. Alwin, and Z. Manfred (2011). "Using panel data to estimate the effect of rainfall shocks on smallholders' food security and vulnerability in rural Ethiopia", *Climatic Change*, 108, 185–206.

Deressa, T., R.M. Hassan, T. Alemu, M. Yesuf, and C. Ringler (2009). *Analyzing the Determinants of Farmers' Choice of Adaptation Methods and Perceptions of Climate Change in the Nile Basin of Ethiopia.* International Food Policy Research Institute (IFPRI). Discussion Paper 00798, Washington, DC.

Food and Agriculture Organization of the United Nations (FAO) (2009). *Food Security and Agricultural Mitigation in Developing Countries: Options for Capturing Synergies.* Rome: FAO.

Growth and Transformation Plan (GTP) (2010). "Federal Democratic Republic of Ethiopia", Ministry of Finance and Economic Development, Addis Ababa, Ethiopia.

Guiteras, R. (2009). "The impact of climate change on Indian agriculture", Manuscript, Department of Economics, University of Maryland, College Park, MD.

Hausmann, J. and W. Taylor (1981). "Panel data and unobservable individual effects", *Econometrica*, 49(6), 1377–1398.

Hussain, S.S. (1989). "Analysis of economic efficiency in Northern Pakistan: Estimation, a uses and policy implications", PhD Dissertation, University of Illinois, Urbana-Champaign.

IPCC (2012). "Managing the risks of extreme events and disasters to advance climate change adaptation; A special report of working groups I and II of the IPCC", Technical Report.

Kassahun, A. (2011). "The impact of climate variability on crop production in Ethiopia: Which crop is more vulnerable to rainfall variability?", Paper presented at the 9th International Conference of EEA, Addis Ababa, Ethiopia.

Kuosmanen, T., D. Pemsl, and J. Wesseler (2006). "Specification and estimation of production functions involving damage control inputs: A two-stage, semi-parametric approach", *American Journal of Agricultural Economics*, 88(2), 499–511.

Kurukulasuriya, P. and R. Mendelsohn (2008). "A Ricardian analysis of the impact of climate change on African cropland", *African Journal of Agricultural and Resource Economics*, 2(1), 1–23.

Lee, J., D. Nadolnyak, and V. Hartarska (2012). "Impact of climate change on agricultural production in Asian countries: Evidence from panel study", Paper prepared for presentation at the Southern Agricultural Economics Association Annual Meeting, Birmingham.

Liangzhi, Y., M.W. Rosegrant, C. Fang, and S. Wood (2005). "Impact of Global Warming on Chinese wheat productivity", EPT Discussion Paper 143, IFPRI.

Lichtenberg, E. and D. Zilberman (1986). "The econometrics of damage control: Why specification matters", *American Journal of Agricultural Economics*, 68, 261–273.

Mendelsohn, R. and A. Dinar (2003). "Climate and rural income", Mimeo, School of Forestry and Environmental Studies, Yale University.

Mendelsohn, R., W. Nordhaus, and D. Shaw (1994). "The impact of global warming on agriculture: A Ricardian analysis", *American Economic Review*, 84, 753–771.

Ministry of Agriculture (MoA) (2000). *Agro-Ecological Zonation of Ethiopia*. Addis Ababa, Ethiopia.

Mintewab, B., S. Di Falco, and M. Alemu (2014). "On the impact of weather variability and climate change on agriculture: Evidence from Ethiopia", Environment for Development, Discussion Paper.

National Meteorological Agency (NMA) (1996). *Climate and Agro-Climatic Resources of Ethiopia, Meteorological Research Report Series, 1(1)*. Addis Ababa, Ethiopia.

National Meteorological Agency (NMA) (2001). *Initial National Communication of Ethiopia to the United Nations Framework Convention on Climate Change*. Addis Ababa, Ethiopia.

Nisrane, F., G. Berhane, S. Asrat, G. Getachew, A.S. Taffesse, and J. Hoddinott (2011). "Sources of inefficiency and growth in agricultural output in subsistence agriculture: A Stochastic Frontier analysis", ESSP II Working Paper 19. Addis Ababa: IFPRI.

O'Brien, K.L. and R.M. Leichenko (2008). "Human security, vulnerability, and sustainable adaptation", Background paper commissioned for the HDR 2007/2008: Fighting Climate Change: Human Solidarity in a Divided World. New York: UNDP.

Ramsey, J.B. (1969). "Tests for specification error in classical linear least squares regression analysis", *Journal of the Royal Statistical Society*, B31, 250–271.

Schlenker, W., W.M. Hanemann, and A.C. Fisher (2006). "The impact of global warming on U.S. agriculture: An econometric analysis of optimal growing conditions", *Review of Economics and Statistics*, 88(1), 113–125.

Shankar, B. and C. Thirtle (2005). "Pesticide productivity and transgenic cotton technology: The South African smallholder case", *Journal of Agricultural Economics*, 56(1), 97–116.

Tchale, H. and J. Suaer (2007). "The efficiency of maize farming in malawi: A bootstrapped translog frontier", *Cahiers d'economie et sociologie rurales*, 82–83, 34–56.

Tesfay, G., R. Ruben, J. Pender, and A. Kuyvenhoven (2005). "Resource use efficiency on own and share cropping plots", in *Northern Ethiopia: Determinants and Implications for Sustainability*, in *Sustainable poverty reduction in less-favored areas*, p 181.

UN-OHRLLS (2009). *The Impact of Climate Change on the Development Project of the Least Developed Countries and Small Island Developing States.* Available at: http://unohrlls.org.

Wooldridge, J.M. (2002). *Econometric Analysis of Cross-section and Panel Data.* Cambridge, MA: The MIT Press.

The World Bank (2003). *Risk and Vulnerability Assessment, Draft Report for Ethiopia.* Washington, DC: The World Bank.

The World Bank (2006). *Managing Water Resources to Maximize Sustainable Growth: A Country Water Resources Assistance Strategy for Ethiopia.* Washington, DC: The World Bank.

3 Vulnerability and impact assessment of climate change on East African wildlife tourism

A study of the Maasai Mara ecosystem

Richard Kerongo Mose

1. Introduction

The tourism industry is a major contributor to global economic development, especially as an employer in developing economies and regions where tourism commonly represents the main source of national foreign incomes (Bigano et al., 2007). UNWTO has determined that tourism is a primary source of foreign exchange earnings in 46 of 50 of the world's least developed countries (LDCs) (UNWTO, 2007a). The sector is directly and indirectly responsible for 8.8 per cent of the world's jobs (258 million); 9.1 per cent of the world's GDP (USD 6 trillion); 5.8 per cent of the world's exports (USD 1.1 trillion); and 4.5 per cent of the world's investments (USD 652 billion) (WTTC, 2012). Travel and tourism generated USD 7.6 trillion (10 per cent of global GDP) and 277 million jobs (one in 11 jobs) for the global economy in 2014 (WTTC Kenya, 2015).

According to the World Travel and Tourism Council the industry is projected to continue growing linearly in the coming years (Figure 3.1).

1.1 Tourism's contribution to the East African economy

Tourism generated an estimated USD 1.2 billion revenue in Kenya in 2012 and USD 1.3 billion in Tanzania in 2011 (KNBS, 2013; RoT, 2011). In 2014 the tourism industry directly supported 206,500 jobs (3.5 per cent of the total employment) in Kenya. This is expected to increase by 2.9 per cent per annum to 277,000 jobs (3.4 per cent of the total employment) in 2025. In 2014 the industry contributed USD 5.618 billion (10.5 per cent of GDP) to Kenya's total GDP; this is forecast to increase by 5.1 per cent per annum to USD 9.642 billion (10.3 per cent of the country's GDP) in 2025 (WTTC Kenya, 2015). In Tanzania, travel and tourism directly supported 467,000 jobs (4.3 per cent of the total employment). This is expected to increase by 2.3 per cent per annum to 551,000 jobs (3.7 per cent of the total employment) in

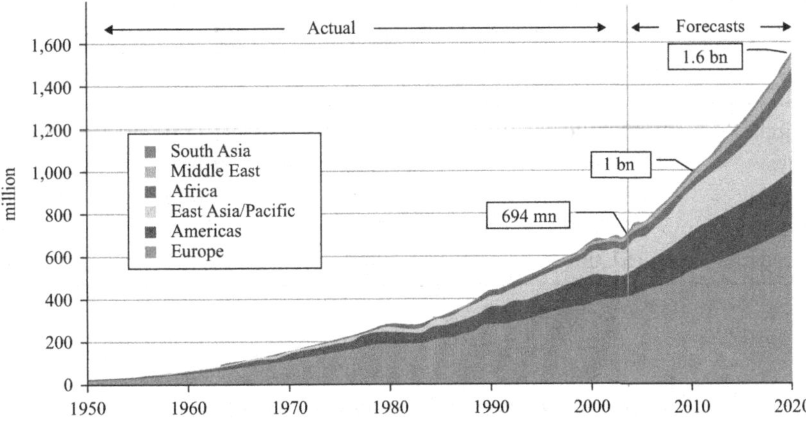

Figure 3.1 World inbound tourist numbers

Source: Adapted from WTTC (2012)

2025. The total contribution of travel and tourism to the Tanzania's GDP was USD 4.127 billion (14.0 per cent of GDP) in 2014 and is forecast to rise by 6.6 per cent per annum to USD 7.942 billion (13.2 per cent of GDP) in 2025 (WTTC Tanzania, 2015). In Uganda, travel and tourism's direct contribution to the country's GDP was USD 0.931 billion (4.3 per cent of the country's total GDP) in 2014, and is forecast to rise by 6.4 per cent per annum between 2015–25 to USD 1.8493 billion (4.3 per cent of the country's total GDP). The industry supported 247,000 jobs (3.6 per cent of the total employment); this is expected to increase by 3.7 per cent per annum to 377,000 jobs (3.7 per cent of the total employment) by 2025. While in Rwanda, travel and tourism directly contributed USD 0.2671 billion (3.6 per cent to the country's total GDP) in 2014 and provided 66,000 jobs (3.0 per cent of the total employment); it is forecast to increase by 4.1 per cent per annum in 2015–25 to USD 0.4243 billion (2.9 per cent of the country's total GDP) (WTTC Rwanda, 2015; WTTC Uganda, 2015). Looking at these figures it is evident that travel and tourism is a very important industry in East African economies. Over 60 per cent of the tourism attractions in East African countries are wildlife based. In Tanzania, for example, the northern safari circuit – which is the main attraction of which the Serengeti-Mara wildebeest migration is a part – generated an estimated USD 550 million in 2008 (Mitchell et al., 2009). Any loss to wildlife migration or their habitats could undermine some of East Africa's key tourism products with significant impacts on national economies (Ogutu et al., 2013). The number of foreign tourists visiting East African countries has continued to grow (Table 3.1).

Table 3.1 Number of inbound tourists per year per country in East African countries

Country	*Number of inbound tourists per year (2011–14)*			
	2011	*2012*	*2013*	*2014*
Ethiopia	523,000	597,000	681,000	770,000
Kenya	1,750,000	1,619,000	1,434,000	1,261,000
Rwanda	688,000	815,000	864,000	926,000
Tanzania	843,000	1,043,000	1,063,000	1,113,000
Uganda	1,151,000	1,197,000	1,206,000	1,266,000

Source: The World Bank (2015)

1.2 Climate change and East African wildlife tourism

The Intergovernmental Panel on Climate Change (IPCC) declared that 'warming of the climate system is unequivocal' (IPCC, 2007a). The global mean temperature increased by 0.76°C between 1850–99 and 2001–05 and IPCC concluded that most of the observed increase in global average temperatures since the mid-20th century was 'very likely' (> 90 per cent probability) the result of human activities that were increasing greenhouse gas (GHG) concentrations in the atmosphere. IPCC (2007a) also predicts that the pace of climate change is 'very likely' (> 90 per cent probability) to accelerate with continued GHG emissions at or above current rates, with globally average surface temperatures estimated to rise by 1.8°C to 4.0°C by the end of the 21st century. These predicted changes highlight the need for awareness and preparedness for natural hazards at the local level through systematic capacity building and strategies for disaster risk management (IPCC, 2007a; UNWTO, 2007a).

Despite its insignificant contribution to GHGs that cause global warming, Africa is one of the most vulnerable regions to the adverse impact of climate change (Hope, 2009). Many areas in Africa are recognized as having climates that are among the most variable in the world on seasonal and decadal time scales (Boko et al., 2007; Conway and Schipper, 2011; Hope, 2009; Kumssa and Jones, 2010)

UNFCCC states that Kenya's climate has been changing considerably over the years. Average annual temperatures increased by 1°C (a 15 per cent rise) between 1960 and 2003, with most of the warming taking place during the long rainy season (March–May), meaning that there were relatively more hot days during the long rainy season by an additional 18.8 per cent (McSweeney et al., 2010; UNFCCC, 2007).

Kenya's substantial arid and semi-arid areas and coastline increase its vulnerability (Munyiri, 2015). According to a response strategy report of the Government of Kenya, the level of knowledge about Kenya's vulnerability to climate change impact is not accurately known (GoK, 2010). What is known, however, is that the country is vulnerable to climate change because of her dependence on climate-sensitive sectors such as agriculture, water and tourism (Munyiri, 2015).

Tourism is a highly climate-sensitive industry. IPCC and UNWTO have stated that tourism will be greatly affected by climate change (UNWTO, 2007a). Research on tourism demand indicates that a gradual shift in the attractiveness of climatic conditions for tourism and consequently a shift in international tourism demand towards higher latitudes and altitudes are very likely (Boko et al., 2007; Hamilton et al., 2005; UNWTO, 2007b). For example, a study carried out by Scott et al. (2012), using a global scale simulation model, projected that tourists from temperate nations that currently dominate international travel will spend more holidays in their home countries or nearby regions. Consequently, relative demand for international travel to sub-tropical and tropical nations is projected to decline. Studies on climate and tourism demand which use econometric models also show temperature to be statistically significant in determining demand for a variety of tourism products (Hamilton et al., 2005; Weaver, 2011).

Nature-based tourism is an important and growing segment of tourism. This is tourism which includes travelling to undeveloped areas for the purpose of enjoying nature. In countries such as Kenya, New Zealand and Nepal, this sector accounts for as much as 40–60 per cent of all international tourists (Nyaupane and Chhetri, 2009). Climate change significantly affects the tourism industry, most importantly due to its effect on the attractiveness of tourism destinations and tourist flows (Amelung et al., 2007). Nature-based tourism depends on natural resources such as water, coastlines, landscapes and biodiversity. These influence the potential attraction of destinations. However, climate change threatens the loss of some of these relevant natural resources (Gössling and Hall, 2006). Despite significant growth in research on tourism and climate change, there are considerable gaps in research on specific regions especially in developing countries. There is a significant research gap particularly in the context of vulnerabilities and impact of climate change on wildlife and wildlife-based tourism in developing countries and small island states (Nyaupane and Chhetri, 2009).

2. Purpose and methodology

The purpose of this study is to examine the vulnerability and impact of climate change on wildlife tourism and to develop a model for identifying vulnerability indicators and conceptual frameworks and come up with an empirical model.

Data was collected from the management of the Maasai Mara Game Reserve, wildlife conservancies within Maasai Mara, the managements of hotels and lodges and from drivers and tour guides working in the Maasai Mara Game Reserve. The sample size was 30 hotels and lodges, which represented 30 per cent of the accommodation facilities, and three conservancies representing 27 per cent of the conservancies sampled, with a 95 per cent confidence level (0.5 margin of error based on the Yamane (1967) formula). The accommodation facilities and game ranches were sampled using a purposive stratified sampling technique so that every type of accommodation facility was represented. The sample size comprised of 30 hotel and lodge managers, three conservancy managers and 384 tour guides and drivers. This sample size was based on the Cochran (1963) formula. Informal structured interviews using an open-ended interview schedule were used to collect data using a snowball sampling technique. A self-administering questionnaire was also used to collect data. The questionnaire and interview schedule were pre-tested to ensure that they collected the desired data. Non-participatory observations were also used to collect data. Secondary data was collected from library research and the internet. The primary focus was wildlife tourism in the Maasai Mara ecosystem and data collected was analyzed using qualitative methods. Very little research has been done on how climate change has impacted wildlife tourism in East Africa. This study adds to information about this contemporary area.

The Cochran formula

$$n_0 = \frac{Z^2 * p * (1-p)}{e^2} \quad (1)$$

n_0 – sample size
Z_2 – abscissa of the normal curve that cuts-off an area α at the tails
e – acceptable sampling error
p – estimated proportion of an attribute that is present in the population

The Yamane formula

$$n = \frac{N}{1 + N * (e)^2} \quad (2)$$

n – sample size; N – population size; e – acceptable sampling error
* 95 per cent confidence level and $p = 0.5$ are assumed

3. Literature review

Climate change vulnerability is a concept that is used to denote a condition whereby a system or any of its components is susceptible or prone to and is unable to cope with adverse effects of climate change (IPCC, 2007c). Impacts are defined as the effects that one thing has on another (IPCC, 2007c). According to IPCC (2007c) the impact of climate change is defined as the effects that climate change has on the biophysical environment. Tourism is regarded as a sector that is highly vulnerable to climate change because it is highly connected to the natural environment (Richardson and Witkowski, 2010). Climate change impacts the resource base (attractions) upon which tourism depends to attract visitors (Richardson and Witkowski, 2010; Scott et al., 2012; Simpson et al., 2008; UNWTO-UNEP-WMO, 2008). The impact of climate on tourism can bring negative and/or positive effects to tourism enterprises and communities. According to UNWTO two things determine the attractiveness of a tourism destination: the natural environment and the security of the destination (UNWTO, 2007a).

According to Mkiramweni (2014) the impacts of climate change on wildlife tourism can be direct or indirect and they are linked to variations in precipitation, temperature, humidity and landform transformations resulting from increased encroachments and activities associated with human habitations.

Some countries and regions are more vulnerable than others to the impact of climate change and there may also be some benefits for certain regions. The level of knowledge about potential climate change impact also varies greatly between regions (Simpson et al., 2008) (Table 3.2).

To develop and understand the concept of wildlife tourism in Maasai Mara and East Africa, a profile of the main stakeholders in the sector needs to be established. Table 3.3 gives a list of the main stakeholders in wildlife tourism in Maasai Mara.

3.1 Vulnerability and impact of climate change on communities in Maasai Mara

Communities that depend on wildlife tourism will be impacted if climate change leads to a decline in visitors (Hambira et al., 2013). Similarly, climate change has the potential to affect the resource base from which local communities derive

Table 3.2 Relative level of tourism-specific climate change knowledge and estimated impact and vulnerability of climate change on tourism by region

Region	*Estimated vulnerability of climate change on tourism*	*Estimated impact of climate change on tourism*	*Relative level of tourism-specific climate change knowledge*
Africa	Extremely high	Moderately-strongly negative	Extremely poor
Asia	Extremely high	Weakly-moderately negative	Extremely poor
Australia and New Zealand	Very high	Moderately-strongly negative	Poor-moderate (high in the Great Barrier Reef)
Europe	High	Weakly-moderately negative	Moderate (high in the alpine areas)
Latin America	Very high	Weakly-moderately negative	Poor
North America	High	Weakly negative	Moderate (high in coastal and ski areas)
Polar regions	Very high	Weakly negative – weakly positive	Poor
Small islands	Extremely high	Strongly negative	Moderate (highest with respect to impacts on reef systems)

Source: Adapted from Simpson et al. (2008)

Table 3.3 Key wildlife tourism stakeholders in Maasai Mara

Stakeholders	Primary goals/expected benefits from wildlife tourism
Visitors	Access to an affordable, high-quality wildlife tourism experience. Learn local cultures and experiences.
Tour business operators	Promotion and advertising for wildlife tourism products. Maximize short-term profits to individual operators and members of the travel trade. Provide high-quality tourism operations and experiences.
Government agencies both local and central	Policy formulation and enforcement. Research and training. Promoting and advertising wildlife tourism.
Host communities (indigenous and community surrounding parks)	Protect environment and maximize profits from wildlife tourism. Increased access to natural resources (water, grazing/agricultural land and forests). Improved livelihoods and well-being. Involvement in decision-making. Compensation of lost property caused by wildlife/tourism/conservation.
Conservationists and environmental managers	Minimize threats to wildlife resources. Satisfy public recreation goals. Use tourism to support conservation goals. Law enforcement in protected areas. Participation in policy formulation and enforcement.
Non-governmental organizations (NGOs)	Protection of wildlife habitats, biodiversity and the general environment. Provide support (such as water projects) to local communities. Use tourism to support conservation goals. Consequences of tourism.
Wildlife	Main attractions for tourists. Source of data for biodiversity researchers. Require to be conserved and protected.

Source: Adapted from Mkiramweni (2014)

their livelihoods (Gössling et al., 2008). It is likely that affected communities will disrupt immediate wildlife resources in order to cope with the impact of climate change (Mkiramweni, 2014). In Maasai Mara climate change is exacerbating an already worsening situation. An increase in human population around the Mara ecosystem has led to an increase in the demand for housing and food for the ballooning population. Shanties have sprung up, taking up land meant for wildlife. Demand for food has led to an increase in the acreage under food crops such as wheat and maize, which has eaten into wildlife land.

3.2 *Impact of climate change on the tourist and tourism businesses in Maasai Mara*

According to The Climate Institute (2006), climate change will pose risks to businesses including physical impacts, regulations, competition, changing markets, investments, effects on the price of energy, energy infrastructure, litigation and shareholder activism. All sectors will be affected including finance, property, insurance, agriculture, energy and infrastructure. Tourism property owners and energy users are likely to have the highest exposure to these impacts. These risks arise from the physical impacts of climate change and also from the responses of governments, investors, shareholders, competitors, customers, consumers, the public and the media.

Maasai Mara has numerous tourism-based businesses ranging from curio sellers, hotels, lodges, camping sites and tented camps. The ecosystem has about 7,000 beds in hotels, tented camps and lodges which range from five star lodges to ramshackle accommodation facilities (MoT Kenya, 2013). The other increasingly thriving business is that of commercial sex workers, which has grown rapidly in recent years. The highest number of visitors is recorded in June through October. These are the months when the great wildebeest migration takes place from the Serengeti to Mara (June through August) and back to Serengeti (September and October), sometimes extending to November (Ogutu et al., 2009; Owen-Smith and Ogut, 2012).

3.3 *Impact of climate change on wildlife and ecosystems in Maasai Mara*

According to Lusweti (2011), climate change affects biodiversity including wildlife. With a change in climate comes a change in wildlife reproduction cycles. Wildlife usually synchronizes its reproduction cycles to follow the weather conditions; this is more so for herbivores who want to reproduce just at the onset of the rains when there is plenty of food for lactating mothers and the grass is long enough to hide the young ones from marauding predators. As climate changes, animals are increasingly being forced to change their reproductive behavior and migration patterns.

Kenya is a mega bio-diverse country with over 35,000 species of flora and fauna in variable ecosystems ranging from marine, tropical dry land, forests and arid land (Lusweti, 2011).

Maasai Mara is home to the wildebeests, topis, zebras, Thomson's gazelles, hippopotami, Nile crocodiles, leopards, hyenas, cheetahs, jackals and nocturnal bat-eared foxes (which are not found anywhere else). Antelopes that can be found here include the Grant's gazelles, impalas, duikers and Coke's hartebeests. The plains are also home to the distinctive Maasai giraffe and the large roan antelope (Lusweti, 2011; Ogutu et al., 2009; Owen-Smith and Ogutu, 2012).

Staffan (2002) writes that the wildebeest are famous for their annual long-distance migration, seemingly timed to coincide with the annual pattern of rainfall and grass growth. The timing of their migration in both the rainy and dry seasons can vary considerably (by months) from year to year. At the end of the rainy season (May or June in East Africa), wildebeest migrate to dry-season areas in response to a lack of surface (drinking) water. When the rainy season begins again (months later), the animals quickly move back to their wet-season ranges. Factors that affect their migration include food abundance, surface water availability, predators and phosphorus content in grasses (The Heinz Center, 2012). Phosphorus is a crucial element for all life forms, particularly for lactating female bovid. As a result during the rainy season, wildebeest select grazing areas that contain particularly high phosphorus levels since this is the time when female animals are lactating.

In Maasai Mara there are two wildebeest migration routes. One involves about 1,300,000 wildebeests, 500,000 Thomson's gazelles, 97,000 topis, 18,000 elands and 200,000 zebras migrating from Serengeti to Mara and back every year, and the other involves about 30,000 wildebeest migrating from the Loita plains in Kenya to Mara and back every year (The Heinz Center, 2012; MoT Kenya, 2013). These migrants are followed by hungry predators, most notably lions, cheetahs and hyenas, and other herbivores such as elands, zebras and antelopes. The migrating animals help feed the crocodiles in the transboundary Mara River and they also help fertilize the Mara ecosystem through their millions of tons of droppings. This spurs growth of new vegetation thus helping to feed the other ungulates and grazers in this ecosystem. Anything that interferes with the migration will thus be interfering with the real survival of the entire ecosystem. Climate change will affect rainfall patterns across Africa and wildebeest may not be able to migrate in search of better conditions. The increased frequency of droughts due to climate change will increase the need for blue wildebeest to make long migrations (The Heinz Center, 2012). Climate change has already made the wet season drier and warmer and the dry season wetter; therefore, blue wildebeest are arriving two months earlier for the wet season and moving south when land there is still barren. This can result in lower quality forage for lactating females (Chidumayo, 2011; IUCN, 2008).

IPCC (2012) states that climate change is a new and growing threat to wildlife migrations in the East African savannas. The increased frequency and severity of droughts and floods that is expected to occur will modify vegetation growth and hence food availability for the migrating animals. For example, in the Amboseli ecosystem, a severe drought caused the wildebeest population to crash by more than 85 per cent in 2009 (GoK, 2011). By 2010, the population numbered only 3,000 animals, down from over 15,000 before the drought, the lowest observed for more than 30 years (GoK, 2013).

The main factor influencing wildebeest migration is rainfall through its effect on forage and soil salinity. Yet, wildebeest numbers are negatively correlated with annual rainfall in the Mara-Serengeti ecosystem. The survival of wildebeest in the changing weather patterns therefore depends on their migratory behavior (Ogutu et al., 2011; Sitati et al., 2014; Sitati and Wishitemi, 2003).The ability of migrants to respond to changing climatic conditions is likely to be impaired by such man-made threats as habitat loss and fragmentation. As migratory corridors and dispersal areas are lost due to land use change, migratory movements will be curtailed and this will compromise the ability of migrants to cope with the widening climatic variability that are expected as a consequence of global warming (Ogutu et al., 2009; Owen-Smith and Ogutu, 2012).

Due to changing climatic conditions, Maasai Mara is already experiencing a change in its biodiversity. Invader plant species such as *Ipomea spp.* and *Solanum spp.* are reportedly increasing. This is due to overgrazing as a result of reduced forage due to reduced rainfall. The emergence of these plant species will negatively impact the ability of the ecosystem to support large numbers of grazers as those seen during the migration. In the long run this will affect the migration of the wildebeest and other animals that tag along, eventually affecting the entire tourism business in the area. Long wet weather in Maasai Mara is not favored by the migratory wildebeest because the soils in the Mara ecosystem are mainly clay and they become waterlogged with prolonged rains. The waterlogged soil causes the foot rot disease among the wildebeest and this also makes the vegetation less nutritious. Hence, the wildebeest prefer the drier south, thus making them migrate back to Serengeti earlier than expected (MENR, 2012).

Due to climate change and climate variability, the productivity of the ecosystems will be greatly affected, meaning that wildlife will increasingly find it difficult to get enough water and food in their natural ecosystems. The result will be increased competition for the increasingly scarce resources leading to increased resource conflicts including increased human–wildlife conflicts as the animals struggle to survive in a changing environment.

With a change in the wildlife's migratory patterns due to the changing climate, wildlife will increasingly move out of the conservation areas to people's farms. In Maasai Mara elephants are increasingly moving to the north due to increased competition for forage in the game reserve. The elephants' northward movement exacerbates poverty in that region since they destroy crops, increasing human–wildlife conflicts (Table 3.4).

3.4 *Conceptual frameworks*

Vulnerability is a function of exposure, sensitivity and adaptive capacity (IPCC, 2007a). Vulnerability assessment (VA) is a practical action in climate change research and policy formulation. It is intended to provide an understanding of the system's exposure, sensitivity and adaptive capacity. In other words, vulnerability assessment provides an understanding of the degree to which a system is vulnerable or resilient to shocks and stressors and this understanding provides policymakers and tourism practitioners grounds for developing adaptation strategies (Hinkel and Klein, 2009). As vulnerability is place and context specific, VA has to be place and context based in order to understand the vulnerability and resilience in the context considered in the study (Scott et al., 2012; UNWTO-UNEP-WMO, 2008).

To properly understand the direct and indirect effects of climate change on wildlife tourism, a comprehensive conceptual framework needs to be established. Figure 3.2 illustrates the vulnerability and impact of climate change on wildlife tourism. The framework incorporates both direct and indirect impacts of climate change to wildlife and wildlife tourism. It should be noted that the impact of

Table 3.4 Impacts and vulnerabilities of climate change in Africa relevant for tourism

Impacts	*Vulnerabilities*
Temperature	Terrestrial ecosystems
Higher warming (x1.5) throughout the continent and in all seasons compared to the global average	Drying and desertification in many areas, particularly the Sahel and southern Africa. Deforestation and forest fires.
Drier subtropical regions may become warmer than the moister tropics	Degradation of grasslands reducing their carrying capacity
Precipitation	25–40% animal species in national parks in sub-Saharan Africa expected to become endangered
Decrease in annual rainfall in much of Mediterranean Africa and northern Sahara with a greater likelihood of decreasing rainfall as the Mediterranean coast is approached	Change in animals' migratory patterns
Decrease in rainfall in southern and eastern Africa in much of the winter rainfall region and western margins	Emergence of invader species of plants in natural ecosystems
Increase in annual mean rainfall in East Africa	Increased animal diseases
Increase in rainfall in the dry Sahel may be counteracted through evaporation	Coastal Zones
Extreme Events	Coastal erosion is already destroying infrastructure and tourism facilities
Increase in frequency and intensity of extreme events including droughts and floods, as well as events occurring in new areas	Threat of inundation along coasts in eastern Africa and coastal deltas such as the Nile delta and in many major cities due to a rise in sea levels, coastal erosion and extreme events
Increase in natural resource conflicts	Degradation of marine ecosystems including coral reefs and mangroves off the East African coast. Cost of adaptation to sea level rise could amount to at least 5–10% GDP.
	A 30% loss of corals resulted in reduced tourism in Mombasa and Zanzibar, and caused financial losses of about USD 12–18 million
	80% of the glaciers on Mt Kilimanjaro are gone. Water pollution-related diseases in low-lying regions (coastal areas).
	Research
	Large gaps in research on climate variability impacts, vulnerability and changes in tourism
	Generally
	Pole-ward shift of centers of tourist activity and a shift from lowland to highland tourism

Source: Adapted from Munyiri (2015)

climate change on wildlife directly and indirectly affects wildlife-based tourism. In Maasai Mara, for example, climate change negatively impacts the migration patterns of the wildebeest, whose migration across the transboundary Mara River forms the cornerstone of tourism's survival. An impact on these animals then impacts wildlife tourism both directly and indirectly.

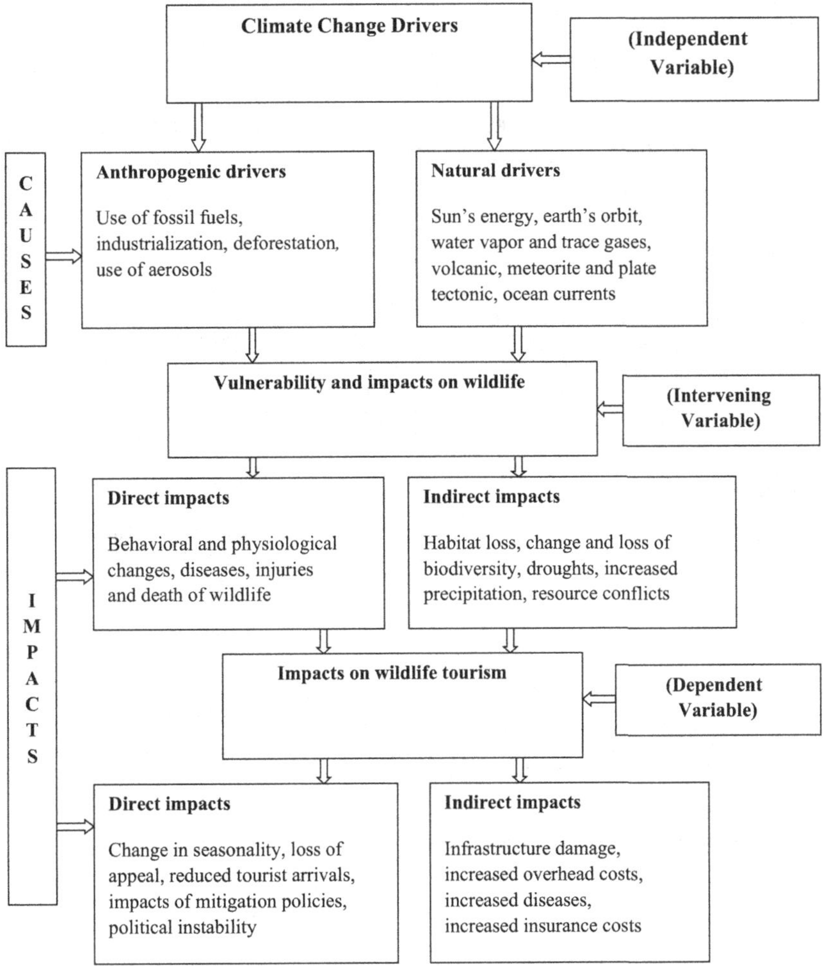

Figure 3.2 Wildlife tourism and climate change vulnerability conceptual framework

Source: Adapted from Calgaro (2011)

Calgaro (2011) has developed the most comprehensive model of vulnerability assessment and adaptation to climate change specifically for tourism destinations (Figure 3.3). In his model the exposure of destinations, vulnerability sensitivity, adaptation and their interactions are explained. This framework incorporates four major activities that featured the most in the climate change adaptation frameworks that were reviewed: (1) a case study analysis, (2) vulnerability assessment, (3) improving adaptive capacity through adaptation, and (4) monitoring and evaluating adaptations.

Key vulnerabilities are associated with many climate-sensitive systems including food supply, infrastructure, health, water resources, coastal systems, ecosystems,

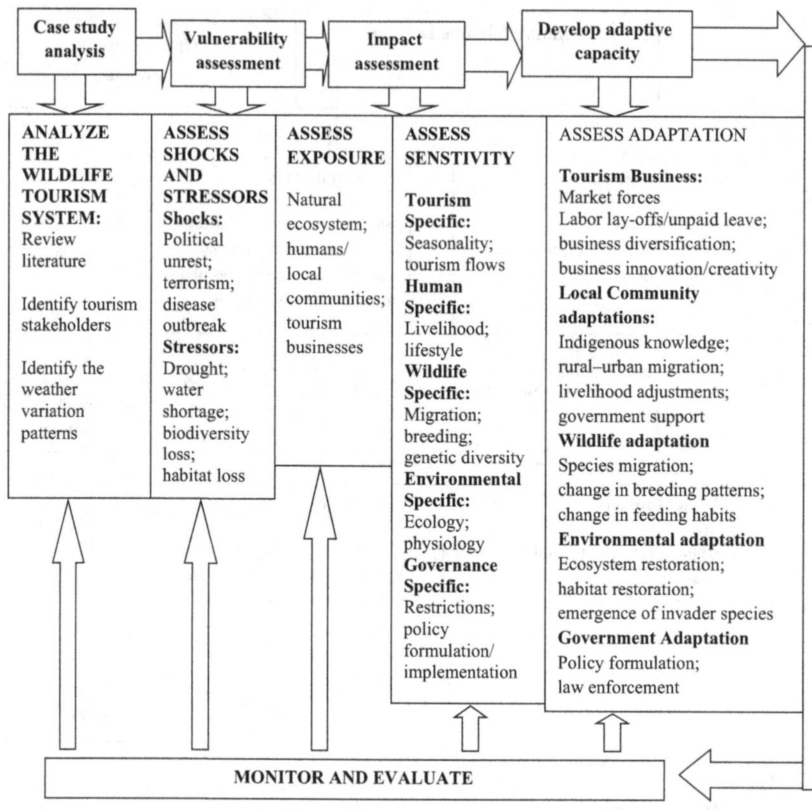

Figure 3.3 Wildlife tourism climate change vulnerability assessment framework
Source: Adapted from Calgaro (2011)

global bio-geochemical cycles, ice sheets and modes of oceanic and atmospheric circulations (Schneider et al., 2007). The vulnerabilities can be assessed using criteria developed by Schneider et al. (2007):

- Magnitude of impacts,
- Timing of impacts,
- Persistence and reversibility of impacts,
- Likelihood (estimates of uncertainty) of impacts and vulnerabilities and confidence in those estimates,
- Potential for adaptation,
- Distributional aspects of impacts and vulnerabilities, and
- Importance of the system(s) at risk.

3.5 *Vulnerability indicators*

It is noteworthy that with very good vulnerability assessment tools (VA tools) and conceptual frameworks, a good understanding and identification of specific climate change vulnerability indicators for each of the major players in wildlife tourism is important. Figure 3.4 shows how to arrive at vulnerability indicators for each of the sectors.

According to Birkmann (2007), there are nine different phases in the development of indicators: first, a relevant goal is identified, selected and defined. Then a scoping process is performed in order to identify the target group and the associated purposes for which the indicators will be used. The third phase presumes the identification of an appropriate conceptual framework, which means structuring the potential themes and indicators into a structural framework. The fourth phase involves the definition of the selection criteria for the potential indicators. The fifth phase is the identification of a set of potential indicators. Then there is the evaluation and selection of each indicator taking into account the criteria developed at an earlier stage, which results in a final set of indicators. The last phases of the indicator development are preparing a report and

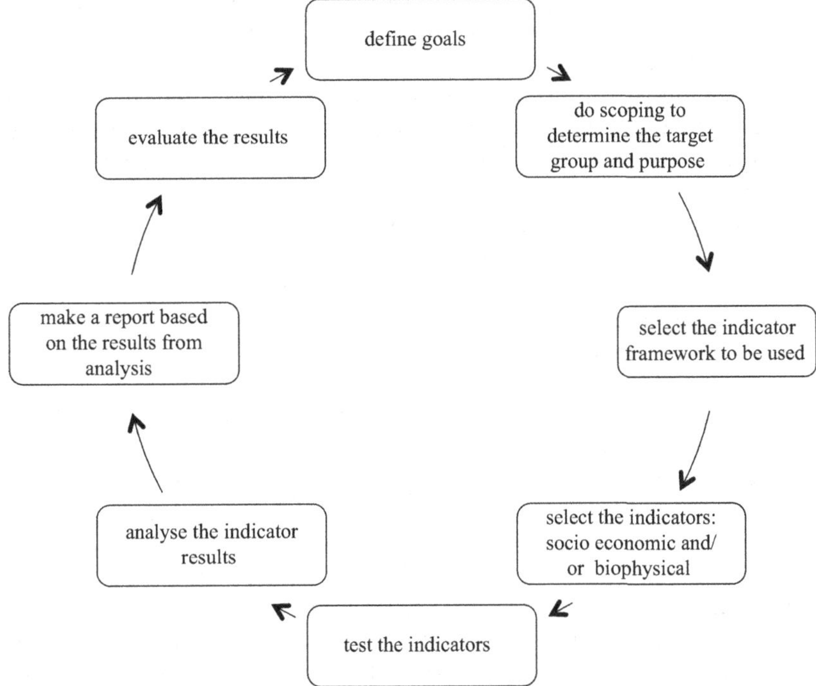

Figure 3.4 Vulnerability Indicator development process

Source: Adapted from Birkmann (2007)

assessing the indicator performance, which may result in a re-evaluation of the results depending on the outcome obtained.

The indicators for vulnerability of wildlife tourism to climate change may be biophysical, social-cultural or economic. The biophysical indicators include change in precipitation, changes in temperature, wind, humidity, increase in wildlife diseases, change in vegetation species including appearance of new species and edaphic factors. The social-cultural indicators include increase in human–human conflicts and human–wildlife conflicts while economic factors include increases in damage to infrastructure including roads, electric poles and inflation rates.

4. Results and discussion

Climate change is affecting the Maasai Mara ecosystem. Tourism businesses and the entire tourism industry in Maasai Mara greatly depend on the migration of the wildebeest. In 2009, for example, when the Mara River waters were very low, the migration was not as spectacular as expected and this led to massive tourist bookings being cancelled. In 2013 the changing rainfall patterns resulted in the wildebeest migrating late (July–August) and they also left early in September. This again led to massive hotel bookings being cancelled.

The flash floods that come with changing rainfall patterns and intensity have been reported to destroy roads and other infrastructure including electricity connectivity. This usually affects the tourists directly, leading to some of them missing flights, increasing their costs of stay. Hotels and lodges are also increasingly incurring extra overhead costs as electricity goes off and the roads are damaged. This reduces the attractiveness of wildlife tourism in this area. A disruption in the flow of tourists to Mara is affecting livelihoods and reducing income bases.

Over 60 per cent of the hotels and lodges in Maasai Mara have been negatively impacted by climate change. The impacts include increased hotel room cancellations (sometimes up to 80 per cent). There has been an up to 70 per cent increase in overhead costs and uncertainty, which too has led to 30 per cent staff lay-offs in some establishments.

Sixty-five per cent of tourists reported that they had been negatively affected. The main impacts were reduced attractiveness of the wildlife (60 per cent) and increased expenditure on the tour (55 per cent).

Over 80 per cent of the conservancies, especially those on the northern side of the reserve, reported incidences of increased human–wildlife conflicts. The main reason for this is loss of livestock to predators and loss of crops to wild ungulates.

Changing weather is also resulting in reduced pastures for cows (the main economic activity in Maasai) with the result that the community is encroaching further and further into the game reserve, leading to human–wildlife conflicts. For example, there has been frequent poisoning of lions and hyenas by the community. This is reducing the attractiveness of wildlife tourism as an economic activity in this marginalized area. These disruptions in livelihoods are set to exacerbate poverty levels among the Maasai people.

4.1 Tourism destination climate change vulnerability empirical model

The vulnerability (V) of a tourism destination to climate change equals the exposure (E) of the place to climate change impact, combined with the sensitivity (S) of the place to these impacts, minus the destination's capacity to adapt to these impacts (AC) and the destination's resilience ability. These can be modeled as:

$$V = (E + S) - (AC + R) \tag{3}$$

where V = vulnerability, E = exposure, S = sensitivity, R = resilience and AC = adaptive capacity.

If $(AC + R)$ is more than $(E + S)$ then V will be negative, indicating extreme vulnerability, while if $(AC + R)$ is less than $(E + S)$ then V will be positive, indicating that the destination is in no danger from climate change; whereas when $(AC + R)$ is equal to $(E + S)$, then the destination is able to resist climate change. It should be noted though that the elements in this model are all empirical and they will vary from place to place and from time to time. These elements are greatly dependent on the ability to develop and use good vulnerability indicators.

Often vulnerability is discussed in relation to biophysical impacts or indicators such as a rise in sea level, bushfires or coastal erosion; however, it is important that the socioeconomic impacts are also considered. For example, what is the likely effect of the aforementioned impacts on destination appeal, tourist numbers and seasonality? The breakdown of impacts into biophysical and socioeconomic factors can help gain a clearer understanding of destination specific impacts, which in turn can assist in developing targeted adaptation strategies. Birkmann (2007) and Jopp et al. (2013) state that a review of vulnerability should include two stages:

- What are the potential biophysical impacts of climate change?
- What are the likely socioeconomic implications?

Jopp et al.'s (2013) biophysical and socioeconomic dimensions of vulnerability for tourism are now summarized.

Biophysical dimensions

- Environmental fragility (air, water, land)
- Dependency on environment for tourism activities and appeal

Socioeconomic dimensions

- Vulnerability of different social groups
- Role of social networks (coping ability)
- Vulnerability of different tourist groups (elderly, business, disabled, etc.)
- Vulnerability of different tourism sub-sectors (accommodation, transportation)

Wildlife tourism in Maasai Mara is very vulnerable to climate change. The exposure and sensitivity side – that is, $(E + S)$ – indicates an industry that is highly exposed to biophysical elements such as increased change in precipitation patterns, increased invader plant species, increased change of migratory patterns of wildlife and socioeconomic factors such as increased human–wildlife conflicts and reduced tourist flows. The adaptation and resilience side reveals an industry with low resilience and adaptive capacity due to lack of enough concise data, lack of proper support mechanisms from the government and other quarters and lack of a proper adaptation framework

4.2 Importance of vulnerability and impact assessments

In East Africa, climate change comes with devastating impacts on the economies. Apart from terrorism, drought and floods have caused the top 10 disasters in East Africa in the last four decades. It is forecast that an increase in temperature by 1.5°C by 2040 will result in a 1.7 per cent decrease in Africa's GDP (IPCC, 2007a).

Most of the East African wildlife is found in rural and marginalized areas. These are areas that are characterized by economic activities that are mainly subsistence in nature. Poverty levels are high in these areas. Wildlife tourism is slowly being accepted as a community-based natural resource management style that will economically benefit the locals in these areas and at the same time also help conserve biodiversity. Through wildlife tourism, communities benefit directly by getting jobs, selling their tourism products (for example, curios), showcasing their culture and earning an income. The people benefit directly through improved infrastructure, improved healthcare and improved security. The fiscal impact of tourism in East African countries varies based on a country's policies and the natural resources available.

Climate change is set to negate this positive human–wildlife interaction and coexistence. With increased unreliability and unpredictability in weather conditions, wild animals are increasingly moving out of their reserved conservation areas to community farms, destroying crops. Humans are also encroaching more and more into the conservation areas to expand the land under arable farming since climate change has led to reduced yields. The result is an increase in human–wildlife conflicts, which is disruptive for tourism, and the result will be increased poverty for these marginalized communities and increased biodiversity loss.

An understanding of the vulnerability and impact of climate change will be a great step forward in preparing a nature-based tourism community, most of whose members are in rural areas that are marginalized so that they are able to anticipate and prepare for adaptation. Once a community has developed its own clear climate change indicators, it will be able to develop better adaptation strategies. A better prepared community will have reduced disruptions to its lives and livelihoods. A study of climate change vulnerability and impact assessment in East Africa is a timely intervention, especially since little research has been done in the area.

5. Conclusion and recommendations

It is now recognized that regardless of emission reduction efforts, there is an inevitable need for societies around the world to adapt to unavoidable changes in climate (IPCC, 2007b). Therefore, greater emphasis on research that specifically addresses the informational needs of tourism stakeholders should be considered (Scott and Becken, 2010). Consequently, an assessment of vulnerability and adaptation is crucial in responding to changing climate. However, vulnerability and adaptation assessment methodologies and models are still very preliminary (Carter et al., 2007; Jopp et al., 2010).

A tourism industry that anticipates potential changes is more likely to be less affected by these changes (less vulnerable), has more possibilities of recovering from external and internal shocks (more resilient), has more opportunities to take advantage of in the emerging conditions and is more likely to be successful in the current era of rapid change (Gössling et al., 2012; IPCC, 2007b; Jopp et al., 2010).

Since climate change vulnerability is very place, context, time and situation specific, it is important that wildlife tourism stakeholders in East Africa develop a clear understanding of their specific indicators so that they are able to establish how vulnerable they are and how much they will be impacted by climate change.

Tourism stakeholders in the Mara ecosystem and in East Africa must be able to come up with suitable climate change vulnerability assessment tools and frameworks that will then be used to assess the specific climate change impacts so that proper adaptation tools that are very specific to particular vulnerabilities and impacts can be developed. The adaptation frameworks and tools developed must include enactment of good legislations and their enforcement. Furthermore, the process of formulating frameworks and tools must be all inclusive so that all stakeholders have a voice and a say in the process and thus can own the final adaption strategy that is agreed upon. It is from this understanding that appropriate adaptation strategies can be developed. In practical terms, vulnerability can only be assessed after the factors that influence exposure, sensitivity and adaptive capacity of a studied system have also been assessed (Calgaro et al., 2014). In a coupled human-environmental system, such as the wildlife tourism system, this assessment enables a researcher to understand differential vulnerabilities of the system's components (such as communities, tourism businesses, visitors, landscapes and ecosystems) in order to identify the most vulnerable component (Calgaro et al., 2014). Thus, this knowledge is needed prior to developing adaptation actions.

This study provides a way forward on how to assess vulnerability and impact of climate change on wildlife tourism by showing how to come up with place-specific indicators; the indicators can then be applied on the empirical model developed in the study to show how vulnerable, resilient or adaptive the tourism business is to the effects of climate change.

East African countries should be encouraged to share data on climate change and to train more manpower on climate change adaptation and resilience development. The governments should also empower communities for climate change resilience and adaptation by providing necessary financial resources for shock absorption, concise information in a timely manner and funding for further research in this area.

References

Amelung, B., S. Nicholls, and D. Viner (2007). “Implications of global climate change for tourism flows and seasonality”, *Journal of Travel Research*, 45(3), 285–296.

Bigano, A., J.M. Hamilton, and R.S.J. Tol (2007). “The impact of climate change on domestic and international tourism: A simulation study”, *The Integrated Assessment Journal*, 7, 25–49.

Birkmann, J. (2007). “Risk and Vulnerability indicators at different scales: Applicability, usefulness and policy implications”, *Environmental Hazards*, 7, 20–31.

Boko, M., I. Niang, A. Nyong, C. Vogel, A. Githeko, M. Medany, B. Osman-Elasha, R. Tabo, and P. Yanda (2007). “Africa”, in M.L. Parry, O.F. Canziani, J.P. Palutikof, P.J. van der Linden, and C.E. Hanson (eds), *Climate Change 2007: Impacts, Adaptation and Vulnerability. Contribution of Working Group II to the Fourth Assessment Report of the Intergovernmental Panel on Climate Change.* Cambridge: Cambridge University Press, pp. 433–467.

Calgaro, E. (2011). “Building resilient tourism destination futures in a world of uncertainty: Assessing destination vulnerability, in Khao Lak, Patong and Phi Phi Don, Thailand to the 2004 Tsunami”, Macquarie University Research Online.

Calgaro, E., D. Dominey-Howes, and K. Lloyd (2014). “Application of the destination sustainability framework to explore the drivers of vulnerability in Thailand following the 2004 Indian Ocean tsunami”, *Journal of Sustainable Tourism*, 22(3), 361–383.

Carter, T.R., R.N. Jones, X. Lu, S. Bhadwal, C. Conde, L.O. Mearns, B.C. O‘Neill, M.D.A. Rounsevell, and M.B. Zurek (2007). “New assessment methods and the characterization of future conditions”, in M.L. Parry, O.F. Canziani, J.P. Palutikof, P.J. van der Linden, and C.E. Hanson (eds), *Climate Change 2007: Impacts, Adaptation and Vulnerability. Contribution of Working Group II to the Fourth Assessment Report of the Intergovernmental Panel on Climate Change.* Cambridge: Cambridge University Press, pp. 133–171.

Chidumayo, E. (2011). “Climate change and wildlife resources in East and Southern Africa”, in E. Chidumayo, D. Okali, G. Kowero, and M. Larwanou (eds), *Climate Change and African Forest and Wildlife Resources.* Nairobi: African Forest Forum, pp. 135–148.

The Climate Institute (2006). *Climate Change: Risks and Opportunities for Australian Business.* The Climate Institute Australia.

Cochran, W.G. (1963). *Sampling Techniques* (2nd ed.). New York: John Wiley and Sons, Inc.

Conway, D. and E.L. Schipper (2011). “Adaptation to climate change in Africa: Challenges and opportunities identified from Ethiopia”, *Global Environmental Change*, 21, 227–237.

GoK (Government of Kenya) (2010). *National Climate Change Response Strategy.* Nairobi: Government Printers.

GoK (Government of Kenya) (2011). *State of the Environment and Outlook 2010.* Nairobi: Government Printers.

GoK (Government of Kenya) (2013). *National Climate Change Action Plan 2013–2017.* Nairobi: Government Printers.

Gössling, S. and C.M. Hall (2006). "An introduction to tourism and global environmental change", in Gössling, S. and Hall, C.M. (eds), *Tourism and Global Environmental Change*. London: Routledge, pp. 1–34.

Gössling, S., P. Peeters, and D. Scott (2008). "Consequences of climate policy or international tourist arrivals in developing countries", *Third World Quarterly*, 29(5), 701–805

Gössling, S., D. Scott, M. Hall, J. Ceron, and G. Dubois (2012). "Consumer behaviour and demand response of tourists to climate change", *Annals of Tourism Research*, 39(1), 36–58.

Hambira, W.L., J. Saarinen, H. Manwa, and J.R. Atlhopheng (2013). "Climate change adaptation practices in nature-based tourism in Maun in the Okavango Delta area, Botswana: How prepared are the tourism businesses?", *Tourism Review International*, 17(1), 19–29.

Hamilton, J., D. Maddison, and R. Tol (2005). "Effects of climate change on international tourism", *Climate Research*, 29, 245–254.

The Heinz Center (2012). *Climate-Change Vulnerability and Adaptation Strategies for Africa's Charismatic Megafauna*. Washington, DC: The Heinz Center, p. 56.

Hinkel, J. and R. Klein (2009). "Integrating knowledge to assess coastal vulnerability to sea-level rise: The development of the DIVA tool", *Global Environmental Change*, 19, 384–395.

Hope, K.R. (2009). "Climate change and poverty in Africa", *International Journal of Sustainable Development & World Ecology*, 16(6), 451–461.

IPCC (2007a). "Assessing Key Vulnerabilities and Risks from Climate Change", in M.L. Parry, O.F. Canziani, J.P. Palutikof, P.J. van der Linden, and C.E. Hanson (eds), *Climate Change 2007: Impacts, Adaptation and Vulnerability. Contribution of Working Group II to the Fourth Assessment Report of the Intergovernmental Panel on Climate Change*. Cambridge: Cambridge University Press, pp. 701–805.

IPCC (2007b). "Summary for policymakers", in M.L. Parry, O.F. Canziani, J.P. Palutikof, P.J. van der Linden, and C.E. Hanson (eds), *Climate Change 2007: Impacts, Adaptation and Vulnerability. Contribution of Working Group II to the Fourth Assessment Report of the Intergovernmental Panel on Climate Change*. Cambridge: Cambridge University Press, pp. 7–22.

IPCC (2007c). *The Intergovernmental Panel on Climate Change*. Available at: www.ipcc.

IPCC (2012). *Managing the Risks of Extreme Events and Disasters to Advance Climate Change Adaptation: A Special Report of Working Groups I and II of the Intergovernmental Panel on Climate Change*. Cambridge, UK and New York: Cambridge University Press.

IUCN SSC Antelope Specialist Group (2008). *Connochaetes Taurinus*. Available at: www.iucnredlist.org.

Jopp, R., T. DeLacy, and J. Mair (2010). "Developing a framework for regional destination adaptation to climate change", *Current Issues in Tourism*, 13(6), 591–605.

Jopp, R., J. Mair, T. DeLacy, and M. Fluker (2013). "Using a regional tourism adaptation framework to determine climate change adaptation options for Victoria's Surf Coast", *Asia Pacific Journal of Tourism Research* 18(1–2), 144–169.

KNBS (2013). "Economic survey 2013 highlights", Ministry of Devolution and Planning, Kenya National Bureau of Statistics. Available at: www.knbs.or.ke/Economic%20Surveys/Cabinet_Secretary_Presentation_on_Economic_Survey_May_2013.pdf.

Kumssa, A. and J. Jones (2010). "Climate change and human security in Africa", *International Journal of Sustainable Development & World Ecology*, 17(6), 453–461.

Lusweti, A.M. (2011). *Biodiversity Conservation in Kenya: Institute of Economic Affairs*. Available at: www.ieakenya.or.ke/publications/doc.

McSweeney, C., M. New, and G. Lizcano (2010). *UNDP Climate Change Country Profiles: Afghanistan*. Available at: http://country-profiles.geog.ox.ac.uk/.

MENR (2012). *Mapping Wildlife Dispersal Areas and Migratory Routes/Corridor (Part I): Southern Kenya Rangelands* (Draft Version March 2012). Nairobi: Ministry of Environment and Natural Resources (MENR).

Mitchell, J., J. Keane, and J. Laidlaw (2009). "Making success work for the poor: Package tourism in Northern Tanzania", ODI/SNV.

Mkiramweni, P.N. (2014). "Sustainable wildlife tourism in the context of climate change: The case study of Ngorongoro conservation area, Tanzania", Unpublished PhD Thesis, College of Business, Victoria University Melbourne, Australia.

MoT (Ministry of Tourism Kenya) (2013). *Destination Facts by Region*. Available at: www.tourism.go.ke/ministry.nsf/pages/destinationfacts.

Munyiri, E.K. (2015). "Vulnerability and adaptation of the tourism sector to climate change in Nairobi, coast and central tourist circuits in Kenya", Unpublished PhD Thesis, Kenyatta University, Nairobi, Kenya.

Nyaupane, G. and N. Chhetri (2009). "Vulnerability to climate change of nature-based tourism in the Nepalese Himalayas", *Tourism Geographies*, 11(1), 95–119.

Ogutu, J., N. Owen-Smith, H.P. Piepho, and M.Y. Said (2011). "Continuing wildlife population declines and range contraction in the Mara region of Kenya during 1977–2009", *Journal of Zoology*, 285, 99–109.

Ogutu, J., N. Owen-Smith, H. Piepho, M. Said, S. Kifugo, R. Reid, H. Gichohi, P. Kahumbu, and S. Andanje (2013). "Changing wildlife populations in Nairobi National Park and adjoining Athi-Kaputiei plains: Collapse of the migratory wildebeest", *Open Conservation Biology Journal*, 7, 11–26.

Ogutu, J., H.P. Piepho, H. Dublin, N. Bhola, and R. Reid (2009). "Dynamics of Mara–Serengeti ungulates in relation to land use changes", *Journal of Zoology*, 278(1), 1–14.

Owen-Smith, N. and J. Ogutu (2012). "Changing rainfall and obstructed movements: Impact on African ungulates", Wildlife Conservation in a Changing.

Richardson, R.B. and K. Witkowski (2010). "Economic vulnerability to climate change for tourism-dependent nations", *Journal of Tourism Analysis*, 15(3), 315–330.

RoT (2011). "The economic survey 2011", Dar es Salaam: President's Office, Planning Commission. Available at: www.mof.go.tz/mofdocs/Micro/Economic%20Survey%202011.pdf.

Schneider, S.H., S. Semenov, A. Patwardhan, I. Burton, C.H.D. Magadza, M. Oppenheimer, A.B. Pittock, A. Rahman, J.B. Smith, A. Suarez, and F. Yamin (2007). "Assessing key vulnerabilities and the risk from climate change", in M.L. Parry, O.F. Canziani, J.P. Palutikof, P.J. van der Linden, and C.E. Hanson (eds), *Climate Change 2007: Impacts, Adaptation and Vulnerability. Contribution of*

Working Group II to the Fourth Assessment Report of the Intergovernmental Panel on Climate Change. Cambridge: Cambridge University Press, pp. 779–810.

Scott, D. and S. Becken (2010). "Adapting to climate change and climate policy: Progress, problems and potentials", *Journal of Sustainable Tourism*, 18(3), 283–295.

Scott, D., C.M. Hall, and S. Gossling (2012). *Tourism and Climate Change: Impacts, Adaptation and Mitigation*. London: Routledge.

Simpson, M., S. Gössling, D. Scott, C.M. Hall, and E. Gladin (2008). *Climate Change. Adaptation and Mitigation in the Tourism Sector: Frameworks, Tools and Practices*. Paris: UNEP.

Sitati, N.W. and B.E.L. Wishitemi (2003). "Wildebeest migration and tourism seasonality pattern and dynamics in the Mara ecosystem, Kenya", *African Journal of Business and Economics*, 2(1).

Sitati, N., K. Lekishon, S. Bakari, F. Warinwa, S.N. Mwiu, N. Gichohi, E. Bitok, M. Mwita, H.K. Ija, and J. Mukeka (2014). "Wildebeest (*Connochaetes taurinus*) population densities and distribution in dry and wet season in the Kilimanjaro landscape", *Natural Resources*, 5, 810–821. Available at: http://dx.doi.org/10.4236/nr.2014.513070.

Staffan, U. (2002). *Savannah Lives: Animal Life and Human Evolution in Africa*. Oxford: Oxford University Press.

UNFCCC (2007). *Climate Change: Impacts, Vulnerabilities and Adaptation in Developing Countries*. Bonn: UNFCCC.

UNWTO (2007a). *Ministers' Summit on Tourism and Climate Change*. London.

UNWTO (2007b). "Second International Conference on Climate Change and Tourism. Davos Declaration: Climate Change and Tourism Responding to Global Challenges, Davos, Switzerland, 3 October". Madrid: United Nations World Tourism Organization.

UNWTO (2007c). *Tourism Development and Climate Change: Understanding, Anticipating, Adapting, Participating in the Common Effort*. Available at: www.unwto.org/sites/.../summarydavose.pdf.

UNWTO. United Nations World Tourism Organization, United Nations Environment Program, World. Meteorological Organization (UNWTO-UNEP-WMO) (2008). *Climate Change and Tourism: Responding to Global Challenges*. Madrid: UNWTO.

Weaver, D. (2011). "Can sustainable tourism survive climate change?", *Journal of Sustainable Tourism*, 19(1), 5–15.

The World Bank (2015). *International Tourism Number of Arrivals*. Available at: www.data.worldbank.org/indicator/ST.INT.ARVL.

WTTC (2012). *Travel & Tourism Economic Impact 2012, Africa*. Available at: www.wttc.org.

WTTC Kenya (2015). *Travel & Tourism Economic Impact 2015 Kenya*. Available at: www.wttc.org.

WTTC Rwanda (2015). *Travel & Tourism Economic Impact 2015 Rwanda*. Available at: www.wttc.org.

WTTC Tanzania (2015). *Travel & Tourism Economic Impact 2015 Uganda*. Available at: www.wttc.org.

Yamane, T. (1967). *Statistics: An Introductory Analysis* (2nd ed.). New York: Harper and Row.

4 Multidimensional measure of household energy poverty and its determinants in Ethiopia[1]

Mekonnen Bersisa

1. Introduction

Energy is used in cooking, lighting, production, communication, heating and cooling. It is crucial for the well-being of society. In general, energy is an important ingredient for attaining good education, health and a good quality of life. Access to modern energy is crucial for economic development, as it contributes to improved health conditions, reduces indoor air pollution, increases production and productivity using modern technologies and machinery, saves time and adds to further education and expansion of health facilities (Barnes et al., 2011). Lack of access (both physical and economical) to reliable energy is believed to hamper economic growth and reducing the welfare of citizens (Chakravarty and Tavoni, 2013).

Moreover, energy is central in addressing many of today's global development challenges such as poverty, inequalities, health, education, digital divide, connectivity and climate change (Foster et al., 2013; Nussbaumer et al., 2012). Despite the massive contribution of energy to economic progress and the important role that it plays in the process of economic development, there are indicators that the global energy system will face various challenges that will question issues of sustainability and energy security in the future. Among the challenges are increasing risks of shortages of energy supply, especially non-renewable sources; the threat to the environment caused by fossil fuel energy production and use; and persistent energy poverty. These challenges can be remedied only through strong and coordinated government action and public support (Birol, 2007).

Access to and use of modern energy sources, both physically and economically, for most poor households is inconceivable. In the case of rural parts in developing countries, not only economic access but physical access too is a major problem. The only dominant source of safe energy is electricity generated by using various primary energy sources but with limited physical access. Access to reliable and affordable energy as well as energy security has shown limited promising improvements for developing countries. As a result, the issue has been on the academic and policy agendas for a considerable time. Even though this has been a concern for developing countries since the 1980s, the problem of energy poverty has not yet been resolved in these countries (Barnes et al., 2011; Birol, 2007; Li et al., 2014; Pereira et al., 2010).

In the context of development, energy is mainly used for lighting, cooking, production and communication. Energy poverty is considered one of the most important issues related to development. It is believed to be both the cause and the manifestation of poverty. 'Energy poor' is defined as households that cannot meet their basic energy consumption needs. Breaking the vicious circle of energy poverty and eradicating energy poverty and achieving sustainable development in developing countries will be realized only with concerted efforts of researchers, policymakers, donor organizations and state governments (Birol, 2007; OFID, 2008).

Strikingly, in recent years about 1.4 billion people in developing countries have had lack of access to electricity and about 3 billion people have relied on inefficient and polluting fires for cooking and other household needs. Most of the electricity-deprived populations are in sub-Saharan Africa and South Asia. Further, about 80 per cent of those without access to electricity live in rural areas (UNDP and WHO, 2009; WEO, 2014). Ethiopia, ranked 157th on the Human Development Index (HDI), is one of the least developed countries in the world. It has one of the lowest rates of access to modern energy services. Its energy supply is primarily based on biomass. About 90 per cent of the primary energy source in the country is biomass while oil accounts for about 7 per cent and hydropower for 0.9 per cent. Additionally, the energy use pattern in the country shows that households account for 88 per cent of the total energy consumption followed by industry (4 per cent), transport (3 per cent), services and others (5 per cent). Regardless of its high potential for production of modern energy, only about 23 per cent of the population in Ethiopia has access to electricity[2] (Dawit, 2012; WEO, 2013, 2014).

As a response to development challenges and aspirations of having inclusive and sustainable development, Ethiopia launched an ambitious medium-term development plan – the Growth and Transformation Plan (GTP) in 2011. The country put a target of attaining middle-income status by 2025 and the plan aligned its growth path with climate resilient green growth. In line with this plan, the country embarked on an expansion of modern energy sources and its energy sector is considered an important pillar for realizing green growth and accelerating development in the country (FDRE, 2011a, 2011b). However, currently the country's energy use pattern questions the sustainability and security of its energy use. Moreover, a majority of the households, especially in the rural parts, rely on traditional sources of energy. This signals persistence of energy poverty in the country.

Globally there is a lot of literature on energy (fuel) poverty (Barnes et al., 2011; Boardman, 1991; Chakravarty and Tavoni, 2013; Foster et al., 2000; Nussbaumer et al., 2012; Walkera et al., 2014). However, only a few studies on energy poverty are available for sub-Saharan African countries (Edoumiekumo et al., 2013; Tchereni et al., 2013). There is a paucity of research on energy poverty in Ethiopia, especially of studies employing a multidimensional measurement approach. For instance, a study by Bekele et al. (2015) only examines the extent and determinants of multidimensional energy poverty in Ethiopia's capital Addis Ababa. Thus, the present study contributes to general literature on energy poverty and provides a concrete metric for Ethiopia. Using a rich dataset of the household survey, the study analyzes the extent and determinants of energy poverty in Ethiopia. This study is expected to deepen an understanding of the causes and extent of energy poverty. It also investigates the most important attributes of multidimensional energy poverty and examines the extent of energy poverty for different groups of households in rural and small towns in Ethiopia. This is expected to indicate policy instruments for the post-2015 sustainable development strategy and will bridge the existing knowledge gap in the causes of energy poverty and indicate the way forward for a smooth transition to a modern energy system.

This research elaborates on several aspects of energy poverty with implications for the well-being of society, including the many dimensions of energy poverty, the implications of persistence in energy poverty and poverty reduction, and the association between energy poverty traps and specific household characteristics. A number of research questions were formulated to do an analysis:

- What is the most important dimension of energy poverty?
- What does this mean for a country with persistent energy poverty such as Ethiopia?
- Do household characteristics really matter in energy poverty?

The rest of this study is organized as follows. Section 2 provides a brief summary of access to energy, reviews the definitions of energy poverty and presents a metric of the multidimensional measure. It further discusses literature, summarizing empirical works on energy poverty. Section 3 presents the data and methodology while Section 4 discusses the results. The final section gives a conclusion and policy recommendations for achieving the sustainable development goals (SDGs).

2. Issues in energy poverty

2.1 Energy potential and access

Access to modern energy is related to the level of economic development. In particular, the electrification rate seems to parallel a country's economic status. According to WEO's (2013) report, lower electrification rates and larger numbers of people without access to electricity are more prevalent in developing countries. Globally in 2011 about 1.4 billion people had no access to electricity regardless of impressive electrification rates of about 81.9 per cent (an urban electrification rate of 93.7 per cent and a rural electrification rate of only 69 per cent) (Table 4.1).

Developing countries are home to almost entire populations without access to electricity. Nearly half of these people are in Africa where the overall electrification rates are only 42.6 per cent (urban electrification rate of 65.2 per cent

Table 4.1 Electricity access in 2011 (regional aggregates)

Region	*Population without electricity (in million)*	*Electrification rate (per cent)*	*Urban electrification rate (per cent)*	*Rural electrification rate (per cent)*
Developing countries	1,257.0	76.5	90.6	65.1
Africa	599.7	42.6	65.2	27.8
North Africa	1.0	99.4	100.0	98.7
Sub-Saharan Africa	598.7	31.8	55.2	18.3
Developing Asia	614.7	83.1	95.0	74.9
India	306.1	75.3	93.9	66.9
Rest of developing Asia	308.6	87.1	95.3	80.2
Latin America	23.8	94.8	98.5	81.1
Middle East	18.7	91.0	98.5	75.8
Transition economies and OECD	1.1	99.9	100.0	99.7
World	1258.1	81.9	93.7	69.0

Source: Adapted from the WEO (2013) database

and rural electrification rate of 27.8 per cent). These figures are very alarming for sub-Saharan African (SSA) countries. About 47.5 per cent of the population without access to electricity is living in SSA countries. Here the overall electrification rates are only 31.8 per cent (urban electrification rate of 55.2 per cent and rural electrification rate of 18.3 per cent). Ethiopia is among the countries with lower electrification rates in SSA countries. Even though more than half of Ethiopia's population is geographically close to the electricity grid, about 70 million people do not have access to electricity. The overall electrification rate in the country is about 23 per cent (urban electrification rate of 85 per cent and rural electrification rate of only 11 per cent). The country is performing well as compared to Africa and SSA countries' average urban electrification rates. However, it is performing poorly in rural electrification, which is below the average SSA rural electrification rate (18.3 per cent). The country's per capita domestic electricity consumption is less than 100 kWh per year lower than the SSA countries' average level (317 kWh per year) and less than what a refrigerator uses per year in a developed country (Power Africa, 2015; WEO, 2013, 2014).

Even though it is underdeveloped, Ethiopia is endowed with diversified energy sources. It has huge potential of various energy sources that are underdeveloped but promisingly exploitable at different scales. So far the renewable energy potential of the country is predominantly generated from hydropower, which is far below the capacity of the country. Energy potential from biomass remains dominant and is exploited in the rural parts (Table 4.2).

Table 4.2 Ethiopia's renewable energy potential

Resource	*Unit*	*Exploitable reserve*	*Exploited*	
			Amount	*Per cent*
Hydropower	MW	45,000	~2100	<5 per cent
Solar/day	kWh/m2	4–6		<1 per cent
Wind power	GW	1350	171MW	<1 per cent
Geothermal	MW	7000	7.3 MW	<1 per cent
Wood	Million tons	1120	560	50 per cent
Agricultural waste	Million tons	15–20	~6	30 per cent
Natural gas	Billion m3	113	-	0 per cent
Coal	Million tons	>300	-	0 per cent
Oil shale	Million tons	253	-	0 per cent

Source: Compiled from different documents of the Ethiopian Ministry of Water and Energy

Ethiopia's capacity for electricity generation is increasing at an impressive rate. Its generation rate has grown by about 200 per cent as compared to the 2008 level. Ninety per cent of the electricity is generated from hydropower sources. However, this direction needs cautious movement, as hydropower is highly susceptible to droughts, which may risk the sustainability of electricity supply in the country. Despite this potential, the rural parts of the country predominantly meet their energy needs from non-renewable sources.

2.2 Definition of energy poverty

Considerable efforts have been devoted to defining energy poverty. However, the standards that have been developed rest on arbitrary assumptions with regard to the energy devices used and on a normative definition of what a set of basic needs consist of. The contexts in which the definition is used, such as differences in cultural and climatic conditions, are of paramount importance. This has complicated the universality of a definition of energy poverty (Barnes et al., 2011).

Nevertheless, it is possible to have a commonly used definition of energy poverty. It can be defined as the state of deprivation where a household is barely able to meet its most minimum energy requirements for basic needs (Foster et al., 2000; Modi et al., 2006; OECD and IEA, 2010). It is also defined as lack of access to modern energy services (Li et al., 2014). Further, the concept of energy poverty has been expanded to 'an absence of sufficient choice in accessing adequate, affordable, reliable, high quality, safe and environmentally benign energy services to support economic and human development'. 'Energy poor' has been defined as households that cannot meet their basic energy needs by estimating a minimum limit of energy consumption (Parajuli, 2011; Pereira et al., 2011). Additionally, expenditure or income parameters are used for defining energy poverty. For instance, energy poverty has been defined in terms of the percentage of income spent on energy consumption. Households that spend more than 10 per cent of their incomes on energy are considered energy poor. On top of this, the multidimensional measure of energy poverty has been employed by extending energy use and access as being multidimensional in nature (Gowon and Moses, 2014; Nussbaumer et al., 2012; Sher et al., 2014). Regardless of the immense efforts devoted to the issue, as of today there is no unified definition of the concept of energy poverty. The multidimensional measure, which was originally developed in the context of poverty and inequality, seems to be consistent with the notion of the SDGs.

Literature on energy poverty differentiates between energy poverty and fuel poverty. Some attribute these concepts to concerns of different countries on the basis of their economic status and energy systems. Energy poverty is the issue of accessibility to modern energy whereas fuel poverty is an issue of affordability. The former is a concern in developing countries, at least under the current economic status, whereas the latter is more of a concern in developed countries (Boardman, 2012). (A detailed review of the definitions of fuel poverty is available in Moore, 2012.)

2.3 Measures of energy poverty

Various measures of energy poverty have been developed and applied in literature on energy poverty. These metrics can be categorized as unidimensional and composite index measures. The former provide a powerful and unbiased measure that is easy to interpret with regard to one specific dimension and is simple to compute. However, it is not suitable for less tangible issues such as sustainable development or poverty measures. The unidimensional measure of energy poverty tries to give metrics that could parallel the income measure of poverty with the World Bank's poverty line of $1.25 per day. Composite indices, on the other hand, are single numerals calculated from a number of variables that represent the aggregated value of a dimension. These are advantageous over the unidimensional (dashboard) approach, where we evaluate each dimension against some pre-determined cut-off points. In the composite indices we find a single number, which basically facilitates a comparison across various groups. The composite indices include the following measures:

- The Multidimensional Energy Poverty Index (MEPI)
- The Energy Development Index (EDI)

Both MEPI and EDI (Ravallion, 2010) measure access to modern energy sources. But MEPI evaluates energy poverty whereas EDI is a measure of an energy system's transition towards modern fuels (Nussbaumer et al., 2012). The development of the multidimensional energy poverty measure, which parallels multidimensional poverty measures, is a reflection of capabilities and functioning. The method is both data intensive and comprehensive, as it considers non-income dimensions in the (energy) poverty measure. Notwithstanding its merits and relevance from the perspective of poverty, the method is less applicable due to a paucity of data for less-developed countries.

As a component of the multidimensional measures and a base for unidimensional measures, various indices have been developed for assessing the level and extent of energy poverty. The commonly used index of poverty measure is by Foster et al. (1984), which has been adopted to measure energy poverty as well. The three metric measures – the headcount index of energy poverty, the energy poverty gap index and the squared energy poverty gap index – are frequently computed to assess the energy poverty status of households. Following Foster et al. (2000), these indices of energy poverty can be formulated as *P*:

$$P_{\alpha} = \sum_{E_i \leq Z} \left(\frac{w_i}{N}\right)\left(1 - \frac{E_i}{Z}\right)^{\theta} \tag{1}$$

where P_{α} stands for the energy poverty index; wi stands for the weight for household *I*; E_i stands for energy consumption for household *I*; *Z* stands for the fuel poverty line; and *N* stands for population size. This index provides three metrics of energy poverty: intensity (headcount ratio), severity (poverty gap) and depth (squared poverty gap) for α = 0, 1 and 2, respectively.

However, the striking issue in energy poverty literature is determining the energy poverty line. For over 20 years many researchers have been using the definition given as the minimum quantity of physical energy needed to perform such basic tasks as cooking and lighting. Others have also used a definition of the energy poverty line as the level of energy used by households below the known expenditure or income poverty line. The underlying assumption of this approach is that expenditure-based poor households are necessarily energy poor as well, which may or may not be the case (Foster et al., 2000).

Further, energy expenditure as a proportion of total income has been used to determine the energy poverty line (Boardman, 1991). This method was derived from the fact that relatively speaking poor households spent a higher percentage of their incomes on energy than wealthier ones, and spending more than a certain share of income may deprive them of other necessary goods. A cut-off point of 10 per cent of the total income has been used as the maximum share of energy expenditure allowed to remain non-poor (Barnes et al., 2011). One of the advantages of this approach is its insensitivity to price change. It is a relative energy poverty index allowing for heterogeneity in the poverty line by income classes and locations. The same authors have also developed another method that is similar to the expenditure method to define the energy poverty line. For the alternative method they use a demand-based approach as the threshold point at which energy consumption begins to rise with an increase in household income. At or below this threshold point, households consume a bare minimum level of energy and should be considered energy poor. Besides this, some authors have also proposed a median approach when income distribution is skewed to determine the energy poverty line.

Definition of energy poverty and determining the cut-off (the energy poverty line), however, need to be approached with caution. The conventional way of defining poverty and the poverty line does not serve this purpose. In the case of conventional goods, higher consumption means a higher level of welfare or lower level of poverty. But for energy goods, more consumption may not necessarily lead to higher welfare due to the fact that the demand for energy is a derived demand. Higher consumption of energy perhaps leads to lower welfare due to its repercussions on the environment, human health and budget claims. In this paper we employ the multidimensional measure of energy poverty following the Nussbaumer et al. (2012) methodology.

2.4 *Empirical literature*

This section presents a summary of empirical works on energy poverty for different regions. The survey is chronologically presented in Table 4.3 to show past developments and the state of research at present.

Various researchers have examined energy poverty in different countries. This brief review of the developments in literature on the measurement of energy poverty for different countries indicates that researchers have used various methods and the results of their analyses vary considerably. Even though energy poverty is a pressing issue for developing countries, especially for sub-Saharan Africa, there are very few studies on this issue in SSA countries. For example,

Table 4.3 A summary of empirical studies on energy poverty

No	*Author(s)*	*Year*	*Country*	*Energy poverty definition and analysis*
1	Pachauri and Spreng	2004	India	Two-dimensional/ Engineering method
2	Barnes et al.	2011	Bangladesh	Demand based
3	Pereira et al.	2011	Brazil	Used the conventional analytical framework (Lorenz curve, Gini coefficient, etc.)
4	Nassbaumer et al.	2012	Some African countries	Multidimensional Energy Poverty Index
5	Khandker et al.	2012	India	Demand based
6	Tchereni et al.	2013	Malawi	Energy expenditure
7	Edoumiekumo et al.	2013	Nigeria	Multidimensional Energy Poverty Index
8	Bekele et al.	2015	Ethiopia	Multidimensional Energy Poverty Index

Tchereni et al. (2013) conducted an economic analysis of energy poverty for Malawi. They showed that various socioeconomic variables determined the energy poverty status of households. Similarly, Edoumiekumo et al. (2013) employed the multidimensional measure of energy poverty to show the extent and determinants of energy poverty in Nigeria. Their results of multidimensional energy poverty showed that the country had severe energy poverty with some regional variations. Moreover, their regression results from the multinonial logit model showed that socioeconomic, geographic and demographic variables affected the probability of households falling into different energy poverty statuses.

There is paucity of research on this issue for Ethiopia. Very few studies are available and those which are available have limitations in terms of the area covered and the methodology employed. For instance, Bekele et al.'s (2015) study is geographically limited only to Addis Ababa. Therefore, it is expected that the current paper will bridge this gap in literature. Further, our study employs the multidimensional measure of energy poverty following the family of decomposable measures of multidimensional poverty proposed by Alkire and Foster (2007) and recently modified as the multidimensional measure of energy poverty index (MEPI) by Nussbaumer et al. (2012).

3. Data and methodology

3.1 Data sources and types

The data used for this study is a combination of secondary data obtained from various sources. Primarily, the study relied on secondary data collected by the Central Statistical Agency of Ethiopia (CSA) and the World Bank (WB). It also employed data from the International Energy Agency–World Energy Outlook database. Two waves of data from the Ethiopian Socioeconomic Survey (ESS), which is a collaborative project between CSA and the World Bank Living Standards Survey, were also used. The first wave of the data was collected in 2011 and the second in 2014, which was finally released in March 2015. The survey is a very comprehensive and multi-topic survey that can be flexibly used for welfare analyses using different attributes. The first wave of the survey covered almost all the rural parts of the country and small towns.

As part of the first survey, information was collected from 3,969 respondents in all regions of the country. In its second wave, the survey extended the sampling frame by including respondents from large urban areas, including the capital Addis Ababa. By doing this, it tried to maintain the representativeness of the data collected from the sample respondents. The second round of the survey collected information from 5,262 respondents, of which 3,776 were from the first wave. The two waves are expected to gradually form panel data where households are observed over time. The panel attrition rate between the two current waves is only 5 per cent or the two-year panel success rate is about 95 per cent, which can be safely used for a simple panel data analysis following households' energy use behavior over time. As a result, our study used information from 3,776 respondents in rural and small towns in Ethiopia who were covered in both the rounds of the survey. (For a detailed description of the dataset, see CSA and WB, 2011, 2015.)

3.2 The multidimensional measure of energy poverty

The striking issue in measuring energy poverty is availability of detailed data on various dimensions of households' energy use. The selection of variables/ indicators in constructing MEPI is subject to the availability of data. Moreover, determining the relative importance of each variable in constructing MEPI is crucial. Following literature on the multidimensional measure of energy poverty and data available, the following attributes are identified as indicators of energy use status of households in rural and small towns in Ethiopia.

The index is composed of five indicators forming an index with four dimensions. The first indicator identified is type of energy sources used by households for cooking. It is clear that all households use energy for cooking their daily food. However, the type of energy sources they use to generate this heat affects their welfare. Use of traditional energy sources (firewood, charcoal, dung or crop residuals) cause many inconveniences and entail great opportunity costs (such as time allocated for collecting them). The second dimension is extent of indoor air pollution. Dependence on traditional sources of energy and using inefficient energy use technologies among other things exposes households to higher risks of indoor air pollution. Indoor air pollution threatens the health and lives of many rural households in developing countries. Women and children are highly prone to the externalities of cooking. This in turn creates health risks and reduces the welfare of the households (HDR, 2014; WHO, 2002). As a result, inclusion of variables that can proxy this problem is very crucial for computing the multidimensional index of energy poverty. Two variables are used to measure the risk and health burden of indoor air pollution: kitchen and type of stove used. The third indicator is type of energy used for lighting and, finally, ownership of entertainment and educational assets are used to construct the MEPI. Details of the variables, indicators, weights used and deprivation cut-offs for computing MEPI are given in Table 4.4.

On the other hand, multidimensional energy poverty is analytically constructed from the dimensions identified with weights estimated or assigned to show the level of energy deprivations that may affect households' welfare. The construction of MEPI follows the multidimensional poverty measure developed by scholars at the Oxford Poverty and Human Development Initiative (OPHI) (Alkire, 2007; Alkire and Foster, 2007, 2011; Alkire and Santos, 2014). Their initiative was influenced by Amartya Sen's groundbreaking work on deprivations and capabilities with the central argument that human poverty should be considered as the absence of opportunities and choices for living a basic human life (Sen, 1990).

The energy deprivation status of a household was constructed using four dimensions with five indicators. A household was said to be energy poor if the deprivation exceeded pre-defined cut-off points. Following Nussbaumer et al.

Table 4.4 A description of attributes, variables and their cut-off points for computing MEPI

No	*Dimension*	*Indictor*	*Variables (weight)*	*Deprivation cut-off (poor if . . .)*
1	Cooking (C_i)	Modern cooking fuel	Type of cooking fuel (0.25)	Use traditional sources of energy* for cooking
2	Pollution (IP_i)	Indoor air pollution	Kitchen is separate (0.15)	Use same residential house for cooking or no kitchen
			Type of oven/*mited* used for cooking (0.15)	Use traditional cook stove or use a three stone cook stove
3	Lighting (HF_i)		Type of energy used for lighting (0.25)	Household is deprived if it does not have electricity for lighting
4	Entertainment and Education (EE_i)	Entertainment or educational appliance ownership	Has a radio, tap, TV or satellite dish (0.20)	A household is considered poor/deprived if it has none of these assets

Note: * = Traditional sources of energy in this context refer to biomass such as firewood, charcoal, dung and crop residuals while modern energy sources include electricity, kerosene, LPG and natural gas

(2012), we defined multidimensional energy poverty status of households as: multidimensional energy poverty was measured in d variables for the sampled households (n). A vector $Y = \{y_{ij}\}$ represented the $n \times d$ matrix of achievements for i households across j variables. The value of $y_{ij} > 0$, therefore, represented household i's achievement in the jth variable. From these household-level achievements using the dual cut-off approach, we constructed the extent and severity of multidimensional energy poverty for each household and aggregated it to the population level.

A multidimensional energy poverty line of 0.33 was adopted. A household was energy poor if it was deprived of more than 33 per cent of the indicators. Hence, a household whose sum of weighted deprivation was greater than or equal to 0.33 was categorized as energy poor and a household whose sum of weighted deprivation was less than 0.33 was energy non-poor.

MEPI was then computed as:

Energy Poverty Headcount:

$$H = \frac{1}{N}\sum_{i=1}^{q} c_i > k \,, \tag{2}$$

where k stands for the energy poverty line and c_i stands for households whose deprivation score is higher than the cut-off point. The energy poverty headcount (H) measures the incidence of energy poverty; it is the percentage of households whose deprivation score is above the cut-off point.

Energy poverty intensity:

$$A = \frac{\sum_{i=1}^{q} c_i(k)}{\sum_{i=1}^{q} c_i}, \tag{3}$$

where $\sum_{i=1}^{q} c_i(k)$ is the censored weighted deprivation score of the household. Finally, MEPI is computed from both incidence and intensity of energy poverty as:

$$\text{MEPI} = H * A \tag{4}$$

3.3 An econometric analysis of energy poverty

The aim of this study is to determine the energy poverty state of households. The index computed provides a measure of energy poverty. In line with literature, in the second step the households were classified as energy poor and energy non-poor. This allowed analyzing the multidimensional measure of energy poverty and its determinants using a panel logit model. In the logit model the dependent variable was the Multidimensional Energy Poverty Index. It was transformed into binary choice by using a specified deprivation cut-off point for the energy poverty index. If the index was greater than 0.33 the household was considered to be energy poor multi-dimensionally. The threshold was chosen based on the assumption of minimum required energy to satisfy the normal needs of a household considering the four dimensions described earlier.

3.4 Specification of the econometric model

The theoretical foundation for the specification of this model was driven from the latent variable approach. Suppose that a household's energy use is specified as:

$$y^*_{it} = x_{it}\beta + c_i + u_{it} \tag{5}$$

However, y^*_{it} is not observable by a researcher; what the researcher observes is whether, based on the threshold, the household under consideration is energy poor or not. As a result, the analyst can initiate specifications and estimations of binary choice models from the latent variable specification to identify and estimate the effects of the determinants of household energy poverty:

$$y_{it} = \begin{cases} 1 & \text{if } y^*_{it} > 0 \\ 0, & \text{otherwise.} \end{cases} \tag{6}$$

Now the probability that y_{it} takes the value of 1 of the given covariates and individual unobserved heterogeneity can be written as:

$$pr\left(y_{it}=1 \mid x_{it}, c_i\right)=F\left(x_{it}\beta+c_i\right), \tag{7}$$

where $F(.)$ is either the standard normal CDF (probit model) or the logistic CDF (logit model). From this non-linear model, individual heterogeneity (c_i) cannot be removed easily by differencing using within-transformation or inclusion of the individual dummy variable to estimate (c_i) since it results in biased estimates unless t is very large. This will lead to the problem of incidental parameters (small T bias) (Cameron and Trivedi, 2005). Thus, we can estimate non-linear panel models with random effect or fixed effect logit or probit models. In this paper assuming the logistic distribution, we can specify our logit model as:

$$\begin{aligned} pr\left(y_{it}=1 \mid x_{it}, c_i\right) &= \Lambda\left(x_{it}\beta+c_i\right) \\ pr\left(y_{it}=1 \mid x_{it}, c_i\right) &= \frac{\exp\left(x_{it}\beta+c_i\right)}{1+\exp\left(x_{it}\beta+c_i\right)} \end{aligned} \tag{8}$$

The traditional random effect logit model under the following assumption was used to estimate the determinants of multidimensional energy poverty in rural and small towns in Ethiopia. It required strict exogeneity and zero correlation between the explanatory variables (x) and individual heterogeneity (c_i). The final estimable model for identifying and examining the effects of the determinants of multidimensional energy poverty in rural and small towns in Ethiopia used characteristics of a household head (age, sex, education level, marital status); household characteristics (family size, expenditure on energy, total household expenditure, credit use and number of rooms); and nature of residential area (rural or small town). After the estimation of the random effect logit model, the log odds ratio and marginal effects were estimated to get interpretable results.

The odds ratio obtained from the logit model, which shows the ratio of success to failure, can be specified as:

$$\begin{aligned} \left(\frac{pr\left(y_{it}=1 \mid x_{it}, c_i\right)}{pr\left(y_{it}=0 \mid x_{it}, c_i\right)}\right) &= \frac{\exp\left(x_{it}\beta+c_i\right)}{1+\exp\left(x_{it}\beta+c_i\right)} \Bigg/ 1-\frac{\exp\left(x_{it}\beta+c_i\right)}{1+\exp\left(x_{it}\beta+c_i\right)} \\ &= \exp\left(x_{it}\beta+c_i\right) \end{aligned} \tag{9}$$

If we take the log of the odds ratio we get the log odds ratio as:

$$\begin{aligned} \log\left(\frac{pr\left(y_{it}=1 \mid x_{it}, c_i\right)}{pr\left(y_{it}=0 \mid x_{it}, c_i\right)}\right) &= \log\left(\exp\left(x_{it}\beta+c_i\right)\right) \\ &= x_{it}\beta+c_i \end{aligned} \tag{10}$$

Finally the marginal effect for the determinants of energy poverty based on the logit model parameter estimates was obtained from the following relation:

$$\partial \Pr(y_{it} = 1 \mid x_{it}, c_i) \Big/ \partial x_{jit} = \beta_j \Lambda(x_{it}\beta + c_i)\{1 - \Lambda(x_{it}\beta + c_i)\} \quad (11)$$

The odds ratio and marginal effects were among the generated results that were used for an interpretation. As we can see from Eq. 11, the marginal effect of the *x*-variables based on the logit is non-linear. This implies that the interpretation of the logit model should be treated with caution. Depending on the test of panel versus pool data results, we have reported the pooled logit model results.

4. Results and discussion

The first part of this section presents descriptive statistics of important variables to highlight and give a clear picture of the data used for the study. It starts with a presentation and discussion of the demographic characteristics of the respondents. It then extends to a description of the socioeconomic characteristics of the households. It finally presents the status of households in energy-related activities with due emphasis on the variables used for constructing the Multidimensional Energy Poverty Index. This part gives the energy access and energy use technology ownership status of the households. As such it shows the energy poverty status of the households qualitatively or gives the dashboard indicator of the deprivation levels of households. The second part of the section gives an analysis of energy poverty using a multidimensional approach in detail. It then presents the econometric results to examine the determinants of multidimensional energy poverty in rural and small towns in Ethiopia.

4.1 *Descriptive statistics of demographic characteristics*

The demographic characteristics of the households and their heads for the two waves of the data are presented in Table 4.5.

Table 4.5 Household size, age and sex of head (by year)

Variable	*Year*			
	2011		*2014*	
	Mean	*Std. Dev.*	*Mean*	*Std. Dev.*
Household size (in number)	4.86	2.38	5.00	2.39
Household head's age (in years)	44.24	15.64	45.84	15.32

Source: Researcher's computation

As can be seen from Table 4.5, family size of the sample respondents was about 4.86 in 2011 with a standard deviation of 2.38. In the second round of data collection, the mean family size was slightly higher than it was in the first round. In 2014 average family size of the respondents was five persons per household with a standard deviation of 2.39. This tells us that family planning needs to be reconsidered if the country wants to keep population growth within reasonable dynamics. Further, Table 4.5 shows that the average age of the household head was about 44.24 and 45.84 years in 2011 and 2014, respectively, or the average age of the head of the household was slightly higher in 2014 as compared to 2011.

A detailed exploration of the data in Table 4.6 shows that there was not much variation in the headship and religion of the head of the household in the two rounds of the survey. The headship role was predominantly played by males, which calls for various policies to empower women and their role in resource use and decisions in the household. Furthermore, the religion of the head of the household showed a slight variation in the two survey periods.

The marital status of the head of the household shows that a majority of the respondents were married (about 76.28 and 74.49 per cent in 2011 and 2014, respectively). Table 4.6 further shows that a very low proportion of the respondents was single or separated in both the rounds of the survey.

Table 4.7 presents the expenditure patterns of households on different items in 2011 and 2014. There is an observable variation in expenditure patterns in the survey years. In the first round, food and energy expenditures were on

Table 4.6 Sex, religion and marital status of the head of the household (by year) (percentage)

Variable	*Year*	
	2011	*2014*
	Per cent	*Per cent*
Household head's sex Male 7	5.48	74.12
Household head's sex Female	24.52	25.88
Household head's religion Orthodox	43.83	43.77
Household head's religion Muslim	32.79	33.23
Household head's religion Protestant	19.65	19.70
Household head's religion Others	3.73	3.30
Single	3.83	3.36
Married	76.28	74.49
Divorced	5.47	6.83
Separated	1.91	1.36
Widowed	12.52	13.96

Source: Researcher's computation

Table 4.7 Descriptive statistics of important variables (by year)

Variable	*Year*			
	2011		*2014*	
	Mean	*Std. Dev.*	*Mean*	*Std. Dev.*
Annual food expenditure	8,843.56	48,391.32	6,723.93	10,573.76
Annual energy expenditure	665.97	6,179.88	642.35	2,067.00
Annual non-food expenditure	1,439.25	8,879.73	1,631.07	3,070.07
Annual non-food expenditure (fixed assets)	2,224.09	13,886.54	2,964.07	5,356.31
Annual total expenditure	12,506.91	53,249.59	11,319.07	14,101.73

Source: Researcher's computation

average higher than they were in 2014. But expenditure on non-food items shows slightly higher value on average in 2014 as compared to 2011. Moreover, the pattern of expenditure shows that there was wider dispersion, which indicates the extent of inequality in the study area and hence implies relevant policy interventions to improve the situation.

4.2 *Descriptive statistics of energy sources and technology use of households*

The data from the two rounds of the survey contain important information about the energy use status of households. Residents in most developing countries, especially in rural parts, rely on inefficient energy use technologies and energy sources to meet their daily needs. This is partly due to the non-availability of alternative sources and due to their non-affordability. As we can see from Table 4.8, a majority of the households used biomass as a source of energy for cooking. Firewood (either collected or purchased) was the major source of energy for cooking for about 87 per cent of the households in rural and small urban areas. This predominance of energy use for cooking has significant implications for health, time use and negative environmental impacts. Very few households used modern energy sources as a major source of cooking energy.

Table 4.8 shows that electricity, solar, kerosene and butane/gas made an almost insignificant proportion of energy sources for cooking in rural and small towns in Ethiopia. This requires an aggressive energy policy and interventions to ameliorate the situation.

Table 4.9 shows the status of energy sources for lighting in rural and small towns in Ethiopia. A further look at the data shows that the primary energy source for lighting was kerosene light (local *kuraz*), which accounted for about 41 and 35 per cent in 2011 and 2014, respectively. About 17 and 20 per cent of the respondents used electricity from different sources for lighting in 2011

Table 4.8 Main sources of cooking fuel

Variable	*Year*	
	2011	*2014*
	Per cent	*Per cent*
Collecting firewood	78.04	77.62
Purchase firewood	9.80	9.71
Charcoal	1.61	1.52
Crop residuals/leaves	3.24	3.30
Dung/manure	5.01	5.30
Sawdust	0.08	0.03
Kerosene	0.62	0.69
Butane/gas	0.03	0.11
Electricity	0.13	0.64
Solar	0.03	0.00
Other sources	1.42	1.10

Source: Researcher's computation

Table 4.9 Main source of energy for lighting households (by year)

Variable	*Year*	
	2011	*2014*
	Per cent	*Per cent*
Electricity meter–private	7.64	7.90
Electricity meter–shared	9.65	12.35
Electricity from generator	0.45	0.50
Solar energy	0.13	3.05
Electric battery	0.29	0.50
Light from dry cell with switch	17.29	25.64
Kerosene light lamp (imported)	9.75	5.78
Kerosene light lamp (local kuraz)	41.23	33.54
Candle/wax	0.24	0.08
Firewood	12.99	9.68
Other sources	0.32	0.98

Source: Researcher's computation

and 2014, respectively. Light from dry cells with switch, firewood and imported kerosene lamps contributed significantly to households' source of energy for lighting. Despite the fact that Ethiopia is a country with sunshine throughout the year, solar energy as a source contributed a very small proportion of households' source of energy for lighting. This signals that solar energy as an alternative source of energy for the country is poorly developed, which calls for appropriate policy interventions in the area.

Indoor air pollution is a very severe problem in developing countries, which predominantly use traditional sources of energy for preparing their food (see Table 4.10). Besides the type of energy used, the type of kitchen and energy use technologies play a crucial role in reducing indoor air pollution. Energy use technology has an immense role in reducing indoor air pollution, quantity of energy used for cooking or lighting and saving time for households. Cooking in most of the developing countries demands a lot of time, uses considerable energy and claims a higher resource budget of poor households. As a result, improving energy use efficiencies of these technologies and promoting technologies will reduce energy use-related burdens on the environment and enhance households' welfare to a greater extent. As can be seen from Table 4.11, about 97 per cent of the households used traditional stoves for cooking. This figure does not show any improvement in the 2014 survey.

Table 4.10 Type of kitchen used by households

Variable	*Year*	
	2011	*2014*
	Per cent	*Per cent*
A room used as a modern kitchen outside	0.35	0.56
A room used as a modern kitchen inside	0.32	0.64
A room used as a traditional kitchen outside	32.70	36.40
A room used as a traditional kitchen inside	23.27	28.95
No kitchen	43.36	33.46

Source: Researcher's computation

Table 4.11 Primary type of stove (*mitad*) used – baking *enjera*

Variable	*Year*	
	2011	*2014*
	Per cent	*Per cent*
Traditional *mitad* (removable)	68.68	72.48
Traditional *mitad* (not removable)	28.33	25.24
Improved energy saving *mitad* (rural tech.)	2.70	1.91
Electric *mitad*	0.29	0.93

Source: Researcher's computation

4.3 Extent of energy poverty in rural and small towns in Ethiopia

The results of the deprivation analysis show that the sample households were severely deprived of modern energy services and hence we see evidence of widespread energy poverty in rural and small towns in Ethiopia. The headcount measure of the deprivation status of households when it comes to energy services is presented in Table 4.12.

As can be seen from Table 4.12, the dashboard approach shows the extent of deprivation of energy sources or services by each indicator. A further look at the results shows that there was some improvement in deprivation levels in 2014 as compared to 2011. However, the change is not very impressive, which suggests that the sector needs concerted policy interventions. The results also show that about 82.72 and 81.35 per cent of the households were below energy poverty line in 2011 and 2014, respectively.

Energy poverty is prevalent in most developing countries. The situation is peculiar for rural parts of SSA countries, where most of the population is deprived of access to modern energy sources. Modern energy sources are both physically and economically not accessible in rural parts. Physical accessibility means the availability of energy sources in the area. For example, the rate of rural electrification is very low, which implies that electricity is not physically accessible to rural residents. More importantly, economic accessibility is challenging for rural residents for switching to modern energy and improved energy technologies. Low-income/poor households cannot afford to pay for modern energy and improved technologies, which forces them to use traditional sources of energy and energy use technologies.

The case is acute for rural and small urban areas in Ethiopia. As we can see from Table 4.13, the multidimensional measure of energy poverty shows the existence of severe energy poverty. About 74 per cent of the households were

Table 4.12 Incidences of energy poverty by year (headcount energy poverty, *H*)

Year	*Values*	*Type of cooking fuel*	*Kitchen is separate*	*Type of oven/* mited *used for cooking*	*Type of energy used for lighting*	*Has a radio, tap, TV or satellite dish*	*Incidence of energy poverty (H)*
	Weights	0.25	0.15	0.15	0.25	0.20	1.00
2011	Per cent	99.21	66.92	97.03	82.28	63.80	
	Weighted value	24.80	10.04	14.55	20.57	12.76	82.72
2014	Per cent	98.57	62.42	97.17	76.22	68.54	
	Weighted value	24.64	9.36	14.58	19.06	13.71	81.35

Source: Researcher's computation

Table 4.13 Multidimensional index of energy poverty indices by year (the Alkire and Foster, AF, 2007 method)

Group variable	*Year*	
	2011	*2014*
	MEPI	*MEPI*
Male	73.3	71.3
Female	78.9	76.6
Population	74.4	73.2

Source: Researcher's computation

Table 4.14 Relative contribution of dimensions to Alkire and Foster (*AF*) MEP indices estimated as population share (in per cent)

Dimensions	*Year*	
	2011	*2014*
	MEPI	*MEPI*
Type of cooking fuel	43.20	40.43
Type of kitchen used	18.12	20.37
Type of stove used	10.60	15.52
Source of energy for lighting	8.48	10.36
Ownership of educational/ entertainment appliances	19.6	13.32

Source: Researcher's computation

multi-dimensionally energy poor in 2011 while there was only a slight decline in this figure in the second round of the survey. Female-headed households were more energy poor as compared to male-headed households in both the years.

Table 4.14 shows the contribution of each dimension to the multidimensional index of energy poverty for households. This information can be used for targeting each dimension if one wants to reduce energy poverty in the study area. The dimensional deprivation shows that any attempts to solve the problem of energy poverty in the study area should target each dimension with varying degrees of emphasis.

4.4 *Determinants of MEPI in rural and small towns in Ethiopia*

Once we had examined the extent of energy poverty in the study area, the next step was to examine the factors that were responsible for this level of energy poverty for the households. Using the random effect logit model, we examined the determinants of multidimensional energy poverty for households in rural and small urban areas in Ethiopia. The regression results using socioeconomic

Table 4.15 Logit regression results of determinants of MEPI

MEPI_index	*Coefficients*	*Std. Err.*	*p-value*
Household's size	0.13	0.06	0.022
Sex of HH head (male = 1, female = 0)	0.69	0.32	0.031
Household head's age	–0.02	0 .01	0.047
Literacy (1 literate, 0 otherwise)	1.62	0.38	0.000
Area of residence	1.80	0.27	0.000
Number of rooms for HH	–0.34	0.08	0.000
Credit use (1 if used, 0 otherwise)	–0.26	0.30	0.384
HH energy expenditure (log)	–0.05	0.10	0.654
HH total expenditure (log)	–0.72	0.15	0.000
Marital status (married = 1 or 0 otherwise)	0.82	0.41	0.045
Marital status (divorced = 1 or 0 otherwise)	1.48	0.60	0.013
Marital status (separated = 1 or 0 otherwise)	0.53	1.10	0.631
Marital status (widowed = 1 or 0 otherwise)	1.37	0.64	0.032
Constant	8.13	1.22	0.000

Note: N = 6,533, Log likelihood = –322.91, Pseudo R^2 = 0.30, Wald $chi^2(13)$ = 211.49

characteristics, household head's characteristics and community characteristics are given in Table 4.15. Before running the regression, we conducted a series of diagnostic tests to see whether the data fulfilled some desirable properties. The presence of multicollinearity, normality of the variables and specification tests were conducted using appropriate tools. The pair-wise correlation coefficient showed that there was no significant correlation between the independent variables. To correct for unknown forms of the heteroscedasticity problem that may reduce efficiency of the estimated coefficients, we used White's heteroscedasticity consistent standard error (robust estimation). The results of the random effect logit model and marginal effects after logit are given in Tables 4.15 and 4.16, respectively.

Since the logit model's results were not directly interpretable, we had to compute either the log odds ratio to interpret the estimated results as the effect of independent variables on the probability of success to failure ratio, or alternatively we could compute marginal effects after logit and interpret the results directly as the effect of covariates on the probability of being energy poor. We preferred the results of the marginal effect after logit since these give us the effect of covariates on the probability of being multi-dimensionally energy poor.

The results in Table 4.16 show that as household size increased by one member the probability of the household falling into multidimensional energy poverty increased by 0.0004, which was significant at the 5 per cent level of significance. Male-headed households had about 0.0024 higher probability of becoming multi-dimensionally energy poor as compared to female-headed households. A one-year increase in the age of the head of the household decreased

Table 4.16 Marginal effect after the logit model

Variable	*dy/dx*	*Std. Err.*	*P>|z|*
Household's size	0.0004	0.0002	0.028
Sex of HH head (male = 1, female = 0)	0.0024	0.0014	0.093
Household head's age	-0.00005	0 .00003	0.058
Literacy (1 literate, 0 otherwise)	0.005	0.0011	0.000
Area of residence	0.011	0.0034	0.001
Number of rooms for HH	-0.001	0.0003	0.002
Credit use (1 if used, 0 otherwise)	-0.00074	0.00086	0.385
HH energy expenditure (log)	-0.00013	0.0002	0.655
HH total expenditure (log)	-0.002	0.0005	0.000
Marital status (married = 1 or 0 otherwise)	0.003	0.0020	0.135
Marital status (Divorced = 1 or 0 otherwise)	0.002	0.0007	0.001
Marital status (Separated = 1 or 0 otherwise)	0.001	0.0018	0.520
Marital status (Widowed = 1 or 0 otherwise)	0.002	0.0009	0.008

Source: Authors calculations.

the probability of the household becoming multi-dimensionally energy poor by 0.00005 and was significant at the 10 per cent level. Access to credit, more rooms occupied and higher household total expenditure significantly reduced the probability of a household falling into energy poverty.

5. Conclusions, recommendations and policy implications

5.1 *Conclusions and recommendations*

This study examined in detail the extent and determinants of energy poverty in rural and small towns in Ethiopia. The study used two rounds of overlapping data from a survey conducted as a joint project of the Central Statistical Agency of Ethiopia and the World Bank as part of the Living Standards Survey. With the primary objective of analyzing the extent and determinants of multidimensional energy poverty in the study area, the paper highlighted the status of households with regard to energy use and energy use technologies in the area. The descriptive statistics' results clearly revealed energy use status of the respondents in both the survey years.

The study also examined the extent of energy poverty in the area using the multidimensional measure following the Nussbaumer et al. (2012) methodology adopted from Alkire and Foster (2007) as the multidimensional measure of poverty. The results of the Multidimensional Energy Poverty Index show that about 74.4 and 73.2 per cent of the respondents were multi-dimensionally energy poor in 2011 and 2014, respectively. The results also show that there was no significant improvement in the energy poverty status of the households in the survey periods with a three-year difference. The relative contribution and decomposition of multidimensional energy poverty by dimension can help policymakers and development planners direct resources and efforts in appropriate intervention areas. Specifically, policy interventions for improving households' energy poverty should consider each attribute and design appropriate tools for public intervention.

On the other hand, results from the random effect logit model showed determinants of the MEP status of the households. Households with larger family size; married, widowed or divorced household heads; and located in rural areas had a higher probability of being multi-dimensionally energy poor. On the contrary, higher age of the head of the household, access to credit, more rooms occupied and higher total household expenditure (proxy for income) reduced the probability of households being multi-dimensionally energy poor. As noted in literature and confirmed by the positive coefficient of income on energy poverty from the regression results of this study, energy poverty is highly correlated with income poverty. As incomes increase, the energy poverty levels decrease, which implies that affordability of energy sources and energy use technologies require a series of policy interventions. Policies promoting clean energy technology and clean energy sources should be supported to enhance households' incomes. Moreover, the results of the study show that the government of Ethiopia has a long way to go still to realize rural clean energy access regardless of the relentless efforts that have been put in so far. More efforts are required for promoting rural clean energy and energy use technologies (for example, through rural electrification and promoting solar energy) coupled with an appropriate pricing mix (subsidy) to reach the poor, thus reducing energy poverty.

5.2 *Policy implications of energy poverty for poverty reduction*

It is an undeniable fact that poverty is the most fundamental realities of developing countries. Energy poverty is a new dimension of poverty. Most incidences of energy poverty emanate from lack of access to clean, affordable and modern energy services. Unlike income poverty, this can be improved through price reduction, improving energy efficiency, expanding modern energy and increasing household incomes. In effect, energy efficiency plays a prominent role in reducing energy poverty. Such an approach will make the energy that is necessary for basic needs affordable at a lower expenditure. It has a double dividend benefits. It makes energy required for basic life to be affordable at lower costs and helps in mitigating global warming through reducing emissions related to energy use. Reducing energy poverty provides enormous welfare benefits to poor households. It contributes to reducing poverty through improvements in the health of household members and lower indoor air pollution, which means lower respiratory diseases and lower health expenditure. Moreover, use of modern energy and technologies increase productivity and leave scope for new opportunities for additional incomes and reduces the time and labor spent on household activities. Modern technologies for energy use, especially in the rural parts of a developing country, contribute to poverty reduction, improving health and education and promoting development in the area. Policymakers can use the results of this study for synergizing poverty reduction and energy poverty reduction policies. The results could also be used for domesticating international goals such as SDGs to national realities.

Notes

1 This research is supported by the Jönköping International Business School (JIBS), Jönköping University, Sweden, in collaboration with Addis Ababa University for doctoral studies in Economics, a project supported by the Swedish International Development Cooperation Agency (SIDA). The author would like to thank Professor Almas Heshmati, Professor Andreas Stephan, Dr Alemu Mekonnen and other participants of a seminar at Jonkoping International Business School for their comments and suggestions on an earlier version of this research.

2 https://energypedia.info/wiki/Ethiopian_Energy_situation accessed on 11/19/2013.

References

Alkire, S. (2007). "Choosing dimensions: The capability approach and multidimensional poverty", CPRC Working Paper No. 88.

Alkire, S. and J.E. Foster (2007). "Counting and multidimensional poverty measurement", OPHI Working Paper No. 7.

Alkire, S. and J.E. Foster (2011). "Counting and multidimensional poverty measurement", *Journal of Public Economics*, 95, 476–487.

Alkire, S. and M.E. Santos (2014). "Measuring acute poverty in the developing world: Robustness and scope of the multidimensional poverty index", *World Development*, 59, 251–274.

Barnes, D.F., S.R. Khandker, and H.A. Samad (2011). "Energy poverty in rural Bangladesh", *Energy Policy*, 39, 894–904.

Bekele, G., W. Negatu, and G. Eshete (2015). "Energy poverty in Addis Ababa city, Ethiopia", *Journal of Economics and Sustainable Development*, 6(3), 26–34.

Birol, F. (2007). "Energy economics: A place for energy poverty in the agenda?", *The Energy Journal*, 28(3), 1–6.

Boardman, B. (1991). *Fuel Poverty: From Cold Homes to Affordable Warmth*. London: Belhaven Press.

Boardman, B. (2012). "Fuel poverty synthesis: Lessons learnt, actions needed", *Energy Policy*, 49, 143–148.

Cameron, A.C. and P.K. Trivedi (2005). *Microeconometrics: Methods and Applications*. New York: Cambridge University Press.

Chakravarty, S. and M. Tavoni (2013). "Energy poverty alleviation and climate change mitigation: Is there a trade off?", *Energy Economics*, 40, 567–573.

CSA and WB (2011). *Living Standards Measurement Study-Integrated Surveys on Agriculture (LSMS-ISA): Ethiopia Rural Socioeconomic Survey (ERSS) Basic Information Document*. Available at: siteresources.worldbank.org/INTLSMS/Resources/33589861233781970982/5800988-1367841456879/91700251367841502220/ERSS_Basic_Information_Sept_2013.pdf.

CSA and WB (2015). *Living Standards Measurement Study-Integrated Surveys on Agriculture (LSMS-ISA): Ethiopia Rural Socioeconomic Survey (ERSS) Basic Information Document*. Available at: http://siteresources.worldbank.org/INTLSMS/Resources/3358986123378197 0982/5800988-1367841456879/9170025142714424 7562/Basic_Information_Document_Wave_2.pdf.

Dawit, D. (2012). "Assessment of biomass fuel resource potential and Utilization in Ethiopia: Sourcing strategies for renewable energies", *International Journal of Renewable Energy Research*, 2(1), 131–139.

Edoumiekumo, S.G., S.S. Tombofa, and T.M. Karimo (2013). "Multidimensional energy poverty in the south-south geopolitical zone of Nigeria", *Journal of Economics and Sustainable Development*, 4(20), 96–103.

FDRE (2011a). *Country Strategy Paper 2011–2015*. Addis Ababa, Ethiopia.

FDRE (2011b). *Ethiopia's Climate Resilient Green Economy*. Addis Ababa, Ethiopia: Green Economy Strategy.

Foster, J., J. Greer, and E. Thorbecke (1984). "Notes and comments: A class of decomposable poverty measures", *Econometrica*, 52(3), 761–766.

Foster, J., S. Seth, M. Likshin, and Z. Sajaia (2013). *A Unified Approach to Measuring Poverty and Inequality: Theory and Practice*. Washington, DC: The World Bank.

Foster, V., J.P. Tre, and Q. Wodon (2000). *Energy Prices, Energy Efficiency, and Fuel Poverty*. Washington, DC: Latin America and Caribbean Regional Studies Programme, the World Bank.

Gowon, E.S. and K.T. Moses (2014). "Multidimensional energy poverty in Bayelsa State of Nigeria: Implications for sustainable development", *African Journal of Social Sciences*, 4(1), 135–145.

HDR (2014). *Sustaining Human Progress: Reducing Vulnerabilities and Building Resilience*. New York: United Nations Development Programme.

Khandker, S.R., D.F. Barnes, and H.A. Samad (2012). "Are the energy poor also income poor? Evidence from India", *Energy Policy*, 47, 1–12.

Li, K., B. Lloyd, X.J. Liang, and Y.M. Wei (2014). "Energy poor or fuel poor: What are the differences?", *Energy Policy*, 68, 476–481.

Modi, V., S. McDade, D. Lallement, and J. Saghir (2006). *Energy and the Millennium Development Goals*. New York: Energy Sector Management Assistance Programme, United Nations Development Programme, United Nations Millennium Project and the World Bank.

Moore, R. (2012). "Definitions of fuel poverty: Implications for policy", *Energy Policy*, 49, 19–26.

Nussbaumer, P., M. Bazilian, and V. Modi (2012). "Measuring energy poverty: Focusing on what matters. Renewable and sustainable", *Energy Reviews*, 16, 231–243.

OECD and IEA (2010). *World Energy Outlook*. Paris: OECD.

OFID (2008). "Energy poverty in Africa: Proceedings of a workshop held by OFID", OFID Pumphlet Series, Abuja, Nigeria.

Pachauri, S. and D. Spreng (2004). "Energy use and energy access in relation to poverty", *Economic and Political Weekly*, 39(3), 271–278.

Parajuli, R. (2011). "Access to energy in Mid/Far west region-Nepal from the perspective of energy poverty", *Renewable Energy*, 36, 2299–2304.

Pereira, M.G., M.A.V. Freitas, and N.F. DeSilva (2010). "Rural electrification and energy poverty: Empirical evidences from Brazil", *Renewable and Sustainable Energy Reviews*, 14, 1229–1240.

Pereira, M.G., M.A.V. Freitas, and N.F. DeSilva (2011). "The challenge of energy poverty: Brazilian case study", *Energy Policy*, 39, 167–175.

Power Africa (2015). *Investment Brief for the Energy Sector of Ethiopia*. Addis Ababa. Available at: www.usaid.gov/powerafrica.

Ravallion, M. (2010). "Mashup indices of development", The World Bank, Policy Research Working Paper 5432.

Sen, A. (1990). *Development as Capability Expansion*. Cambridge, MA: Harvard University Press.

Sher, F., A. Abbas, and R.U. Awan (2014). "An investigation of multidimensional energy poverty in Pakistan: A province level analysis", *International Journal of Energy Economics and Policy*, 4(1), 65–75.

Tchereni, B.H.M., W. Grobler, and S.H. Dunga (2013). "Economic analysis of energy poverty in South Lunzu, Malawi", *Journal of Economics and Sustainable Development*, 4(4), 154–163.

UNDP and WHO (2009). *The Energy Access Situation in Developing Countries: A Review on the Least Developed Countries and Sub-Saharan Africa*. Available at: http://content-ext.undp.org/aplaws_assets/2205620/2205620.pdf.

Walkera, R., P. McKenziea, C. Liddellb, and C. Morris (2014). "Estimating fuel poverty at household level: An integrated approach", *Energy and Buildings*, 80, 469–479.

WEO (2013). *World Energy Outlook 2013-Electricity Access Database*. Paris: Cedex 15, France.

WEO (2014). *African Energy Outlook: A Focus on Energy Prospect of Sub-Saharan Africa*. International Energy Agency. Paris: Cedex 15, France.

WHO (2002). *Addressing the Links Between Indoor Air Pollution, Household Energy and Human Health*. Washington, DC: World Health Organization.

5 Household food security and school enrollment

Evidence from Malawi

Sunyoung Lee

1. Introduction

This paper studies how food availability affected school enrollment rates in Malawi in 2010–11. Many previous works have found the relationship between income/wealth and child labor, but not many studies specify the relationship between food consumption levels and school enrollment. This paper discusses the question: how do parental decisions for a child's schooling vary in terms of food consumption levels as a proxy of poverty? It also discusses how incomes and school dropout rates are associated just below or just above subsistence levels, respectively. This paper is interesting in that it uses a subjective measure of the subsistence level according to which a household considers its food consumption level enough or not.

Previous works have shown a negative relationship between income and child labor and a positive relationship between income and schooling within a country or across countries. They also show that schooling and child labor are deeply related (Khanam, 2008; Psacharopoulos, 1997; Ravallion and Wodon, 2000). The main assumption of the previous papers is that parents send their children to work when their own wages are not sufficient to meet the basic needs of the family. Basu (2000) argues that parents withdraw their children from work if they have sufficient resources for their basic needs, while others show that labor supply of children starts decreasing once subsistence needs are met. The present paper uses food availability levels as a proxy for subsistence and studies the relationship between 'enough' food consumption and school enrollment and also shows that perceived food consumption levels could be a better tool than income to explain schooling in a developing and rural country.

This paper used the Probit and OLS models to estimate the relationship between school enrollment rates and food consumption levels. The food consumption variable is defined as *enoughfood*, which is equal to 1 if a family has never faced a situation that members had to skip a meal because they did not have anything to eat for a year before the survey. Thus, if *enoughfood* is 1, then the family is considered to be above the subsistence level at least regarding food concerns. An income variable and the interaction term with the *enoughfood* variable are also included. The research used the Malawi Third Integrated Survey

(2010–11), which is the first wave of cross-section panel datasets from World Bank data. The sample size was over 20,000 children aged 6–18 years, which gives it substantial statistical power.

The paper found that having enough food had a significant relationship with dropout rates whether or not income was controlled. Children consuming enough food were 1.6 per cent less likely to drop out of school than children not having enough food, controlling for income, individual, household and community characteristics. However, the dropout rates increased as incomes increased for children consuming enough food. However, a 100-dollar increase in income increased the dropout rate by 0.3 per cent. This increase may be caused by economic opportunities outside school and poor teaching quality, which made the opportunity cost of sending children to school high and so parents preferred keeping their children at work. The study also found that the income levels themselves did not have any significant relationship with dropout rates without the *enoughfood* variable included in the regressions. This may be because income alone cannot capture financial resources in a poor country such as Malawi.

2. Literature review

There are two main streams on child labor and schooling. The first is child labor caused by poverty and the other is non-poverty issues such as owning a farm in a developing country leading to child labor (Basu et al., 2010). Incomes, wages or household wealth play an important role in decisions on child labor and school enrollments. For example, Edmonds (2005) found that child labor declined as the economic status improved in Vietnam between 1993 and 1997. According to his study, an increase in anticipated income was related to an increase in schooling and a decrease in the hours worked. Beegle et al. (2006) assert that there was a significant relationship between transitory household income shocks and increase in child labor.

However, income was not considered an important factor at every income level. Among most of the research on child labor and income, there is an agreement on when child labor occurs: when a household income drops below its subsistence level. For example, Dessing (2001) found that near the subsistence level, the income effect was greater than the substitution effect, thus there was negative elasticity of family labor supply. In other words, as family wages decreased, members had to put more time into work to meet their basic needs. If the wage of a primary worker in a household was not enough for all the family members, then secondary workers such as children were needed to work. Basu et al. (2010) also point out that at above subsistence level, an adult's wage was high enough to support a family and children were not required to work, but below the subsistence level, because the adult's wage was very low and could not support a family, children had to work for survival.

Our paper used perceived food security as a proxy for subsistence level to estimate the relationship between schooling and subsistence in terms of household food security. For a year before the survey, if a household had never faced a situation of skipping meals because of lack of food, it was postulated as 'above subsistence level'; if a household had skipped a meal, then it was 'below subsistence level'. The food poverty measure has several advantages over simple income or consumption variables. First, enough food consumption could be a better yardstick to bifurcate households above subsistence and below subsistence levels as compared to usual income poverty lines because it captures the issues of each household holistically as survey questions usually miss aspects such as degree of family illness, money management skills or food price levels or fluctuations in each village. Second, income or consumption will hardly be measured accurately in a poor rural country such as Malawi considering the fact that a substantial part of its population is involved in family farming or getting paid in in-kind wages.

3. Background of agriculture and education in Malawi

Malawi is a landlocked country in the southeast of Africa; it also has the smallest territory in Africa. Malawi is among the least developed countries in the world and its economy is heavily dependent on agriculture, which accounts for over 30 per cent of its GDP and over 90 per cent of its export revenues. As of 2008, 47 per cent of its population was engaged in agriculture and 84 per cent of the population lived in a rural area. Unemployment in Malawi was relatively low at 6 per cent and the ratio of economically active male to female population in agriculture was 1.05. The rate of undernourished people in the total population was 29 per cent during 2004–06. Malawi's GDP in 2008 was USD 2,920 million, GNI per capita was USD 289, agricultural GDP on total GDO was 34.7 per cent and 32 per cent of its national budget was spent on agriculture.[1]

The education system in Malawi is divided into three levels – primary, lower secondary and upper secondary. Primary education is free but not compulsory. Students take a test called the Primary School Leaving Certificate Examination (PSLCE) in the last year of primary education, the results of which are used for secondary school entrance, as there are limited seats at this level. According to UNESCO, as of 2010, the official age of school entrance was six years and 4.6 million students were enrolled in schools. Primary school is for six years; lower secondary for four years; and upper secondary for two years.[2] According to the Education Policy and Data Center (EPDC), as of 2010, 57 per cent of the youth (aged 15–24 years) had not even completed primary education, and 5 per cent of the youth had not obtained any education. Only 7 per cent of the youth had completed secondary education. The out-of-school rate in primary education was 11 per cent (11 per cent male and 10 per cent female). Five per cent urban children and 11 per cent rural children were not attending school. At the secondary level 27 per cent children were out of school (23 per cent male and 32 per cent female). There were substantial gender differences at the secondary school while there was almost no gender difference at the primary level. Geographically, out-of-school rates were 23 and 28 per cent in urban and rural areas, respectively.[3]

4. Theoretical models

Our paper mainly used two theories: Basu and Van (1998) and Dessing (2001). Basu and Van's luxury axiom on child labor says 'a family will send the children to the labor market only if the family's income from non-child-labor sources drops very low.' In other words, this axiom carries the message that a child not working is a luxury for a family which can afford it.

$$L^c\left(W^a\right) = \begin{cases} 0, \ if \ W^a < W^s \\ 1, \ if \ W^a \geq W^s \end{cases} \tag{1}$$

Eq. 1 assumes that all households are identical with one child and one adult, and child labor supply (L^c) is a function of adult wages (W^a). If adult wages drop below the subsistence wage (W^s), then an adult prefers children working; on the other hand, if adult wages move above the subsistence level, then the adult prefers children not working.

Dessing (2001) explains the household-level labor supply model in terms of primary and secondary workers. His model is detailed in labor supply dynamics including substitution effect, income effect and even nutrition for the extreme poor. He argues that if the wages of a primary worker go below or approach near subsistence levels, then income effects dominate substitution effects and thus labor leading to supply of secondary workers going up. Near the substitution level, even a small amount of additional income would be welcomed by a poor family that needs to use up all its labor to maintain subsistence consumption levels. Thus, if we consider a secondary worker as a child in Dessing's labor supply model, then Dessing's labor supply curve is equivalent to Basu and Van's child labor curve near the subsistence level in that subsistence wage is the determinant of child labor.

The other child labor model used in this paper addresses parental utility as a function of current consumption levels and human capital that children will achieve in the future (Emerson and Souza, 2003). This model claims that parents assume a utility function as:

$$U_t = U\,(c_t, h_{t+1}) \tag{2}$$

where c_t is the current household consumption level and h_{t+1} is human capital achieved by a child in the next period. Parents, as rational decision makers struggling near the subsistence level, will have to determine whether they can increase current consumption by not sending kids to school and the expected future utility of children thanks to schooling. If a utility of current consumption of a family outweighs the utility of human capital of children in the future, then parents will send their children to work rather than sending them to school.

5. Data description

The main dataset used for this study is the Malawi Third Integrated Household Survey 2010 (IHS3) collected by the National Statistical Office of the Republic of Malawi. The Malawi government does this survey every five years to monitor changes in general living conditions of the people of Malawi. This is a cross-section dataset and has extensive information including migration, education, poverty and agriculture at the individual, household and community levels. IHS3 data is collected in three main regions – north, center and south – and these regions are stratified into two categories – urban and rural. Only the regions Lilongwe City, Blantyre City, Mzuzu City and the Municipality of Zomba are urban areas while the rest are rural areas. Among the 3,247 households in the survey, 864 households lived in urban areas and 2,400 households in rural areas.

This paper restricts the sample to children aged 6–18 years and the unit of observation is an individual child. There were over 20,000 children in this age range, which gives the sample significant statistical power. The reason for choosing this as the age range was that it spans normal primary and secondary school age groups.

Although it has a large number of observations, there is the possibility that income or consumption was not measured correctly because the questions on income and consumption largely relied on memory and estimations. For example, 'how much did you sell your crop for last year?' or, 'how much did were you paid per kilogram in average last year?' Thus, there are chances that the people did not remember correctly and gave incorrect answers, thus leading to biases in the estimates. Another reason for answers not being exact is that the people trade or get paid in kind such as crops or chicken and they also grow and consume crops. These in-kind wages or payments require conjectures about wages and consumption, so it is difficult to get exact data. This is especially the case in a country in which most of the population resides in rural areas.

6. Summary statistics

Table 5.1 presents descriptive statistics of IHS3 data. It shows that 83 per cent of children aged 6–18 years were enrolled in schools in Malawi during the survey period (2010–11). Primary school enrollment rates were 11 while for secondary school they were 73 per cent. Gender differences in school enrollment were negligible at the primary level (1 percentage point higher for female pupils) but became substantial at the secondary level as the rate was 32 and 23 per cent for boys and girls, respectively. For the entire sample, only 0.903 per cent of the population had ever attended school; 77 per cent of school-going-age children said they had attended school in the previous year.

The main variables of interest are 'enough food' and 'consumption'. Enough food is equal to 1 if for a year before the survey a household had never faced a situation that its members had to skip a meal because of lack of food, otherwise it is zero. Thus, instead of looking at households above or below the subsistence level using an objective and unilateral standard (USD 1.50 per day), this paper tries to capture the real situation that a household might or might not have experienced in the past. Unfortunately, Malawi is one of the poorest

Table 5.1 Summary statistics

Variable	*Description*	*Mean*	*Std. Err.*	*Min*	*Max*
Dependent variables					
Enrolled	1 if enrolled in school, 0 otherwise				
schoolexp	1 if ever attended school, 0 otherwise	0.903	0.296	0	1
Variables of interest					
enoughfood	1 if household never skipped a meal because of lack of food for a year, 0 otherwise	0.509	0.500	0	1
foodworried	1 if household worried about lack of food for a year, 0 otherwise	0.334	0.472	0	1
consumption	Total spending of HH in USD	415	506	29	10303
Other characteristics					
Age	in years	11.308	3.728	6	18
female	1 if female, 0 otherwise	0.505	0.500	0	1
married	1 if married, 0 otherwise	0.019	0.136	0	1
fatherdied	1 if one's father died, 0 otherwise	0.601	0.490	0	1
poverty	1 if below poverty line, 0 otherwise	0.547	0.498	0	1
houseowned	1 if household owned a house, 0 otherwise	0.838	0.368	0	1
hhsize	Number of household	6.224	2.153	1	19
rural	1 if resided in rural area, 0 otherwise	0.833	0.373	0	1
hhedu	Level of education of household head	1.474	0.842	1	4
noreligion	1 if had no religion, 0 otherwise	0.004	0.066	0	1
trareligion	1 if traditional religion, 0 otherwise	0.005	0.069	0	1
Christian	1 if Christian, 0 otherwise	0.398	0.489	0	1
Muslim	1 if Muslim, 0 otherwise	0.054	0.225	0	1
othreligion	1 if religion other than specified, 0 otherwise	0.003	0.058	0	1

Source: The Malawi Third Integrated Household Survey

even among sub-Saharan African countries, and more than half the students (0.509) were from households that had nothing to eat for a year. Along with food consumption levels, household total expenditure was also considered and the 'consumption' variable showed the total expenditure of a household in dollars. The minimum was USD 29 and the maximum was USD 10,303.

Other personal, household and regional characteristics were also included for control. 'Age' shows that the age in years and the mean age of the sample was 11 because the sample population was restricted to 6 to 18 years. The variable 'female' was equal to 1 if female, otherwise 0. 'Married' was 1 if married, zero otherwise, and the mean of this variable for children aged 6–18 years was 0.019. The mean of 'poverty' that indicated that an individual was below the poverty line was 0.547. The proportion of students from a household that owned a house was relatively large at 83.8 per cent, but 'owning a house' is totally different from what this means in developed countries. The average household size was 6.2 (minimum 1 to maximum 19). In the sample, about 83 per cent of the children resided in rural areas and 37 per cent in urban areas. The average education levels of household heads was lower secondary education at 1.47 (1 for primary education completed, 2 for lower secondary completed, 3 for upper secondary completed and 4 for higher education completed). Christians were in a majority, while Muslims were at second place.

7. Empirical strategy

The dependent variable is enrollment rate, a binary variable, which is 1 if a child has dropped out of school; the variables of interest are enough food and consumption. The enough food variable is also a binary indicator which bifurcates families into two categories – families consuming or not consuming enough food – and was used as a proxy for the subsistence level. Along with the enough food variable, the consumption level variable was also included. By doing so, it was possible to examine the different effects of consumption across the households above and below the subsistence level, respectively. β_2 shows the relationship between household income levels and school dropout rates for households with inadequate food consumption, and β_3 for households with adequate food consumption. Control variables were added to control for individual, household, school and community factors. Individual controls (X_i) include age and gender; household controls (X_h) include monthly income, household size, the education level of the household head, credit and land; school controls (X_s) include whether or not the school had a building and books; and community control includes the rural/urban area variable. The Probit model was used to estimate the dropout rates, as the enrollment variable is a binary indicator (Eq. 3).

$$\begin{aligned} &P(Enrollment_i) \\ &= \beta_0 + \beta_1 enoughfood_h + \beta_2 consumption_h \\ &+ \beta_3 enoughfood_h * consumption_h + \beta_4 age_i \\ &+ \beta_5 female_i + \beta_6 married_h + \beta_7 hhedu_h \\ &+ \beta_8 fatherdied_h + \beta_9 houseowned_h + \beta_{10} religion_h \\ &+ \beta_{11} rural_c + \varepsilon_i \end{aligned} \tag{3}$$

8. Regression results

The results on variables of interest are interesting. The 'enough food' variable explains enrollment rates among students much better than 'consumption'. As regression 6 in Table 5.2 shows, the coefficients of consumption and enough food*consumption variables were zero, while the 'enough food' variable generated statistically significant results with great magnitude for all regressions in which

Table 5.2 Regression results

Variable names	*Dependent variable: enrolled*					
	OLS			*Probit*		
	(1)	*(2)*	*(3)*	*(4)*	*(5)*	*(6)*
Enoughfood	0.039***		0.065***	0.169***		0.263***
	(0.005)		(0.007)	(0.023)		(0.033)
Consumption		0.000	0.000***		0.000	0.000***
(USD)		(0.000)	(0.000)		(0.000)	(0.000)
Enoughfood			0.000***			0.000***
*Consumption			(0.000)			(0.000)
Age	−0.003***	−0.005	−0.003***	−0.014***	−0.014***	−0.014***
	(0.001)	(0.001)	(0.001)	(0.003)	(0.003)	(0.003)
Female	0.009*	0.008*	0.009*	0.038*	0.036*	0.037*
	(0.005)	(0.007)	(0.005)	(0.022)	(0.022)	(0.022)
Married	−0.779***	−0.774***	−0.781***	−3.118***	−3.108***	−3.127***
	(0.019)	(0.020)	(0.019)	(0.182)	(0.182)	(0.181)
HH size	0.005***	0.005***	0.004***	0.022***	0.018***	0.017***
	(0.001)	(0.001)	(0.001)	(0.005)	(0.006)	(0.006)
HH education	0.043***	0.046***	0.043***	0.236***	0.243***	0.232***
	(0.003)	(0.004)	(0.004)	(0.018)	(0.018)	(0.018)
Fatherdied	0.018***	0.020***	0.017***	0.082***	0.089***	0.077***
	(0.005)	(0.005)	(0.005)	(0.023)	(0.023)	(0.024)

(*Continued*)

Table 5.2 (Continued)

Variable names	*Dependent variable: enrolled*					
	OLS			*Probit*		
	(1)	*(2)*	*(3)*	*(4)*	*(5)*	*(6)*
Houseowned	0.004	0.003	0.005	0.020	0.017	0.024
	(0.008)	(0.008)	(0.008)	(0.037)	(0.036)	(0.037)
Rural	–0.001	–0.003	0.003	–0.001	–0.003	0.019
	(0.008)	(0.008)	(0.008)	(0.036)	(0.037)	(0.037)
No religion	–0.249***	–0.249***	–0.248***	–0.753***	–0.748***	–0.751***
	(0.038)	(0.039)	(0.038)	(0.138)	(0.138)	(0.138)
Traditional religion	–0.115***	–0.115***	–0.111***	–0.375***	–0.393***	–0.359***
	(0.036)	(0.037)	(0.036)	(0.139)	(0.138)	(0.139)
Muslim	–0.067***	–0.067***	–0.068***	–0.247***	–0.251***	–0.249***
	(0.011)	(0.014)	(0.011)	(0.046)	(0.046)	(0.046)
Other religion	–0.037	–0.037	–0.035	–0.132	–0.143	–0.126
	(0.043)	(0.044)	(0.043)	(0.182)	(0.181)	(0.181)
constant	0.753***	0.783***	0.736***	0.571***	0.637***	0.508***
	0.016	(0.018)	(0.016)	(0.070)	(0.069)	(0.071)
R-squared	0.115	0.112	0.1156	0.101	0.099	0.103
N	19,999	19,999	19,999	19,999	19,999	19,999

Source: The Malawi Third Integrated Household Survey

Note: (1)-(3) OLS models and (4)-(6) Probit models. Standard errors in parenthesis. Statistically significant at: ***: 1% level, ** 5% level, and * 10% level. Income in US-dollar, changed using MWK-dollar exchange rate at the time of interview (1 USD = 710 MWK).

it was included. The regression results show the discontinuity of school enrollment around the subsistent economic level. In Table 5.2, OLS (3) and Probit (6) are the main results of this study. As can be seen from regression 1, having enough food and controlling for other variables increased the possibility of school enrollment by a degree of 0.039, and this result was statistically significant at the 1 per cent level. On the other hand, consumption showed no effect on school enrollments, the coefficient of consumption appeared to be 0.000 at the 1 per cent significance level. By including the 'enough food*consumption' variable in regression 3, the effects of consumption on school enrollments were compared in separate groups of having enough food and not having enough food. Surprisingly, for both groups, consumption could not explain school enrollments. Although the coefficients of 'consumption' and 'enough food*consumption' were zero, including them increased the magnitude of the coefficient 'enough food'. Probit models (4) ~ (6) give us the same results on the relationship between school enrollment rates, having enough food and consumption.

Second, a look at other individual, household and regional control variables shows that 'age' had a negative effect on school enrollments but the magnitude was not big and only negative by 0.003. Among the household factors including household size, education levels of household heads, the death of the father and owning a house, education levels of household heads had the biggest magnitude at 0.043, holding other things constant. This means that if the education levels of the household heads increased by one level, then children were more likely to be enrolled in school by 4.3 per cent. Additionally, the association between owning a house and school enrollment appears to be negligible. This could be because owning a house has a different meaning in Malawi as compared to what it means in developed countries. Even if they owned a 'house', many families lived in poor structures built with mud with almost no facilities. This was especially the case in poor rural areas. In addition, religion was significant in this study. There are five religious groups – Christians, Muslims, traditional religions, other religions and no religion in Malawi. Christianity is the majority religion and has been omitted in the regression models for comparison. It turns out that Christian children were more likely to be enrolled in school than those from any other religion, as all other religious group variables had negative coefficients.

8.1 Enough food consumption as a necessary condition

According to Table 5.2, 'enough food' always remains significant whether or not consumption is included and whichever model is used. Regressions (1) ~ (3) are obtained by using OLS models and (4) ~ (6) are from the Probit models. The OLS regression model (1) reports that enrollment rate of children from households consuming enough food was 3.9 per cent higher than children from households not consuming enough food. The magnitude of enoughfood got bigger controlling for consumption in regression 3; having enough food increased enrollment rates by 6.5 per cent and was statistically significant at the 1 per cent level. Probit models (4) ~ (6) give more significant coefficients and Table 5.3 shows the marginal effects of the Probit model calculated at the

Table 5.3 Marginal effects of the Probit model

Variable names	*Dependent variable: enrolled*					
	Probit			*Marginal effects at mean*		
	(1)	*(2)*	*(3)*	*(4)*	*(5)*	*(6)*
Enoughfood	0.169***		0.263***	0.041***		0.064***
	(0.023)		(0.033)			
Consumption (USD)		0.000	0.000***		0.000	0.000***
		(0.000)	(0.000)			
Enoughfood *Consumption			0.000***			0.000***
			(0.000)			
Age	−0.014***	−0.014***	−0.014***	0.009***	0.009***	0.009***
	(0.003)	(0.003)	(0.003)			
Female	0.038*	0.036*	0.037*	0.005*	0.004*	0.006*
	(0.022)	(0.022)	(0.022)			
Married	−3.118***	−3.108***	−3.127***	−0.759***	−0.758***	−0.761***
	(0.182)	(0.182)	(0.181)			
HH size	0.022***	0.018***	0.017***	0.020***	0.022***	0.019***
	(0.005)	(0.006)	(0.006)			
HH education	0.236***	0.243***	0.232***	−0.003***	−0.003***	−0.003***
	(0.018)	(0.018)	(0.018)			
Fatherdied	0.082***	0.089***	0.077***	0.005***	0.004***	0.004***
	(0.023)	(0.023)	(0.024)			
Houseowned	0.020	0.017	0.024	0.000	−0.001	0.005
	(0.037)	(0.036)	(0.037)			

Rural	−0.001	−0.003	0.019	0.058	0.059	0.057
	(0.036)	(0.037)	(0.037)			
No religion	−0.753***	−0.748***	−0.751***	−0.183***	−0.182***	−0.183***
	(0.138)	(0.138)	(0.138)			
Traditional religion	−0.375***	−0.393***	−0.359***	−0.091***	−0.096***	−0.087***
	(0.139)	(0.138)	(0.139)			
Muslim	−0.247***	−0.251***	−0.249***	−0.060***	−0.061***	−0.061***
	(0.046)	(0.046)	(0.046)			
Other religion	−0.132	−0.143	−0.126	−0.032	−0.035	−0.031
	(0.182)	(0.181)	(0.181)			
constant	0.571***	0.637***	0.508***			
	(0.070)	(0.069)	(0.071)			
R-squared	0.101	0.099	0.103			
N	19,999	19,999	19,999			

Source: Author's computations

mean. Columns (4) ~ (6) in Table 5.3 show the marginal effects at the mean, where the coefficient of *enoughfood* is 0.039 in the Probit model in column 4 and the marginal effect at the mean is 0.041. This means that, controlling for individual, household, community and school factors, children having enough food showed a 4.1 per cent higher possibility of being enrolled in school than children who did not consume enough food. Column 6 in Table 5.3 shows that the marginal effect of *enoughfood* on enrollment was 0.064 at the mean, controlling for income and other factors. There was a 6.4 per cent higher possibility, which is high given that public education is offered free and total enrollment rates are about 83 per cent. In sum, if a household reached a certain level so that its subsistent needs were met, then parents were 6.4 per cent more likely to send their children to school.

8.2 Income is not a good measure in a poor rural region

In regressions 2 and 5, it was found that there was no significant relationship between consumption levels and enrollment rates. This does not mean that a family's financial situation was not related to school dropout rates or child labor, as many studies in literature address the significant relationship between household wealth/income and child labor (Basu et al., 1998; Beegle et al., 2006; Edmonds, 2005). Instead, it means that an income or consumption measurement error is what makes the consumption variable insignificant in the regression in Malawi's rural areas. It is very difficult to get accurate consumption or income data in the context of a poor rural region where people are commonly pay in-kind wages and they consume own-produced goods. Besides, many of them farm for their families' needs. Thus, it is even harder to track their consumption accurately. This may be one of the main reasons why the consumption variable barely generates a significant relationship between a household's economic situation and school enrollment in this research.

8.3 Sufficient condition for schooling

The consumption variable explains the relationship between consumption and enrollment rates for children not having enough food; and the *consumption*enoughfood* variable explains this for the children having enough food. In regressions 3 and 6, the coefficient of consumption is zero, and so is the *consumption*enoughfood* variable. This means that for both groups below and above subsistence levels, the consumption level will not affect school enrollment rates. But, as mentioned earlier, the simple and naïve conclusion that consumption levels will not affect school enrollments is not correct and it would be beneficial to scrutinize the results of the two groups separately to explain the outcomes.

Meeting subsistence levels is the most critical and urgent goal for any household below the subsistence level. The relationship between incomes and dropout rates in a developing country can be explained by Emerson and Souza's (2003) model that parental utility is a function of current consumption levels and human capital achievement by children in the future. If the utility of extra consumption is greater than the utility of educating children, parents prefer sending their children to work over sending them to school. This is more likely the case when there are many economic opportunities in a community and the quality of education is poor. Baschieri and Falkingham (2009) found the same results that economic opportunities had a negative effect on school attendance in Malawi. They argue that 'children living in communities where a high proportion of land has a slope of less than 5 degrees (i.e. is potentially arable) are less likely to be enrolled than other children.' What this means is that as agricultural job opportunities increased, the opportunity cost of educating children went up because parents had to give up additional agricultural income.

The utility gap between the two choices got bigger where education did not seem to give a better future to the children due to its low quality. Thus, the more economic opportunities in the community and the lower the quality of schooling, the greater opportunity costs that parents have to pay. Baschieri and Falkingham (2009) also maintain that in Malawi in 2003, 'almost 40 per cent of the difference in district variance is explained by the availability of income-generating opportunities in the area, and almost 25 per cent is explained by differences in perceptions of school quality.' Therefore, if higher income or consumption levels do not explain school enrollment rates, the possible reasons include economic opportunities and low education quality or a failing school system that the benefits of education seem negligible. This is a plausible claim considering that the Malawi public school system has been failing, as there is a shortage of classrooms and qualified teachers and the quality of education is decreasing as a consequence.[4]

It can be assumed that till the necessary conditions are met for subsistence, an increase in incomes cannot help raise school enrollment rates. Below the subsistence level (not having enough food), the coefficient of income turns out to be not significant, but above the subsistence level (having enough food), the dropout rates slightly increase as incomes increase. In other words, if income is still below the subsistence level, increasing it cannot affect schooling decisions because sending children to school is still a luxury no matter how much money families make below the subsistence level. However, above the subsistence level, parents have options to decide between the two utilities of current consumption and future returns of educating children. The slight positive relationship between dropout rates and school enrollments tells us that parents still choose not to send their children to school even though the households are above the subsistence level when the utility of return to education is not greater than the utility of economic opportunities in a community. The conclusion that can be drawn is that reaching a certain subsistence level plays an important role in sending children to school in general but this is not the only reason.

In conclusion, the economic level at which a household is able to consume enough food may play an important role in sending children to school. However, if parents find the utility of increasing current consumption levels to be greater than educating children, an increase in income will not lead to an increase in school enrollments because subsistence is a necessary condition and parents will require other sufficient conditions to be met. In addition, there was no significant relationship between incomes and dropouts. This could be because income is not a precise measure to capture financial situations in a rural poor country or because there are many complicated issues between current utility of consumption and investing in the children's future.

8.4 Subjective measure of subsistence level

Another interesting finding of this research is that the subjective measure 'worrying about food' also produces similar results. The 'food worried' variable is equal to 1 if a household had been worried about lack of food for a year before the survey, zero otherwise. As can be seen from Tables 5.4 and 5.5, only the 'food worried' variable gives an explanation regarding school enrollment rates but the consumption and the integrated term of 'consumption' and 'food worried' remains zero. From this result, the subjective measure is found to be reliable in showing poverty levels in a country with poverty.

9. Conclusion

The research question of this paper was how food security as a proxy for subsistence levels affected school enrollment in Malawi. The results suggest that parents need two conditions in general to send their children to school: one is a necessary condition which is the economic level that can afford minimum needs, and the other is a sufficient condition, which is that the utility from educating children is greater than the utility from increasing current consumption levels.

The Probit and OLS models were used to examine the effects of having enough food and incomes on schooling decisions. The Probit model showed that having enough food increased school enrollments by 6.4 per cent at the mean. There was no significant association between incomes and dropout rates for children not consuming enough food. Also, the regression results suggested that consumption levels cannot explain schooling in a developing rural country. Without the *enoughfood* variable, both OLS and Probit models did not generate any significant association between enrollment rates and consumption. The results of income estimates may become biased due to income measurement errors in rural areas, where in-kind payments are common instead of getting a paycheck or cash. On top of this, income distribution in Malawi is in the shape of a right angle with huge income gaps between different income groups.

In a more detailed study to estimate a more precise income effect, it will be useful to check if the dataset has a big enough sample size even after the sample is restricted to the population that gets paid in cash. However, it should be noted that the possibility of the population getting paid by check or in cash

Table 5.4 Effect of worrying about food on school enrollment

Variable	*Dependent variable: Enrolled*					
	OLS			*Probit*		
	1	*2*	*3*	*4*	*5*	*6*
Food worried	−0.033***		−0.050***	−0.133***		−0.199***
	(0.005)		(0.008)	(0.023)		(0.034)
Consumption		0.000	0.000***		0.000	0.000***
		(0.000)	(0.000)		(0.000)	(0.000)
Food worried			0.000***			0.000***
*Consumption			(0.000)			(0.000)
Age	−0.003***	−0.005***	−0.003***	−0.013***	−0.014***	−0.014***
	(0.001)	(0.001)	(0.001)	(0.003)	(0.003)	(0.003)
Female	0.008*	0.008*	0.008*	0.036	0.036	0.035
	(0.005)	(0.007)	(0.005)	(0.022)	(0.022)	(0.022)
HH size	0.005***	0.005***	0.004***	0.022***	0.018***	0.017***
	(0.001)	(0.001)	(0.001)	(0.005)	(0.006)	(0.006)
HH education	0.045***	0.046***	0.044***	0.245***	0.243***	0.236***
	(0.003)	(0.004)	(0.004)	(0.017)	(0.018)	(0.018)
Fatherdied	0.018***	0.020***	0.018***	0.078***	0.089***	0.078***
	(0.005)	(0.005)	(0.005)	(0.024)	(0.023)	(0.024)
Married	−0.779***	−0.774***	−0.780***	−3.117***	−3.108***	−3.122***
	(0.019)	(0.020)	(0.019)	(0.181)	(0.182)	(0.181)

(Continued)

Table 5.4 (Continued)

Variable	*Dependent variable: Enrolled*					
	OLS			*Probit*		
	1	*2*	*3*	*4*	*5*	*6*
Houseowned	0.003	0.003	0.003	0.014	0.017	0.014
	(0.008)	(0.008)	(0.008)	(0.036)	(0.036)	(0.036)
Rural	–0.004	–0.003	0.000	–0.014	–0.003	0.006
	(0.008)	(0.008)	(0.008)	(0.036)	(0.037)	(0.037)
No religion	–0.249***	–0.249***	–0.247***	–0.751***	–0.748***	–0.746***
	(0.038)	(0.039)	(0.038)	(0.138)	(0.138)	(0.138)
Traditional religion	–0.116***	–0.115***	–0.114***	–0.384***	–0.393***	–0.372***
	(0.036)	(0.037)	(0.036)	(0.139)	(0.138)	(0.139)
Muslim	–0.072***	–0.067***	–0.073***	–0.267***	–0.251***	–0.269***
	(0.011)	(0.014)	(0.011)	(0.046)	(0.046)	(0.046)
Other religion	–0.043	–0.037	–0.041	–0.160	–0.143	–0.150
	(0.043)	(0.044)	(0.043)	(0.181)	(0.181)	(0.181)
constant	0.785***	0.783***	0.789***	0.703***	0.637***	0.720***
	(0.016)	(0.018)	(0.016)	(0.070)	(0.069)	(0.070)
R-squared	0.114	0.112	0.114	0.100	0.099	0.101
N	19,999	19,999	19,999	19,999	19,999	19,999

Source: Author's computations

Table 5.5 Marginal effect of Probit model at the mean

Variable	*Dependent variable: enrolled*					
	Probit			*Marginal effects at mean*		
	1	*2*	*3*	*4*	*5*	*6*
Food worried	–0.133***		–0.199***	–0.032***		–0.048***
	(0.023)		(0.034)			
Consumption		0.000	0.000***		0.000	0.000***
		(0.000)	(0.000)			
Food worried *Consumption			0.000***			0.000***
			(0.000)			
Age	–0.013***	–0.014***	–0.014***	0.009***	0.009***	0.009***
	(0.003)	(0.003)	(0.003)			
Female	0.036	0.036	0.035	0.003	0.004	0.003
	(0.022)	(0.022)	(0.022)			
Married	0.022***	0.018***	0.017***	–0.76***	–0.757***	–0.76***
	(0.005)	(0.006)	(0.006)			
HH size	0.245***	0.243***	0.236***	0.019***	0.022***	0.019***
	(0.017)	(0.018)	(0.018)			
HH education	0.078***	0.089***	0.078***	–0.003***	–0.005***	–0.003***
	(0.024)	(0.023)	(0.024)			
Fatherdied	–3.117***	–3.108***	–3.122***	0.005***	0.004***	0.004***
	(0.181)	(0.182)	(0.181)			

(*Continued*)

Table 5.5 (Continued)

Variable	*Dependent variable: enrolled*					
	Probit			*Marginal effects at mean*		
	1	*2*	*3*	*4*	*5*	*6*
Houseowned	0.014	0.017	0.014	−0.004	−0.001	0.001
	(0.036)	(0.036)	(0.036)			
Rural	−0.014	−0.003	0.006	0.06	0.059	0.058
	(0.036)	(0.037)	(0.037)			
No religion	−0.751***	−0.748***	−0.746***	−0.183***	−0.17***	−0.182***
	(0.138)	(0.138)	(0.138)			
Traditional religion	−0.384***	−0.393***	−0.372***	−0.094***	−0.084***	−0.091***
	(0.139)	(0.138)	(0.139)			
Muslim	−0.267***	−0.251***	−0.269***	−0.065***	−0.05***	−0.066***
	(0.046)	(0.046)	(0.046)			
Other religion	−0.160	−0.143	−0.150	−0.039	−0.023	−0.037
	(0.181)	(0.181)	(0.181)			
constant	0.703***	0.637***	0.720***	−0.032***	−0.037***	−0.048***
	(0.070)	(0.069)	(0.070)			
R-squared	0.100	0.099	0.101			
N	19,999	19,999	19,999			

Source: Author's computations

is biased and does not represent the whole population in developing countries. Another possible option will be using consumption instead of income. To do this, precise local average prices to get the values of food or other non-food items from interviewees' own production will be useful.

The claims of this paper would have been much more persuasive if panel data was available to control for individual and community characteristics that do not change over time. In such a case, households that go through changes in subsistence status – change from consuming enough food to lack of food or from lack of food to enough food – could carry incisive messages about the relationship between subsistence levels and school enrollments. Then it would be ideal to measure perceived poverty and schooling because of the personal characteristics that could affect both perceived food consumption and dropout rates.

Notes

1 FAOSTAT (http://faostat3.fao.org/browse/area/130/en).
2 UNESCO Institute for Statistics.
3 EPDC (www.epdc.org/sites/default/files/documents/EPDC%20NEP_Malawi.pdf).
4 Ripple Africa (www.rippleafrica.org/education-in-malawi-africa/general-education-in-malawi-africa).

References

Baschieri, A. and J. Falkingham (2009). "Staying in school: Assessing the role of access, availability, and economic opportunities – The case of Malawi", *Population, Space, and Place*, 15(1), 205–224.

Basu, B. (2000). "The intriguing relation between adult minimum wage and child labour", *The Economic Journal*, 110(462), 50–61.

Basu, K., S. Das, and B. Dutta (2010). "Child labor and household wealth: Theory and empirical evidence of an inverted-U", *Journal of Development Economics*, 91(1), 8–14.

Basu, K. and P. Hoang Van (1998). "Economics of child labor", *American Economic Review*, 88(3), 412–427.

Beegle, K., R.H. Dehejia, and R. Gatti (2006). "Child labor and agricultural shocks", *Journal of Development Economics*, 81(1), 80–96.

Dessing, M. (2001). "Labor supply, the family and poverty: The S-shaped labor supply curve", *Journal of Economic Behavior & Organization*, 49(4), 433–458.

Edmonds, E.V. (2005). "Does child labor decline with improving economic status?", *The Journal of Human Resources*, XL(1), 77–99.

Emerson, P.M. and A. Portela Souza (2003). "Is there a child labor trap? Intergenerational persistence of child labor in Brazil", *Economic Development and Cultural Change*, 51(2), 375–398.

Khanam, R. (2008). "Child labour and school attendance: Evidence from Bangladesh", *International Journal of Social Economics*, 36(1/2), 77–98.

Psacharopoulos, G. (1997). "Child labor versus educational attainment some evidence from Latin America", *Journal of Population Economics*, 10(4), 377–386.

Ravallion, M. and Q. Wodon (2000). "Does child labour displace schooling? Evidence on behavioural responses to an enrollment subsidy", *The Economic Journal*, 110(462), C158–C175.

6 Analysis of poverty and its determinants in Rwanda

Masoomeh Rashidghalam

1. Introduction

Poverty has been a phenomenon throughout human history and the evolution of human society. It is the main cause of hunger; it concerns all nations, especially developing countries (Liu and Xu, 2016). It is the principal cause of hunger and undernourishment. Poverty is seen as the oldest and the most resistant virus that brings about a devastating disease in the third world or in developing countries (Tazoacha, 2001). The measurement and analysis of poverty are important for different reasons. First, they are crucial for cognitive purposes in order to identify what the situation is. Second, they are important for analytical purposes to recognize which factors cause poverty in a society. Third, they are important for policymaking purposes to design best solutions to deal with poverty. Finally, they are also needed for evaluation purposes to monitor if the current policies are effective and whether the poverty situation is changing.

Among the world's continents, Africa is the poorest. The swelling number of Africans living in poverty has increasingly attracted the attention of governments, international donors and researchers to development strategies that are 'pro-poor'. There are lots of reasons for African poverty. According to Addae-Korankye (2014), it is caused by corruption and poor governance, poor land utilization and land tenure systems, civil wars and unending political conflicts, poor infrastructure, diseases and poor health facilities and the World Bank and IMF's reform policies, among others.

According to data retrieved from the World Bank Development Indicators, Rwanda is one of the poorest countries in Africa. Rwanda is a landlocked, resource-poor country that is ranked 15 out of the 25 poorest countries in Africa with a gross domestic product (GDP) per capita of USD 689 in 2016.[1] It was also ranked 167 out of 182 countries in the 2009 United Nations Development Program's Human Development Index (HDI).

Rwanda has made vast improvements in reducing poverty in the past decade. The country reduced the percentage of people living below the poverty line from 57 per cent in 2005 to 39.1 per cent in 2014. Nevertheless, 63 per cent of the population still lives in extreme poverty, defined by the World Bank as individuals living on less than \$1.25 a day.[2]

Rwanda's population is about 11.75 million, of which 3.15 million lived in rural areas in 2016. Considered to be among the smallest countries on the continent, Rwanda's total area is estimated to be 26,334 square kilometers (NISR, 2015). Rwanda is the most densely populated country in Africa, with about 446.9 persons/km^2. The 1994 genocide, which killed about a million people, changed the demographic structure of the country. Women now account for 54 per cent of the population, as the heads of many households were killed in the genocide. About 44 per cent of Rwandan children suffer from stunting. This means that they are unable to grow to their full potential because of lack of adequate nutrition.

About 90 per cent of the Rwandan population is engaged in agriculture as a means of survival. Since the country is densely populated and is landlocked, access to natural resources is very low. Moreover, the non-competitive industrial sector has failed to contribute toward its GDP in the last few decades.[3] Agriculture employs 80 per cent of the labor force, but only accounts for a third of the country's GDP. Nearly half of Rwandan agricultural households experience food insecurity.[4] Rwanda's major exports are coffee, tea, minerals (tin, cassiterite and wolframite) and pyrethrum. In fact Rwanda is currently managing its economy through the export of coffee and tea. Coffee is the main export revenue contributor and makes up a quarter of its total export value, while Rwanda's mountain-grown tea is considered to be one of the finest in the world.[5]

Given these statistics, which project an urgent need of reducing poverty in Rwanda, our paper studies poverty in different provinces and districts in the country. It first identifies the poverty line at the province and district levels and then computes headcount, poverty gap and poverty severity at the individual household level. Second, it computes the poverty gap to rank the different provinces and districts by their level of poverty. Third, it estimates the effects of different household characteristics on poverty. Finally, it assists decision makers who want to access the information needed to monitor poverty in Rwanda and engage in policy decisions about poverty reduction.

The rest of the paper is organized as follows. Section 2 gives a literature review. Section 3 introduces the data used in the empirical part of the study. The next section gives estimations of the poverty line and poverty severity results; this is followed by an analysis of poverty determinants' estimations. Section 5 gives an analysis of the results while Section 6 gives a conclusion.

2. Literature review

Empirical literature has studied the designation of poverty in Africa. Addae-Korankye (2014) found that poverty could be fought in the presence of strong institutions and equitable distribution of resources, both of which require a non-corrupt government. According to his study, the programs designed to fight against African poverty are not fully implemented because the funds end up in the hands of corrupt individuals. Mwabu and Thorbecke (2004) argue that rural-based policies in sub-Saharan Africa have the potential to reduce poverty.

They found that although African agriculture remained the principal source of employment and income for most rural people, its dynamism depended critically on conditions prevailing in rural non-farm sectors. Also, growth in non-farm sectors created opportunities for higher incomes and employment in agriculture. Thus, agriculture and the rural non-farm sector complemented each other in the process of rural development.

Pauw and Leibbrandt (2012) developed a general equilibrium micro-simulation model to simulate the economy-wide effects of minimum wages in South Africa. Their study showed that minimum wages led to a marginal decline in poverty and overall inequality. They also found that job losses were more likely to affect the poorest among minimum wage workers, while rising production costs reduced overall household welfare. McFerson (2010) reviewed the interaction of traditional restrictions on women's property rights, weak governance and violent civil conflict in perpetuating gender discrimination and women's poverty in sub-Saharan Africa. Neutel and Heshmati (2006) studied the relationship between globalization and poverty and income inequality using data from 65 developing countries. The results of their study show that globalization has led to poverty reduction and it has also reduced income inequalities and the relationship between globalization and poverty remained significant when controlled for regional heterogeneity. A non-linear analysis showed that poverty had diminishing returns to benefits from globalization. Other researchers too have written on poverty, including Achia et al. (2010), Alkire and Foster (2011), Dzanku et al. (2015), Grobler (2016), Menon et al. (2015), Shepherd et al. (2013), and Ucal (2014).

3. Estimation methods

The first step in modeling determinants of poverty in a society is measuring poverty. Three methods can be used for this:

- Choosing relevant dimensions and indicators of well-being, which include monetary and non-monetary indicators of poverty. In monetary indicators, one has a choice between using income or consumption as the indicator of well-being. On the other hand, in non-monetary indicators, poverty is associated with health, nutrition and literacy, and also with deficient social relations, insecurity and low self-esteem and powerlessness.
- Selecting poverty lines that are cut-off points separating the poor from the non-poor. They can be monetary (for example, a certain level of consumption) or non-monetary (for example, a certain level of literacy).
- Selecting a poverty measure to be used for reporting for the population as a whole or for a population sub-group only (Coudouel et al., 2001).

We use the poverty lines method to measure poverty in our study. In this regard, once income per capita is defined at the household level, the next step is to define poverty lines. There are two ways of setting poverty lines: relative and absolute poverty lines. A **relative poverty line** is defined in relation to the overall distribution of income or consumption in a country (for example, the poverty line is defined as half the median or mean household income per capita of the total population (OECD, 2016)). Relative poverty is the condition in which people lack the minimum amount of income needed to maintain an average standard of living in the society in which they live. Relative poverty is considered the easiest way of measuring the level of poverty in an individual country. It is defined relative to the members of a society and, therefore, differs across countries.[6] On the other hand, an **absolute poverty line** refers to a condition where a person does not have the minimum amount of income needed to meet the minimum requirements for one or more basic living needs over an extended period of time, including food, safe drinking water, sanitation facilities, health, shelter, education, information and access to services. Absolute poverty lines are often based on estimates of the cost of basic food needs such as the cost of a nutritional basket considered minimal for the healthy survival of a typical family.[7]

Once we have computed income per capita, we need to measure the relative poverty line. Hence, the next step is determining whether that amount places the household 'in poverty' or it defines the household as 'non-poor'.

After identifying who is poor, this is aggregated into one poverty index. The frequently used one is the headcount, which is expressed as (Hanna, 2004):

$$headcount = \frac{Number\ of\ people\ whose\ income\ is\ below\ poverty\ line}{Total\ size\ of\ population}$$

In the next step, we need to compute the 'poverty gap' and 'poverty severity'. Poverty gap is defined as the average shortfall of the total population from the poverty line. It is obtained by adding up all the shortfalls of the poor (assuming that the non-poor have a shortfall of zero) and dividing the total by the population. In other words, it estimates the total resources needed to bring all the poor to the level of the poverty line (divided by the number of individuals in the population) and helps refine the poverty rate by providing an indication of the poverty level in a country (OECD, 2016). Poverty severity (squared poverty gap) helps construct a measure of poverty that takes into account the inequalities among the poor; some researchers also use the squared poverty gap (The World Bank Institute, 2005). This takes into account not only the distance separating the poor from the poverty line (the poverty gap), but also the inequalities among the poor. That is, a higher weight is placed on those households that are further away from the poverty line. The measures of depth and severity of poverty are important complements of the incidence of poverty. It might be the case that some groups have high poverty incidence but a low poverty gap (when numerous members are just below the poverty line), while other groups have a low poverty incidence but a high poverty gap for those who are poor (when relatively few members are below the poverty line but with extremely low levels of consumption or income) (Coudouel et al., 2001).

After defining poverty gap and poverty severity, the second step is to run probit and tobit regressions to study the incidence of poverty determinants. In these regressions the dependent variable in the probit model is a binary variable with 1 representing an individual being poor and zero representing non-poor, while it is the magnitude of the poverty gap and severity in the generalized tobit model. The generalized tobit model is a combined two-step probit and OLS model estimated by the maximum likelihood method accounting for a sample selection bias resulting in differences in probabilities of the poor and non-poor.

Determinants of poverty in every society can be ordered into two groups: macroeconomics and microeconomics. On the micro level (which is the scope of our study), the determinants can be divided into regional-level, community-level and household-level characteristics; each of them is divided into different sub-groups. On the regional level, these determinants are geographic conditions; regional governance; level and development of public services; communication; infrastructure; and economic, political and market stability. Community-level determinants include accessibility to public goods (for example, roads, electricity, healthcare and education). Household characteristics can be sub-grouped into demographic characteristics (for example, household size, dependency ratio and the gender of household head), economic characteristics (for example, household employment, household consumption and household assets) and social characteristics (for example, health, education and shelter) (Hanna, 2004).

To characterize the total poor in the study area, we deployed a probability model so as to forecast the chances of arriving at the poverty line. Given the dependent variable of main interest that classifies households as poor or non-poor, a binary probit model was appropriate for the analysis and is expressed as:

$$Y^* = X'\beta' + \varepsilon_i \tag{1}$$

where Y^* is the unobservable magnitude that considers the net probability of an individual poor, X is a vector of individual household characteristics, β is a vector of parameters and ε_i is the disturbance term. The outcome of the response variable is expressed as:

$$\begin{aligned} Y_i &= 1 \;\; if \;\; Y^* \leq 0, \text{ the poor and} \\ Y_i &= 0 \;\; if \;\; Y^* > 0, \text{ non-poor} \end{aligned} \tag{2}$$

The coefficients in Eq. 1 show the sign effect of the variables on the probability of poor or non-poor.

4. Data

In 2006, the 12 provinces of Rwanda were abolished and replaced with five new provinces of Kigali City, Eastern Province, Western Province, Northern Province and Southern Province, which were sub-divided into 30 districts. Each district in turn was divided into sectors leading to 416 sectors.[8]

The data used in this study is from Rwanda's household survey. The initial dataset consisted of 6,748 household-level observations in Rwanda's different provinces and districts in 2012. Data for determining poverty is location defined as rural, semi-urban and urban areas; population density; population growth; distance to road; distance to market; age of household head; literacy of head; marital status of head; gender of head; number of people in the household; access to credit; migration and remittances; farmland; vegetable gardens; number of animals; number of crops; cash crop products; and number of banana trees owned by a household. Income is defined in terms of per capita household income in 2012 prices.

5. Analysis of the results

Table 6.1 provides summary statistics of the data for various household characteristics, poverty lines and demographic characteristics used in the study.

In order to check for collinearity among the explanatory variables, correlation coefficients among all the 19 variables used in our study are given in Table 6.2.

Table 6.1 Summary statistics of means of data (N = 6,748)

Variables	*Definition*	*Mean*	*Std. Dev.*	*Minimum*	*Maximum*
hhnr	Household id	5361.9	2533.28	977.00	9747.00
distnr	District number	344.69	116.05	201.00	507.00
hhsize	Number of people in the household	4.92	2.13	1.00	18.00
tincome	Total income from all income-generating primary activities	39183.15	77911.71	0.00	2544000.00
income	Income	14488.76	50654.18	0.00	2544000.00
pline1	Relative poverty line	2134.88	812.37	1094.37	4947.50
poor1	Headcount poverty ratio by relative poverty line	0.30	0.46	0.00	1.00
pgap1	Poverty gap by relative poverty line	306.58	611.94	0.00	4934.17
pgap1s	Poverty severity by relative poverty line	468409.00	1414148.00	0.00	24346001.00
pline2	Absolute poverty line	23250.00	0.00	23250.00	23250.00
poor 2	Headcount poverty ratio by absolute poverty line	0.88	0.33	0.00	1.00
pgap2	Poverty gap by relative absolute line	15859.39	7642.62	0.00	23250.00

(*Continued*)

Table 6.1 (Continued)

Variables	*Definition*	*Mean*	*Std. Dev.*	*Minimum*	*Maximum*
pgap2s	Poverty severity by absolute poverty line	3.1E+08	1.82E+08	0.00	5.41E+08
rural	Rural area	0.87	0.33	0.00	1.00
semiurb	Semi-urban area	0.08	0.27	0.00	1.00
popdens	Population density number of inhabitants per square kilometer	757.54	1038.59	2.29	13009.00
populg	Population growth	3.23	3.32	-5.67	25.02
distroad	Distance to road	3839.56	3700.98	0.00	21924.65
distmark	Distance to market	76.64	71.22	0.00	1200.00
agehead	Age of household head	47.33	15.74	15.00	103.00
lithead	Household head can read and write a simple message	0.55	0.50	0.00	1.00
mshead	Marital state of head, equals 1 if the head is married	0.56	0.50	0.00	1.00
dfemale	Gender of head, equals 1 if the head is female	0.29	0.45	0.00	1.00
nrincome	Number of income-generating activities undertaken by household	1.67	0.64	0.00	10.00
credd	Access to credit	0.16	0.36	0.00	1.00
worksend	Working elsewhere and sending home remittances	0.06	0.24	0.00	1.00
fland	Access to farmland	0.90	0.30	0.00	1.00
vegetd	Vegetable garden (= 1 if household owns a vegetable garden)	0.60	0.49	0.00	1.00
nranimal	Number of animals	2.85	5.41	0.00	203.00
nrcrops	Number of crops	3.03	1.69	0.00	10.00
cashcrop	Cash crop products	0.06	0.24	0.00	1.00
bantrnr	Number of banana trees owned by the household	0.40	1.06	0.00	4.00

Source: Author's computations

Table 6.2 Correlation matrix of the variables (N = 6,748)

	Househ. size	*Total income*	*Income per capita*	*Povline relative*	*Povgap relative*	*Povgap2 relative*	*Povgap absolute*	*povgap2 absolute*	*Populg growth*	*Distance road*	*Distance market*	*Age head*	*Nr income*	*Farm-land*	*Vegetable garden*	*Nr animal*	*Nr crops*	*Cash crops*	*Banana tees nr*
Househ size	1.00																		
Total income	–0.24	1.00																	
	(0.00)																		
Income per cap	–0.30	0.83	1.00																
	(0.00)	(0.00)																	
Povline relative	0.02	0.13	0.07	1.00															
	(0.00)	(0.00)	(0.00)																
Povgap relative	0.44	–0.21	–0.13	0.19	1.00														
	(0.00)	(0.00)	(0.00)	(0.00)															
Pgap2 relative	0.32	–0.14	–0.09	0.28	0.90	1.00													
	(0.00)	(0.00)	(0.00)	(0.00)	(0.00)														
Povgap absolute	0.59	–0.58	–0.44	–0.19	0.42	0.28	1.00												
	(0.00)	(0.00)	(0.00)	(0.00)	(0.00)	(0.00)													
povgap2 absolute	0.61	–0.53	–0.38	–0.20	0.52	0.35	0.97	1.00											
	(0.00)	(0.00)	(0.00)	(0.00)	(0.00)	(0.00)	(0.00)												
Popul growth	0.07	0.07	0.01	0.15	0.03	0.03	–0.05	–0.05	1.00										
	(0.00)	(0.00)	0.30	(0.00)	(0.02)	(0.00)	(0.00)	(0.00)											
Distance road	–0.02	–0.05	–0.02	–0.07	0.01	–0.01	0.04	0.04	0.08	1.00									
	(0.05)	(0.00)	(0.00)	(0.00)	(0.57)	(0.29)	(0.00)	(0.00)	(0.00)										
Distance market	–0.03	–0.06	–0.03	–0.02	0.01	0.00	0.04	0.04	–0.03	0.15	1.00								
	(0.01)	(0.00)	(0.01)	0.04)	(0.25)	(0.88)	(0.00)	(0.00)	(0.01)	(0.00)									
Age head	–0.03	0.01	0.04	–0.02	0.04	0.03	–0.09	–0.06	–0.02	–0.03	–0.02	1.00							
	(0.02)	(0.49)	(0.00)	(0.05)	(0.00)	(0.01)	(0.00)	(0.00)	(0.14)	(0.02)	(0.14)								

Source: Author's computations

(*Continued*)

Table 6.2 (Continued)

	Househ. size	*Total income*	*Income per capita*	*Povline relative*	*Povgap relative*	*Povgap2 relative*	*Povgap absolute*	*povgap2 absolute*	*Populg growth*	*Distance road*	*Distance market*	*Age head*	*Nr income*	*Farm-land*	*Vegetable garden*	*Nr animal*	*Nr crops*	*Cash crops*	*Banana tees nr*
Nr	0.17	–0.01	–0.04	0.10	0.04	0.05	0.06	0.05	–0.02	0.01	0.02	–0.12	1.00						
income	(0.00)	(0.49)	(0.00)	(0.00)	(0.00)	(0.00)	(0.00)	(0.00)	(0.11)	(0.32)	(0.09)	(0.00)							
Farmland	0.05	–0.13	–0.10	–0.14	0.03	0.01	0.13	0.13	–0.11	0.12	0.10	0.09	0.25	1.00					
	(0.00)	(0.00)	(0.00)	(0.00)	(0.02)	(0.57)	(0.00)	(0.00)	(0.00)	(0.00)	(0.00)	(0.00)	(0.00)						
Vegetable	0.13	–0.03	–0.06	–0.03	0.00	–0.02	0.07	0.06	0.01	0.01	0.01	0.01	0.10	0.10	1.00				
garden	(0.00)	(0.01)	(0.00)	(0.04)	(0.84)	(0.21)	(0.00)	(0.00)	(0.43)	(0.39)	(0.52)	(0.23)	(0.00)	(0.00)					
Nr animal	0.17	0.03	–0.01	–0.01	0.00	0.00	0.03	0.03	0.03	0.03	–0.02	0.07	0.15	0.13	0.11	1.00			
	(0.00)	(0.02)	(0.34	(0.61)	(0.78)	(0.69)	(0.01)	(0.02)	(0.01)	(0.01)	(0.20)	(0.00)	(0.00)	(0.00)	(0.00)				
Nr crops	0.11	–0.08	–0.08	–0.06	0.06	0.04	0.12	0.12	0.00	0.13	0.02	0.06	0.21	0.55	0.13	0.23	1.00		
	(0.00)	(0.00)	(0.00)	(0.00)	(0.00)	(0.00)	(0.00)	(0.00)	(0.99)	(0.00)	(0.10)	(0.00)	(0.00)	(0.00)	(0.00)	(0.00)			
Cash crops	0.05	0.03	0.00	–0.02	–0.03	–0.03	0.00	0.00	–0.04	0.00	–0.01	0.04	0.04	0.08	0.07	0.05	0.15	1.00	
	(0.00)	(0.02)	(0.75)	(0.17)	(0.02)	(0.02)	(0.84)	(0.91)	(0.00)	(0.70)	(0.47)	(0.00)	(0.00)	(0.00)	(0.00)	(0.00)	(0.00)		
Banana tree	0.05	0.02	0.02	0.02	0.02	0.01	0.00	0.01	0.14	0.10	–0.01	0.05	0.06	0.12	0.07	0.11	0.21	0.02	1.0
Nr	(0.00)	(0.06)	(0.20)	(0.18)	(0.08)	(0.41)	(0.99)	0.63	(0.00)	(0.00)	0.62)	(0.00)	(0.00)	(0.00)	(0.00)	(0.00)	(0.00)	(0.13)	

Source: Author's computations

Household size, as expected, was unconditionally positively and significantly correlated with relative and absolute poverty; it was also correlated with poverty severity. Income and household size were negatively correlated. Income and total income had a negative correlation with poverty and poverty severity. Age of the head of the household was positively correlated with relative poverty and poverty severity. On the other hand, distance to road and the market were correlated negatively with income and positively with the relative poverty line. Between all these pairs, only household size, total income, absolute poverty and poverty gap showed a correlation higher than 0.50, indicating serious multi-collinearity and possible confounded estimated effects. The remaining pairs were low correlated with each other and did not show any signs of serious multi-collinearity.

Variations in the different variables such as total income, relative and absolute poverty lines, the headcount poverty ratio, poverty gap, and poverty severity can be decomposed into changes among districts, provinces and regions. The rest of the analysis sheds light on district, provincial and regional heterogeneity in incidence of poverty and its intensity.

Table 6.3, Part I reports the means of household size, total income, income, relative poverty line, headcount and poverty gap on the basis of relative and absolute poverty lines and also poverty severity for each district. Mean of household total income was the highest for Cyuve and lowest for district Buruhukiro. In this regard, the relative poverty line, poverty gap and poverty severity were the highest for Cyuve.

Table 6.3, Part II shows the variables mentioned earlier at the provincial level. Province 2 had the lowest amount of income and total income; it also had the lowest poverty line. On the other hand, the maximum headcount poverty ratio, poverty gap and poverty severity were in this province. The results show that the high/low ranked provinces according to different variables were: income (Province 5/Province 2), total income (Province 5/Province 2), relative poverty line (Province 4/Province 2), headcount by relative poverty line (Provinces 4, 2/Provinces 3, 1), headcount by absolute poverty line (Province 2/Province 4), relative poverty gap (Province 4/Province 2), absolute poverty gap (Province 2/Province 4), relative poverty severity (Province 4/Province 2) and absolute poverty severity (Province 2/Province 5).

The data is divided into three groups by regional location as urban, semi-urban and rural. According to Table 6.3, Part III, the poverty headcount ratio, poverty gap and poverty severity were the highest in rural areas. On the other hand, income, total income and the relative poverty line were the lowest in rural areas. Table 6.3, Part III shows that the poverty headcount ratio, poverty gap and poverty severity were minimum in urban areas.

After defining poverty lines, poverty gap and poverty severity, the next step is modeling poverty determinants. Table 6.4 presents estimation results for six different models of incidence of poverty, poverty gap and poverty severity. The models differ in the way in which the poverty line is measured, namely relative and absolute approaches.

Table 6.3 Means of variables by district, province and area

	hhsize	*Total income*	*Income Per capita*	*Relative Povline*	*Absolute Povpline*	*Head C Relative*	*Head C Absolute*	*Gap Relative*	*Relative Absolute*	*Gap2 Relative*	*Gap2 Absolute*
A. Means by district											
Busoro	4.6	20607	6958	1211	23250	0.26	0.92	141	18051	98049	367439953
Kansi	4.7	30226	13471	1846	23250	0.30	0.92	278	16577	319682	327236392
Busanze	5.4	23502	7947	1561	23250	0.30	0.95	228	18162	231723	365539459
Karama	5.0	43067	14780	2750	23250	0.35	0.89	446	15330	743723	289891192
Buruhukiro	5.0	38985	14757	1875	23250	0.32	0.88	312	16187	389503	320572807
Bweramana	4.7	40820	15648	2645	23250	0.28	0.86	355	14568	598108	276042152
Cyeza	4.5	27650	11577	1667	23250	0.32	0.91	293	16988	322117	340291676
Gacurabwenge	5.1	20533	7356	1094	23250	0.28	0.93	134	18244	88317	373456725
Gishyita	4.5	47515	20442	2813	23250	0.29	0.85	398	14543	700658	273452247
Boneza	5.2	43170	13033	2083	23250	0.31	0.86	286	15379	365009	301380281
Cyanzarwe	5.5	54920	13417	3206	23250	0.30	0.85	502	14134	1013420	260974399
Jenda	5.2	43339	12162	2025	23250	0.22	0.92	144	16602	145828	317115320
Kabaya	4.7	20239	7608	1341	23250	0.31	0.95	217	18079	191628	363821925
Butare	5.0	58814	21877	2535	23250	0.30	0.82	335	14221	543847	271299347
Bushenge	5.4	29855	10191	1667	23250	0.30	0.91	250	17021	273282	337954306
Bushoki	4.8	32634	11369	1744	23250	0.28	0.89	241	16551	273909	327912984
Busengo	4.6	25646	9595	1200	23250	0.28	0.88	153	16794	117768	341715857
Cyuve	4.7	62514	23589	4948	23250	0.32	0.77	711	11782	2116912	204779824
Butaro	5.0	43680	16895	1875	23250	0.33	0.84	316	15310	376349	304930341
Bukure	5.1	41989	12828	1875	23250	0.30	0.88	272	15901	320288	312951318

Karenge	4.9	47036	22822	1852	23250	0.32	0.88	327	16145	396454	318666159
Gatunda	5.4	61792	22095	3600	23250	0.27	0.80	475	13024	1056591	236766184
Kageyo	4.9	31712	12535	1875	23250	0.27	0.88	226	15785	240373	306930445
Kabare	4.7	50421	18339	2540	23250	0.28	0.83	317	14405	494733	274148264
Kigarama	4.8	41097	16771	2354	23250	0.34	0.87	399	15730	620748	304617053
Jarama	4.5	43513	23695	1701	23250	0.27	0.84	237	15543	252063	308903958
Mayange	4.9	32675	9453	1761	23250	0.29	0.92	286	17142	355979	338923642
B. Means by province number											
2	4.9	30674	11562	1831	23250	0.30	0.91	273	16763	348903	332558794
3	5.1	42547	14101	2238	23250	0.29	0.88	304	15712	461816	303731277
4	4.8	41293	14855	2328	23250	0.30	0.85	339	15268	641045	298458065
5	4.9	44042	17962	2241	23250	0.29	0.86	324	15396	488276	298417379
C. Means by area											
Urban	5.0	62971	24091	2308	23250	0.22	0.77	287	13146	554756	249101537
Semi-urban	4.9	42639	18889	2473	23250	0.34	0.88	440	15808	849507	306853835
Rural	4.9	37608	13572	2094	23250	0.30	0.88	295	16007	428264	313409831

Source: Author's computations

First, to model the headcount or incidence of poverty with the relative poverty line and headcount based on absolute poverty, the probit model was used to give the binary character of the dependent variable. These models are named Model 1 and Model 2, respectively. The dependent variable is equal to 1 if a household is not considered poor; it equals zero if the household is in poverty. According to Models 1 and 2, households which lived in villages were poorer. This indicates that poverty was predominant among rural dwellers, which might be due to limited access to opportunities and infrastructure in rural areas. Infrastructure such as roads, water, sanitation and electricity are seldom available in the rural areas in Rwanda. Living in towns decreased the probability of relative and absolute poverty. The negative and significant coefficient of the population density variable indicates that a household would be more likely to be non-poor in areas with high population densities. Population growth also had a negative effect on the probability of being relatively or absolutely poor. If a household was far from the road and the market, it was more exposed to poverty.

Household- and individual-level characteristics such as household size, age of household head, education, marital status and gender of the household head form another category that affected the probability of being poor. According to Table 6.4, larger households were more prone to identify themselves as poor. Other studies also conclude that people living in larger and (generally) younger households are typically poorer. Households with older heads tend to have a higher likelihood of poverty. It is widely believed that the gender of the household head significantly influences household poverty and more specifically that households headed by women are poorer than those headed by men since they have low levels of literacy, are paid lower wages and have less access to land or equal employment. The positive coefficient of this variable in Table 6.4 confirms these findings. We found that if a household head could read and write a simple message in any language, the probability of the household remaining below the poverty line decreased. Other studies (for example, Berg, 2008; Javed and Asif, 2011) support this result. Households with married heads were more likely to be poor.

An additional group of variables appears to be important in Rwanda. Here the incidence of poverty is clearly linked to possession of property. The property of a household includes its tangible goods (farmland, vegetable garden, livestock and crops) and its financial assets (access to credit and the number of income-generating activities). A vegetable garden and banana trees are assets with enormous importance for rural dwellers in Africa (Table 6.4). According to the negative coefficients of these variables in our two models, possessing these two decreased the probability of households being relatively and absolutely poor in Rwanda. As expected, having access to credit decreased the probability of being poor. Also if the number of income-generating activities increased, the households were less likely to be poor.

In the next step, we estimated four tobit models; two models for the poverty gap (Models 3 and 4) and two poverty severity models (Models 5 and 6) for relative and absolute poverty lines. Income was measured in per capita

Table 6.4 Probit and tobit models' estimation results

	Probit, Headcount				*Tobit, Poverty gap*				*Tobit, Poverty severity*			
	Model 1: Relative		*Model 2: Absolute*		*Model 3: Relative*		*Model 4: Absolute*		*Model 5: Relative*		*Model 6: Absolute*	
	Coeff.	*StdErr*	*Coeff.*	*StdErr*	*Coeff.*	*StdErr*	*Coeff.*	*StdErr*	*Coeff.*	*StdErr*	*Coeff.*	*StdErr*
Intercept	−2.9110	0.1551	−0.9854	0.1730	−19.7520	1.7054	5.1478	0.6054	−137.2700	11.740	46.8503	5.9036
Rural	0.2510	0.1009	0.3110	0.1077	1.7064	0.5818	0.8588	0.1970	10.9962	3.9955	8.9105	1.9219
Semiurb	0.5110	0.1166	0.4865	0.1360	3.2816	0.6639	1.1045	0.2322	22.4715	4.5592	11.3965	2.2645
Popdens	−0.0001	0.0000	−0.0001	0.0000	0.0812	0.1806	−0.1899	0.0679	0.6876	1.2437	−1.9671	0.6622
Populg	−0.0150	0.0062	−0.0290	0.0083	−0.0957	0.0337	−0.0510	0.0125	−0.6186	0.2315	−0.5793	0.1218
Distroad	0.0000	0.0000	0.0000	0.0000	0.2182	0.0671	0.0346	0.0238	1.4686	0.4621	0.3893	0.2318
Distmark	0.0008	0.0003	0.0007	0.0004	0.4910	0.0887	0.0976	0.0315	3.4099	0.6112	1.0308	0.3074
Agehead	0.0007	0.0014	−0.0081	0.0016	0.0009	0.0081	−0.0280	0.0028	0.0124	0.0556	−0.2803	0.0273
Lithead	−0.1510	0.0404	−0.2752	0.0590	−0.8519	0.2295	−0.3768	0.0867	−5.9984	1.5799	−3.8401	0.8450
Mshead	0.0010	0.0544	0.0016	0.0704	0.1644	0.3121	0.2353	0.1125	1.3796	2.1512	2.2691	1.0967
Dfemale	0.0610	0.0611	0.0391	0.0730	0.3796	0.3509	0.0521	0.1238	2.9753	2.4186	0.5169	1.2071
Hhsize	0.4210	0.0113	0.6225	0.0214	2.3053	0.0626	0.8078	0.0203	16.0001	0.4306	8.6241	0.1983
Nrincome	−0.1248	0.0301	−0.1330	0.0425	−0.7297	0.1702	−0.1594	0.0643	−4.9544	1.1715	−1.9120	0.6264
Credd	−0.1399	0.0511	−0.4488	0.0683	−0.8943	0.2902	−0.6668	0.1083	−5.6828	1.9960	−6.9688	1.0560
Worksend	−0.0674	0.0819	−0.0289	0.0963	−0.2632	0.4688	−0.1346	0.1659	−1.1851	3.2207	−1.4066	1.6181
Fland	0.1919	0.0813	0.3910	0.0963	1.1926	0.4621	0.9064	0.1627	7.5553	3.1788	9.4317	1.5863
Vegetd	−0.0848	0.0384	0.0116	0.0513	−0.4880	0.2191	0.1013	0.0812	−3.6621	1.5085	0.9070	0.7916
Mranimal	−0.0294	0.0044	−0.0241	0.0039	−0.7535	0.1305	−0.2297	0.0487	−5.3300	0.8991	−2.3505	0.4752
Nrcrops	0.0361	0.0135	0.0304	0.0191	0.2293	0.0769	0.0957	0.0290	1.6606	0.5292	0.9629	0.2828
Cashcrop	−0.3160	0.0799	−0.1977	0.1065	−1.7653	0.4573	−0.3515	0.1644	−12.647	3.1550	−3.7084	1.6030
Bantrnr	−0.0162	0.0178	−0.0817	0.0236	−0.0342	0.1007	−0.1356	0.0380	−0.1587	0.6930	−1.2373	0.3701

Source: Author's computations

household income. Because the poverty gap and poverty severity are continuous for households below the poverty line, we investigated whether the independent variables were more strongly associated with different degrees of poverty. Table 6.4 gives the results from the tobit models for Rwanda. Living in rural areas increased the depth of poverty and poverty severity.

Estimation results for poverty gap and poverty severity indicate that all the factors mentioned earlier except for 'distance to market' influenced poverty, poverty gap and poverty severity in the same direction and were consistent with each other. Accordingly, living in rural areas, distance to market, family size, marital status and age of household head, female-headed household, population density and population growth increased the poverty gap and poverty severity. But literate household heads and ownership of property and assets reduced the probability of falling into poverty severity and poverty gap.

6. Conclusion

The aim of our research was to do an analysis of poverty in Rwanda and determine a household's characteristics that influenced the probability of the household falling into poverty and its effects on poverty gap and poverty severity. We used data that covered 6,748 households in 2012.

First, we defined relative and absolute poverty lines in different districts and provinces of Rwanda. Our results showed that Province 4 and Province 2 had the highest and lowest poverty lines, respectively. On the other hand, the relative poverty line, poverty gap and poverty severity were the highest for Cyuve. Income was measured in per capita household income.

Second, for the purpose of analyzing poverty determinants, we defined three different poverty specifications: relative and absolute poverty, poverty gap and poverty severity. All three specifications were regressed on the set of household characteristics. Two probit models were used to model headcount poverty and four tobit models for factors affecting poverty gap and poverty severity of poor households. The use of combined probit and tobit (generalized tobit) allowed us to correct for sample selection bias. The results at this stage showed that living in a rural area, distance to market, family size, marital status and age of household head, female-headed household, population density and population growth increased the probability of being poor and these variables also increased the depth and severity of poverty. On the other hand, literate household heads and ownership of property and assets reduced the probability of falling into poverty and intensity of poverty.

Notes

1 www.africanvault.com/poorest-countries-in-africa/.
2 www.ruralpovertyportal.org/country/home/tags/rwanda.
3 www.africanvault.com/poorest-countries-in-africa/.
4 http://borgenproject.org/10-things-you-didnt-know-about-poverty-in-rwanda/.
5 www.rw.undp.org/content/rwanda/en/home/countryinfo.html.

6 http://study.com/academy/lesson/what-is-relative-poverty-definition-causes-examples.html.
7 http://web.worldbank.org/WBSITE/EXTERNAL/TOPICS/EXTPOVERTY/EXTPA/0,,contentMDK:20242879~menuPK:435055~pagePK:148956~piPK:216618~theSitePK:430367~isCURL:Y~isCURL:Y~isCURL:Y~isCURL:Y,00.html).
8 The Republic of Rwanda after Territorial Reform (2008).

References

Achia, T.N.O., A. Wangombe, and N. Khadioli (2010). "A logistic regression model to identify key determinants of poverty using demographic and health survey data", *European Journal of Social Sciences*, 13(1), 38–45.

Addae-Korankye, A. (2014). "Causes of poverty in Africa: A review of literature", *American International Journal of Social Science*, 3(7), 147–153.

Alkire, S. and J. Foster (2011). "Counting and multidimensional poverty measurement", *Journal of Public Economics*, 95(7), 476–487.

Berg, S. (2008). *Poverty and Education*. Paris: International Institute for Educational Planning and International Academy of Education.

Coudouel, A., J. Hentschel, and Q. Wodon (2001). *Poverty Measurement and Analysis* (Chapter 1 of PRSP Sourcebook). Available at: www.worldbank.org/poverty/strategies/chapters/data/data.htm#.

Dzanku, F.M., M. Jirstrom, and H. Marstrop (2015). "Yield gap-based poverty gaps in rural Sub-Saharan Africa", *World Development*, 67, 336–362.

Grobler, W.C.J. (2016). "Perceptions of poverty: A study of food secure and food insecure households in an urban area in South Africa", *Procedia Economics and Finance*, 35, 224–231.

Hanna, F. (2004). "The determinants of poverty in Ukraine", MSc Thesis in Economics, National University of Kyiv-Mohyla Academy.

Javed, Z.H. and A. Asif (2011). "Female households and poverty: A case study of Faisalabad District", *International Journal of Peace and Development Studies*, 2(2), 37–44.

Liu, Y. and Y. Xu (2016). "A geographic identification of multidimensional poverty in rural China under the framework of sustainable livelihoods analysis", *Applied Geography*, 73, 62–76.

McFerson, H.M. (2010). "Poverty among women in Sub-Saharan Africa: A review of selected issues", *Journal of International Women's Studies*, 11(4), 49–72.

Menon, J., N. Vijayakumar, J.K. Joseph, P.C. David, M.N. Menon, S. Mukundan, P.D. Dorphy, and A. Banerjee (2015). "Below the poverty line and non-communicable diseases in Kerala: The epidemiology of non-communicable diseases in rural areas (ENDIRA) study", *International Journal of Cardiology*, 187, 519–524.

Mwabu, G. and E. Thorbecke (2004). "Rural development, growth and poverty in Africa", *Journal of African Economies*, 13(1), 116–165.

Neutel, M. and A. Heshmati (2006). "Globalisation, inequality and poverty relationships: A cross country evidence", IZA Discussion Paper Series.

NISR (2015). *Rwanda's National Institute of Statistics*. Kigali, Rwanda: Government of Rwanda.

OECD (2016). Poverty Gap (Indicator). Paris Cedex, France. Available at: data.oecd.org/inequality/poverty-rate.htm.

Pauw, K. and M. Leibbrandt (2012). "Minimum wages and household poverty: General equilibrium macro–micro simulations for South Africa", *World Development*, 40(4), 771–783.

Republic of Rwanda after Territorial Reform (2008). *Ministry of Local Government, Government of Rwanda*. Available at: www.minaloc.gov.rw.

Shepherd, A., T. Mitchell, K. Lewis, A. Lenhardt, L. Jones, L. Scott, and R.M. Wood (2013). *The Geography of Poverty, Disasters and Climate Extremes in 2030*. London: Department for International Development (DFID).

Tazoacha, F. (2001). "The causes and impact of poverty on sustainable development in Africa", Paper presented at the conference held in Bordeaux, France, 22–23 November.

Ucal, M.Ş. (2014). "Panel data analysis of foreign direct investment and poverty from the perspective of developing countries", *Procedia – Social and Behavioral Sciences*, 109, 1101–1105.

World Bank Institute (2005). *Introduction to Poverty*. World Bank Institute, August 2005. Available at: siteresources.worldbank.org/PGLP/Resources/PovertyManual.pdf.

Part II

Taxes, trade openness and capital

7 Assessing the revenue implications of indirect tax reforms in Rwanda

Etienne Ndemezo[1] *and*
Francis Menjo-Baye[2]

1. Introduction

Indirect tax reforms modify the structure of consumption expenditure and so also the tax revenue collected. According to Crossley et al. (2009), a change in indirect tax rates affects consumption through two channels: the income effect and the substitution effect. The substitution effect is a consequence of the changes in relative prices, whereas the income effect is a reflection of a change in a household's purchasing power.

For Feldstein (2008) the impact of a tax reform on tax revenue has three components: (1) mechanical change, (2) behavioral change and (3) excess tax burden. Mechanical change is the extra tax revenue when consumption expenditure does not vary. Behavioral change is the extra revenue that depends on the response to the change in the tax rate. And excess tax burden, or deadweight loss, is the additional tax cost endured by a taxpayer because of price distortions (Hines Jr., 2007). The excess tax burden itself is not tax revenue; it is a tax surcharge that the tax reform gets taxpayers to pay by lowering consumption. Thus, an analysis of the revenue implications of a tax policy should not be limited to tax productivity, but should also include its inefficiency regarding deadweight loss.

Value added tax (VAT) was introduced in the Rwandan tax system in January 2001 at a flat rate of 15 per cent. The tax reform of January 2002 increased the VAT tax rate to 18 per cent. Indubitably, this tax reform entailed many consequences, among them a change in tax yields. Therefore, the main objective of this paper is to evaluate the revenue consequences of the VAT rate reform. More specifically, this article aims: (1) to examine the effects of the 2002 increase in the VAT rate on the consumption expenditure of Rwandan households and (2) to determine the impact of this VAT rate reform on the government's tax revenues.

To address these two objectives, we adopted the methodological framework of the elasticity of the taxable base with respect to the tax rate (Gruber and Saez, 2002). Gruber's and Saez's (2002) article is a seminal work in the field of labor income taxation. However, to the best of our knowledge, no attempt has been made to apply their methodology to indirect taxation. Also, even if indirect taxes constitute the main source of tax revenue in low-income countries, to our knowledge no empirical study has been done to assess the behavioral consequences of an indirect tax in a developing country. Thus, the merit of this article is mainly empirical.

The data used are from the second Integrated Survey on the Living Standards of Rwandan Households (EICV2), which took place from 12 October 2005 to 3 October 2006. The choice of this survey is justified by the post-reform period during which it was conducted. The consumption expenditure collected in this survey contains post-reform prices, which can be useful in judging the behavioral response of household consumption to a change in prices following the 2002 VAT rate reform.

The main outcome is that the increase in VAT rate in 2002 slightly increased Rwandan households' expenditures. This slight increase in households' spending was accompanied by a substantial increase in tax revenues of about 20 per cent. This attests that a mechanical change mainly dominated this increase in revenue. The behavioral component was only 0.5 per cent and was mainly borne by poor households. Moreover, the 2002 VAT reform resulted in low tax inefficiency, as for 100 Rwandan francs of extra revenue that were collected, households only experienced an excess tax burden valued at about 3 Rwandan francs.

The rest of the paper is organized as follows. The next section gives a literature review; Section 3 describes the methodology used while Section 4 is dedicated to empirical results and a discussion. The last section gives a conclusion.

2. Literature review

From Dupuit (1844) it is known that the relationship between tax rate and tax revenue is not linear because of a change in consumption behavior with respect to the tax rate (Laffer, 2004; Wanniski, 1978). According to Saez (2001) the tax base reacts to a change in the tax rate. Hence, depending on taxpayer behavior, an increase in the tax rate can lead to a decrease in the taxable base. For individuals who have more opportunities to escape the tax burden by tax evasion or by an inter-temporal tax base shifting, the taxable base is very sensitive to the tax rate. In contrast, those who do not have enough opportunities to minimize tax incidence, the tax base is insensitive to the tax rate (Sillamaa and Veall, 2001).

An analysis of the linkage between tax rate and tax base is mainly developed within the income taxation theory. Saez et al. (2012) did a critical review in this area. In indirect taxation, there are limited analyses of the relationship between the tax rate and taxable base. The few studies that exist have been done in developed countries and mainly concern selective taxes (which apply to the volume and not to the goods' value).

In the context of import regulations within the European Union, Crawford and Tanner (1995) conducted a study in the United Kingdom to determine the revenue effect of a tax rate reduction on alcoholic drink products. Using data from the Irish Family Budget survey over 20 years (1978–96), they estimated the model of domestic demand and pointed out the elasticity of demand for these goods with respect to excise tax rates. Their results show that beer and wine were relatively insensitive to price and that tax rates in force were below the Laffer (2004) tax rate. Therefore, they concluded that a decline in the tax rate on alcoholic beverages would lower revenues. Crawford and Tanner's (1995) study showed that liquor is sufficiently sensitive to price and they did not reject the hypothesis that its tax rate was a Laffer one. This implies that a decline in the tax rate on liquor would raise tax revenues from this commodity.

Crawford et al. (1999) resumed the same study and analyzed the long-term effects of a change in tax rates on alcoholic beverages by integrating the cross-price elasticity that had been ignored in their previous study. Comparing wine and liquor, they found that these two drinks were substitutes. On the other hand, beer and wine, and beer and liquor, were complements.

Like Crawford and Tanner (1995) they ignored cross-price elasticity and found that lowering the tax rate on liquor could increase the tax revenue collected from it. Further, taking into account the cross-price elasticity, Crawford et al. (1999) found that tax revenue from wine grew with a decline in the tax rate on liquor. Moreover, they found that a decline in the tax rate on wine resulted in increasing demand for beer and a decline in demand for liquor. This could result in an increase in the tax revenue from beer and wine and in a decrease in revenue from liquor. Therefore, the authors recommended not raising the tax rate on liquor because, overall, this would result in a decrease in revenue from alcoholic drinks. Ultimately, their result was the same as Crawford and Tanner's (1995).

The common methodological characteristic of these two studies is that they are based only on the substitution effect and ignore the income effect of revenue change. However, according to Crossley et al. (2009), the change in tax revenue due to a change in the tax rate is separated into income effect and substitution effect. Income effect implies that a decrease in the tax rate increases households' purchasing power. Depending on the value of the income-elasticity of demand, the income effect may increase or decrease consumer spending. The substitution effect concerns a change in household expenditure in response to a change in relative (or inter-temporal) prices.[1]

Studying the revenue impact of the 2009 decline in the VAT rate in England, Crossley et al. (2009) found that the inter-temporal substitution effect prevailed on the income effect. The explanation for this phenomenon is that the decline in VAT rate was reflected in the prices of luxuries rather than in the prices of necessities. Indeed, luxuries are easier to postpone than necessities (Browning and Crossley, 2000). Further, Barrell and Weale (2009) identified an increase in expenditure on non-perishable goods during the period of the VAT rate decline and called this phenomenon the *trade-off* effect.

Cashin and Unayama (2016) studied the revenue impact of a VAT rate increase in Japan. Contrary to expectations, these authors found that households did not increase their expenditure in the period following the increase in VAT rate. On the other hand, anticipating an increase in the VAT rate, Japanese households increased their expenditure during the period directly following the announcement of an increase in this rate. This inter-temporal substitution especially had to do with durables and storable non-durables. In terms of revenue, the substitution effect that followed the announcement of an increase in the VAT rate resulted in a minor loss of tax revenue and the actual effect of the increase in the VAT rate was revenue neutral.

Concerning marginal excess tax burden, Harberger (1964) theorized a unit tax and personal income tax. Comparing these two taxes he concluded that personal income tax generated a less marginal excess tax burden than the unit indirect tax.

However, Feldstein (1999) used the Harberger method and showed that the marginal excess tax burden of wage income tax, measured in terms of taxable income supply rather than in terms of labor supply, was more important. Compared to the flat tax, Feldstein (1999) showed that the extra tax cost of the wage income tax was 12 times higher than the extra tax cost approximated by Harberger (1964).

Using the method of behavioral change in tax revenue, Saez (2004) showed that taking account of the sources and destinations of a change in taxable income, the marginal excess tax burden of the wage income tax decreased enormously. On the other hand, he also showed that the marginal excess tax burden was almost non-existent for lower income brackets as compared to the richest income bracket.

Comparing the before-tax situation to the after-tax situation of a taxpayer, Saez's (2004) method respects the Pigou conception of excess tax burden (Lind and Granqvist, 2010). This is its main difference from Harberger's triangle method, which compares the after-tax situation of a taxpayer to that which would prevail if a hypothetical flat tax replaced this tax.

Apart from the Harberger's (1964) approximation, to the best of our knowledge no other study has been conducted on the approximation of the efficiency cost of an indirect tax rate reform. Therefore, our study constitutes advancement in this empirical literature.

3. Methods

The base of indirect taxes is made up of consumer spending.[2] This is likely to increase or decrease following a change in the tax rate and households' preferences. To analyze the effects of a change in the tax rate on consumption expenditure, we refer to the methodological framework of the elasticity of taxable income with respect to the marginal tax rate (Gruber and Saez, 2002).

3.1 Elasticity of taxable income with respect to the marginal tax rate

Seeking to assess the elasticity of taxable income with respect to the marginal tax rate, Gruber and Saez (2002) maintained that a taxpayer satisfies his utility using two types of commodities: consumption goods and income. Maximizing the taxpayer's utility, they showed that the supply function of taxable income was:

$$z = z(1 - t, I) \tag{1}$$

where z is the taxable income, t is the marginal tax rate and I is the exogenous income. Here exogenous income designates all types of non-taxable income.

Eq. 1 highlights two variables that represent arguments of the supply function of taxable income – marginal tax rate and exogenous income. Gruber and Saez (2002) showed that the two variables influence the supply of the taxable income as:

$$\frac{dz}{z} = -\zeta^{c}\frac{dt}{1-t} + \eta\frac{dI - zdt}{z(1-t)} \tag{2}$$

with $(dI - zdt)$ defined as a change in post-tax income following a change in the marginal tax rate. For these authors, this value is equivalent to a change in the tax revenue from taxpayers who have a taxable income z. Parameters ζ^{C} and η represent the compensated elasticity of taxable income with respect to the marginal tax rate and the income effect, respectively, whereas dz, dt and dI represent the infinitesimal change in taxable income, in marginal tax rate and in exogenous income, respectively.

The specificity of Eq. 2 is that it introduces the income effect in an assessment of the elasticity of a taxable base with respect to the tax rate. However, it is more suitable for personal income taxation rather than for consumption expenditure taxation. To adapt it to indirect taxation, we refer to the theory of the consumer by replacing the supply of taxable income by the supply of taxable expenditure and replacing the marginal tax rate by the implicit tax rate.[3]

3.2 *Elasticity of taxable expenditure with respect to the implicit tax rate*

We define the taxable expenditure of household h on commodity i as:

$$E_i^h = E_i^h(q, I_h) \tag{3}$$

where E_i^h means the expenditure tax-included on commodity i by household h, q refers to the vector of prices tax-included and I_h designates the income of household h. We assume that only the consumption expenditure is taxable and that household income is not taxed.

Taxable expenditure depends on the vector of final prices and household income. A change in the indirect tax rate has no effect on household income. Therefore, we assume that a change in the implicit tax rate fully passes through the consumer price: $dq_i = p_i d\pi_i$ where P_i is the price tax-excluded on commodity i; dq_i and $d\pi_i$ are, respectively, the changes in price tax-included for commodity i and the change in the implicit tax rate on commodity i.

For household h, after a change in the tax rate, the change in consumption expenditure is induced by a combination of the change in the vector of prices and the change in real income:

$$dE_i^h = \frac{\partial E_i^h}{\partial q_i} dq_i + \sum_{j \neq i} \frac{\partial E_i^h}{\partial q_j} dq_j + \frac{\partial E_i^h}{\partial I_h} dI_h \tag{4}$$

where dE_i^h is the change in consumption expenditure tax-included of household h on the commodity i; $\frac{\partial E_i^h}{\partial q_i}$ and $\frac{\partial E_i^h}{\partial q_j}$ are the derivatives of the expenditure tax-included of household h on commodity i with respect to the price of the goods i and j, respectively; dI_h and $\frac{\partial E_i^h}{\partial I_h}$ are changes in the real income of household h and the derivative of the expenditure tax-included of household h on commodity i with respect to the real income of household h.

After rearrangement, the change in the consumption expenditure can be written as:

$$\frac{dE_i}{E_i} = \left[\left(1 + \varepsilon_{ii}^u\right) \frac{d\pi_i}{1 + \pi_i} + \sum_{i \neq j} \varepsilon_{ij}^u \frac{d\pi_j}{1 + \pi_j} \right] + \eta_i \frac{dI}{I} \tag{5}$$

with ε_{ii}^u, ε_{ij}^u, η_i respectively designating the uncompensated own price elasticity of demand for commodity i, the cross-price elasticity of demand for commodity i with respect to the price of commodity j; and variables π_i and $d\pi_i$ representing the implicit tax rate on commodity i and its infinitesimal change, respectively. Here variables E_i and dE_i, I and dI are, respectively, total expenditure on commodity i and its change post the reform and total household income and its change post the reform.

With some rearrangements, Eq. 5 becomes:

$$\frac{dE_i}{E_i} = \zeta_{ii}^u \frac{d\pi_i}{1 + \pi_i} + \eta_i \frac{dI}{I} \tag{6}$$

The parameter $\zeta_{ii}^u \left[= 1 + \varepsilon_{ii}^u + \sum_{i \neq j} \varepsilon_{ji}^u \right]$ is the uncompensated price elasticity of the expenditure of household m on commodity i. Here, ε_{ji}^u designates the cross-price elasticity of demand for commodity j with respect to the price of commodity i. Other variables are defined as earlier.

On the right hand side of Eq. 6, the first term represents the substitution effect, while the last term is the income effect. The substitution effect is negative in terms of quantity consumed. However, in terms of expenditure, the sign of the substitution effect may be positive or negative. It is non-positive if the demand for the concerned commodity is elastic and it is non-negative when the demand for this commodity is inelastic. In terms of expenditure, the income effect is non-negative for normal goods and non-positive for inferior goods.

Eq. 6 highlights the elasticity of expenditure with respect to the tax rate and with respect to household income. Through this expression, the aggregate elasticity of expenditure with respect to the tax rate and with respect to household income can be estimated using, as explicative variables, the change in the implicit tax rate borne by each household and the change in household income; the independent variable being the household expenditure tax-included.

However, for this, it is imperative to possess panel data on two cohorts at least, with at least one cohort relating to the pre-reform period. To overcome the lack of panel data, we replaced the elasticity of expenditure with respect to the tax rate by the price elasticity of expenditure.

In order to facilitate calculations, and using the Roy identity ($dI/I = w_i dq_i/q_i$), Eq. 6 was transformed as:

$$\frac{dE_i}{E_i} = \zeta_{ii}^u \frac{d\pi_i}{1+\pi_i} + w_i\eta_i \frac{d\pi_i}{1+\pi_i} \tag{7}$$

with w_i representing the budget share of commodity i; the other variables defined as earlier. Here, $w_i\eta_i$ designates the income effect coefficient, while ζ_{ii}^u is the substitution effect coefficient of the change in consumption expenditure.

The limitation of using this approach is that it takes account of only taxable goods whose tax rates were modified. This technique assumes that indirect tax reforms do not influence the consumption expenditure of non-taxable goods.

3.3 *Implications in terms of revenue yields*

We recall that the revenue yield of an indirect tax rate reform can be split into two components: behavioral change and mechanical change. Behavioral change in tax revenue is derived from Eq. 7, using the Slutsky equation $\left(\varepsilon_{ii}^u = \varepsilon_{ii}^c - w_i\eta_i\right)$:

$$\Delta B_i = E_i \pi_i \zeta_{ii}^c \frac{\Delta\pi_i}{1+\pi_i} \tag{8}$$

where ΔB_i is the behavioral change in tax revenue, E_i is the total expenditure tax-included on commodity i; π_i and $\Delta\pi_i$ are, respectively, the implicit tax rate applicable to commodity i and its change post-reform; $\zeta_{ii}^c \left(= 1 + \varepsilon_{ii}^c + \sum_{i \neq j} \varepsilon_{ji}^u\right)$ is the compensated price elasticity of the consumption expenditure on commodity i. Other parameters are defined as earlier.

Depending on the sign of the price elasticity of consumption expenditure, the behavioral change in tax revenue may be positive or negative. Otherwise, the behavioral change is negative for luxuries and positive for necessities.

The mechanical change in tax revenue is given by:

$$\Delta M_i = E_i \frac{\Delta\pi_i}{1+\pi_i} \tag{9}$$

with ΔM_i referring to the mechanical change in tax revenue; the other variables are defined as previously.

Mechanical change is always non-negative. The total growth of tax revenue is the sum of mechanical change and behavioral change:

$$\Delta R_i = E_i\left[1+\pi_i\zeta_{ii}^c\right]\frac{\Delta\pi_i}{1+\pi_i} \tag{10}$$

with ΔR_i designating the total change in tax revenue from expenditure from commodity i; π_i and $\Delta\pi_i$ are the implicit tax rates on commodity i before the tax reform and its post-reform change; other variables are defined as earlier.

3.4 *Implications in terms of marginal excess tax burden*

To compute the marginal excess tax burden, we adopted the Saez (2004) approach. According to Saez, the additional excess tax burden is measured in terms of the ratio of behavioral change in tax revenue over a change in total tax revenue. However, we only counted the negative behavioral change because the positive one cannot be considered as an additional excess tax burden because it is counted in the total additional government revenue:

$$\Delta EB_i = \frac{|\Delta B_i|}{|\Delta R_i|} = \frac{|\pi_i\zeta_i^c|}{|1+\pi_i\zeta_i^c|} \tag{11}$$

where ΔEB_i represents the additional excess tax burden due to an increase in the indirect tax rate on commodity i; other variables are defined as earlier. The bars that surround the values in Eq. 11 indicate that the concerned amount is in absolute value. Therefore, the total extra excess tax burden is the added additional excess tax burden borne by all commodities.

According to Eq. 11, the higher the implicit tax rate and more the price elasticity of expenditure, more significant is the additional excess tax burden. Therefore, a marginal excess tax burden is important for goods whose demand is much more elastic than others, that is, for goods which are considered luxuries.

4. Variables and data

The variables required to implement Eqs. (7) to (11) are:

1 Consumption expenditures tax-included (before and after the VAT rate reform),
2 Implicit tax rates and their changes post-reform, and
3 Uncompensated and compensated price elasticity of expenditure.

Data on consumption expenditure is from the second Integrated Survey on the Living Standards of Rwandan Households (EICV2). This survey was conducted in 2005–06 by the National Institute of Statistics of Rwanda (NISR). Thus, consumption expenditure collected by EICV2 contains post-reform prices.

Tax data is from implicit tax rates calculated using the VAT rate and the excise duty rates prevailing in 2001 and in 2006. In order to compute the change in implicit tax rates, we compared the implicit tax rates in 2006 and in 2001.

Price elasticities of expenditure were estimated using the Linear Expenditure System (LES) model as extended by Creedy and Sleeman (2006). Data used to estimate the LES model was consumption expenditure from EICV2.

5. Empirical findings and discussion

We first focus on the effects of the VAT rate reform on the structure of household expenditure and then analyze the effects of the increase in the VAT rate on tax revenue and on excess tax burden.

5.1 *Effects of increase in the VAT rate on household expenditure*

The increase in the VAT rate in January 2002 slightly modified the consumption habits of Rwandan households. The increase in the VAT rate resulted in the growth of all the implicit tax rates applicable to different commodity groups. Moreover, this change in the implicit tax rate caused several slight changes in households' choices. Table 7.1 summarizes the splitting of behavioral effects of indirect taxes computed through Eq. 7.

Most of the commodity groups experienced slight increases in spending. Overall, the increase in households' spending was valued at about 0.29 per cent of pre-reform expenditure. The substitution effect was estimated at 0.07 per cent and the income effect was approximated at 0.22 per cent of a household's pre-reform spending. The positive sign of the substitution effect means that the increase in relative prices was borne much more by necessities than by luxuries.

Further, two commodity groups experienced a positive substitution effect greater than 1 per cent: private fuel (2.4 per cent) and communication (1.9 per cent). These two commodity groups are luxuries; but also, according to cross-price elasticity, they complemented all other commodity groups and their related spending increased with an increase in the prices of other goods. Despite a very low income effect, the significance of the substitution effect gave these two commodity groups the first two ranks in the total behavioral changes in consumption expenditure.

The income effect is positive everywhere, attesting that all commodities were normal. It exceeded 0.3 per cent of the post-reform expenditure for three commodity groups: clothing (0.62 per cent), hygiene products (0.36 per cent) and housing (0.30 per cent). The budget shares of these three commodity groups were very high (greater than 12 per cent). This implies that they were represented more than the others in households' consumption bundles. As a result, a significant portion of a household's budget was devoted to them and they benefitted more from the income effect.

The conjunction of income and substitution effects indicates that three commodity groups experienced a very slight decline in their spending because they were luxuries: (in descending order) leisure and recreation, beer and personal effects. Four commodity groups underwent a higher total behavioral effect compared to others: private fuel (2.4 per cent), communication (2.0 per cent), clothing (0.9 per cent) and preventive health (0.6 per cent). All these commodities

Table 7.1 Splitting the behavioral effect of the VAT rate increase on indirect tax revenue per commodity group (in per cent)

Products	*Substitution effect*	*Income effect*	*Total behavioral effect*
Agricultural foods	0.000	0.000	0.000
Manufactured foods	0.323	0.033	0.356
Non-alcoholic beverages	0.307	0.009	0.316
Beer	-0.012	0.005	-0.007
Wine and liquor	0.433	0.000	0.433
Outside meals	0.125	0.019	0.144
Tobacco	0.047	0.060	0.107
Clothing	0.238	0.620	0.858
Personal effects	-0.050	0.047	-0.003
Leisure and recreation	-0.162	0.100	-0.062
Housing	-0.140	0.300	0.160
Furnishings and appliances	-0.161	0.214	0.053
Home water and energy	0.223	0.023	0.246
Home repairs	0.200	0.001	0.201
Private fuel	2.384	0.002	2.387
Public transport	0.000	0.000	0.000
Preventive health	0.571	0.004	0.575
Curative health	0.069	0.116	0.185
Hygiene products	-0.057	0.355	0.298
Communication	1.901	0.096	1.997
Education	0.000	0.000	0.000
Total	0.073	0.215	0.288
per cent	*25.3*	*74.7*	*100.0*

Source: Authors' computations using EICV2 data

had a positive and higher substitution effect. Further, clothing had a higher average budget share (29 per cent) and, consequently, a bigger income effect.

Ultimately, the increase in the VAT rate forced households to increase their spending to cope with the increase in prices. However, this does not necessarily imply that the increase in the VAT rate increased the quantity consumed; our analysis concerns only expenditure modifications.

5.2 *Effects of an increase in the VAT rate on tax revenue*

The growth in household expenditure is reflected in the behavioral component of an increase in tax revenue, which was about 0.5 per cent (Table 7.2). The behavioral increase in revenue exceeded the increase in expenditure. As seen earlier, this attests that a change in the VAT rate mainly resulted in an increase in money being spent on goods that were heavily taxed (communication and

Table 7.2 Splitting the 2002 VAT rate increase effects on tax revenue (in per cent)

Products	*Behavioral change*			*Mechanical change*	*Total change*
	Substitution	*Income*	*Total*		
Agricultural foods	0.000	0.000	0.000	0.000	0.000
Manufactured	0.371	0.038	0.409	20.000	20.409
Non-alcoholic	0.491	0.015	0.506	7.602	8.108
Beer	-0.022	0.009	-0.013	5.847	5.835
Wine and liquor	0.846	0.001	0.847	5.340	6.187
Outside meals	0.144	0.022	0.165	20.000	20.165
Tobacco	0.086	0.110	0.196	5.714	5.910
Clothing	0.274	0.713	0.986	20.000	20.986
Personal effects	-0.057	0.054	-0.003	20.000	19.997
Leisure	-0.186	0.115	-0.071	20.000	19.929
Housing	-0.161	0.345	0.184	20.000	20.184
Furnishings	-0.185	0.246	0.061	20.000	20.061
Water and energy	0.256	0.026	0.282	20.000	20.282
Home repairs	0.230	0.002	0.232	20.000	20.232
Private fuel	3.756	0.004	3.760	7.142	10.902
Public transport	0.000	0.000	0.000	0.000	0.000
Preventive health	0.656	0.005	0.661	20.000	20.661
Curative health	0.080	0.133	0.213	20.000	20.213
Hygiene products	-0.066	0.408	0.342	20.000	20.342
Communication	2.186	0.110	2.296	43.600	45.896
Education	0.000	0.000	0.000	0.000	0.000
Total	0.152	0.334	0.486	19.523	20.009
per cent	*31.340*	*68.660*	*100.000*	–	–
	0.761	*1.668*	*2.429*	*97.571*	*100.000*

Source: Authors' calculations using EICV2 data

private fuel) or more consumed (clothing, hygiene products and housing). Moreover, this outcome means that indirect tax revenue was elastic with respect to its tax base; this elasticity can be estimated at 1.6875 (that is, 0.486/0.288).

Further, even if the behavioral growth of tax revenue remained low, the increase in the VAT rate overall increased indirect tax revenue (about 20 per cent of the previous revenue). The total growth in indirect tax revenue was widely dominated by the mechanical component (97.6 per cent). Behavioral growth represented only 2.4 per cent of the total increase in indirect tax revenue. Overall, the substitution effect was less than the income effect, thus justifying that the VAT rate change effect was more proportional to budget shares. The effect of the VAT rate reform on relative prices and so on the structure of consumer bundles was less significant than its effect on households' real income.

However, compared to the change in consumer expenditure, the income effect of the VAT rate reform on tax revenue was lower. As mentioned earlier, this certifies that an increase in households' spending on highly taxed goods was mainly from the substitution effect. Further, at the individual level the substitution effect in absolute value outweighed the income effect for most commodity groups. Goods that did not meet this 'rule' are tobacco, clothing, housing, furnishings and appliances, curative health and hygiene products. All previous products had a greater average budget share (above 2 per cent) and, consequently, experienced a significant income effect.

The unequal significance of the substitution effect indicates that the impact of the VAT rate was unequal among commodities and that it restructured households' consumption baskets. The substitution effect and the trade-off effect (Barrell and Weale, 2009) were low for goods, which represented little immediate interest (durable goods and luxury goods) compared to other goods deemed most essential by households, such as manufactured food products, preventive health, private fuel and home water and energy.

The total behavioral effect was negative for three commodity groups (in descending order): (1) leisure and recreation, (2) beer and (3) personal effects. These three commodity groups are luxuries, which experienced a higher negative substitution effect that outweighed the income effect. On the other hand, the behavioral effect was positive and greater than 1 per cent for two commodity groups: private fuel (3.8 per cent) and communication (2.3 per cent). As discussed earlier, these two groups complement other commodities and benefit more from a price increase following an increase in the VAT rate.

Ultimately, on the one hand, the behavioral effect of the increase in the VAT rate was negative for luxury commodities and, on the other hand, it was positive and relatively high for goods which complement others, even if they were luxuries. The former are easy to postpone when there is an increase in indirect tax rates (Browning and Crossley, 2000), whereas the latter have a higher positive substitution effect thanks to an increase in the relative prices of other commodity groups, particularly of necessities.

Further, only mechanical change in revenue from the commodity groups that bear excise taxes was different from 20 per cent (which is also the percentage increase in the VAT rate). In absolute value, these taxable goods experienced higher growth in their tax rates at about 5 per cent or more. We can interpret this as: the higher growth in tax revenue from communication is explained by the significant increase in its tax rate during the post-reform period while slow growth in tax revenue from other goods bearing excise duties originated from their pre-reform higher tax rates.

Considering households' standard of living, the behavioral growth of tax revenue was relatively higher among households in the first three quintiles and relatively lower among households in the last two quintiles (see Figure 7.1). This attests that facing an increase in market prices, relatively poor households increased their spending rather than non-poor households. This fact also confirms the finding shown earlier that indirect taxes are mainly levied on necessities.

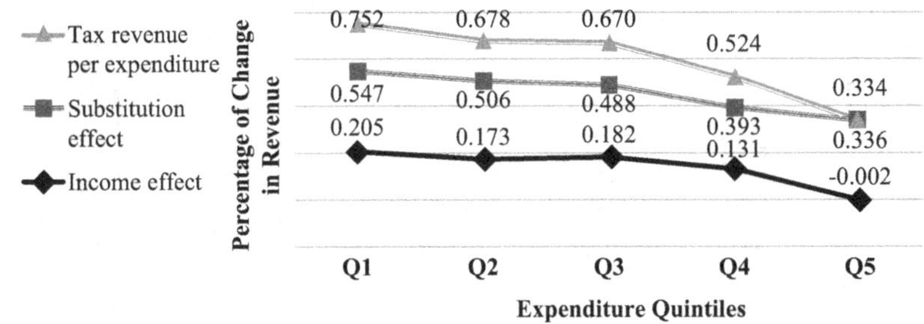

Figure 7.1 Splitting behavioral change in tax revenue per expenditure quintile (in per cent)

Source: Authors' calculations using EICV2 data

Behavioral growth of tax revenue among poor households was about 0.7 per cent, while it was about 0.5 per cent in the fourth quintile and 0.3 per cent among households in the last quintile. However, it is important to mention here that the change in tax revenue was widely dominated by the mechanical component for all household categories. Thus, the decreasing behavioral response cannot be interpreted as a regressiveness of the VAT rate reform of January 2002.

Further, behavioral change in tax revenue was influenced more by the income effect (over 70 per cent) for all households. The substitution effect was slightly negative in the last quintile. Thus, the low participation of wealthy households in the behavioral growth of tax revenue came partly from their negative reactions to a change in relative prices. Also, the first quintile experienced the most important substitution effect and a higher behavioral growth in tax revenue. This attests that households in this quintile were much more insensitive to changes in prices as compared to others.

These results are consistent with Saez's (2002) results about commodity taxation with non-linear optimal direct taxation. For Saez in order to increase tax revenue, it is optimal to tax those goods lesser which are consumed more by wealthy households. This means overall that the elasticity of consumption expenditure with respect to indirect tax rates is lower among richer households and higher among poor households. This also conforms with the inverse-elasticity rule, which states that tax rates on goods should be inversely related to their compensated elasticity of demand if redistribution does not count.

However, considering total growth[4] instead of behavioral growth of tax revenue, the contribution of households in the last quintile is predominant (see Figure 7.2). Total revenue growth in the last quintile was in the order of 20.2 per cent, thus slightly exceeding the overall average of 20 per cent. This was a consequence of the predominance of wealthier households' consumption expenditure on taxable goods.

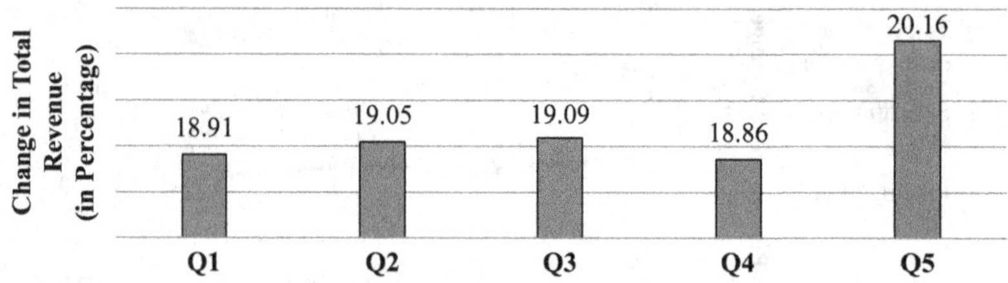

Figure 7.2 Households' contribution to total tax revenue growth per quintile (in per cent)

Source: Authors' computations using EICV2 data

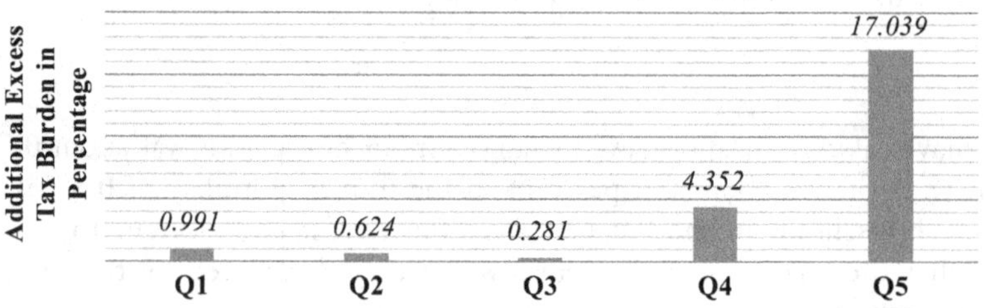

Figure 7.3 Additional excess burden resulting from the 2002 VAT rate reform

Source: Authors' calculations using EICV2 data

Households which were comparatively less wealthy participated in the total growth in indirect tax revenue at a much lower rate (below average), which varied from 18.7 per cent (fourth quintile) to 19.1 per cent (second and third quintile). As compared to households in the other quintiles, the fourth quintile consumed relatively less taxable goods. However, overall, the total growth in tax revenue was progressive.

5.3 Effect of the VAT rate reform on excess tax burden

The overall utility loss resulting from the VAT rate reform was valued at about 2.878 Rwandan francs[5] (RWF) for 100 additional Rwandan francs collected as indirect taxes. The marginal excess tax burden due to an increase in the VAT rate was greater for leisure and recreation, which are luxury goods.

Considering the standard of living (Figure 7.3), households in the third quintile were less disadvantaged; they consumed relatively less taxable luxuries. The last two quintiles were the most disadvantaged. Overall, they experienced a tax surcharge equivalent to 4.352 per cent and 17.039 per cent for the fourth and the last quintile, respectively. This explains that these wealthier households consumed much more luxuries as compared to poorer households, particularly leisure and recreation commodities. More detailed information about contributions of taxable products to total indirect tax revenue after the VAT reform (in percentage) is provided in Appendix Figures 7.A and 7.B.

5.4 *Implications in terms of poverty reduction policies*

In general even if most economists believe that public expenditures are a better instrument for targeting the poor, this study demonstrates that it is possible to improve the welfare of poor families by using the indirect tax system. This can be done by zero-rating or even subsidizing basic necessities such as manufactured foods and home water and energy because they are relatively more consumed by poorer households who were also much more affected by the 2002 VAT rate reform.

Manufactured foods and home water and energy together generated less than 2 per cent of total indirect tax revenue. Certainly, their removal will be revenue costly, but it is possible to compensate this revenue reduction by changing tax rates on other commodities that generate more revenue; for example, a decrease in the tax rate applicable to leisure and recreation. As seen earlier, lowering tax rate on leisure and recreation will increase their consumption and, consequently, raise government revenues.

6. Summary and conclusion

In this article we computed the change in household expenditure and in indirect tax revenue consecutive to an increase in the VAT rate in January 2002 in Rwanda. For this purpose, we adapted the methodological framework of a change in the income tax base with respect to the marginal tax rate (Gruber and Saez, 2002), in order to conform it to indirect taxation. As compared to Gruber and Saez's (2002) method, our adaptation has the merit of using data which is easy to collect and to archive in developing countries.

Our analysis resulted in two main outcomes. First, the increase in VAT rate in January 2002 caused a slight growth in consumption expenditure (of 0.3 per cent) among Rwandan households. This growth in household expenditure was reflected in the behavioral component of the tax revenue increase which was about 0.5 per cent; this was mainly borne by the poorest households. The second outcome concerns the increase in tax revenue which was significant (about 20 per cent of the pre-reform revenue). Therefore, the mechanical effect of the increase in the VAT rate largely prevailed on the behavioral effect. Moreover, the excess tax burden remained modest because it represented only approximately 3 RWF for 100 RWF of extra revenue collected. It was borne by luxuries, mainly the leisure and recreation group.

These outcomes permit us to recommend some tax arrangements in order to compensate the poorest households because they were affected much more by the VAT rate reform. This can be done, for example, by zero-rating or even subsidizing basic necessities such as manufactured foods and home water and energy. However, the main target of indirect taxes must remain revenue yield. This seems to be true, as our analysis shows that during the period studied, indirect tax revenue was elastic with respect to consumption expenditure.

Appendix A

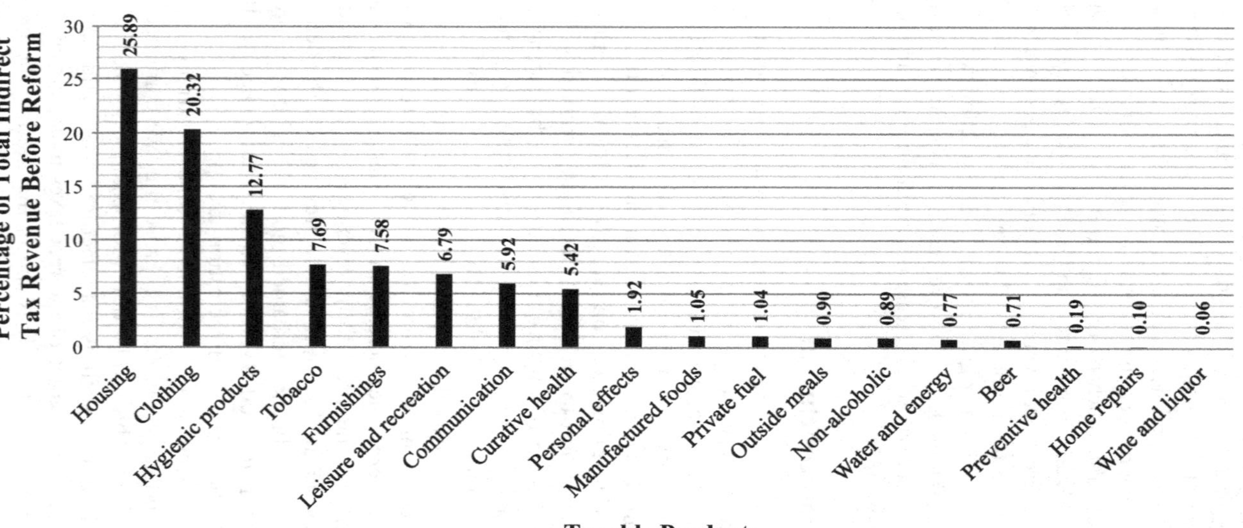

Figure 7.A Contribution of taxable products to total indirect tax revenue before the VAT reform (in percentage)

Source: Authors' computations using EICV2 data

Appendix B

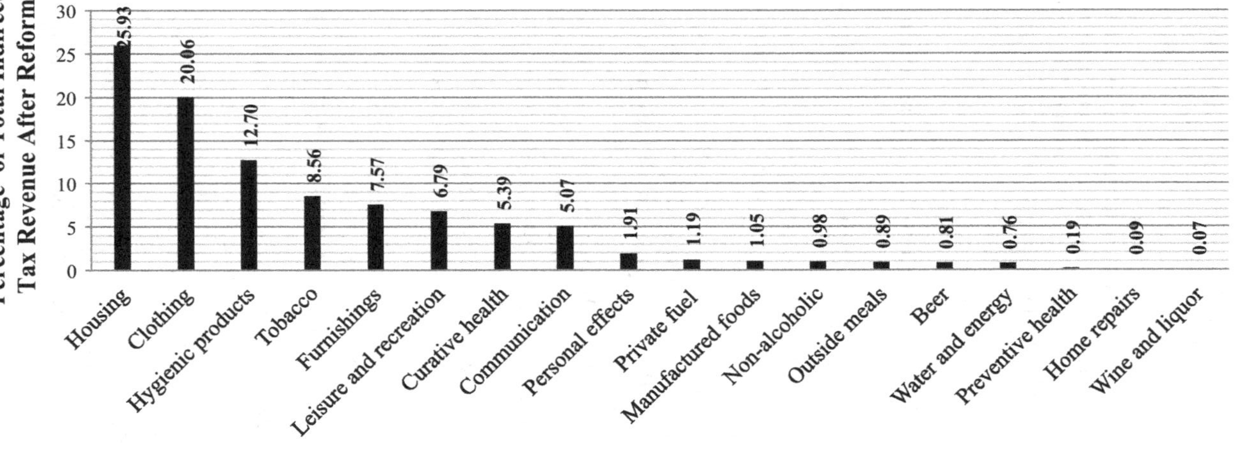

Figure 7.B Contribution of taxable products to total indirect tax revenue after the VAT reform (in percentage)

Source: Authors' computations using EICV2 data

Note: According to Appendix 1 and 2, eight products contributed separately to the total indirect tax revenue by more than 5 per cent before and after the VAT reform: Housing, Clothing, Hygiene Products, Tobacco, Communication, Furnishings and Appliances, Leisure and Recreation and Curative Health. The collective contribution of these eight products exceeded 92 per cent before and after the VAT reform. Consequently, the remaining 10 products contributed to indirect tax revenues by less than 8 per cent.

Notes

1 Crossley et al.'s (2009) study refers to change in consumption due to a temporal decline in the VAT rate. However, it is even valid in the case of a consistent decline in the tax rate.
2 This methodological approach borrows mainly from Ndemezo and Baye (2016:185–186).
3 We define the implicit tax rate as: $\pi_i = v_i + \tau_i + \tau_i v_i$, where π_i represents the implicit tax rate, τ_i is the excise duty rate on good i and v_i is the VAT rate on good i.
4 Total growth in indirect tax revenue is a combination of behavioral change and of mechanical change in indirect tax revenue.
5 Rwandan franc (RWF) is the currency used in Rwanda. On 21 October 2016, 1 USD was equal to 807.683 RWF. The overall excess tax burden is calculated as a weighted average of the excess tax burden per quintile. The weight used is the share of households' expenditures per quintile.

References

Barrell, R. and M. Weale (2009). "The economics of a reduction in VAT", *Fiscal Studies*, 30, 17–30.

Browning, M. and T.F. Crossley (2000). "Luxuries are easier to postpone: A proof", *Journal of Political Economy*, 108(5), 1022–1026.

Cashin, D. and T. Unayama (2016). "Measuring intertemporal substitution in consumption: Evidence from a VAT increase in Japan", *The Review of Economics and Statistics*, 98(2), 285–297.

Crawford, I., Z. Smithand, and S. Tanner (1999). "Alcohol taxes, tax revenues and the Single European Market", *Fiscal Studies*, 20(3), 287–304.

Crawford, I. and S. Tanner (1995). "Bringing it all back home: Alcohol taxation and cross-border shopping", *Fiscal Studies*, 16(2), 94–114.

Creedy, J. and C. Sleeman (2006). "Indirect taxation and progressivity: Revenue and welfare changes", *FinanzArchiv/Public Finance Analysis*, 62(1), 50–67.

Crossley, T.F., H. Low, and M. Wakefield (2009). "The economics of a temporary VAT cut", *Fiscal Studies*, 30(1), 3–16.

Dupuit, J. (1844). "On the measurement of the utility of public works", in K.J. Arrow and T. Scitovsky (eds), *Readings in Welfare Economics* (1969). London: Allen and Unwin, pp. 255–283.

Feldstein, M. (1999). "Tax avoidance and the deadweight loss of the income tax", *The Review of Economics and Statistics*, 81(4), 674–680.

Feldstein, M. (2008). "Effects of taxes on economic behavior", *National Tax Journal*, 61(1), 131–139.

Gruber, J. and E. Saez (2002). "The elasticity of taxable income: Evidence and implications", *Journal of Public Economics*, 84, 1–32.

Harberger, A.C. (1964). "Taxation, resource allocation, and welfare", in J. Due (ed), *The Role of Direct and Indirect Taxes in the Federal Revenue System*. Princeton, NJ: Princeton University Press, pp. 25–80.

Hines Jr., J.R. (2007). "Excess burden of taxation", Working Paper No. 2007-1, Michigan Ross School of Business.

Laffer, A.B. (2004). "The Laffer curve: Past, present, and future", *The Heritage Foundation* 1765.

Lind, H. and R. Granqvist (2010). "A note on the concept of excess burden", *Economic Analysis and Policy*, 40(1), 63–73.

Ndemezo, E. and M.F. Baye (2016). "Evaluation of redistributive and welfare impacts of indirect taxes reform in Rwanda", in A. Heshmati (ed), *Poverty and Well-Being in East Africa: A Multi-faceted Economic Approach*. Economic Studies in Inequality, Social Exclusion and Well-Being Series, XV. Switzerland: Springer International Publishing, pp. 165–195.

Saez, E. (2001). "Using elasticities to derive optimal income tax rates", *Review of Economic Studies*, 68, 205–229.

Saez, E. (2002). "The desirability of commodity taxation under non-linear income taxation and heterogeneous tastes", *Journal of Public Economics*, 83, 217–230.

Saez, E. (2004). "Reported incomes and marginal tax rates, 1960–2000: Evidence and policy implications", in J.M. Poterba (ed), *Tax Policy and the Economy*. Cambridge, MA: The MIT Press, pp. 117–173.

Saez, E., J. Slemrod, and S.H. Giertz (2012). "The elasticity of taxable income with respect to marginal tax rates: A critical review", *Journal of Economic Literature*, 50(1), 3–50.

Sillamaa, M.A. and M.R. Veall (2001). "The effect of marginal tax rates on taxable income: A panel study of the 1988 tax flattening in Canada", *Journal of Public Economics*, 80, 341–356.

Wanniski, J. (1978). "Taxes, revenues, and the Laffer curve", *The Public Interest*, (50), 3–16.

8 Differential impact of trade liberalization and rural–urban income inequalities on poverty in African countries

Kahsay Berhane

1. Introduction

In the past three decades African countries have engaged in widespread trade liberalization and poverty reduction strategies. Almost all developing countries have believed that trade liberalization is a favorable condition for economic growth. In addition to classical economists' argument about the comparative advantage, trade liberalization enhances strong competition, promotes goods in a larger market and transfers technology. It hence increases efficiency in production. Thus, many developing countries have undertaken multilateral and regional efforts to liberalize trade, which involves reduction of tariff and non-tariff barriers and providing more uniform levels of protection among member countries.

Despite African countries' engagement with economic openness and trade liberalization since the late 1980s, Africa remains the poorest continent in the world. Based on Beegle et al.'s (2015) argument, due to rapid population growth in Africa, there were 330 million poor people in 2012 as compared to 280 million poor people in 1990. Moreover, the projections show that the world's poor will gradually be more concentrated in Africa, keeping the continent at the forefront of the global poverty agenda even in an era of globalization.

Available theoretical literature on the traditional trade theory predicts welfare gains from openness at the country level through specialization, better resource allocation, productivity improvement, technology transfer from developed countries and its spillover effects in host countries, and increased investments in innovation. However, the theoretical and empirical results on the impact of trade on the poor remain uncertain; in fact there are conflicting views on the effect of trade liberalization on poverty in developing countries. The first view argues that in the long run open economies are better in aggregate than closed economies and relatively open economic policies contribute significantly to development (Abuka et al., 2007; Carneiro and Arbache, 2003). The second view claims that trade liberalization tends to make the poor poorer and the rich richer, thus widening income inequalities among people and that, even in the longer run, successful open countries may leave some people behind in poverty (Evans, 2001; Harrison et al., 2003; Lofgren, 2000). So, theoretical and empirical literature shows that developing countries do not gain equally from the opportunities arising out of increased access to international markets in the developed world.

This paper contributes to literature on the impact of trade liberalization on poverty in Africa in four different ways (see Appendix A for a list of African countries studied). First, from an estimation point of view, we apply a novel approach, the recently developed methodology of common correlated effects mean group (CCEMG) estimator of Pesaran (2006) and the augmented mean group (AMG) estimator (Bond and Eberhardt, 2013; Eberhardt and Bond, 2009; Eberhardt and Teal, 2010). Taking into account cross-sectional dependency and slope heterogeneity, this study produces more robust and country-specific results. Second, the analysis uses a larger sample of countries (42), including North African countries and updated datasets that cover the period from 1996 to 2014 as compared to other recent studies, which cover 30 countries in sub-Saharan Africa from 1981 to 2010 (Le Goff and Singh, 2014). Third, we use private household consumption expenditure per capita as a proxy for poverty levels and a ratio of agricultural value added to the summation of industries and service sector value added as proxy for rural–urban income inequalities in Africa. Fourth, this paper develops all the necessary steps for estimating the impact of trade liberalization on poverty in Africa.

The rest of the paper is structured as follows. The next section presents theoretical and empirical literature on trade openness and poverty. It then takes a detailed look at the channels through which trade policy could affect poverty levels. Section 3 presents the model's specifications, data sources and methodology used to estimate the potential effect of trade openness on the rate of poverty reduction in Africa. The data is analyzed in Section 4. The final section provides a conclusion and gives policy recommendations based on the results.

2. Literature review

Though many international trade theories exist (both old and newer ones that are more relevant in today's era of globalization), economic theory does not provide a framework for analyzing the effects on poverty due to trade reforms. Changes in trade policy can offer considerable opportunities to improve the living standards of poor households, but at the same time these changes can also increase their vulnerabilities to external shocks that have short- to medium-term adverse impacts. For example, changes in trade policy effect consumer prices, factor incomes or employment, productivity, economic growth, and government revenue and spending; all these are discussed in literature.

The theories are powerful but they fail to explain the impact of trade liberalization when other things such as non-tradable goods, specific factors or segmented labor markets are taken into account (Winters, 2002). Moreover, trade openness can have two counteracting effects. On the one hand, it induces the development of labor-intensive sectors and creates employment and incomes for a large part of the population in labor-endowed countries, particularly for the poor. But, on the other hand, openness in trade may hurt protected industries and their employment status, resulting in income distributional effects. To offset this and to ensure net overall gains, trade adjustment assistance is often recommended as reimbursement for losses arising due to trade liberalization (Cicowiez and Conconi, 2008).Therefore, properly addressing the impact of trade policy on the well-being of the poor needs a thorough investigation of its consequences and the possible channels for these effects to trickle down to the poor become a necessary step in this study.

Hence, the next section starts by reviewing the most common transmission channels developed by Winters et al. (2004). These are presented with some slight modifications; that is, the framework identifies four general channels through which trade reforms affect poverty. It first reviews the trade and growth poverty linkage. Second, it focuses on how poverty is affected by household consumption and production through changes in prices of goods and services. Third, it discusses the labor market through factor price, wage and employment, and how these channels are affected by government revenues and thus possibly the scope for more spending on the poor or where it leads to taxation that may put a disproportionate burden on the poor due to trade reforms. This will help us understand and identify the effect that trade liberalization has on the poor.

Economic growth and stability

Economists agree that economic growth is potentially the most important channel for reducing poverty and that trade might play an important role in this process of economic growth. To validate this argument, we first need to study the relationship between trade openness and economic growth, and then demonstrate how trade-induced economic growth might affect poverty in developing countries.

Theoretically, the relationship between trade openness and growth still remains ambiguous, particularly for developing countries that might not have comparative advantages in sectors that create dynamic gains from trade liberalization (Rodriguez and Rodrik, 2001). According to the Heckscher-Ohlin-Samuelson trade theory, the hypothesis of factor input mobility across sectors suggests that openness to international trade may generate substantial gains by reallocating resources between tradable and non-tradable sectors. Other theoretical models, however, suggest that free trade may hurt growth in incomes in underdeveloped or agrarian economies due to external competition and shocks.

Despite enormous empirical literature, there is still no general consensus concerning the relationship between trade openness and growth. A number of empirical studies show a positive and significant relationship. For example, according to Myint (1958), openness to international trade in developing economies provides an efficient means for overcoming the narrowness of the domestic market and provides an exit for extra products relative to domestic demand. Daumal and Özyurt (2010) show that an open economy can improve the skills and effectiveness of the labor force as it can learn by exporting hypotheses. Further, opening up to the external sector leads to the integration of an economy into global innovation and international marketing contacts, which provide ideas to local producers to innovate, imitate and develop new products.

Then again, Young (1991) argues about the positive effect of openness, asserting that trade liberalization made it possible for some economies to specialize in low value-added activities such as extraction and exploration of natural resources and production of primary goods. In effect, these non-dynamic sectors faced a low tendency for technological improvements, which was unfavorable in the long-run economic growth. Studies by Harrison (1996) and Rodriguez and Rodrik (2001) are also uncertain about the robustness and significance of the positive growth effects of openness. According to Rodriguez and Rodrik (2001) the various indicators of openness used by researchers are poor measures of indicators of trade barriers. After a methodological review of studies such as those by Ben-David (1993), Dollar (1992), Edwards (1998) and Sachs et al. (1995), they find little evidence that openness to international trade is significantly associated with economic growth.

Eriş and Ulaşan (2013) used the Bayesian model averaging techniques from a cross-section of countries over the period 1960–2000. Their results show no evidence that trade openness is directly and robustly correlated with economic growth in the long run. Similarly, Tekin (2012), using a panel of least developed countries (LDCs) using the Granger causality testing approach and taking into account cross-sectional dependence and slope heterogeneity, shows that there is no significant causality relation between openness to trade and economic growth. The results obtained by Amadou (2013) examined the causal relationship between openness and economic growth in the West African Economic and Monetary Union (WAEMU) countries and found that besides Côte d'Ivoire, trade openness did not lead to economic growth in WAEMU countries. A more recent study using a dynamic panel data framework by Ula an (2015) observes the openness–growth nexus using various openness indicators. His findings show that lower trade barriers are not linked to higher growth, implying that trade openness by itself does not enhance economic growth.

Therefore, in order to show how trade openness affects poverty via growth, one needs to examine how trade-induced economic growth affects poverty, a link which is very difficult to establish. In general, economic growth is necessary for reducing poverty, but it needs a complementary policy to do so. Poor people benefit from trade-induced economic growth when growth is distributed by a proper institution and when governments used policy interventions to facilitate employment-centered structural transformations of their economies as the most important stage (Dollar and Kraay, 2002, 2004).

Price transferring channels and accessibility of goods and services

Trade liberalization policies can affect the poor through the effects that tariff changes have on relative prices of goods and services. Price variations in goods and services affect poor people through direct and indirect ways, as these depend on a wide range of factors, including institutional, poor infrastructure, trade facilities, world price levels, exchange rates, domestic taxes and market integration over time and space. Therefore, the direct poverty impact of changes in prices mainly depends on whether households are net consumers or net producers of goods and services in the international market. The poor may also benefit from accessibility of goods and services due to relaxation and removal of export and import bans and duties in the international market. An open trade regime also permits imports of technologies that can help the poor in the production process, such as the provision of improved seeds and fertilizers, water purification chemicals, simple packaging processes for perishable goods and so on (Bannister and Thugge, 2001). However, there are also indirect effects that should be taken into consideration as price shocks are transmitted into other market and multiplier effects or have local spillovers. A decrease in prices will benefit net consumers and harm net producers and vice versa.

Labor markets: the factor price, income and employment link

Trade openness can affect households via factor prices, wages and employment. Winters et al. (2004) noticed that being employed was often a vital factor on whether an individual was considered poor or not since most individuals got their incomes from labor. Based on the traditional trade theory of the Heckscher-Ohlin model, if labor-intensive countries export labor, an augmented demand will lead to an increased demand for labor (Krugman et al., 2016). Depending on the elasticity of labor supply, two extremes can occur in the labor market: an increase in demand will either lead to an increase in wages or an increase in the level of employment. However, there is also a possibility of something between these two extreme outcomes; that is, employment as well as wages might increase at the same time (Winters et al., 2004). Moreover, country studies show that labor is not as mobile from one sector to another, as the HO trade theory model assumes; for comparative advantages to increase incomes of unskilled labor, they need to be able to shift from contracting sectors to expanding sectors. Another explanation for why the poor may not gain from trade liberalization is that developing countries have historically protected sectors that use unskilled labor such as agriculture, textiles and apparel products.

The government revenue and spending channel

The effect of trade openness on a government's revenue losses has been identified as one of the key transmission channels for many developing countries (Winters et al., 2004). The share of trade taxes in total revenue is negatively associated with the level of economic development, with many low-income countries earning half or more of their revenues from trade taxes. However, the effect of trade reforms on government revenues is complex. If initial tariffs are prohibitively high, reducing them and eliminating non-tariff barriers can result in higher trade flows and reduce incentives for smuggling and corruption, thus boosting revenues. Simplifying tariff rules to create a more homogeneous structure, with just a few tariff rates, improves collective efficiency, which could increase government tax revenues.

The government may use alternative sources of revenue to compensate for the losses due to tariff reduction, such as value added tax and widening the tax base, because of which the poor may be adversely affected (Hertel and Reimer, 2005). Empirical evidence indicates that developing countries have not managed to fully recover lost tariff revenues. But empirical evidence that links trade openness with poverty levels has found contrasting results depending on the methodology and country studied. Keen and Baunsgaard (2005) analyzed data on tax revenues in a search for evidence on whether countries actually recovered the revenues lost from other sources during past episodes of trade liberalization. They found that high-income countries had clearly done so and that for middle-income countries, the recovery was of the order of 45–60 per cent.

3. Data, variables and model specifications

This section describes and defines the data used for empirical results of poverty and trade liberalization, rural–urban inequalities, other control variables and the sources of the data. It also explains in detail the model specifications and the econometric technique used.

3.1 Data and definition of variables

Several sources were used to collect data for this study, of which the major ones were the World Development Indicators (The World Bank, 2015a) and the United Nations Conference on Trade and Development (UNCTAD, 2015). Institutional variables were collected from World Governance Indicators (The World Bank, 2015b). The period and the number of countries included in this study were dictated by the availability of consistent time series data for all the countries. Therefore, the final data covers a balanced panel of 42 African countries over the period 1996–2014. The selected countries are listed in Appendix A. The study includes the following variables.

Household consumption expenditure per capita (proxy for poverty)

There are many definitions and measures of poverty, but the most popular indicator is the poverty headcount index, which measures the percentage of the population living with consumption or income per person below a certain poverty line. It is a measure of absolute poverty. Another popular measure is the poverty gap, which measures the mean distance below the poverty line as a proportion of the poverty line. However, due to lack of time series data on the above poverty line variables, in this study we use private household consumption expenditure per capita as a proxy for poverty (LHCEPP).[1] This measure is consistent with the World Bank's definition of poverty as 'the inability to attain a minimal standard of living' measured in terms of basic consumption needs (The World Bank, 1990). Moreover, consumption expenditure among the poor is usually more reliably reported and more stable than income (Datt and Ravallion, 1992; Odhiambo, 2009, 2010; Quartey, 2008).

Trade openness

Trade share in GDP (that is, (Exports + Import)/GDP) is the most commonly used proxy for trade openness, as the trade performance of countries captures the most important dimension of openness in general. However, we define trade openness in real terms and in logarithms (LTO)[2] (that is, trade openness based on constant 2005 US dollars). Trade openness appears to be beneficial for economic growth on average; its effect varies considerably across countries and depends on a variety of conditions related to the structure of the economy and its institutions. For robustness checking we used the log of merchandise trade as percentage of GDP (LMTG) as proxy for trade openness.

Rural–urban inequalities (RUI)

This is measured by the ratio of agricultural value added to summation of industrial and service value added as share of GDP, a measure of rural–urban income inequality (LRUI).[3] The ratio of agricultural to industrial value added as a share of GDP has also been used by Baliamoune-Lutz and Lutz (2004), Shahbaz et al. (2007) and Tiwari et al. (2013) as proxy for rural–urban income inequalities.

Economic growth

To measure economic growth, we used the log of real GDP per capita (LRGDP) (PGDP, constant at 2005 US dollars).

Control variables

We used additional control variables that are commonly used in household consumption expenditure equations. The first one is inflation to control macroeconomic instability. Inflation is a factor that is worsening poverty because it reduces the purchasing power of all individuals, but it is more harmful for the poor and the middle-income class than it is for the rich class because wealthy individuals can reduce their risks by hedging their exposure to inflationary situations by accessing financial services (see Easterly and Fischer, 2001; Kpodar and Singh, 2011). This is measured by consumer price changes (annual per cent) (CPIG) available in the World Bank database. The second variable is foreign direct investment (FDI) as a spillover effect of foreign production and consumption behavior in the domestic market.

3.2 *Model specification*

Based on this review and following the frameworks posited by Berg and Krueger (2003), Dollar and Kraay (2002) and Ghura et al. (2002), as well as using the basic trade-growth-poverty model use by Ravallion (2005) and Ravallion and Chen (1997) and empirical works of Agénor (2004, 2005), Anyanwu and Erhijakpor (2009, 2010), and Islam (2004), the relationship that we want to estimate is a classical poverty model, which is represented for a country i at time t as:

$$Pov_{it} = f(TO_{it}, RUI, RGDP_{it}, X_{it}). \tag{1}$$

The simple linear functional formulation of Eq. 1 is represented as:

$$\begin{aligned} \text{In } Pov_{it} = \alpha + \beta_i \text{ In } TO_{it} + \phi_i \text{ In } RUI_{it} + \beta_j \text{ In } RGDP_{it} + \\ \theta_k \text{ In } X_{it} + \gamma_t + \mu_i + \varepsilon_{it} \end{aligned} \tag{2}$$

where i and t represent country and time period, respectively. In Pov_{it} is log real per capita household consumption expenditure as a proxy for the poverty level for country i at time t. In TO_{it} is trade openness (that is, log of per cent of exports and imports to GDP) for country i at time t. In RUI_{it} is rural–urban income inequality (measured as agricultural to the summation of industrial and service value added as share of GDP); to measure economic growth we used real GDP per capita (ln PGDP, constant at 2005 US dollar) for country i at time t. X_{it} is a vector of control variables for country i at time t. γ_t and μ_i correspond to time effects and unobserved country-specific effects, respectively. Finally, ε_{it} is the regression error term.

4. Econometric methodology

This section discusses the estimation methods that address major potential problems of a long macro-econometrics panel model in this study. First, the panel dataset has a reasonably long time dimension and thus non-stationarity of the variables in the model needs to be addressed. In addition, since this is a macroeconomic panel data study on poverty, where many of the determinants cannot be included due to data availability, these effects need to be controlled for to avoid omitted variable bias. We also discuss methods to allow the effects of explanatory variables and unobserved common factors to vary across countries to fulfill the aims of this study.

Exemplarily, for a poverty model, we consider the equation:

$$y_{it} = \underbrace{\alpha_i CO_t + \theta_i z_{it}}_{\beta_i x_{it}} + \underbrace{\gamma_i CUO_t + \varepsilon_{it}}_{\mu_{it}}. \tag{3}$$

where y_{it} is the vector of dependent variable, x_{it} be the matrix of explanatory variables which is composed of a vector of observed individual specific regressor and common observable variables represented by z_{it} and CO_t, respectively. And

β_i are the country parameters for the variables of x_{it}. Moreover, the error term μ_{it} is determined by the vector of unobserved common factors and white noise error term. α_i ***and*** γ_i are country specific factor loadings associated with the common observable and common unobservable, respectively. If the common observable and common unobservable factors are correlated, then an endogeneity problem arises and we end up with inconsistent and biased estimates, as the coefficient β_i is not properly identified.

Therefore, we discuss the estimation of model 3 by using two different econometric models; that is, restricting the vector of coefficients to be homogeneous and allowing it to vary across countries (heterogeneous slope). First, it can be seen that the Pooled OLS (POLS) estimator uses conventional least squares regression based on pooling all the observations without considering country-specific effects, which could lead to biased estimates. In addition, in POLS estimates, the effects of explanatory variables x_{it} are restricted to be constant across countries ($\beta_i = \beta$). Unobserved common factors (CUO_t) might be taken into account by introducing time dummies into the POLS regression model. However, the time dummies can only capture common shocks to log of household consumption expenditure per capita (LPOV) that have the same effects across countries, and thus the effects of CUO_t on LPOV are constrained to be homogeneous across countries ($\gamma_i = \gamma$) in POLS estimates.

Second, in the fixed effects (FE) and random effects (RE) estimators, time-invariant country-specific effects are taken into account and treated as fixed and random in the regression, respectively. To decide between the FE and RE estimators, we can run a Hausman test, where the null hypothesis is that the preferred model is RE versus the alternative being FE. However, in the FE and RE estimators, the slope parameters of x_{it} are constrained to be identical across countries ($\beta_i = \beta$). In addition, as in the Pooled OLS estimation, CUO_t may be taken into account by including time dummies in the FE and RE regression models, and thus the influence of CUO_t on poverty is restricted to be constant across countries ($\gamma_i = \gamma$) by both the FE and RE estimators.

However, the POLS estimator as well as the fixed effect and random effect models encounter a number of econometric issues with the large macro panel dataset. All estimators fail to account for the presence of cross-section dependence and parameter heterogeneity across the countries. Hence, to address the problem of cross-section dependence and the issue of parameter heterogeneity, we apply a different set of novel methods, including the mean group (MG) estimator (Pesaran and Smith, 1995), the common correlated effects mean group (CCEMG) estimator (Pesaran, 2006) and the augmented mean group (AMG) estimator (Bond and Eberhardt, 2013; Eberhardt and Bond, 2009; Eberhardt and Teal, 2010). The MG method applies time-series ordinary least squares (OLS) to each panel (or country in this paper) separately, including an intercept to capture fixed effects and a linear trend to capture time-variant unobservables. The method then averages the estimated individual-specific slopes with or without weights. In the dynamic case, when the coefficients are heterogeneous across groups, the MG estimators are consistent for large T and N (Pesaran and Smith, 1995). But still the MG estimator does not incorporate any information on common factors that may be present in the panel dataset. Common factors are time-specific effects that are common across countries. By adding the cross-section averages of the dependent and independent variables as additional regressors when applying OLS to each unit, the common correlated effects mean group (CCEMG) estimator allows for cross-sectional dependence and time-variant unobservables with heterogeneous impact across panel members (Pesaran, 2006). Represented by these cross-sectional averages, the unobserved common factors can be any fixed number. With satisfactory small sample properties and a robust estimator of short-run dynamics, the CCEMG estimator is also very robust to structural breaks, non-stationary and non-cointegrated common factors and certain serial correlations (Kapetanios et al., 2011). As an alternative approach, the augmented mean group (AMG) approach first estimates a pooled model augmented with year dummies by first-order difference OLS. Estimators on the year dummies are collected to form a new variable that represents the common dynamic process and is used as an additional regressor for each group-specific regression model apart from an intercept to capture time-invariant fixed effects. Like the CCEMG estimator, AMG also deals with non-stationary variables and multifactor error terms, especially taking into account cross-sectional dependence (Bond and Eberhardt, 2013; Eberhardt and Bond, 2009).

The advantage of the AMG approach over the CCEMG approach is treating the set of unobservable common factors as a common dynamic process that, depending upon the context, may have useful interpretations instead of being treated as a nuisance. In addition, Bond and Eberhardt (2013) using Monte Carlo simulations showed that the AMG estimator is unbiased and commonly most efficient for different combinations of N and T. However, the MG estimators found that the bias of the MG estimator increases in T and decreases in N. This implies that this estimator is more suitable for a panel where $N > T$.

In our study we also report the estimations result by POLS, dynamic FE and RE estimators (Appendix B) and the MG, CCEMG and AMG estimators for robustness checks. Before estimating the standard panel model that is a vector of homogeneous coefficients and the newly developed model that assumes there is heterogeneous coefficient across the panel, three vital steps are needed in the empirical estimation. First, a cross-sectional dependency test to determine if unobserved common factors need to be accounted for in the estimation process and to decide an appropriate unit root test. Second, a panel unit root test to determine the time series properties of the data. Last, selecting an appropriate estimation technique based on the result of the cross-sectional test and panel unit root test.

4.1 Cross-sectional dependence test

In order to determine the presence of cross-sectional dependence (hereafter CD) in our data, we implement the simple test suggested by Pesaran (2004). The test statistical is based on the correlation coefficient between the time series for each of the panel members on all of the variables. The CD test is based on an average of all pair-wise correlations of the ordinary least squares (OLS) residuals from the individual regressions in the panel data model:

$$y_{it} = \alpha_i + \beta_i x_{it} + \mu_{it} \tag{4}$$

where y_{it} is the dependent variable, ($i = 1, \ldots, N$), N is the number of panel members, ($t = 1, \ldots, T$) is time period and x_{it} is the vector of observed explanatory variables. α_i and β_i refer to the intercepts and the slope coefficients are allowed to vary across the panel members.

The Pesaran (2004) CD-test statistic can generally be expressed as:

$$CD = \sqrt{\frac{2T}{N(N-1)}}\left(\sum_{i=1}^{N-1}\sum_{j=i+1}^{N}\hat{\rho}_{ij}\right) \rightarrow N(0,1). \tag{5}$$

where $\hat{\rho}_{ij}$ refers to the sample estimate of the pair-wise correlation of the OLS residuals, μ_{it} associated with Eq. 4:

$$\hat{\rho}_{ij} = \frac{\sum_{t=1}^{T}\hat{\mu}_{it}\hat{\mu}_{jt}}{\sqrt{\sum_{t=1}^{T}\hat{\mu}_{it}^2}\sqrt{\sum_{t=1}^{T}\hat{\mu}_{jt}^2}} = \hat{\rho}_{ji}. \tag{6}$$

The null hypothesis for this test is cross-sectional independence, and under this the statistic is distributed as standard normal for $T > 3$ and large value (Pesaran, 2004). The CD-test statistic from various simulations shows it is robust to non-stationarity, structural breaks, parameter heterogeneity and, above all, performs well in small samples. This test is applicable both to the variables and also to the estimated residuals.

4.2 *Panel unit root tests*

Before proceeding to the panel estimation methods, this study needs to discuss unit root tests that will be applied in the empirical analysis to check for stationarity of the variables using first and second generation of panel unit root tests. From the former, the IPS panel unit root test (Im et al., 2003; Maddala and Wu, 1999) and, from the latter, the CIPS panel test (Pesaran, 2007) were generated that take into account cross-sectional dependence among panel members used in this study.

4.2.1 *Panel unit root tests without cross-sectional dependence*

THE IM-PESARAN-SHIN (IPS) TEST

Im, Pesaran and Shin (hereafter IPS), proposed a test for the presence of unit roots in panels that combines information from the time series dimension with that from the cross-section dimension, such that fewer time observations are required for the test to have power. Since the IPS test has been found to have superior test powers by researchers in economics to analyze long-run relationships in panel data, we also employed this procedure in this study. IPS begins by specifying a separate Augmented Dickey-Fuller (ADF) regression for each cross-section with individual effects and no time trend:

$$\Delta y_{it} = \alpha_i + \rho_i y_{i,t-1} + \sum_{j=1}^{p_i} \beta_{ij} \Delta y_{i,t-j} + \varepsilon_{i,t} \tag{7}$$

where $i = 1, \ldots, N$, $t = 1, \ldots, T$ and yi,t stand for each series under consideration for the country i at time t. The null hypothesis is that all series contain a unit root, $\rho_i = 1$ for all i (with $i = 1, 2, \ldots, N$), while the alternative hypothesis assumes that some of the N panel units are stationary with individual specific autoregressive coefficients.

Im et al. (2003) propose a test based on the average of the ADF statistics computed for each individual in the panel. Specifically, the IPS statistic is based on the ADF statistics averaged across groups. Let $t_{i,T}(i = 1, 2 \ldots, N)$ denote the t-statistics for testing for unit root in individual series i, and let $E(t_{i,T}) = \mu$ and $V(t_{i,T}) = \sigma^2$. Then:

$$\bar{t}_{N,T} = \frac{1}{N}\sum_{i=1}^{N} t_{iT} \text{ and } \sqrt{N}\frac{\left(\bar{t}_{N,T} - \mu\right)}{\sigma} \overset{N}{\Rightarrow} N(0,1). \tag{8}$$

The t-bar is then standardized and it is shown that the standardized *t-bar* statistic converges to the standard normal distribution as N and $T \to \infty$ and under the assumption of cross-sectional independence.

MADDALA AND WU TEST

Maddala and Wu (hereafter MW) (1999) propose a panel unit root test that allows for the autoregressive coefficients to vary across panels. In particular, this test combines the significance levels of individual Phillips-Perron or ADF unit root tests for each cross-section i to construct an overall test statistic based on a test suggested by Fisher (1932):

$$\lambda = -2\sum\nolimits_{i=1}^{N} \ln \phi_i. \tag{9}$$

where ϕ_i is the p-value of a unit root test for country i.

This is used to test the null hypothesis that all panels have a unit root versus the alternative hypothesis that at least one panel is stationary. Since $(-2\ln \phi_i)$ is distributed as χ^2 with two degrees of freedom, λ has a χ^2 distribution with $2N$ degrees of freedom where N denotes the number of panels.

4.2.2 *Panel unit root tests with cross-sectional dependence*

Both the IPS and MW tests are based on the restrictive assumption that the series are independent across country i, suffer from serious size distortions and restricted power in the presence of cross-sectional dependence. In order to overcome this, Pesaran (2007) (hereafter CIPS) suggests a simple approach that controls for the possible presence of cross-section dependence.

The null hypothesis in this test is that all panels (here, countries) have a unit root against the alternative hypothesis that a fraction of panels are stationary. In particular, the method of this test is based on augmenting the standard ADF regression with the cross-section averages of lagged levels and first-differences of the individual series to capture cross-sectional dependence. Pesaran calls this a cross-sectionally augmented Dickey-Fuller (CADF) test. The simple CADF regression used for the ith cross-section unit is defined as:

$$\Delta y_{it} = \alpha_i + \rho_i y_{i,t-1} + \theta_i \overline{y}_{i,t-i} + \sum_{j=0}^{p_i} \beta_{ij} \Delta \overline{y}_{i,t-j} + \sum_{j=1}^{p_i} \beta_{ij} \Delta y_{i,t-j} + \varepsilon_{it}. \tag{10}$$

where $\overline{y}_{t-1} = N^{-1} \sum_{i=1}^{N} y_{i,t-1}$ *and* $\Delta \overline{y}_t = N^{-1} \sum_{i=1}^{N} y_{i,t} = \overline{y}_t - \overline{y}_{t-1}$. The CIPS test is based on the average of individual cross-sectionally ADF statistic (CADF) as:

$$CIPS = \frac{1}{N} \sum_{i=1}^{N} t_i (N,T). \tag{11}$$

Simulated critical values of CIPS are listed in Pesaran (2007). Baltagi et al. (2007) show that the CIPS test is found to be robust to the presence of other sources of cross-sectional dependence such as the spatial form.

5. Empirical results

At the first stage of the analysis the study tested for cross-sectional dependence and then to avoid the possibility of spurious regressions the properties of the variables needed to be checked. In order to perform an analysis of sensitivity and robustness, this study employed first generation panel unit root tests of Im et al. (2003) and Maddala and Wu (1999) and second generation panel unit root test of Pesaran (2007; CIPS).

The results of the CD test are given in Table 8.1. These results clearly show that the null hypothesis of cross-sectional independence is rejected at the 1 per cent significance level for all variables.

Table 8.1 Average correlation coefficients and the Pesaran (2004) CD test

Variables	*CD-Test*	*P-value*
Household consumption expenditure per capita in log (LHCEPC)	101.08	0.000
Trade openness as percentage of GDP in log (LTO)	22.58	0.000
Rural–urban income inequalities in log (LRUI)	37.63	0.000
Real GDP per capital in log (LRGDP)	59.5	0.000
Consumer price index growth (inflation) (CPIG)	24.32	0.000
Foreign direct investment as % GDP in log (FDIG)	8.85	0.000
Merchandise trade as percentage of GDP (MTG)	31.7	0.000
Real GDP growth (constant 2005 USD) (RGDPG)	5.84	0.000

Note: Under the null hypothesis of cross-section independence CD ~ N(0,1)

Table 8.2 Pesaran (2007) panel unit root test (CIPS)

Variable	*without trend* *P-value*	*with trend* *P-value*
Log HH consumption expenditure per capital (LHCEPC)	0.000	0.000
Log of trade openness index (LTO)	0.005	0.642
Log of rural–urban income inequalities (LRUI)	0.000	0.032
Log of real GDP per capital (LRGDP)	0.996	0.885
Consumer price index growth (CPIG)	0.000	0.000
Log of foreign direct investment (% of LFDI)	0.000	0.002
Log of life expectancy for both males and females (LLEXB)	0.000	0.001
First difference of LTO and LRGDPC		
DLTO	0.000	0.000
DLRGDPC	0.000	0.000

Note: Pesaran (2007) runs a test for unit root in a heterogeneous panel with cross-sectional dependence. The null hypothesis assumes that all series are non-stationary.

Hence, among the three unit root tests, the CIPS results are preferred because this test allows for the heterogeneity of autoregressive coefficients across panels and can control for cross-sectional dependence (Pesaran, 2007).

The results reported in Table 8.2 show that the log variables at levels of all variables are stationary at the 1 per cent significance level except for two variables; that is, log trade openness (LTO) and log of real gross domestic product (LRGDP). When we take the first difference, it becomes stationary.

In order to check the stationarity of the variables at appropriate critical values of the unit root test statistic, our study plotted trade openness and gross domestic product variables over time to determine the correct panel unit root test with or without a trend. If the unit root test does not specify the deterministic terms correctly, then this may lead to an over- or under-rejection of the null hypothesis.

As we can see from Figure 8.1, both variables seem to be trended, and thus our study focuses on tests with trend values. The results of these tests are reported in Table 8.2. The results of CIPS tests reject that the variables have a unit root at the 1 per cent significance level.

For a dynamic model with homogeneous slope using Pooled OLS (POLS), random effects (RE) and fixed effects (FE), estimated results are presented in Appendix B. The estimated dynamic models in cases of heterogeneous slopes were estimated using recently developed techniques including mean group (MG), common correlated effects mean group (CCEMG) and augmented mean group (AMG). The estimators are given in Table 8.3.

The predicted residual from POLS, RE and FE estimations found that the results of the CIPS and CD tests did not reject the hypothesis[4] of the presence of a unit root and cross-sectional dependence, implying that the conventional panel data estimation regression results are inconsistent and biased. Therefore, we need an estimation technique that takes into account parameter heterogeneity and cross-section dependence along with allowing for non-stationary properties.

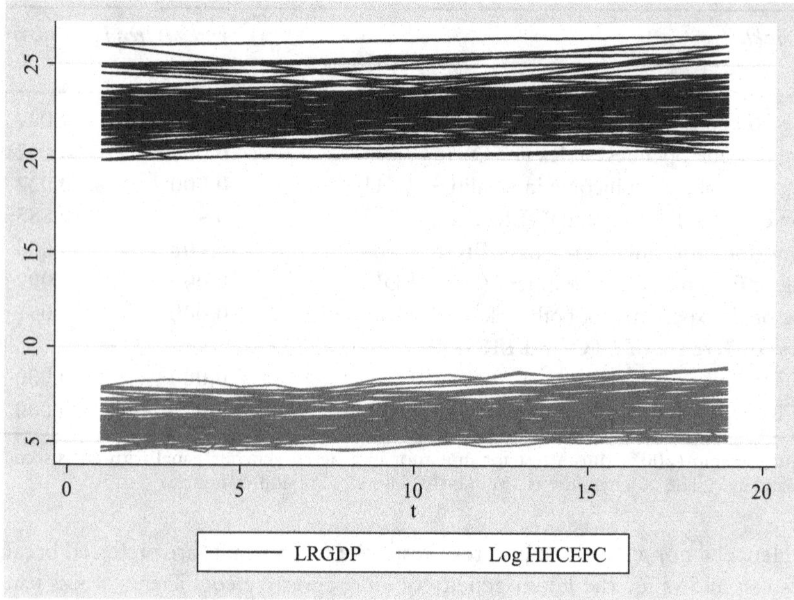

Figure 8.1 Poverty and trade openness trend over time

Table 8.3 Dynamic heterogeneous estimation results

Variables	*MG*		*CCEMG*		*AMG*	
	Coef	*se*	*Coef*	*Se*	*Coef*	*Se*
LHCEPC(-1)	0.372***	0.044	0.364***	0.033	0.495***	0.039
DLTO	-0.342***	0.110	-0.222***	0.074	-0.247***	0.058
LRUI	-0.034	0.085	-0.174***	0.066	-0.072	0.048
CPIG	0.004	0.003	-0.002**	0.001	-0.003***	0.001
DLRGDP	1.447***	0.117	0.745***	0.175	0.291***	0.089
c_d_p					1.043***	0.075
CD P-value	0.001		0.157		0.125	
N	718		718		718	
RMSE	0.0911		0.0290		0.0518	
_cons	-25.972***	2.395	-11.064***	2.368	1.105	1.941

Notes:
1. Author's calculations based on secondary data
2. ***, **, and * level of significance 1%, 5% and 10%, respectively

Hence, in this study we applied mean group (MG) estimator (Pesaran and Smith, 1995), the common correlated effects mean group (CCEMG) estimator (Pesaran, 2006) and the augmented mean group (AMG) estimator (Bond and Eberhardt, 2013; Eberhardt and Bond, 2009; Eberhardt and Teal, 2010).

As a way to compare the MG, CCEMG and AMG models, the root mean squared error (RMSE) is provided for all cases. Based on the results presented in Table 8.3, the root mean square errors (RMSE) of MG and AMG methods were generally larger than their corresponding estimate using CCEMG. Moreover, the MG estimator was less satisfactory because it did not technically address the residual cross-sectional dependence. Therefore, the CCEMG and AMG models have a better fit than the MG model.

The results of CCEMG estimation (Table 8.3) show that the estimated coefficient of all the variables included the trade openness index (export plus import per GDP), rural–urban inequalities (the ratio of agricultural value added per the summation of industry and service value added), the economy size (real gross domestic product 2005 US dollar) and inflation (the consumer price index growth, CPIG), which were significant at the 1 per cent level. The elasticities of trade openness index (DLTO), rural–urban inequalities (LRUI), inflation (CIPG) and real gross domestic product (DLRGDP) were -0.222, -0.174, -0.002 and 0.745, respectively. This estimated result implies that a 1 per cent increase in trade openness, rural–urban inequalities and inflation, on average, decreases the household consumption expenditure per capita by 0.22, 0.17 and 0.002 per cent, respectively, whereas, a 1 per cent increase real gross domestic product, on average, increases the household consumption expenditure per capita by 0.75 per cent.

One of the advantages of the CCEMG estimator is that it is possible to see the effect of the explanatory variable on the outcome variables in specific countries. As we can see from Table 8.4 and Figure 8.1 the coefficient on trade openness

Table 8.4 Country-specific significant coefficients only on trade openness, rural–urban inequality and gross domestic product

No.	*Countries*	*DLTO*	*Countries*	*DLRGD*	*Countries*	*LRUI*
1	Benin	-0.3***	Benin	2.4***	Botswana	-0.66***
2	Burkina Faso	-0.33***	Burkina F	2.9***	Cameroon	-0.68***
3	Chad	0.61***	Ethiopia	2.31***	Chad	0.24***
4	Congo, DR	0.59***	Kenya	-2.94***	Congo, DR	-1.02***
5	Congo, Rep.	-1.21***	Madagascar	1.73***	Ghana	-1.14***
6	Egypt,	-0.8***	Mauritius	1.3***	Guinea	-0.76***
7	Ethiopia	-1.1***	Rwanda	1.74***	Mauritius	-0.32***
8	Gambia, The	-0.95***	Seychelles	1.29***	Seychelles	-0.96***
9	Madagascar	-0.55***	Togo	1.06***	Uganda	-0.39***
10	Mozambique	-0.95***	Uganda	0.94***	Kenya	0.62**
11	Uganda	-0.65***	Cameroon	0.91**	Madagascar	-1.01**
12	Guinea-Bissau	-0.71**	Congo, Rep.	2.02**	Rwanda	0.4*
13	Namibia	0.28*	Malawi	0.86**		
14	Seychelles	-0.24*	Chad	0.45*		
15	Togo	-0.42*	Congo, DR	1.83*		
16			Niger	-0.53*		

Note: ***, **, and * level of significance 1%, 5% and 10%, respectively

index ranged from -1.21 for the Democratic Republic of Congo to 0.61 for Chad, and the coefficient for rural–urban inequalities varied from -1.14 for Ghana to 0.61 for Kenya. Likewise, the coefficient of gross domestic product varied from -2.94 for Kenya up to 2.9 for Burkina Faso (also see Appendix C).

6. Conclusions and policy recommendations

While trade liberalization has been well established in literature as an important component of growth and poverty reduction strategies in developing countries, both theoretically and empirically, its impact on poverty is ambiguous. This study attempted to fill this gap by examining the differential impact of trade liberalization and rural–urban inequalities on poverty in African countries using the recently developed methodology by the common correlated effects mean group (CCEMG) estimator (Pesaran, 2006) and the augmented mean group (AMG) estimator (Bond and Eberhardt, 2013; Eberhardt and Bond, 2009; Eberhardt and Teal, 2010) for a panel of 42 African countries over the period 1996–2014. The findings of this research show that, on average, trade liberalization did not seem to be associated with lower poverty, while rural–urban inequalities were significantly and negatively associated with poverty. Moreover, the impact of trade openness on poverty varied from country to country; therefore the one-policy-fits-all approach will not work in Africa.

These results are consistent with recent literature, which argues that the benefits of trade liberalization are not automatic and that policies that accompany the opening of trade are needed. These policies should aim at encouraging innovations and investments in human capital, attracting FDI, providing effective resolution to conflicts and governance, and having the ability to adjust and learn new skills. This accompanying policy agenda will allow resources to be reallocated away from less productive activities to more promising ones.

Therefore, trade liberalization should not be seen in isolation and additional policies will be needed to enhance its impact, including on poverty. This also means that poor policies and institutions, weak human capital and limited financial development not only have a direct negative effect on countries' welfare, they also prevent the poor in developing countries from benefiting from the gains of trade liberalization.

In order to minimize the negative effects of trade openness on poverty in the short run and ensure that the impact reverses into positive outcomes, trade openness needs to be accompanied by a range of supporting reforms that enable growth, prices, firms and labor to adjust easily within a more dynamic and competitive global environment. Even though there have been policies to increase economic and export growth, Africa's economic growth performance has been mediocre as evaluated by similar developing countries' economies. This is one of the main reasons why the countries have failed to create adequate economic growth to reduce poverty in Africa. Africa's trade performance is relatively low due to various factors such as weak institutional set-ups, low infrastructure, lack of skilled labor and high costs of intermediate inputs. All of these factors need to be considered to ensure sustainable economic and export growth. Moreover, an improved international price competitiveness policy the designing of appropriate policies to ensure that lower international prices are passed on to poor consumers and the speeding up of labor market adjustments policies in each country depending on country-specific characteristics are also needed.

Appendices

Appendix A List of African countries included in the study

Algeria	Malawi
Benin	Mali
Botswana	Mauritania
Burkina Faso	Mauritius
Burundi	Morocco
Cameroon	Mozambique
Central African Republic	Namibia
Chad	Niger
Congo, Dem. Rep.	Nigeria
Congo, Rep.	Rwanda
Cote d'Ivoire	Senegal
Egypt, Arab Rep.	Seychelles
Ethiopia	Sierra Leone
Gabon	South Africa
Gambia, The	Sudan
Ghana	Swaziland
Guinea	Tanzania
Guinea-Bissau	Togo
Kenya	Tunisia
Lesotho	Uganda
Madagascar	Zimbabwe

Appendix B Dynamic homogeneous estimation results using POLS, RE and FE

Variables	*POLS*		*RE*		*FE*		*POLS*		*RE*		*FE*	
	Coef	*Se*	*Coef*	*Se*	*Coef*	*Se*	*Coef*	*Se*	*Coef*	*Se*	*Coef*	*Se*
LPOV(−1)	0.940***	0.012	0.940***	0.012	0.806***	0.022	0.944***	0.012	0.944***	0.012	0.820***	0.021
DLTO	−0.243***	0.039	−0.243***	0.039	−0.261***	0.038						
DLMTG							−0.318***	0.033	−0.318***	0.033	−0.311***	0.033
KOF	0.004***	0.001	0.004***	0.001	0.009***	0.002	0.004***	0.001	0.004***	0.001	0.008***	0.002
DLRGDP	0.705***	0.124	0.705***	0.124	0.566***	0.128	0.767***	0.119	0.767***	0.119	0.628***	0.124
LRUI	−0.027***	0.008	−0.027***	0.008	−0.088***	0.027	−0.025***	0.008	−0.025***	0.008	−0.096***	0.026
GOVEFF	0.058***	0.010	0.058***	0.010	0.079***	0.015	0.053***	0.010	0.053***	0.010	0.067***	0.015
DLPOP	−2.247***	0.781	−2.247***	0.781	−1.423	1.077	−2.074***	0.752	−2.074***	0.752	−1.383	1.042
LFDIG	0.020	0.019	0.020	0.019	0.032	0.023	0.022	0.018	0.022	0.018	0.029	0.022
LLEXB	0.046	0.046	0.046	0.046	0.244*	0.131	0.045	0.045	0.045	0.045	0.249*	0.127
LRODA	0.000	0.006	0.000	0.006	0.011	0.012	0.001	0.005	0.001	0.005	0.006	0.012
CD P-value	0.000		0.000		0.000		0.000		0.965		0.000	
CIPS P-val	0.000		0.000		0.001							
_cons	−0.019	0.193	−0.019	0.193	−0.521	0.459	−0.042	0.186	−0.042	0.186	−0.521	0.444

Notes:
1. Authors' calculations based on secondary data
2. *, ** and *** indicate statistical significance at 10%, 5% and 1%, respectively
3. The null hypothesis of CIPS is non-stationary
4. The CD test shows that residuals are cross-sectional dependent

Appendix C Country-specific coefficients on trade openness, rural–urban inequalities and GDP

No.	*Countries*	*DLTO*	*LRU*	*LRGD*	*No.*	*Countries*	*DLTO*	*LRU*	*LRGD*
1	Algeria	−0.2	0.0	0.5	22	Malawi	−0.06	−0.23	0.86**
2	Benin	−0.3***	−0.1	2.4***	23	Mali	0.91	−0.50	0.04
3	Botswana	0.6	−0.7***	−1.1	24	Mauritania	−0.24	−0.03	0.66
4	Burkina Faso	−0.3***	−0.7	2.9***	25	Mauritius	−0.45	−0.32***	1.30***
5	Burundi	−0.1	−0.4	1.4	26	Morocco	0.50	−0.58	0.68
6	Cameroon	0.0	−0.7***	0.9**	27	Mozambique	−0.95***	0.04	0.82
7	CAF	−0.3	0.0	0.5	28	Namibia	0.28*	−0.02	0.11
8	Chad	0.6***	0.2***	0.5*	29	Niger	−0.16	−0.01	−0.53*
9	Congo, Dem. Rep.	0.6***	−1.0***	1.8*	30	Nigeria	−0.14	0.08	−0.46
10	Congo, Rep.	−1.2***	0.0	2.0**	31	Rwanda	0.40	−0.33*	1.74***
11	Cote d'Ivoire	0.5	−0.1	0.3	32	Senegal	1.11	−0.16	3.95
12	Egypt, Arab Rep.	−0.8***	−0.2	−0.5	33	Seychelles	−0.24*	−0.96***	1.29***
13	Ethiopia	−1.1***	−0.9	2.3***	34	Sierra Leone	−0.14	−0.50	0.37
14	Gabon	−0.2	0.0	0.3	35	South Africa	0.04	0.00	0.41
15	Gambia, The	−1.0***	−0.1	0.4	36	Sudan	−0.21	0.22	−1.82
16	Ghana	−0.5	−1.1***	2.0	37	Swaziland	−0.09	−0.15	−0.53
17	Guinea	−0.3	−0.8***	0.8	38	Tanzania	−0.08	0.00	−0.51
18	Guinea-Bissau	−0.7**	0.0	1.5	39	Togo	−0.42*	0.02	1.06***
19	Kenya	−0.5	0.6**	−2.9***	40	Tunisia	−0.36	0.13	0.54
20	Lesotho	−0.3	0.3	0.6	41	Uganda	−0.65***	−0.39****	0.94***
21	Madagascar	−0.6***	−1.0**	1.7***	42	Zimbabwe	−0.38	−0.26	0.92

Note: ****, *** and * represents 1%, 5% and 10% level of significance

Notes

1 Log of private household consumption expenditure per capita.
2 Log of trade openness.
3 Log of rural–urban income inequality.
4 From Appendix A, the *p*-value of Pesaran (2004) CD-test is near zero. This implies that the null hypothesis of cross-section independence is rejected.

Reference

Abuka, C.A., M. Atingi-Ego, J. Opolot, and P. Okello (2007). "Determinants of poverty vulnerability in Uganda", Institute for International Integration Studies, IIIS Discussion Paper 2003:203.

Agénor, P. (2004). "Macroeconomic adjustment and the poor: Analytical issues and cross-country evidence", *Journal of Economic Surveys*, 18, 351–408.

Agénor, P. (2005). "Unemployment-poverty tradeoffs", *Central Banking, Analysis, and Economic Policies Book Series*, 8, 115–165.

Amadou, A. (2013). "Is there a causal relation between trade openness and economic growth in the WAEMU countries?", *International Journal of Economics and Finance*, 5, 151.

Anyanwu, J. and A.E. Erhijakpor (2009). *The Impact of Road Infrastructure on Poverty Reduction in Africa, Poverty in Africa*. New York: Nova Science Publishers, pp. 1–40.

Anyanwu, J. and A.E. Erhijakpor (2010). "Do international remittances affect poverty in Africa?", *African Development Review*, 22, 51–91.

Baliamoune-Lutz, M. and S.H. Lutz (2004). Rural-Urban Inequality in Africa: A Panel Study of the Effects of Trade Liberalization and Financial Deepening. Journal of African Development, 57 (1), 1–19.

Baltagi, B.H., G. Bresson, and A. Pirotte (2007). "Panel unit root tests and spatial dependence", *Journal of Applied Econometrics*, 22, 339–360.

Bannister, G.J. and K. Thugge (2001). *International Trade and Poverty Alleviation*. Washington, DC: International Monetary Fund.

Beegle, K., L. Christiaensen, A. Dabalen, and I. Gaddis (2015). *Poverty in a Rising Africa: Overview*. Washington, DC: World Bank Group.

Ben-David, D. (1993). "Equalizing exchange: Trade liberalization and income convergence", *The Quarterly Journal of Economics*, 108, 653–679.

Berg, M.A. and A.O. Krueger (2003). "Trade, growth, and poverty: A selective survey", International Monetary Fund.

Bond, S. and M. Eberhardt (2013). "Accounting for unobserved heterogeneity in panel time series models", Mimeo, Nuffield College, University of Oxford.

Carneiro, F.G. and J.S. Arbache (2003). "The impacts of trade on the Brazilian labor market: A CGE model approach", *World Development*, 31, 1581–1595.

Cicowiez, M. and A. Conconi (2008). "Linking trade and pro-poor growth: A survey", *Trade and Poverty in the Developing World*, Washington, DC: Inter-American Development Bank, 7–29.

Datt, G. and M. Ravallion (1992). "Growth and redistribution components of changes in poverty measures: A decomposition with applications to Brazil and India in the 1980s", *Journal of Development Economics*, 38, 275–295.

Daumal, M. and S. Özyurt (2010). "The impact of international trade flows on economic growth in Brazilian states", *Review of Economics and Institutions*, 2(1), 1–25.

Dollar, D. (1992). "Outward-oriented developing economies really do grow more rapidly: Evidence from 95 LDCs, 1976–1985", *Economic Development and Cultural Change*, 40, 523–544.

Dollar, D. and A. Kraay (2002). "Growth is good for the poor", *Journal of Economic Growth*, 7, 195–225.

Dollar, D. and A. Kraay (2004). "Trade, growth, and poverty", *The Economic Journal*, 114, F22–F49.

Easterly, W. and S. Fischer (2001). "Inflation and the poor", *Journal of Money, Credit and Banking*, (33), 160–178.

Eberhardt, M. and S. Bond (2009). "Cross-section dependence in nonstationary panel models: A novel estimator", MPRA Discussion Paper 2009:17870.

Eberhardt, M. and F. Teal (2010). *Productivity Analysis in Global Manufacturing Production.* Oxford: University of Oxford.

Edwards, S. (1998). "Openness, productivity and growth: What do we really know?", *The Economic Journal*, 108, 383–398.

Eris, M.N. and B. Ulasan (2013). "Trade openness and economic growth: Bayesian model averaging estimate of cross-country growth regressions", *Economic Modelling*, 33, 867–883.

Evans, D. (2001). "Identifying winners and losers in Southern Africa from Global Trade Policy reform: Integrating findings from GTAP and Poverty case studies for a Zambian example", ESRC Development Economics/International Economics Conference, Nottingham University.

Fisher, R.A. (1932). *Statistical Method of Research Workers.* Edinburgh: Oliver and Boyd.

Ghura, D., C. Leite, and C.G. Tsangarides (2002). *Is Growth Enough? Macroeconomic Policy and Poverty Reduction.* Washington, DC: International Monetary Fund.

Harrison, G.W. (1996). "Openness and growth: A time-series, cross-country analysis for developing countries", *Journal of Development Economics*, 48, 419–447.

Harrison, G.W., T.F. Rutherford, and D.G. Tarr (2003). "Trade liberalization, poverty and efficient equity", *Journal of Development Economics*, 71, 97–128.

Hertel, T.W. and J.J. Reimer (2005). "Predicting the poverty impacts of trade reform", *Journal of International Trade & Economic Development*, 14, 377–405.

Im, K.S., M.H. Pesaran, and Y. Shin (2003). "Testing for unit roots in heterogeneous panels", *Journal of Econometrics*, 115, 53–74.

Islam, R. (2004). *The Nexus of Economic Growth, Employment and Poverty Reduction: An Empirical Analysis.* Geneva: International Labour Office: Recovery and Reconstruction Department.

Kapetanios, G., M.H. Pesaran, and T. Yamagata (2011). "Panels with non-stationary multifactor error structures", *Journal of Econometrics*, 160, 326–348.

Keen, M.M. and M.T. Baunsgaard (2005). *Tax Revenue and (or?) Trade Liberalization.* Washington, DC: International Monetary Fund.

Kpodar, K. and R.J. Singh (1 December 2011). "Does financial structure matter for poverty? Evidence from developing countries", Evidence from Developing Countries, World Bank Policy Research Working Paper Series.

Krugman, P.R., Obstfeld, M., & Melitz, M.J. (2015). *International Economics: Theory and Policy* (10th ed.). Boston: Pearson.

Le Goff, M. and R.J. Singh (2014). "Does trade reduce poverty? A view from Africa", *Journal of African Trade*, 1, 5–14.

Lofgren, H. (2000). "Trade reform and the poor in Morocco: A rural-urban general equilibrium analysis of reduced protection", *Earnings Inequality, Unemployment, and Poverty in the Middle East and North Africa*, 51–84.

Maddala, G.S. and S. Wu (1999). "A comparative study of unit root tests with panel data and a new simple test", *Oxford Bulletin of Economics and Statistics*, 61, 631–652.

Myint, H. (1958). "The 'classical theory' of international trade and the underdeveloped countries", *The Economic Journal*, 68, 317–337.

Odhiambo, N.M. (2009). "Finance-growth-poverty nexus in South Africa: A dynamic causality linkage", *The Journal of Socio-Economics*, 38, 320–325.

Odhiambo, N.M. (2010). "Is financial development a spur to poverty reduction? Kenya's experience", *Journal of Economic Studies*, 37, 343–353.

Pesaran, M.H. (2004). "General diagnostic tests for cross section dependence in panels", IZA Discussion Paper 2004:1240.

Pesaran, M.H. (2006). "Estimation and inference in large heterogeneous panels with a multifactor error structure", *Econometrica*, 74, 967–1012.

Pesaran, M.H. (2007). "A simple panel unit root test in the presence of cross-section dependence", *Journal of Applied Econometrics*, 22, 265–312.

Pesaran, M.H. and R. Smith (1995). "Estimating long-run relationships from dynamic heterogeneous panels", *Journal of Econometrics*, 68, 79–113.

Quartey, P. (2008). "Financial sector development, savings mobilization and poverty reduction in Ghana", in Peter Quartey (ed), *Financial Development, Institutions, Growth and Poverty Reduction.* Helsinki: NU WIDER, pp. 87–119.

Ravallion, M. (2005). "Inequality is bad for the poor", World Bank Policy Research Working Paper.

Ravallion, M. and S. Chen (1997). "What can new survey data tell us about recent changes in distribution and poverty?", *The World Bank Economic Review*, 11, 357–382.

Rodriguez, F. and D. Rodrik (2001). "Trade policy and economic growth: A sceptic's guide to the cross-national evidence", in Ben S. Bernanke and Kenneth S. Rogoff (eds.), *NBER Macroeconomics Annual 2000.* Cambridge and London: MIT Press, 261–338.

Sachs, J.D., A. Warner, A. Slund, and S. Fischer (1995). "Economic reform and the process of global integration", *Brookings Papers on Economic Activity*, (1), 1–118.

Shahbaz, M., A. Lodhi, and M.S. Butt (2007). "Financial development under the shade of globalization and financial institutions: The case of Pakistan", *Philippine Review of Economics*, 44(2), 125–148.

Tekin, R.B. (2012). "Development aid, openness to trade and economic growth in least developed countries: Bootstrap panel Granger causality analysis", *Procedia-Social and Behavioral Sciences*, 62, 716–721.

Tiwari, A.K., M. Shahbaz, and F. Islam (2013). "Does financial development increase rural-urban income inequality? Cointegration analysis in the case of Indian economy", *International Journal of Social Economics*, 40, 151–168.

Ulaşan, B. (2015). "Trade openness and economic growth: Panel evidence", *Applied Economics Letters*, 22, 163–167.

UNCTAD (2015). *Foreign Direct Investment Database.* Available at: http://stats.unctad.org/fdi.

Winters, L.A. (2002). “Trade liberalisation and poverty: What are the links?”, *The World Economy*, 25, 1339–1367.

Winters, L.A., N. Mcculloch, and A. McKay (2004). “Trade liberalization and poverty: The evidence so far”, *Journal of Economic Literature*, 42, 72–115.

World Bank (1990). *World Development Report 1990: Poverty*. New York: Oxford University Press.

World Bank (2015a). *World Development Indicators*. Washington, DC: The World Bank. Available at: http://data.worldbank.org/datacatalog/world-development-indicators.

World Bank (2015b). *World Governance Indicators*. Washington, DC: The World Bank. Available at: www.govindicators.org.

Young, A. (1991). “Learning by doing and the dynamic effects of international trade”, National Bureau of Economic Research.

9 Effects of capital flight on growth and poverty reduction in Ethiopia

Evidence from a simulation-based analysis

Alemayehu Geda and Addis Yimer

1. Introduction

Despite growth resurgence in the last two decades, Africa is still saddled with very high and stubborn poverty rates, as well as high and often increasing levels of inequalities (Ndikumana, 2013). One of the fundamental problems that African economies are still facing is that they have not been able to sustain high growth rates for a sufficiently long time to generate meaningful gains in poverty reduction (Ndikumana, 2013).

One of the structural constraints to growth in most African countries is the low level of domestic investments. And one of the reasons for this is the shortage of domestic financing, especially long-term investment capital (Global Financial Integrity and African Development Bank, 2013). Yet, as noted by Ndikumana (2013), the African continent presents a stunning paradox. On the one hand, a majority of the African countries exhibit chronic and even deepening investment-saving gaps. On the other hand, the continent is also a source of large and increasing volumes of capital flight. It is estimated that over the last four decades, the continent has lost up to $1.3 trillion through capital flight (Ndikumana et al., 2015).

As noted by Deppler and Williamson (1987), the fundamental economic concern about capital flight is its tendency to reduce welfare in the sense that it leads to a net loss in the total real resources available to an economy for investments and growth. That is, capital flight is viewed as a diversion of domestic savings away from financing domestic real investments and in favor of foreign financial investments. As a result, the pace of growth and development in the economy is retarded from what it would have been otherwise (Deppler and Williamson, 1987).

Empirical studies on Africa have found a negative relationship between investment and capital flight (Adesoye et al., 2012; AfDB et al., 2012; Ndiaye, 2007, 2011; Saheed and Ayodeji, 2012). They find that as more capital is shifted abroad and invested or stored, the supply of capital available domestically is reduced and the direct and indirect reductions in domestic investment levels get intensified. For example, in Nigeria and Angola, the African Economic Outlook by AfDB et al. (2012) suggests that capital flight reduced investments by USD 10.7 billion and USD 3.6 billion per year in 2000 and 2008, respectively. The report also states that a reduction in the stock of capital flight from Africa by a quarter would have increased the ratio of domestic investments to GDP from 19 to 35 per cent (AfDB et al., 2012; Fofack and Ndikumana, 2010). In general, as noted by Weeks (2015) the loss of foreign exchange through debt services and capital flight in part explains the relatively weak growth in the region.

Previous empirical works on capital flight from Africa have concentrated on estimating its volume and identifying determinants of the phenomenon with limited emphasis on its impact on growth and poverty reduction in the region. Studies on the impact of capital flight on poverty reduction in Africa are very few. Among the existing studies, AfDB et al. (2012) argue that if all capital flight had been invested (assuming the productivity of capital remaining constant), poverty in the continent would have been lower than it currently is. More specifically, the average poverty reduction in the region would have been 4 to 6 percentage points higher per year (AfDB et al., 2012).

Similarly, capital flight is an important issue in Ethiopia because of its deleterious impact on economic growth and welfare, macroeconomic stability and income distribution. Despite the huge problem of capital flight from Ethiopia, it was surprising to find that there have scarcely been any country-specific studies concerning the impact of capital flight on economic growth and poverty reduction in the country. Given the lack of rigorous and exhaustive studies in the country, this paper addresses issues of pervasive poverty and shortage of foreign exchange as evidence of rising capital flight and contributes to literature and policy debate on the growth and poverty reduction impact of capital flight from Africa in general and from Ethiopia in particular.

The contribution of this paper to literature on capital flight from Africa is manifold. First, to the best of our knowledge, this study is among the first country-level studies that quantifies the effect of capital flight both on growth and poverty reduction in Africa. Whereas previous similar country case studies have concentrated on the effect of capital flight on growth, this study goes further to analyze the impact of capital flight on poverty reduction also. In addition, the few available studies that analyze the effect of capital flight on poverty reduction aggregate countries in their analyses (see AfDB et al., 2012; Nkurunziza, 2015). Our study, on the other hand, presents results at the country level, providing information that is more useful for policy and country case studies. Second, we not only used updated estimates of capital flight that cover the period from 1970 to 2012, but also used elasticity of poverty to income and inequality in an analysis of the potential effect of capital flight on the rate of poverty reduction. Third, this paper develops a step-by-step methodology for estimating the effect of capital flight both on growth and poverty reduction efforts.

The rest of the paper is organized as follows. Section 2 discusses the general overview of growth and poverty trends in the country. Section 3 presents the estimated level of capital flight from Ethiopia. A review of related literature is presented in Section 4. Section 5 discusses the methodology employed for an analysis of the effects of capital flight on growth and poverty reduction along with the empirical findings. Section 6 gives a conclusion with some policy recommendations.

2. Overview of growth and poverty trends in Ethiopia

The last two decades have been a period of intense controversy over growth and poverty statistics in Ethiopia. Controversies surfaced concerning the statistics produced by central government data sources, which often showed double-digit economic growth and a very rapid decline in poverty. Whereas the official numbers have been quoted in double digits for the past decade, estimates by the International Monetary Fund (IMF) and a careful examination of the numbers by various academic researchers consistently show a lower GDP growth rate (Geda and Yimer, 2014). Thus, depending on the source of the data, one can find different narratives of GDP growth and poverty prevalence in Ethiopia.

If we base our analysis on official government reports on growth and poverty, the country's record of growth and poverty reduction is an impressive one. According to official statistics, Ethiopia continued to register double-digit economic growth (Figure 9.1). In terms of poverty, the official reports indicate that the headcount ratio of poverty (the percentage of population below the poverty line) declined from 45 per cent in 1994–95 to 30 per cent in 2010–11 (Table 9.1).

Using official data, Ethiopia saw one of the best economic performances since the early 1990s in the last decade (see Figure 9.1). The economic growth was impressive, with an average growth rate of about 9 per cent per annum since 2000. If the abnormal first three years are left out and the growth rate is

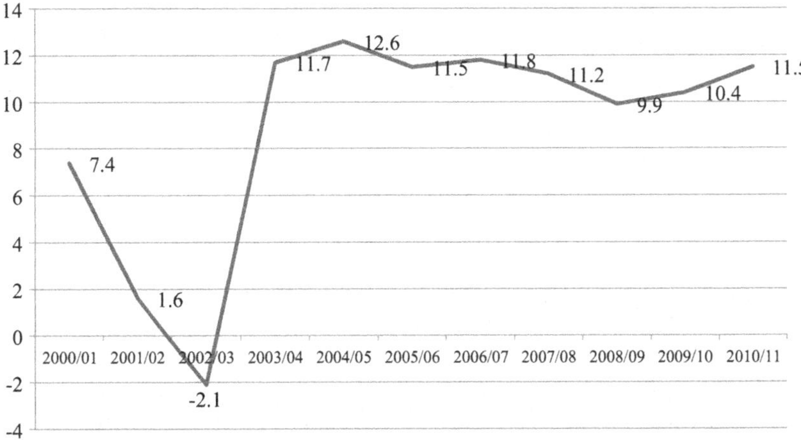

Figure 9.1 Official real GDP growth

Source: Authors' computation based on MOFED (2013)

Table 9.1 Indicators of poverty based on national and department economics data of the Addis Ababa University

Year	*CSA, Nationally Representative Data*			*Dept. of Economics (AAU) Panel Based Data*		
	National	*Urban*	*Rural*	*National*	*Urban*	*Rural*
1994				46	32	48
1995				39	32	40
1995–96						
HCR*	0.45	0.33	0.47			
PGI	0.120	0.099	0.134			
PSI	0.051	0.041	0.053			
1997				29	27	27
1999–2000				NA	NA	NA
HCR	0.44	0.37	0.45			
PGI	0.119	0.101	0.112			
PSI	0.045	0.039	0.046			
2000				41	39	41
2004–05				NA	NA	NA
HCR	0.39	0.35	0.39			
PGI	0.083	0.077	0.085			
PSI	0.027	0.026	0.027			
2010–11				NA	NA	NA
HCR	0.296	0.26	0.30			
PGI	0.078	0.069	0.08			
PSI	0.031	0.027	0.032			

Source: MOFED (2012)

Note: * = HCR is the headcount ratio; PGI is the poverty gap index which measures how far, on average, households are from the poverty line; and PSI is the poverty severity index. PSI is poverty gap squared and measures the severity of poverty. In addition to the poverty gap, it takes into account inequalities among the poor people by implicitly giving more weight for bigger rather than smaller gaps in the process of squaring the gap index.

computed from 2003, the average annual growth rate comes to about 11 per cent for nine consecutive years. However, given the dependence of growth on rain-fed agriculture and low levels of domestic resource mobilization (including shortage of foreign exchange), the sustainability of this growth is questionable.

Table 9.1 shows the trends in poverty in Ethiopia in the last decade. It is based on detailed household-level data collected both by the government and the Department of Economics at the Addis Ababa University in collaboration with various partners (University of Oxford, Gothenburg University and IFPRI). The government's official income poverty level in 2010–11 is computed based on a poverty line of birr 3,781 per year per adult equivalent. This is a daily equivalent of birr 10.50 per adult equivalent (about USD 0.50). The food poverty line is birr 5.4 (USD 0.27). Given the galloping inflation in the country since 2005, this is an extremely small amount of money to live on even by Ethiopian standards. Notwithstanding this, using the official income-based measure (headcount ratio, called the P0 index), the latest information shows that, in 2010–11, 30 per cent of Ethiopians (about 27 million people) were poor – a significant fall from 2004–05 when this figure was 38.7 per cent. Poverty was slightly higher in rural areas (30 per cent) as compared to urban areas (26.1 per cent).

The poverty gap index (called the P1 index) fell from 8.3 per cent in 2004–05 to 7.8 per cent in 2010–11, indicating a reduction in the intensity of poverty. The poverty gap index may be interpreted as the average cost per capita of eradicating poverty as a percentage of the poverty line. The poverty index therefore implies that to eliminate poverty the government of Ethiopia will need to invest 7.8 per cent of the poverty line per capita. Despite the reduction in headcount poverty and the poverty gap, there has been an increase in the severity of poverty as measured by the increase in the poverty gap squared (called the P2 index) from 2.7 per cent in 2004–05 to 3.1 per cent in 2010–11. This means that the poorest people were worse off in 2010–11 as compared to 2004–05. This also implies that the poorest are vulnerable to further poverty if poverty eradication resources and programs do not specifically target and reach them (Table 9.1).

Despite the official picture about poverty reduction, the poverty level in the country is pervasive and enormous. The calculations of the national poverty line are based on birr 10.75 per adult per day, which is half the commonly used rate of USD 1 a day. Thus, assuming optimistically that the registered income growth is equally distributed, and that a rate of USD 1 (or 20 birr) a day is used instead, about 60 per cent of the population will be below the poverty line instead of 30 per cent, as official data proves (Geda and Yimer, 2014). According to The World Bank (2015), doubling the government's nominal poverty line of USD 0.50 (or birr 10.75) shows that this is equivalent to about USD 2.50 at purchasing power parity (PPP). Using this rate, the World Bank has computed the level of poverty to be 71.4 per cent (The World Bank, 2015).

3. Estimated capital flight from Ethiopia

The political economy configuration of the country has been informed by competition for power for centuries. Thus, economic performance in Ethiopia is highly correlated with conflict and the political process that accompanies it. Ethiopia's history is full of conflicts, drastic policy changes and reversals. Such political processes also influence economic agents' behavior. As a continuation of this historic legacy, the last four decades witnessed regimes that exhibited the same phenomenon. Such cyclical political processes and regime shifts are not only unpredictable but also violent. Economic insecurity pervades the system as rule of law, enforcement of contracts and property right securities (in short, institutions) are configured on a shaky political base. Hence, such a political process has an adverse effect not only on growth and poverty reduction efforts, but it also serves as a triggering factor for future potential violent conflicts in the country (Geda, 2005, 2008; Geda and Degfe, 2005). This has made the country vulnerable to conflicts, uncertainty and potential instability, or at least its perception. This is a significant factor for engaging in capital flight both by the ruling political elites as well as the private sector that feels insecure.

Our analysis mainly covers two of the three recent regimes that the country witnessed in the last century: the 'Derg' or the military regime (1974–91) that ousted Emperor Haile-Selassie I, the last king of Ethiopia, and the Ethiopian People Revolutionary Democratic Force (EPRDF), which is the current regime (1991–). The Derg experimented with the socialist ideology of a centralized command economic system that controlled all spheres of socioeconomic policy-making in the country. This regime was characterized by a deliberate repression of market forces, socialization of the production and distribution process and adopting a policy of 'hard control' (Geda, 2008). In this period, economic performance was highly irregular due to wrong policies, the dependence of economic growth on the agricultural sector and the intense conflict that characterized the period (Geda, 2008). These features of the Derg regime were also the factors that triggered capital flight, especially by the private sector, as the sector was destroyed and harassed.

The second period (post-1991 to present) is a period that saw the coming to power of the EPRDF in 1991 that ousted the Derg. In terms of economic policies, there is significant departure from the doctrines of the command system in favor of the free market. The EPRDF regime adopted typical structural adjustment policies of market liberalization with the support of the World Bank and IMF in 1992 (Geda, 2008). Economic performance during this period has improved substantially. This better economic performance appears to be the combined result of reforms pursuing a better economic policy, favorable weather conditions, better political stability and significant inflows of capital during this period (Geda, 2008; Geda and Yimer, 2014). It is in the context of these two regimes that the analysis in this study needs to be understood.

To estimate the capital flight from the country, this study adopted the Boyce and Ndikumana (2001) approach, which is an extension of the 'residual' method developed by The World Bank (1985). For country i in year t, capital flight is computed as:

$$KF_{it} = \Delta DEBTADJ_{it} + FDI_{it} - (CA_{it} + \Delta RES) + MISINV_{it} \qquad (1)$$

where $DEBTADJ$ is the change in the country's stock of external debt (adjusted for cross-currency exchange rate fluctuations so as to take into account the fact that debt is denominated in various currencies and then aggregated in US dollars); FDI is net direct foreign investment; CA is the current account deficit; ΔRES is the change in the stock of international reserves; and $MISINV$ is net trade misinvoicing (that is, under-invoicing of exports and over-invoicing of imports by Ethiopians).

Using this method, capital flight from Ethiopia was estimated for the last 42 years. Table 9.2 summarizes the results. We found the total real capital flight during 1970 to 2012 to be USD 31 billion. On average, the country lost around half a billion dollars annually in the Derg regime. This amount more than doubled to over USD 1 billion per annum during the EPRDF regime. Capital flight amounted to about 50 per cent of the country's average annual exports during the period. The results suggest that Ethiopia was a 'net creditor' to the rest of the world, as the stock of capital flight exceeded its total liabilities. The

Table 9.2 Capital flight from Ethiopia (1970–2012): in millions of real constant USD (2012 = 100)

Year	*Capital Flight (1970–90)* *The Derg Regime**	*Year*	*Capital Flight (1991–2012)* *The EPRDF Regime*
1970	10.7	1991	410.6
1971	-140.9	1992	-725.6
1972	771.6	1993	-420.5
1973	163.9	1994	145.6
1974*	-72.4	1995	91.9
1975	-84.5	1996	-33.3
1976	-324.7	1997	605.7
1977	-138.4	1998	398.3
1978	41.0	1999	-689.5
1979	37.6	2000	170.8
1980	-160.8	2001	2969.6
1981	1457.5	2002	3148.6
1982	2784.0	2003	1700.8
1983	1072.0	2004	1631.3
1984	392.1	2005	-144.5
1985	1272.1	2006	309.6
1986	771.4	2007	2376.2
1987	1794.8	2008	198.4
1988	-561.0	2009	2491.2
1989	-445.9	2010	4096.3
1990	702.2	2011	1818.7
		2012	886.7
Total capital flight	9342.4		21437.1
Average annual capital flight	444.9		974.4
Grand total (1970–2012) = USD 30779.5			
Average annual capital flight (1970–2012) = USD 715.8			

Source: Authors' own computations

Note: * = The Derg regime started in 1974

stock of external debt was just USD 12 billion in 2014. Although we could not distinguish the capital flight carried out by the private sector and the political elites separately in the data, the average annual capital flight during the Derg regime was half the amount in the EPRDF regime. Moreover, the EPRDF regime also accounts for about 70 per cent of the stock of capital flight during the entire period under analysis. Given this significant level of capital flight from a capital-starved poor country where exports covered just 25 per cent of imports in 2014, it is imperative to investigate the implications in terms of missed growth and poverty reduction opportunities.

4. Literature review: the impact of capital flight on growth and poverty reduction

Several channels have been identified in literature through which capital flight affects economic growth. Among these, investments and tax base erosion are the main ones. Capital flight leads to the erosion of the tax base, resulting in a fall in government revenue that consequently induces a decline in public investments and economic growth (Beja, 2007; Boyce, 1992, 1993, 2002; Fofack and Ndikumana, 2009, 2010; Hermes and Lensink, 1992; Ndikumana, 2003, 2006, 2009, 2013; Ndikumana and Boyce, 2011a, 2011b). On the direct effect of capital flight on the financing of investments and hence growth, Fofack and Ndikumana (2010), for instance, report that the repatriation of the flight capital in Nigeria and Angola would imply average additional investments of \$18.4 billion and \$3.2 billion per year, respectively, over 2000–10. In addition, the authors also estimate that if only a quarter of the stock of flight capital from Africa was repatriated to the continent and invested, Africa's domestic investment to GDP ratio would increase from 19 per cent of GDP to 35 per cent of GDP. This would raise Africa's investment to GDP ratio significantly from the lowest to one of the highest in the developing world (Fofack and Ndikumana, 2010).

Irrespective of the channels, recent empirical literature asserts the significant negative effect of capital flight on economic growth in developing countries (Table 9.3). Among others, Gusarova (2009) found that capital flight had a negative impact on economic growth in a sample of 139 developing countries. Similarly, Ndikumana (2013) found this for 39 African countries, Ndiaye (2014) for African Franc Zone countries, Bakare (2011) and Henry (2013) for Nigeria, and Forgha (2008) and Vincent et al. (2014) for Cameroon also found significant negative impacts of capital flight on economic growth.

Literature on the issue of capital flight and poverty in Africa is very scanty. To the best of our knowledge, only two studies (AfDB et al., 2012; Nkurunziza, 2015) have been done to identify the likely impact of capital flight on poverty reduction in Africa.

In both the studies, two simulations were performed to determine the potential effect of capital flight on poverty in Africa. The first was based on the incremental capital output ratio (ICOR) approach, which determines how many units of investment are needed to produce one unit of output. In other words, the simulation determines the additional units of income per capita that would

Table 9.3 Some recent empirical studies on the effect of capital flight on economic growth in developing countries

Authors	*Countries studied*	*Estimation technique*	*Findings*
Nkurunziza (2015)	35 African countries (2000–10)	Simulation using ICOR	Significant negative
Vincent et al. (2014)	Nigeria (1970–2010)	OLS	Significant negative
Ndiaye (2014)	African Franc Zone (1970–2010)	System GMM	Significant negative
Ndikumana (2013)	39 African countries	Simulation using ICOR	Significant negative
Henry (2013)	Nigeria (1980–2011)	OLS	Significant negative
Salandy and Henry (2013)	Trinidad and Tobago (1971–2008)	VECM and GMM	Significant negative
Ajayi (2012)	Nigeria (1970–2009)	Cointegration and Error Correction Mechanism	Significant negative
Bakare (2011)	Nigeria (1988–2010)	VAR	Significant negative
Gusarova (2009)	139 developing countries (2002–06)	Fixed effect and random effect	Significant negative
Lan (2009)	Association of Southeast Asian Nations (1972–2005)	ARDL	Significant negative
Forgha (2008)	Cameroon (1970–2005)	2SLS	Significant negative
Beja (2006)	Philippines (1970–99)	Simulation using ICOR	Significant negative
Cervena (2006)	For some countries in Africa, Latin America, Asia and Eastern Europe	GLS	Significant negative

Source: Authors' compilation

have been generated if all flight capital had been invested in the originating country during the year in which it fled. The simulated effect of capital flight on poverty is derived using pre-determined income-growth elasticity of poverty.

The second simulation used capital stock instead of investment as the variable capturing capital flight. The idea is that investing capital flight in a given year has an effect on incomes not only during the same year but also in subsequent years. Capital stock is computed on the basis of the perpetual inventory method, which derives the current stock of capital by adding current investments to the past stock of capital, net of capital depreciation. Each stock of capital generates a certain level of income, so the additional income per capita due to capital flight is determined using the capital to GDP ratio. The effect on poverty is obtained by multiplying the income-growth elasticity of poverty and growth in GDP per capita that would result from investing flight capital.

The simulation results from AfDB et al. (2012) suggest that over 2000–08, the average rate of poverty reduction for the region would have been 4 to 6 percentage points higher per year. On the other hand, Nkurunziza (2015) suggests that the average annual rate of poverty reduction over 2000–10 could have been 1.9 to 2.5 percentage points above the current rate of poverty reduction per year. The evidence from both studies confirms that capital flight has significantly undermined African countries' efforts to reduce poverty. Assuming that all flight capital had been invested in Africa with at least the same productivity as actual investments, poverty would have been remarkably lower in the region than it currently is.

5. Methodology and discussion of results

Drawing lessons from this literature, the rest of this section computes the effect of capital flight on growth and poverty in Ethiopia. Growth forecasts/planning and financing requirements in many African ministries of finance and economic development/planning are usually done using the Harrod-Domar model and its extension by the World Bank to RMSM-X, which includes the IMF's financial programming models. One of the key parameters used in such an exercise is the incremental capital output ratio (ICOR). This is also the practice in Ethiopia. We used this formulation to simulate growth loss (and hence poverty reduction loss) due to capital flight. The ICOR approach helps relate output growth to capital stock as:

$$K = \beta_k Y \tag{2}$$

where β_k is a constant coefficient, K is capital stock and Y is real GDP.

This coefficient (β_k) could be taken as the capital output ratio. If this ratio is constant, as would be the case if relative prices were constant, the marginal and the average capital output ratio will be the same. The marginal capital output ratio is ICOR. Thus, we may get to an investment equation (and the resultant economic growth) important for our capital flight impact analysis using ICOR as:

$$\Delta K = ICOR * \Delta Y;\ \text{where } \Delta K = I - d * k_{t-1} \text{ and } d \text{ is the deprecation rate} \tag{3}$$

$$I_{gross} = ICOR * \Delta Y + d * K_{t-1} \tag{4}$$

$$I_{gross} = \text{ICOR} * \Delta Y + \text{d} * \text{ICOR} * Y_{t-1} \tag{5}$$

Note: This holds at the initial time where $K = \Delta K$.

The first term in Eq. 4 is the accelerator term, and we see that ICOR is its coefficient. The second term is replacement investment. This formulation helps to easily link investment financing with growth. To use this procedure, we first generated the capital stock using the perpetual method. Having this capital stock, we came up with average ICOR for the period under analysis, which is 3.34. We used this value and the official level of investment to generate the growth rate of the economy for fiscal years 2000–01 to 2012–13 in step one. We took this result as the 'base run' for our exercise. Then we generated the 'would have been growth rate' by adding the capital flight computed in this study to the current level of official investments in the second stage. This gave us another, higher, growth scenario. The difference between these two scenarios offers the growth lost owing to capital flight. This is given in column 1 of Table 9.4 and also in Figure 9.2. Table 9.4 and Figure 9.2 show that the average growth lost during the period 2000–01 to 20012–13 owing to capital flight was 2.2 percentage points per annum.

As Figure 9.2 shows, this average value enormously varied across years. Notwithstanding this result, the use of this approach is tantamount to an implicit assumption that foreign exchange is not a problem in Ethiopia and hence the impact of domestic and foreign capital on growth is the same. Given the significance of capital in the form of foreign currency (as noted in the gap models literature) and the shortage of foreign exchange in Ethiopia almost on a permanent basis, the growth impact of the lost capital might be much more important. If we assume capital in the form of foreign currency to be at least 1.5 times more important (that is, it has that shadow price), the lost growth rate would have been 3.3 percentage points per annum instead (see Table 9.4).

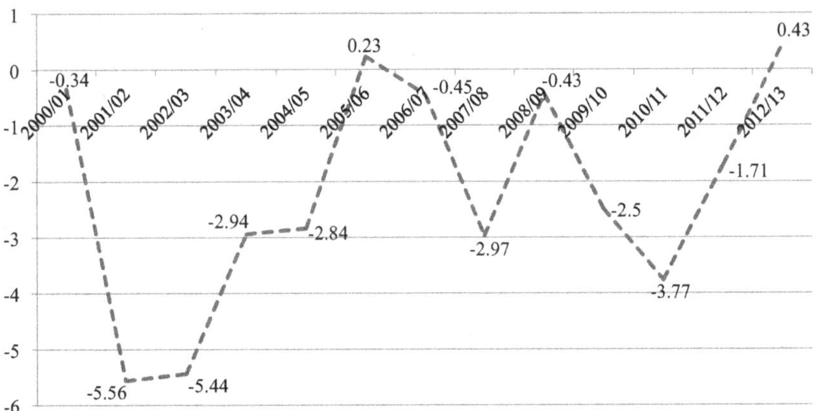

Figure 9.2 The effect of capital flight on growth in Ethiopia 2001–13 (deviation from the base run in percentage points)

Table 9.4 Estimated loss in growth and poverty reduction due to capital flight

Year	*Growth loss due to CF*		*Poverty* (Head count ratio, %)*		*Growth Effect of CF on Poverty*		*Distribution Effect of CF on Poverty (using Gini Coef.)*	
	Percentage points	*1.5CF Loss*	*Base run**	*Including Reversal of CF Effect*	*Base run*	*Including Reversal of CF Effect*	*Base run*	*Including Reversal of CF Effect*
2000–01	–0.34	–0.51	42.1	42.0	–12.2	–13.0	7.9	8.4
2001–02	–5.56	–8.34	42.5	40.5	3.0	–9.9	–1.9	6.4
2002–03	–5.44	–8.17	44.3	40.3	11.3	–1.3	–7.3	0.8
2003–04	–2.94	–4.41	43.9	39.0	–2.4	–9.2	1.6	6.0
2004–05	–2.84	–4.26	38.4	32.8	–9.3	–15.8	6.0	10.2
2005–06	0.23	0.35	37.7	37.8	–9.3	–8.7	6.0	5.6
2006–07	–0.45	–0.67	36.5	36.4	–9.3	–10.3	6.0	6.7
2007–08	–2.97	–4.45	35.3	34.3	–9.3	–16.1	6.0	10.4
2008–09	–0.43	–0.64	34.1	33.1	–9.3	–10.3	6.0	6.6
2009–10	–2.50	–3.74	33.0	31.3	–9.3	–15.0	6.0	9.7
2010–11	–3.77	–5.66	31.9	29.4	–9.3	–18.0	6.0	11.6
2011–12	–1.71	–2.56	30.9	28.0	–9.3	–13.2	6.0	8.6
2012–13	0.43	0.64	29.9	27.2	–9.3	–8.3	6.0	5.4
Average	–2.18	–3.26	37.3	34.8	–6.4	–11.5	4.2	7.4
Average Effect of CF (Percentage points)			–2.5		–5.1		3.2	

Note:* = Extrapolated using elasticity of poverty with respect to growth and inequality, which is –2.316 and 1.546, respectively. With an assumption of a 2.2 per cent population growth, we used 4 per cent per capita income growth (6.5 per cent growth) in getting the poverty trend. Geda and Yimer's (2014) estimates of growth and poverty levels are different from this official figure. Beginning with 2004–05, the AAU panel data-based poverty level is 10 percentage points above the official figures we have in this table, thus making the headcount ratio of 2004–05 as 48.4 per cent (base run) and for 2012–13 as 39.9 per cent instead. This seems most likely to be accurate, as the latest 2009 AAU panel data shows a poverty level of 52 per cent (Stifel and Woldehanna, 2013) while the official figure is about 30 per cent. CF refers to 'Capital Flight'.

Once the impact on growth was known, its potential impact on poverty reduction was simulated using the growth (and inequality) elasticity of poverty that was derived from the relationship specified in Eq. 6. This is based on Datt and Ravallion (1992), where the total change in poverty (P) between two periods, t and $t+n$ (such as $t+1$), can be written as:

$$P_{t+n} - P_t = G(t,t+1) + D(t,t+1) + R(t,t+1) \tag{6}$$

Eq. 6 states that total change in poverty = growth component (G) + redistribution component (D) + residual (R).

Geda et al. (2008) estimated this equation and reported elasticity of poverty to income and inequality of –2.316 and 1.546, respectively, using 22 regional poverty rates, per capita income and Gini figures derived from the 2004–05 household data. Using these elasticity values, the likely level of growth as reported in Table 9.4 and the trend of inequality generated in Geda and Yimer (2014), we computed the most likely level of (income) poverty in the country. For this, we used the realistic average economic growth of 6.5 per cent in the last decade (see Geda and Yimer, 2014). With an estimated population growth rate of about 2.2 per cent, this gives a per capita income growth of about 4 per cent. The national inequality trend is computed using the impact of this growth rate on inequality (the Gini coefficient) based on the results of the estimated elasticities from Eq. 6, which show growth being positively associated with inequality in Ethiopia, especially in urban areas (Geda et al., 2008). The effect of inequality on poverty as derived from these estimated elasticities, together with the income effect of the same growth on the poverty noted, was used to determine the level of poverty in the country. The result of this exercise is given in Table 9.4, columns 3 to 8.

Table 9.4 (column 4) shows that the effect of reversing the capital flight to home on total poverty would have been reducing poverty by an annual average of about 2.5 percentage points during the decade. This is owing to the nature of growth in Ethiopia, which is generally accompanied by rising inequalities; this wiped out part of the positive effect of 'capital flight reversal'-induced growth on poverty reduction. The latest household level-based analysis corroborates this claim (Kacem, 2013; Stifel and Woldehanna, 2013). As the decomposition of change in poverty into income and distribution effects in the last four columns of Table 9.4 shows, had it not been for inequalities that accompanied growth and hence wiped out part of the potential positive effect of growth on poverty reduction, if capital flight had been invested domestically, it would have led to a decline in poverty of about 5 percentage points during the decade. The growth-related distributional impact of capital flight in the last column of Table 9.4 also shows that capital flight worsened the distribution of income measured by a Gini coefficient by a decade average of 3.2 percentage points. This in turn worsened the level of poverty in the country.

6. Conclusion and policy recommendations

6.1 Conclusion

In this study we explored the magnitude and impact of capital flight from Ethiopia on growth and poverty reduction for the period 1970 to 2012. Based on the adjusted residual method, the magnitude of real total capital flight from Ethiopia for 1970–2012 was found to be USD 31 billion. On average, the country lost over half a billion dollars annually during 1970 to 1990–91 (the Derg regime). This figure nearly doubled during 1991–92 to date (the EPRDF regime). The latter is a significant level of loss of capital for a poor country such as Ethiopia, as it amounts to about 50 per cent of the country's average annual export earnings during the same period. This makes Ethiopia a 'net creditor' to the rest of the world, as its private assets held abroad exceed its total liabilities and the stock of external debt which was just USD 12 billion in 2015.

To measure the impact of capital flight on growth, we employed a simulation exercise that was based on a simple ICOR-based growth model. Although there were enormous variations across years, the average growth lost owing to capital flight was found to be about 2.2 percentage points per annum between 2000–01 and 2012–13. Given the significance of capital in the form of foreign currency compared to having it in the domestic currency, the growth (and hence poverty reduction) effect of the lost capital might be much more.

Using an elasticity of poverty to income and inequality, we also found the effect of capital flight on total poverty. Had it not been for capital flight, poverty would have been reduced by about 2.5 percentage points in the last decade. This is, however, owing to the nature of growth in Ethiopia in the last decade, which was accompanied by rising inequalities that wiped out the positive effect of growth on poverty reduction, especially in urban areas. Thus, had it not been for inequalities that accompanied growth, the lost resources through capital flight would have led to a decline in poverty of about 5 percentage points in the last decade instead. This is significant, as on average it had taken the government approximately five years to reduce the poverty level by 5 percentage points in the past.

6.2 Policy recommendations

Capital flight can affect poverty reduction efforts through several channels, including low public service provisions such as education and health as a result of limited budgets for public spending and investments, lost tax revenue and capital flight-fuelled external borrowings (Nkurunziza, 2015). Embezzled public funds that are transferred abroad reduce the amount of resources that can be spent on the development of vital sectors such as agriculture, education, health and infrastructure (Fofack and Ndikumana, 2010). As a capital-starved country, Ethiopia will benefit from investing flight capital in the domestic economy, particularly in the agriculture and infrastructure sectors, where the benefits to the poor are higher than in sectors that are weakly linked with the poor. In turn, higher investments will increase per capita incomes. The resulting growth of per capita incomes will reduce poverty in a proportion determined by the income growth elasticity of poverty. Moreover, as noted by Nkurunziza (2015), capital flight negatively affects tax revenue as private capital fleeing a country is not taxed. Further, there is an indirect effect between capital flight and poverty reduction via capital flight-fuelled external borrowings, as governments may need to borrow more to service their debts, some of them odious (Ndikumana and Boyce, 2011a). Capital flight can also affect poverty through inequalities. Officials who are able to embezzle public resources and can hide them abroad not only contribute to increasing poverty, but this also deepens the cleavage between their group and the majority of the population, particularly those who are more dependent on public services who have to bear the brunt of poor public service provisions (Ndikumana and Boyce, 2011b). As noted by Ravallion (1997), this in turn may create sufficiently high inequalities which can lead to rising poverty. Capital flight also fuels and perpetuates poor governance known to harm poverty reduction efforts by creating an environment that discourages investments, negatively affecting economic growth and poverty reduction.

The analysis based on the simulations presented earlier makes it clear that if Ethiopia is to successfully fight against its high levels of poverty, it will need to mobilize more resources to invest in poverty-reducing programs. Poverty in Ethiopia is pervasive such that traditional sources of investment such as aid and FDI, among others, have had limited effect in addressing the problem. New additional sources of finance are needed. Mobilizing the resources that leave the country in the form of capital flight could provide such needed resources. Hence, the fight against capital flight from Ethiopia should be considered as a fight against poverty.

Tapping capital flight for poverty reduction purposes will not be possible without strong political will. In fact, unless the political leaders are fully on board, they may frustrate the process given that some of them are part of the problem. Provided there is political will, action will be needed on two major fronts: first, the country will have to put in place structures that prevent new resources from illicitly leaving the country and, second, given the size of accumulated resources that have left the country over the years, it will be important to find ways of attracting them back in order to use them as investments in poverty-reducing activities.

A number of measures can be taken to minimize the huge capital flight from the country. First, considering that a large part of such flows results from trade mispricing (Geda and Yimer, 2016; Ndikumana et al., 2015), import and export operations should specifically integrate shipment inspections by specialized agencies. Their role will be to check the conformity of the physical quantities of the goods traded and their value, quality and quantity on export or import documents. Second, the government should be encouraged and urged to ensure transparency and to disclose information relating to financial inflows and outflows. Breaking the secrecy surrounding financial flows to and from the country is crucial in the fight against illicit financial flows. For example, the government should publish accurate and consistent information on how much it receives in debt, FDI and aid, as well as show how these resources are used. Third, improving the general level of economic and political governance will not only lead to the adoption of policies that are more inclusive of the poor but also minimize the corrupt practices that fuel capital flight. This is true since capital flight from the country is mainly driven by corruption and macroeconomic and political instability in the country (Geda and Yimer, 2016; Ndikumana et al., 2015).

References

Adesoye, A.B., O.E. Maku, and A.A. Atanda (2012). "Capital flight and investment dynamics in Nigeria: A time series analysis (1970–2006)", MPRA Paper No. 35836.

AfDB, OECD, UNDP, and UNECA (2012). *African Economic Outlook*. Paris and Tunis: AfDB and OECD.

Ajayi, L.B. (2012). "Capital flight and Nigeria economic growth", *Asian Journal of Finance & Accounting*, 4(2), 277–289.

Bakare, A.S. (2011). "The determinants and roles of capital flight in the growth process of Nigerian economy: Vector autoregressive model approach", *British Journal of Management and Economics*, 1(2), 100–113.

Beja, E. (2006). "Capital flight and the hollowing out of the Philippine economy in the neoliberal regime", *Philippine Journal of Third World Studies*, 21(1), 55–74.

Beja, E. (2007). "Capital flight and economic performance", Munich Personal RePEc Archive, Paper No. 4885.

Boyce, J.K. (1992). "The revolving door? External debt and capital flight: A Philippine case study", *World Development*, 20(3), 335–349.

Boyce, J.K. (1993). *The Philippines: The Political Economy of Growth and Impoverishment in the Marcos Era*. London: Macmillan Press.

Boyce, J.K. (2002). "Unpacking aid", *Development and Change*, 33(2), 239–246.

Boyce, J.K., and L. Ndikumana (2001). "Is Africa a net creditor? New estimates of capital flight from severely indebted sub Saharan African countries, 1970–1996", *Journal of Development Studies*, 38(2), 27–56.

Cervena, M. (2006). "The measurement of capital flight and its impact on long-term economic growth: Empirical evidence from a cross-section of countries", Unpublished Master's Thesis, Comenius University Bratislava.

Datt, G. and M. Ravallion (1992). "Growth and redistribution components of changes in poverty measures", *Journal of Development Economics*, 38, 275–295.

Deppler, M. and M. Williamson (1987). "Capital flight: Concepts, measurement and issues", *Staff Studies of the World Economic Outlook, International Monetary Fund*, (34), 35–58.

Fofack, H. and L. Ndikumana (2009). "Potential gains from capital flight repatriation for Sub Saharan African countries", Policy Research Working Paper No. 5024. Washington, DC: The World Bank.

Fofack, H. and L. Ndikumana (2010). "Capital flight repatriation: Investigation of its potential gains for Sub-Saharan African countries", *African Development Review*, 22(1), 4–22.

Forgha, N.G. (2008). "Capital flight, measurability and economic growth in Cameroon: An econometric investigation", *International Review of Business Research Papers*, 4(2), 74–90.

Geda, A. (2005). "Does conflict explain ethiopian backwardness? Yes and significantly", in A. Geda (ed), *Readings on Ethiopian Economy* (2011). Addis Ababa: Addis Ababa University Press, pp. 662–660.

Geda, A. (2008). "The political economy of growth in Ethiopia", in B. Ndulu, S.A. O'Connell, J.P. Azam, R.H. Bates, A.K. Fosu, J.W. Gunning, and D. Njinkeu (eds), *The Political Economy of Growth in Africa: 1960–2000*. Cambridge: Cambridge University Press, pp. 116–142.

Geda, A. and D. Degfe (2005). "Conflict and economic performance in Ethiopia", in A. Fosu and P. Collier (eds), *Conflict and Post Conflict Economies in Africa*. Basingstoke: Palgrave-Macmillan, pp. 225–142.

Geda, A., A. Shimeles, and J. Weeks (2008). "Growth, poverty and inequality in Ethiopia: Which way for pro poor growth", *Journal of International Development*, 36(9), 1259–1284.

Geda, A. and A. Yimer (2014). "The political economy of growth, poverty and inequality in Ethiopia, 2000–2013", in D. Rahmato, M. Ayenew, A. Kefale, and B. Habermann (eds), *Reflections on Development in Ethiopia: New Trends, Sustainability and Challenges*. Addis Ababa: Forum for Social Studies, pp. 31–66.

Geda, A. and A. Yimer (2016). "Capital flight and its determinants: The case of Ethiopia", *African Development Review*, 28(S1), 39–49.

Global Financial Integrity and African Development Bank (May 2013). *Illicit Financial Flows and the Problem of Net Resource Transfers from Africa: 1980–2009*. Available at: www.gfintegrity.org/report-net-resources-from-africa/.

Gusarova, V. (2009). "The impact of capital flight on economic growth", Unpublished Master's Thesis, Kyiv School of Economics.

Henry, A.W. (2013). "Analysis of the effects of capital flight on economic growth: Evidence from Nigerian economy (1980–2011)", *European Journal of Business and Management*, 5(17), 46–68.

Hermes, N. and R. Lensink (1992). "The magnitude and determinants of capital flight: The case for six sub-Saharan African countries", *De Economist*, 140(4), 515–530.

Kacem, R.B.H. (2013). "Monetary versus Non-Monetary Pro-Poor Growth: Evidence from Rural Ethiopia between 2004 and 2009", *Economics: The Open-Access, Open-Assessment E-Journal*, 7(2013–26), 1–22. Available at: http://dx.doi.org/10.5018/economics-ejournal.ja.2013-26.

Lan, S.K. (2009). "Effects of capital flight on economic growth in selected ASEAN economies", Unpublished PhD Thesis, University Putra Malaysia.

MOFED (2012). *Ethiopia's Progress towards Eradicating Poverty: An Interim Report on Poverty Analysis Study (2010/11)*. Addis Ababa: MOFED.

MOFED (2013). *National Economic Accounts Statistics of Ethiopia: Estimates of the 2010/11 Base Year Series*, Addis Ababa: MOFED.

Ndiaye, A.S. (2007). "Impact of capital flight on domestic investment in the Franc zone", in African Development Bank and United Nations Economic Commission for Africa (eds), *Africa's Development Challenges and Opportunities in the Global Arena – Proceedings of the African Economic Conference*. Paris: Economica, pp. 317–355.

Ndiaye, A.S. (2011). "Capital flight and its determinants in the Franc Zone", AERC Research Paper No. 215. Nairobi: African Economic Research Consortium.

Ndiaye, A.S. (2014). "Is capital flight decisive in explaining economic growth performance in the African Franc zone?", GDN 15th Annual Global Development Conference on Structural Transformation in Africa and Beyond, 18–20 June 2014, Accra, Ghana.

Ndikumana, L. (2003). "Capital flows, capital account regimes, and foreign exchange rate regimes in Africa", Political Economy Research Institute (PERI) Working Paper No. 55, Massachusetts, USA.

Ndikumana, L. (2006). "Corruption and pro-poor growth outcomes: Evidence and lessons for African countries", Political Economy Research Institute (PERI) Working Paper No. 120, Massachusetts, USA.

Ndikumana, L. (2009). "Capital flight", in K. Reinert and R. Rajan (eds), *The Princeton Encyclopedia of the World Economy*. Princeton: Princeton University Press, pp. 1–6.

Ndikumana, L. (2013). "Capital flight and tax havens: Impact on investment and growth in Africa", Department of Economics and Political Economy Research Institute University of Massachusetts at Amherst, 22 December 2013.

Ndikumana, L. and J.K. Boyce. (2011a). *Africa's Odious Debt: How Foreign Loans and Capital Flight Bled a Continent*. London and New York: Zed Books.

Ndikumana, L. and Boyce, J.K. (2011b). "Capital flight from sub-Saharan Africa: Linkages with external borrowing and policy options", *International Review of Applied Economics*, 25(2), 149–170.

Ndikumana, L., J.K. Boyce, and A.S. Ndiaye (2015). "Capital flight from Africa: Measurement and drivers", in S.I. Ajayi and L. Ndikumana (eds), *Capital Flight From Africa: Causes, Effects and Policy Issues*. Oxford: Oxford University Press, pp. 15–54.

Nkurunziza, J.D. (2015). "Capital flight and poverty reduction in Africa", in S.I. Ajayi and L. Ndikumana (eds), *Capital Flight From Africa: Causes, Effects and Policy Issues*. Oxford: Oxford University Press, pp. 81–110.

Ravallion, M. (1997). "Can high inequality developing countries escape absolute poverty?", *Economics Letters*, 56(1), 51–57.

Saheed, Z.S. and S. Ayodeji (2012). "Impact of capital flight on exchange rate and economic growth in Nigeria", *International Journal of Humanities & Social Science*, 2(13), 17–34.

Salandy, M. and L. Henry (October 2013). *The Impact of Capital Flight on Investment and Growth in Trinidad and Tobago, 1971–2008*. St Augustine: Department of Economics. University of the West Indies.

Stifel, D. and T. Woldehanna (2013). "Utility-consistent poverty in Ethiopia, 2000–2011: Welfare improvements in a changing economic landscape", Paper presented at WIDER conference on Inclusive Growth in Africa: Measurement, Causes, and Consequences, September 2013, Helsinki, Finland.

Vincent, A.O., E.K. Ijeoma, F.A. Oluchukwu, and O.U. Nnaemeka (2014). "Is capital flight healthy for Nigerian economic growth? An econometric investigation", *Journal of Empirical Economics*, 3(1), 10–24.

Weeks, J. (2015). "Macroeconomic impact of capital flight in sub-Saharan Africa", in I. Ajayi and L. Ndikumana (eds), *Capital Flight From Africa: Causes, Effects and Policy Issues*. Oxford: Oxford University Press, pp. 81–110.

World Bank (1985). *World Development Report*. Washington, DC: The World Bank.

World Bank (2015). *World Development Indicators*. Washington, DC: The World Bank.

Part III

Employment, gender wage differentials and start-ups

10 Employment and incidence of poverty in urban Ethiopia

Martha Kibru Melese

1. Introduction

Ethiopia has been experiencing fast economic growth in recent years, registering annual per capita growth of 10.8 per cent in the last decade. However, this robust growth is not sufficiently translated into productive employment for the growing labor force. There has been low growth elasticity: each 1 per cent growth resulting in only 0.15 per cent reduction in poverty (The World Bank (WB), 2014). As a result, Ethiopia still remains one of the poorest countries by any standard. A recent human development indicators report by the United Nations Development Program (UNDP) attests to the seriousness and extent of poverty in the country. Ethiopia was ranked 174th out of 189 countries in terms of human development and poverty indices, with a multidimensional poverty index of 0.537, making it the second poorest country in the world (UNDP, 2015). A substantial percentage of the population lived in abject poverty as measured by various socioeconomic indicators. At the national level, about 29.6 per cent of the population lived below the poverty line[1] while in urban areas the poverty headcount index was estimated to be 25.7 per cent (CSA, 2011, 2012). It is now widely recognized that urban poverty is aggravated by rapid growth in urban populations that is beyond what an urban economy can support. Rapid population growth is likely to reduce per capita income growth and well-being, which in turn tend to increase poverty. The effects of poverty become even more serious, especially where there is high rate of urban unemployment and lack of income resulting from recent economic reforms.

The overarching objective of Ethiopian policies has been poverty reduction. A national employment policy was put in place in 2009 to provide a framework to guide interventions aimed at improving employment and poverty outcomes. The government specifically tailored and implemented different urban development programs and strategies to deal with rising unemployment and poverty problems in urban areas (Ministry of Finance and Economic Development (MoFED), 2002).

Poverty reduction requires a thorough knowledge of the phenomena. It cannot be adequately addressed unless there is sufficient information on the characteristics of the poor and how these characteristics determine poverty. Micro-level studies on poverty are appropriate for this. In this context, our study focuses on employment and poverty in urban areas. It looks into the factors that explain the incidence of poverty in urban Ethiopian households using various socio-economic indicators. Specifically, it looks at whether a household with a specific combination of characteristics ends up being poor or not depending on the kind of employment that the household head and its members are engaged in.

The rest of the paper is organized as follows. Section 2 gives the theoretical and empirical literature. It covers the main theories on employment and poverty and summarizes the most important determinants of poverty that have been identified in literature. Section 3 gives an outline of the methodology, while the estimated results are discussed in Section 4. Section 5 gives the conclusion.

2. Literature review

2.1 Theories on measures of poverty

It is possible to assess monetary poverty using household income or consumption expenditure. In most less-developed countries, poverty is better measured using expenditure rather than income for different reasons. Most urban economies in less-developed countries are characterized by large informal sectors. As a result, income is usually erratic and fluctuates a lot, making it difficult to measure it since much of it comes from self-employment in most poor countries. Income is also often understated, as people may be reluctant to disclose the full extent of their incomes for tax purposes. On the other hand, expenditure is less understated relative to income, as it is easier to recall. People are more able and willing to recall what they have spent rather than what they have earned. Thus, consumption provides a better picture of actual standards of living. Further, expenditure represents permanent incomes of households by smoothing out irregularities and so reflects long-term average well-being (Deaton and Zaidi, 2002).

Therefore, this study uses the consumption expenditure-based measure of poverty. First, household size and composition is controlled for by using the adult equivalence scale, recognizing the fact that different household members have different needs and there is the possibility of household economies of scale from joint consumption (Dercon and Krishnan, 1998). Then, households whose per capita consumption expenditure falls below the national poverty line are classified as poor and those above this benchmark are classified as not poor. This study adopts the national poverty line (3,781 Ethiopian birr per adult equivalent per year at 2001 prices) set using the commonly used *cost of basic needs approach*. First an absolute food poverty line is set on the basis of the cost to obtain sufficient food to get 2,200 kilo calories per adult per day, taking into account the typical household diet in Ethiopia. Once this food poverty line is defined for 1995–96, the food poverty line for 2010–11 is obtained using groups of consumption items defined in 1995–96 that generate 2,200 kilo calories; these are valued in 2010–11 national average prices. Then this food poverty line is divided by the average food share of the poorest 25 per cent of the population in order to get the absolute poverty line (MoFED, 2012).

2.2 *Poverty indices*

There are various measures of poverty, but we use the widely accepted Foster, Greer, and Thorbecke (FGT) (1984) poverty indices to measure urban poverty in Ethiopia. The FGT poverty index is based on:

$$P_\alpha = \frac{1}{N}\sum_{i=1}^{n}\left(\frac{z - y_i}{z}\right)^\alpha \tag{1}$$

where N is the size of the sample, n is the number of poor in the sample, z is the poverty line and y_i is consumption expenditure of the household, thus $z - y_i$ is the poverty gap. α is a parameter which takes the value 0, 1 or 2 depending on the degree of concern about poverty. When α is larger, the index puts more weight on the position of the poorest, when $\alpha = 0$, P_α becomes the headcount index (P_0), when $\alpha = 1$, P_α becomes the poverty gap index (P_1) and when $\alpha = 2$, P_α becomes the squared poverty gap (poverty severity) index (P_2).

The FGT index is used because it shows three aspects of poverty: incidence, depth and severity. The headcount index (P_0) measures the proportion of the population that is poor. The headcount index is simple to construct and easy to understand, but it is insensitive to differences in the depth of poverty; it does not show how poor the poor are.

The poverty gap index (P_1) measures the extent to which individuals fall below the poverty line (the poverty gap) as a proportion of the poverty line. The sum of the poverty gaps gives the minimum cost of eliminating poverty if transfers are perfectly targeted. This index is simply the additional income needed by the poor to rise above the poverty line. This measure determines the depth of poverty but ignores its severity; that is, it does not reflect changes in inequalities among the poor.

The squared poverty gap index (P_2) measures the severity of poverty. It averages the squares of poverty gaps relative to the poverty line, thereby putting more emphasis on observations that fall far short of the poverty line rather than those that are closer to it. In other words, this measure takes into account the inequalities among the poor.

2.3 *Theories on the employment-poverty link*

The poor in the labor force refers to the unemployed poor and the working poor where the working poor constitute a major share in the least developed countries. The quantity (un/underemployment) and the quality (in terms of low returns to labor) are the causes of poverty in the labor market (Osmani, 2002). Thus, labor market theories attempt to explain poverty by looking at the reasons behind un/underemployment and the differences in jobs and pay levels.

Different approaches have contributed to an understanding of poverty and have provided ideas for interventions. The major theories are the classical and neoclassical, Keynesian (liberal and neoliberal), Marxist (radical) and the segmented labor market theories (Tomlinson and Walker, 2010).

Classical and neoclassical approaches

For the most part, classical and neoclassical views on poverty correspond to the market-based system where individuals are responsible for their well-being with little to no role for the surrounding social and/or political environment (Davis and Sanchez-Martinez, 2014). Accordingly, poverty is mainly seen as a consequence of the differences in underlying abilities and poor individual choices that affect productivity negatively.

Classical economists argue that labor markets are efficient and so payments are based on productivity (for example, the human capital theory). They attribute differences in jobs and wages to skill disparities (hiring based on merit). They favor supply side policies. Neoclassical economists consider market failures that are beyond individuals' control (such as externalities, moral hazards and adverse selection as well as incomplete information) as reasons that exacerbate poverty (Davis and Sanchez-Martinez, 2014). Examples of market failures include those that exclude the poor from credit markets and barriers to education and employment. Poverty can be aggravated due to failures in the labor market, such as the skill mismatch problem resulting from incomplete/asymmetric information in the labor market or as a result of the cost of education/training that the poor cannot afford. This means that not only quantity but also the type of skill matters in avoiding poverty. Thus, there is a need for limited market regulations to deal with market failures that may lead to poverty.

According to the classical and neoclassical school of thought, the government has a limited role. The government is justified in intervening to address market failures in some cases. For instance, the state might get involved in expanding access to education and credit for the poor, where lack of access to education and credit markets have been identified as causes of poverty.

Classical and neoclassical theories are criticized for their focus on material means to eradicate poverty in addition to their overemphasis on individuals.

The Keynesian (liberal and neoliberal) theory

Keynesians consider poverty to be largely involuntary and mainly caused by macroeconomic forces such as weak aggregate demand, unemployment, excessive inflation, high sovereign debt and asset bubbles (Davis and Sanchez-Martinez, 2014). Therefore, Keynesians emphasize the central role of the government in combating poverty by providing public goods and addressing inequality issues that facilitate the participation of disadvantaged groups and affect dimensions of poverty. New-Keynesians believe that overall growth in income and formation of appropriately designed and financed public capital are effective elements in poverty alleviation.

Marxist/radical and the segmented labor market theories

Unlike the classical theorists, the radical and institutional theorists criticize the efficiency assumption and favor demand side policies. Radical theorists not only associate poverty with efficiency in use of resources, they also consider it as something that is moral and justice (Davis and Sanchez-Martinez, 2014).

Recognizing the fact that individual status depends on the socioeconomic environment, Marxists focus on group characteristics (that is, the concept of class as opposed to the individual) when examining poverty. They also consider the existence of class and group discrimination that prevents the participation of individuals in social, economic and political processes as central to poverty. In other words, they consider poverty to be predominantly a result of inherent structural factors (such as labor market segmentation) that serve to favor certain groups (Hull, 2009).

According to Marxists, growth may not benefit people in certain classes, and thus income growth alone is not sufficient to eradicate poverty (Davis et al., 2014). Rather, there should be sustainable growth, where income growth is accompanied by a fall in variance in income distribution to reduce poverty. They suggest radical changes in the economic system with appropriate legal action and deep market regulations including anti-discrimination laws, labor market reforms and minimum wage laws to prevent workers with the lowest incomes from falling into poverty.

Labor markets in low-income countries tend to be highly segmented, where sectors with different wages and employment conditions exist and there is limited upward mobility for workers from 'less productive' to 'more productive' sectors. As a result, unlike the neoclassical labor market model, factor returns will not equalize across sectors.

Labor market segmentation has important implications for explaining poverty and the relationship between economic growth and poverty reduction. The segmented labor market theories highlight the importance of the labor market and the opportunities created by a segmented labor market and people's access to it as factors explaining poverty. For growth to benefit the poor, it should occur in sectors that the poor are located in; or it should be accompanied by policies that enhance labor mobility across sectors and employment-intensive growth should occur in 'more productive' sectors so that it helps raise wages and productivity-intensive growth should occur in 'less productive' sectors (Hull, 2009).

2.4 Empirical literature

Several empirical studies have been carried out to examine the nature and determinants of poverty in Ethiopia (Ahmed, 2013; Ayalneh et al., 2005; Bigsten and Shimeles, 2008; Dercon and Tadesse, 1999; Kedir and McKay, 2005; Mulat et al., 2003, 2006; Yonas, 2011, 2014). Most of these studies focus on rural areas. For instance, Ahmed (2013) examines the dynamics of poverty in rural Ethiopia during 1994–2009 using the dynamic Probit model. His estimation results show that the likelihood of falling into poverty is associated with various demographic and socioeconomic variables such as the gender of the household head, household size, dependency ratio, land size and ownership of tropical livestock.

While important, the results and insights generated by such rural studies do not necessarily carry over to the urban context. There are obvious differences in poverty contexts and its correlates in rural and urban areas. Dercon and Tadesse (1999) compare rural and urban poverty using the 1994 rounds of the Ethiopian rural and urban household surveys. Their findings suggest that urban poverty was much higher than rural poverty when region-specific food baskets were used. Similarly, Bigsten and Shimeles (2008) investigated poverty transitions and its persistence in Ethiopia using rural and urban household data. Their results indicate that urban households had a higher degree of poverty persistence as compared to rural households.

There are also obvious differences in rural and urban poverty correlates such as household size, education levels and employment status. For instance, Yonas (2014) shows that labor market opportunities are likely to be more diverse in urban as compared to rural areas and thus urban household members are more likely to engage in different ranges of occupations available in urban areas.

Few studies have attempted to examine urban poverty and its associated factors in Ethiopia. Tadesse (1996) analyzed urban poverty in Ethiopia using the 1994 Ethiopian Urban Household Survey and found that there was abject poverty in urban Ethiopia, with 39 per cent of the urban population living below the food poverty line. However, his analysis was limited to food poverty. In 1999, he analyzed the determinants and dynamics of urban poverty using adult equivalent per capita consumption of households as a measure of welfare. He found that fluctuations in the standard of living were mainly triggered by movements in prices, especially that of grains. Thus, he suggested that price stabilization policies were important for abating poverty.

Most of the empirical studies on poverty in Ethiopia solely focus on the relationship between household welfare and demographic characteristics of the household such as age, gender, household composition and size. To my knowledge not much research attention has been paid to the link between poverty and other important socioeconomic factors such as education and employment, except a few preliminary studies. Kedir and McKay (2005) found low levels of education, insecurity in employment and unemployment of household heads together with other factors such as high dependency ratios and lack of asset ownership to be important correlates of chronic poverty in urban areas in Ethiopia. Similarly, in addition to factors such as dependency ratio and geographical location, Bigsten et al. (2003) and Bigsten and Shimeles (2008) identified education and occupational status of household heads as important determinants of poverty in urban areas. Mulat et al. (2006) emphasized the importance of employment on poverty reduction based on their estimated results, which show that being employed had a negative impact on poverty. However, employment in certain groups may not prevent some vulnerable groups from being impoverished. Thus, there is a need for further studies on the impact of different employment statuses on poverty.

Researchers have only looked at the characteristics of the household head and failed to look into the labor market status of other household members. It may be reasonable to proxy household welfare by the characteristics of the household head in countries such as Ethiopia, where traditionally the head of the household is the only earning person in the household. However, taking only the labor market status of the household head as an indicator may not be informative enough when studying poverty in urban areas where there are diverse opportunities. Further, it is important to consider labor market status of other household members – not only that of household heads – when designing anti-poverty policies. Yonas (2014) investigated the persistence of poverty in urban Ethiopia and the role of intra-household heterogeneity in occupations on poverty using rounds of panel data. The results of his study emphasize the important role of labor market status of household heads as well as non-head household members as determinants of households' poverty status. Regression results suggested that households with higher number of own-account workers, casual workers, unemployed members and out-of-the-labor-force members were more likely to be in poverty.

In summary, there is an observable knowledge gap on the issue of urban poverty in Ethiopia. There is rural bias and not much research attention has been given to the possible impact of the differing labor market statuses of a household head and other household members on poverty. Our study fills this gap. It contributes to literature on poverty in Ethiopia by providing evidence on all relevant correlates of poverty (household demographic characteristics and education and employment status of the household head and also its members). Specifically, the study examines whether poverty depends on employment status and conditions. It correctly specifies the model by including interaction terms between the socioeconomic factors included in the model. What distinguishes this study is the use of alternative econometric techniques to corroborate the results by compensating for their limitations.

2.5 *Measured poverty (incidence, depth and severity)*

Despite a substantial decline over the last decade, Ethiopia still has one of the highest urban poverty rates in the world. About 29.6 per cent of its total population was estimated to be poor (CSA, 2011) and the poverty gap index was estimated to be 7.8 per cent and the poverty severity index at 0.031. Poverty seemed to be more pronounced in rural areas relative to urban areas, but it still remained a widespread problem in urban areas (Table 10.1).

It is obvious that poverty still remains a serious social problem in most urban areas in Ethiopia. Its major drivers include rapid population growth and

Table 10.1 Urban poverty measured by different indices

Poverty measure	*Year*		
	1999/00	*2004/05*	*2010/11*
Headcount ratio (incidence)	0.369	0.351	0.257
Poverty gap (depth)	0.101	0.077	0.069
Poverty gap squared (severity)	0.039	0.026	0.027

Source: Calculated based on HICESs of 1999–2000, 2004–05 and 2010–11

unemployment. By the end of 2017, the urban population in the country is estimated to be 19.2 million, accounting for 20 per cent of the entire nation's population. Rapid population growth is likely to reduce per capita income growth and well-being, which tend to increase poverty. The effects of poverty become even more serious, especially where there is high rate of unemployment amongst the economically active population in a country. In 2012, the urban unemployment rate was 18 per cent, with relatively higher recorded rates for female than males: 25 per cent for females against 11 per cent for males (CSA, 2012). There is also new poverty resulting from economic reforms (cuts in public jobs and introduction of cost sharing for public goods) that has led to an increase in urban unemployment and lack of income.

Over the decade covered in this analysis, urban households experienced remarkable progress in well-being. Figure 10.1 shows the fall in poverty as measured by the poverty headcount ratio and the poverty gap indices.

A. Incidence of Poverty

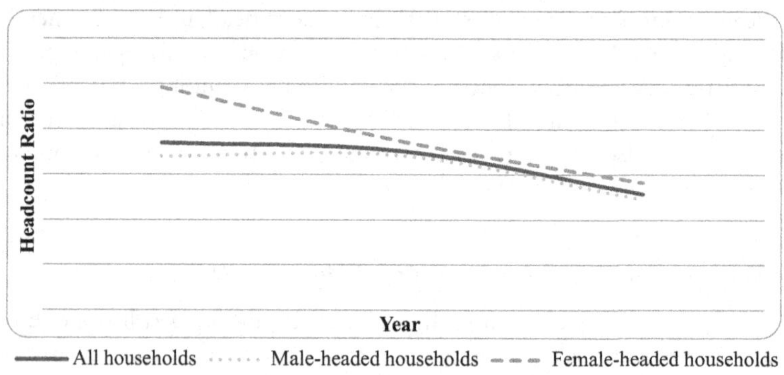

B. Depth of Poverty

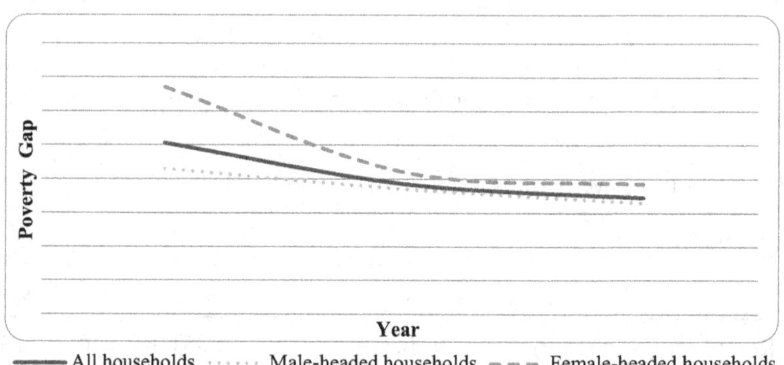

Figure 10.1 Trends in urban poverty

Source: Based on HICESs of 1999–00, 2004–05 and 2010–11

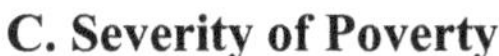

C. Severity of Poverty

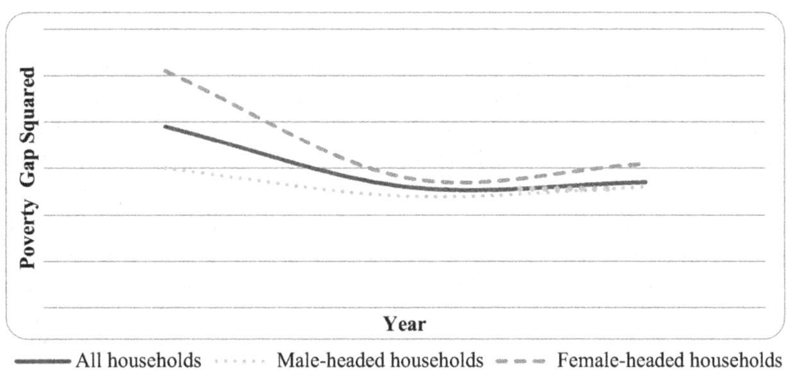

Figure 10.1 (Continued)

As indicated in Figure 10.1A, the proportion of poor people in the country measured by the poverty headcount ratio registered a significant decline especially after 2004–05 (about -27 per cent in the Plan for Accelerated and Sustainable Development to End Poverty (PASDEP) period) while a substantial fall in poverty depth, measured by the poverty gap index, was registered between 1999–00 and 2004–05 (about -24 per cent during the Sustainable Development and Poverty Reduction Program (SDPRP) period) (Figure 10.1B). The reduction in poverty incidence and depth was higher for female-headed households as compared to male-headed households, implying a fall in gender differences. However, the decline in poverty seems to be limited to poverty incidence and poverty depth. Poverty severity (measured by the poverty gap squared index) shows an increasing trend after 2004–05, although it also declined between 1999–00 and 2004–05. This increase in poverty severity implies that the poorest households have become poorer than they were in 2004–05.

The reduction in the incidence and depth of poverty can be attributed to the wide-ranging and multi-faceted pro-poor urban development activities and the ongoing efforts undertaken by the government to create a favorable environment for private sector investments and job creation in the last 10 years (MoFED, 2013). The government of Ethiopia gives due emphasis to poverty reduction through growth and creating employment opportunities, as asserted by its development strategies – the Sustainable Development and Poverty Reduction Program (SDPRP), Plan for Accelerated and Sustainable Development to End Poverty (PASDEP) and the Growth and Transformation Plan (GTP). In urban areas the government's commitment is reflected in the national urban development policy, which has two main packages: the urban development package and the urban good governance package. One objective of the urban development package is to reduce unemployment and poverty. Developing micro- and small-scale enterprises (MSEs) is one program with ambitious goals to attack urban poverty and reduce unemployment in urban areas in the country. Micro-enterprise development has increasingly been seen as an essential ingredient in promoting broad-based growth in improving the well-being of the poor and of women. MSEs have been playing a key role in addressing urban problems in Ethiopia. As per available statistics from the Federal Micro and Small Enterprises Development Agency (FeMSEDA), this sector created jobs for 1.15 million people in 2011–12 alone. According to the country's GTP, there was a plan to create 3.05 million job opportunities in five years (2010–11 to 2014–15). The government of Ethiopia has also paid due attention to the creation of jobs and productivity enhancement. Jobs have been created in both the private and public sectors (for example, jobs in construction, service, trade, manufacturing and urban agriculture sectors). While the government's intention and policy are in the right direction, it is necessary to examine the effects of the policy and the extent to which it has achieved its objectives of employment creation, poverty reduction and business growth in a sustainable way. Evidence in this regard is hard to come by. To date, there has not been an independent assessment of the contribution of the various development strategies in poverty reduction, job creation and business growth either at the federal or regional levels. But it is possible to carry out preliminary estimates to get some indication of the possible efficacy of these programs by considering specific cases.

2.6 Employment status

The latest Urban Employment/Unemployment Survey (UEUS) indicates that almost half of the urban population was employed (60.2 per cent males and 40 per cent females) (CSA, 2011). Looking at the distribution of the urban employed population by employment status, the bulk was constituted by self-employed (38.9 per cent) followed by those employed by private organizations (19.4 per cent). Government employees together with government parstatals accounted for 21.4 per cent of the employed. Paid employees of the government, public enterprises, private organizations and non-governmental organizations together constituted about 49 per cent of the total working population. Unpaid family workers had a substantial share – in 2010 they accounted for 50.3 per cent at the national level (15 per cent in urban areas and about 55 per cent in rural areas). The survey results indicate that paid employment was dominated by males. On the other hand, a higher proportion of females than males were found among domestic employees and unpaid family workers (68.5 per cent of unpaid family workers at the national level were female). The proportion of females in self-employment also exceeded that of males in urban areas.

Nearly three-fourths of the urban employed population in the country was engaged in three almost equally important major occupations: services, shop and market sales workers (24.8 per cent); elementary occupation (22 per cent); and craft and related activities (18.7 per cent). Professionals with technical and associate professionals made up about 13 per cent of the employed population while those working in the legislature and senior officials had the smallest share, constituting a mere 3 per cent of the total employed urban population in the country. In terms of industrial divisions, most were engaged in the service sectors (48.2 per cent), followed by wholesale and retail trade (21.4 per cent), while manufacturing, mining, quarrying and construction industrial divisions accounted for 20.9 per cent of the total employed population in urban areas.

Like many developing economies, the informal sector has been the most important source of employment for the growing population in Ethiopia. A bulk of employment is increasingly being created in the informal sector, where jobs are precarious in nature and productivity levels are comparatively low. In 2009, around 50.6 per cent of urban employment came from the informal sector. A large proportion (about 37.3 per cent) of the urban population was engaged in the private informal sector followed by employment in the public sector, private formal and self-employed informal, in that order. The proportion of women working in the informal sector was significantly higher than their male counterparts. The dominance of informal employment in urban areas confirms that this sector is increasingly serving as a refugee sector, absorbing a larger part of the growing population but at the cost of low labor productivity. The number of people working in the informal sector has been increasing over time, confirming the growing importance of the sector in terms of absorbing employment and serving as a source of income generation for a vast majority of the workers in the country.

3. Model specification

This study is based on cross-section data from the Central Statistical Authority (CSA) of Ethiopia. Specifically, it uses the 2010–11 Household Income Consumption and Expenditure Survey (HICES) and the 2013 labor force surveys (LFS).

Two different methods of analysis (continuous and discrete choice based regressions) are used in order to corroborate the results by compensating for their limitations.

3.1 Logistic regression

This study employs the logit model to estimate the probability of being poor for households in urban Ethiopia conditional upon some characteristics.

Start with the general equation $Y_i = f(X_{1i}, X_{2i}, \ldots, X_{ki})$, where Y_i is the dependent variable representing a household's level of poverty and *X's* are the various household-level socioeconomic and demographic indicators associated with household level of poverty.

Consider a categorical model of a binary poverty regression with a latent variable (Greene, 2003):

$$Y_i^* = \sum_{j=0}^{k} X_{ij}\beta_j + \varepsilon_i \tag{2}$$

Where:

- Y_i^* is the latent underlying response variable and is transformed into a dichotomous response variable Y_i with binary outcomes: taking the value of 1 if the household is poor, zero if not. That is, $Y_i = 1$ if $Y_i^* < Z$, and $Y_i = 0$ otherwise, where Z is the poverty line.

  With the categorical variable models, the probability of having a particular poverty status is determined by the underlying response variable y^* that captures the true economic status of a household: households with adult equivalent per capita consumption expenditure less than the poverty line are considered poor and those with costs greater than the poverty threshold are considered non-poor.

- X_i is a vector of realizations on k explanatory variables for the ith–household. The possible correlates of poverty considered in this study are personal and demographic characteristics (the gender dummy, household size and marital status), educational attainment (literate, primary, secondary and tertiary), employment status of the household head and members (employer, employed worker in the private and public sector, self-employed/on account worker, unpaid family worker), location of residence and interaction terms. Interaction terms between the socioeconomic factors are included in order to account for joint effect and capture the non-linear curvature of the logit link function.
- β is the vector of the k-unknown parameters.
- ε_i refers to the zero mean error terms for the ith household with the underlying logistic cumulative distribution.

It is common to express the model in probability form depending on the outcome. The probability of being poor (which corresponds to $Y_i = 1$) and the alternative event (being non-poor $Y_t = 0$) are derived from the equations and are given as:

$$Prob(Y_i = 1) = Prob(\varepsilon_i > -\sum X_i'\beta) = 1 - F(-\sum X_i'\beta) \tag{3}$$

and

$$Prob(Y_i = 0 / \beta, X_i) = F(-\sum X_i'\beta) \tag{4}$$

where F is the logistic cumulative distribution function for ε_i.

Then it is estimated using a maximum likelihood function, which yields a logistic expression of the form:

$$1 - F(-X_i'\beta) = \frac{e^{X_i'\beta}}{1 + e^{X_i'\beta}} \text{ and } F(-X_i'\beta) = \frac{1}{1 + e^{X_i'\beta}} \tag{5}$$

The probability model is the regression given by:

$$E[Y / X] = 0[1 - F(-X_i'\beta)] + 1[F(-X_i'\beta)] = F(-X_i'\beta) \quad (6)$$

The above probabilities are used to estimate the predicted probabilities given the set of values taken by explanatory variables. Then they are used for deriving the marginal effect of the probability of an event, which is derived by taking partial derivatives with respect to an independent variable.

The logit function to be estimated is written as:

$$\ln \frac{P_i}{1 - P_i} = \sum_{j=1}^{k} \beta_j X_{ij} \quad (7)$$

Where:

- P_i denotes the probability that the ith household is below the poverty line. It is a Bernoulli variable and its distribution depends on the vector of predictors X_i, $P_i(X_i) = \frac{e^{X_i'\beta}}{1 + e^{X_i'\beta}}$
- $\ln \frac{P_i}{1 - P_i}$ is the natural log of the odds in favor of the household falling below the poverty line.
- β_j is the measure of change in the logarithm of the odds ratio of the chance of the poor to non-poor household.

    The results are interpreted through the odds ratio rather than through coefficients. An odds ratio with value greater than 1 indicates a positive relationship; if it is between zero and 1, it implies a negative association; and if it is equal to 1, it implies no relationship between the probability of a household being poor and the explanatory variables.

The rationale for using a logistic regression analysis is that it allows two discrete outcomes and it enables us to explore probabilities of different possible outcomes of a categorically distributed dependent variable from a set of explanatory variables that may be continuous, discrete and dummy, or a mixture of these. To conduct an empirical study on issues dealing with responses of categorical or ordinal data, discrete choice models and limited dependent variable models are suitable and they do not require the data to have a normal distribution with multidimensional dispersion and covariance equal for all variables, unlike general linear models that fail to maintain their desirable asymptotic properties when the errors are heteroscedastic, or non-normal.

Binary models have been widely used instead of level regressions for many reasons. Level regressions do not provide results about poverty in probabilistic terms and they assume that consumption expenditures are negatively related with absolute poverty so the factors that raise consumption reduce poverty at all consumption expenditure levels with no distinction between the effect on the poor and the non-poor (Geda et al., 2005). They impose constant parameters over the entire distribution, which bias the estimate if the poor face constraints that are different from those faced by the non-poor and if the effects of specific characteristics differ between the poor and the non-poor.

One limitation of using binary response models such as the logit model is the unnecessary loss of information in the dependent variable, say when converting household expenditures into a categorical variable and using the latent dichotomous variable instead of the actual continuous variable – we only know the household is poor, but not how poor (Ravallion, 1996). Moreover, the results from the logistic regression mainly ascertain the relationships between variables and only propose possible causal factors.

3.2 Quintile regression

An alternative method of poverty analysis is to perform a quintile regression to assess the determinants of per capita consumption expenditure of households at mean and various other points on the consumption distribution and see potential structural differences in parameter estimates for different consumption groups. These different responses may be interpreted as differences in the response of the per capita consumption expenditure to changes in the regressors at various points in the conditional distribution of consumption (Koenker and Basset, 1978).

The quintile regression model is of the form:

$$y_i = x_i'\beta_\tau + \mu_{i\tau} \tag{8}$$

where y_i is the natural logarithm of the per capita consumption expenditure per year of the ith household, x_i is the ith household's characteristics and τ indicates the quintile number.

This study estimates five quintile regressions as 10, 25, 50, 75 and the 90th quintile. The rationale for using quintile regression is that it provides a more complete description of the underlying conditional distribution compared to other mean-based estimators. Also, quintile regression is robust to outliers and it makes no assumption about the distribution of the error in the model (Koenker and Basset, 1978). However, one limitation of such level regressions is that they do not provide probabilistic statements about poverty status and they assume that consumption is negatively associated with poverty at all consumption expenditure levels.

In this study, we include all relevant variables for an analysis of urban poverty in Ethiopia based on an extensive literature review and economic tests. The simple correlation coefficient is calculated and only those explanatory variables with coefficients less than 0.5 are considered. There is careful selection and construction of variables in order to minimize the possibility of simultaneous causality. An analysis of the determinants of poverty is done only at a single point in time. Regional dummies are included to control for area-specific characteristics. This is helpful in dealing with biases resulting from potential omitted variables.

4. Discussion of results

4.1 Description of the data

The data was drawn from the 2010–11 Household Income Consumption and Expenditure Survey (HICES) of the Central Statistical Authority (CSA) of Ethiopia. It encompassed 17,437 households. Table 10.2 gives the descriptive statistics of some attributes of the reference households. It allows us to draw some initial comparisons on the characteristics of the poor and non-poor households.

Sex of the household head is coded as two dummies, with female as the reference category. As shown in Table 10.2, the proportion of female-headed households was slightly higher for poor households (0.41) as compared to non-poor households (0.36).

The average household size in urban Ethiopia was about 3.8. This average was relatively higher for poor households (5.4) as compared to non-poor households (3.5). The HICSs data confirms that size was the highest in households in the poorest quintile and reduced as per capita expenditure increased.

The education level of the household head is coded as five dummies in response to the household head's highest educational attainment: literate (can only read and write) but not a graduate, primary school, secondary school, technical and vocational education (TVET) and tertiary education; and a literate is attributed as a reference category. Non-poor households had, on average, higher educational attainments than poor households. The averages for secondary and tertiary education for the non-poor were 0.29 and 0.02 while that for the poor were 0.20 and 0.01.

Employment status is coded as four dummies (employer, employed, self-employed and unpaid family workers) with unemployed as a reference category. The proportion of self-employed and unpaid family workers was higher for poor households as compared to non-poor households. The mean for a self-employed head was 0.35 for the poor as compared to 0.31 for the non-poor; and the mean for the number of self-employed members in a household was 0.81 for the poor as compared to 0.41 for the non-poor. Similarly, the mean where the head was doing unpaid family work was 0.34 for the poor as compared to 0.02 for the non-poor; and the mean for the number of unpaid family work members in a household was 0.79 for the poor as compared 0.20 for the non-poor.

There is also a location dummy, which is set to 1 if a household is located in capital Addis Ababa, otherwise it is set at zero. Approximately one-fourth of the poor households are located in capital while only one-fifth of the non-poor reside in the capital.

Table 10.2 Description of data

Variables	*All households*			*Poor households*			*Non-poor households*		
	Mean	*Std. Dev.*	*Obs*	*Mean*	*Std. Dev.*	*Obs*	*Mean*	*Std. Dev.*	*Obs*
Sex (Female = 1)	0.37	0.48	17436	0.41	0.49	3161	0.36	0.48	14275
Household size	3.82	2.32	17436	5.43	2.30	3161	3.46	2.17	14275
Marital status (married = 1)	0.56	0.50	17432	0.60	0.49	3161	0.55	0.50	14271
Education attainment of household head									
Literate (read and write)	0.03	0.17	12612	0.06	0.24	1680	0.03	0.16	10932
Primary	0.45	0.50	12612	0.66	0.47	1680	0.42	0.49	10932
Secondary	0.28	0.45	12612	0.20	0.40	1680	0.29	0.45	10932
Tertiary	0.09	0.28	12612	0.01	0.12	1680	0.02	0.13	2656
Employment status of household head									
Employer	0.02	0.13	3392	0.01	0.12	736	26.26	30.27	2656
Employed	26.64	30.41	3392	28.00	30.86	736	0.36	0.48	2656
Self-employed	0.36	0.48	3392	0.35	0.48	736	0.31	0.46	2656
Unpaid family work	0.32	0.47	3392	0.34	0.47	736	0.02	0.23	14275
Employment status of household members									
No. of employers	0.02	0.27	17436	0.04	0.42	3161	0.37	0.97	14275
No. of employed	0.42	1.06	17436	0.66	1.38	3161	0.45	1.00	14275
No. of self-employed	0.52	1.11	17436	0.81	1.46	3161	0.41	0.95	14275
No. of unpaid family workers	0.48	1.08	17436	0.79	1.50	3161	0.20	0.40	14275
Area of residence									
Addis Ababa	0.21	0.41	17437	0.26	0.44	3162	0.20	0.40	14275

4.2 Results and interpretations

Table 10.3 gives the results of the logistic regression, where the dependent variable is a dichotomous variable taking a value of 1 for poor households (with adult equivalent per capita consumption expenditure less than the poverty

Table 10.3 Results from the logistic regression (2010–11)

Explanatory variables	*Logistic regression*			
	Marginal effects		*Linearized*	
	dy/dx	*Std. Err*	*Odds Ratio*	*Std. Err*
Sex (Female = 1)	–0.0422	0.0261	0.6322	0.1783
Household size	0.0562***	0.0117	1.8595***	0.2495
Household size squared	–0.0021**	0.0011	0.9777*	0.0111
Marital status (relative to unmarried/ separated/divorced/widowed)				
Married	–0.0462**	0.0196	0.5908**	0.1456
Education attainment of household head (relative to literate)				
Primary	–0.0265	0.0319	0.7506	0.2698
Secondary	–0.0721**	0.0325	0.4230*	0.1827
TVET	0.0018***	0.0005	1.0192***	0.0058
Tertiary	–0.0999***	0.0120	0.0740***	0.0536
Employment status of household head (relative to unemployed)				
Employer_cat	0.0386	0.2007	1.4227	2.3797
Employed_cat	0.0033	0.0024	1.0354	0.0267
Self-employed_cat	–0.0443	0.0320	0.5996	0.2497
Family_work_cat	–0.2225*	0.1268	0.0461*	0.0792
Employment status of household members				
No. of employer_total	0.0179	0.0382	1.1941	0.4846
No. of employed_total	–0.0031	0.0106	0.9495	0.1084
No. of self-employed_total	0.0181*	0.0107	1.2003	0.1487
No. of family_work_total	0.0358**	0.0152	1.7814*	0.4960
Area of residence (capital city relative to others)				
Addis_Ababa	0.0217	0.0191	1.2499	0.2411
Interaction Terms				
Female*Married	–0.0393**	0.0171	0.6282*	0.1496
Employer*TVET*Addis Ababa	–0.0028**	0.0014	0.9694*	0.0147
Household size*FamilyWork	–0.0001	0.0002	0.9645	0.0330
Observations	*1922*			
Correctly specified	*84.60%*			

Note: *** = significant at 1%, ** = significant at 5%, * = significant at 10%

line); and taking the value zero for non-poor households (with consumption expenditure greater than the poverty threshold).

The results reported in Table 10.3 prove the existence of a strong relationship between certain socioeconomic characteristics and the probability of a household being poor.

Household size affects poverty through two channels and their effects work in opposite directions – the channel of demographic dependency and the channel of economies of scale. Through the demographic dependency channel, household size contributes positively to the probability of falling into poverty. This is because given a fixed income, an increase in the number of non-working members (dependents who deplete household resources rather than creating them) forces the household to reduce its per capita consumption levels in order to support the additional member(s). Through the economies of scale channel, household size contributes negatively to the probability of falling into poverty. A possible explanation could be related to the composition of households, where a larger household size may indicate a greater number for the labor force with income contributions to the household. The regression results indicate that an increase in *household size* increases the likelihood of being poor but at a decreasing rate (as indicated by the negative coefficient of its square). The significance of the negative quadratic term of household size in the logit model suggests the existence of a turning point (household size = 5), after which an increase in the household size results in improvements in welfare, implying that the effect of household size on poverty through the channel of economies of scale outweighs the effect through the channel of demographic dependency.

Marital status affects poverty status strongly. Households headed by married individuals (as compared to single/divorced/widowed/separated household heads) are less likely to be poor.

The dummies for gender and location of residence are not statistically significant, but they become significant when they interact with other socioeconomic factors. Married female -headed households in urban areas are less likely to be poor as compared to their male counterparts by about 0.48 points, after controlling for all other characteristics.

The level of education (in particular tertiary education relative to the base category-literate – who can only read and write) is found to be an important determinant of poverty status. Having an educated household head is estimated to have a negative impact on the probability of being poor, with the tertiary level of education having the largest marginal effect (–0.10). This probably indicates the increasing returns of higher education in urban Ethiopia. This is as expected because the more the household head is educated, the more probable the household is to earn a better income, cope with risks and uncertainties in incomes and efficiently allocate the resources in hand, which reduces the probability of falling into poverty in the future. This provides strong evidence of the power of education in tackling poverty in urban Ethiopia. Unlike other education indicators, TVET seems to increase the likelihood of being poor. However, it has the opposite effect when it is interacted with employment status and location. Households with TVET graduate heads are less likely to be poor if the head happens to be an employer residing in the capital.

Unfortunately, the logit model regression results do not show significant coefficients for most of the indicators of the labor market status of household heads and members, except unpaid family workers. Household heads with unpaid family workers are less likely to be poor. But, with a greater number of household members engaging in similar family works and self-employment, the household is more likely to be poor.

Table 10.4 reports the results from the five quintile regressions (10, 25, 50, 75 and the 90th quintile) with estimates of poverty determinants at different points in expenditure distribution. The dependent variable is continuous – the natural logarithm of the per capita consumption expenditure.

The results of the quintile regression reinforce the logistic regression results. They share the same coefficient signs for most variables; the only difference is in the magnitude of the coefficients.

The results of the analysis show that female-headed households in urban areas had higher living standards as compared to male-headed households. The gender difference in welfare measured by consumption appears to be higher among those at the top of the expenditure distribution, where female-headed households experience 18 per cent higher per capita expenditure as compared to male-headed households. This is in contrast to most studies from developing countries (Geda et al., 2005; Kedir, 2000; Tomlinson and Walker, 2010), which claim that female-headed households have higher poverty incidence as compared to male-headed households mainly because females have relatively low levels of education, lower levels of physical capital, low labor market participation and low access to markets.

Similar to the results from the logit model, in the short run household size has a negative contribution to household welfare; however, a further increase in household size improves its living standards. The positive effect of household size on household expenditure shows an increase towards higher quintiles.

The regression results explicitly show that households' living standards increase with higher education levels of household heads. Tertiary education has the strongest effect on the welfare of poor households, as can be seen by a fall in the coefficient as we move from the bottom 10th quintile to the top 90th quintile. Belonging to a household whose head has tertiary education increases current living standards by about 59 per cent at the 10th quintile.

Location of residence also has a strong association with household welfare. Households that reside in the capital have higher consumption expenditures as compared to households residing in other urban areas when other factors are held constant. This may be due to the relatively greater number of job opportunities in the capital, mainly as a result of the growing informal sector, which enable individuals to improve their poverty situations.

Like the results from the logit model, the quintile regression results do not show significant coefficients for most indicators of household heads' labor market status. However, the labor market status of household members is found to

Table 10.4 Results of the quintile regressions (2010–11)

Explanatory variables	*Quintile regression*				
	10th	*25th*	*50th*	*75th*	*90th*
	Coef.	*Coef.*	*Coef.*	*Coef.*	*Coef.*
Sex (Female = 1)	0.1411***	0.1038***	0.1297***	0.1929***	0.1775***
Household size	–0.2769***	–0.2243***	–0.2511***	–0.2688***	–0.2516***
Household size squared	0.0139***	0.0106***	0.0150***	0.0175***	0.0162***
Marital status (married relative to unmarried/separated, divorced, widowed)					
Married	0.1710***	0.0645	0.1292***	0.1506***	0.2020***
Education attainment of household head (relative to literate)					
Primary	0.1813**	0.0537	–0.0169	0.0620	0.1127
Secondary	0.2974***	0.1870***	0.1186	0.1674***	0.2042**
TVET	–0.0060***	–0.0046***	–0.0036***	–0.0038***	–0.0036***
Tertiary	0.5891***	0.5693***	0.5128***	0.5805***	0.5235***
Employment status of household head (relative to unemployed)					
Employer_cat	–0.3679*	–0.1357	0.2790	0.0853	–0.0287
Employed_cat	–0.0034*	0.0003	0.0037	0.0050**	–0.0035*
Self-employed_cat	–0.0683	0.0160	0.0363	0.0674	0.1084
Family_work_cat	0.1941*	0.0010	–0.2392	–0.4026**	0.2052

Employment status of household members					
No. of employer_total	0.1238	–0.0143	–0.0369	–0.0180	–0.0727
No. of employed_total	–0.0435**	–0.0413**	–0.0481**	–0.0587***	–0.0784**
No. of self-employed_total	–0.0330	–0.0645***	–0.0853***	–0.1124***	–0.1036***
No. of family_work_total	–0.0354	–0.0616*	–0.0616*	–0.0295	0.0066
Area of residence (capital city relative to others)					
Addis_Ababa	0.1300***	0.1813***	0.1791***	0.1924***	0.1287**
Interaction Terms					
Female*Married	0.1486**	0.2047***	0.0669	0.0170	–0.0993
Employer*TVET*AA	0.0021	0.0041	–0.0022	–0.0034*	–0.0023
hhsize*Family work	–0.0001	0.0002	–0.0002	–0.0005**	–0.0011***
Observations	*1922*	*1922*	*1922*	*1922*	*1922*
Pseudo R2	*0.2103*	*0.2052*	*0.2065*	*0.2135*	*0.1902*

Note: *** = significant at 1%, ** = significant at 5%, * = significant at 10%

significantly affect the welfare of the household. Households with more members engaged in self-employment/own-account workers and unpaid family work have relatively lower living standards as measured by consumption expenditure. The positive association of being an own-account worker with consumption poverty is consistent with the findings of previous studies (Yonas, 2014). A possible explanation could be related to the fact that a significant proportion of own-account workers in urban Ethiopia are engaged in extremely low productivity and low-paying and unstable jobs. For instance, in 2009, 67 per cent of the self-employed were engaged in activities such as petty trading and preparing and selling food and drinks. They did not earn a stable stream of income and lacked access to affordable credit. Hence, it is not surprising that members engaged in such low-paying jobs would were likely to be in consumption poverty. This is one indication of the existence of in-work poverty, where low-paying unskilled job categories exist, which may drag people into poverty confinement. This proves that employment of a certain type may not prevent some vulnerable groups from being impoverished.

5. Conclusion and policy recommendations

This study discussed the extent of urban poverty in Ethiopia and looked at relevant socioeconomic factors associated with poverty using logistic and quintile regressions.

The incidence of poverty has fallen quite substantially over the last 15 years. The proportion of people living in poverty almost halved in this period. Despite this impressive decline, poverty still remains unacceptably high. Further, the intensity/severity of poverty is still on the rise. This means that the poorest of the poor are not significantly seeing the benefits of growth and poverty reduction in the country. Thus, there is a need to identify those households that are severely poor and provide them with appropriate support.

The results of the econometric analysis confirm the expected strong relationship between certain socioeconomic characteristics and the probability of being poor in urban Ethiopia. Female-headed households are less likely to be poor as compared to male-headed households. An increase in household size raises the likelihood of being poor but at a decreasing rate. The level of poverty falls as education levels of the household heads move to higher levels. Households that reside in the capital are less likely to be poor compared to those in regional cities. The findings of this study also confirm the important role of employment in poverty reduction. However, having employment in certain groups does not help the poor reduce their poverty risks. Households with more own-account workers and unpaid family workers are prone to poverty.

Poverty is complex and multidimensional in nature, as it results from various political, social and economic processes and their interactions. Growth is one way of reducing poverty, but it is not enough to eradicate poverty, for which there is a need to create jobs, make investments in social and economic aspects such as quality education, social security and regulation of the labor market, thereby creating opportunities for the poor.

Ethiopia requires more pro-poor growth policies aimed at creating productive employment and at the same time addressing the main constraints of the different sectors where the poor are concentrated. The allocation of public resources to priority sectors such as health and education is essential for building human capital so the poor can ascend from low-productivity and low-return activities to higher yielding sectors easily. There is a dire need to look for ways to deal with the extensive informal sector, which employs a majority of the urban population (for example, extending some of the existing rules and regulations to the informal sector and formalizing these through comprehensive policy packages).

It is important to note that policies should pay particular attention to and be consistent with situations and the needs of the poor. There is a need for more participatory approaches involving the ultimate beneficiaries of development at the grassroots.

Last but not least, the development process and associated poverty reduction strategies must be looked at from a medium- to long-term perspective in order to make them more sustainable. There is also a need for a genuine assessment of institutional set-ups and various policies already implemented/ being implemented.

Note

1 An absolute poverty line is set by the cost of basic needs approach, whereby the minimum per capita yearly expenditure that is required to maintain a specific level of well-being is set as a threshold to separate the poor and the non-poor.

References

Ahmed, M. (2013). "Determinants of poverty in rural Ethiopia: A household level analysis", Master Thesis, Lund University, School of Economics and Management.

Ayalneh, B., K. Hagedorn, and B. Korf (2005). "Determinants of poverty in rural Ethiopia", *Quarterly Journal of International Agriculture*, 44(2), 101–120.

Bigsten, A., B. Kebede, A. Shimeles, and M. Tadesse (2003). "Growth and poverty reduction in Ethiopia: Evidence from household panel surveys", *World Development*, 31(1), 87–106.

Bigsten, A. and A. Shimeles (2008). "Poverty transition and persistence in Ethiopia", *World Development*, 36(9), 1559–1584.

CSA (2011). *Urban Employment Unemployment Survey*. Addis Ababa: CSA.

CSA (2012). *Ethiopia 2011 Demographic and Health Survey*. Addis Ababa: CSA.

Davis, E.P. and M. Sanchez-Martinez (2014). "A review of the economic theories of poverty", Discussion Paper No. 435. National Institute of Economic and Social Research.

Deaton, A. and S. Zaidi (2002). "Guidelines for constructing consumption aggregates for welfare analysis", Living Standards Measurement Survey Working Paper 135. Washington, DC: The World Bank.

Dercon, S. and P. Krishnan (1998). "Changes in poverty in rural Ethiopia 1989–1995: Measurement, robustness tests and decomposition", Working Paper, Centre for the Study of African Economies, University of Oxford.

Dercon, S. and M. Tadesse (1999). "A comparison of poverty in rural and urban Ethiopia", *Ethiopian Journal of Economics*, 8(1), 83–98.

Foster, J., J. Greer, and E. Thorbecke (1984). "A class of decomposable poverty measures", *Econometrica*, 52(3), 761–766.

Geda, A., N. de Jong, M.S. Kimenyi, and G. Mwabu (2005). "Determinants of poverty in Kenya: A household level analysis", Working Paper No. 2005–44, Department of Economics Working Paper Series, University of Connecticut.

Greene, W.H. (2003). *Econometric Analysis* (2nd ed.). Engelwood Cliffs, NJ: Prentice Hall.

Hull, K. (2009). "Understanding the relationship between economic growth, employment and poverty reduction", Promoting Pro-Poor Growth: Employment – © OECD.

Kedir, A. (2000). "Modelling poverty and its determinants for urban Ethiopia: The multinomial logit selection model", *Ethiopian Journal of Economics*, 6(2), 1–36.

Kedir, A. and A. McKay (2005). "Chronic poverty in Ethiopia: Panel data evidence", *International Planning Studies*, 10(1), 49–67.

Koenker, R. and G. Bassett Jr. (1978). "Regression quintiles", *Econometrica: Journal of the Econometric Society*, 46(1), 33–50.

MoFED (2002). *Poverty Profile of Ethiopia: Analysis Based on the 1999/00 HICE and WM Survey Results.* Addis Ababa: Welfare Monitoring Unit (WMU).

MoFED (2012). *Ethiopia's Progress Towards Eradicating Poverty: An Interim Report on Poverty Analysis Study (2010/11).* Addis Ababa: Development Planning and Research Department (DPRD).

MoFED (2013). *Development and Poverty in Ethiopia (1995/96–2010/11).* Addis Ababa: Development Planning and Research Department (DPRD).

Mulat, D., F. Guta and T. Ferede (2003). "Growth, employment, poverty and policies in Ethiopia: An empirical investigation", Issues in Employment and Poverty Discussion Paper 12. Geneva: ILO.

Mulat, D., F. Guta and T. Ferede (2006). "Towards a more employment-intensive and pro-poor economic growth in Ethiopia: Issues and policies", Issues in Employment and Poverty Discussion Paper. Geneva: ILO, Employment Strategy Department.

Osmani, R. (2002). "Exploring the employment nexus: Topics in employment and poverty", A report prepared for the Task Force on the Joint ILO-UNDP Programme on Employment and Poverty, University of Ulster, UK.

Ravallion, M. (1996). "Issues in measuring and modeling poverty", *The Economic Journal*, 106, 1328–1343.

Tadesse, M. (1996). "Food consumption and poverty in urban Ethiopia: A preliminary assessment", in B. Kebede and M. Tadesse (eds), *Proceedings of the Fifth Annual Conference on the Ethiopian Economy.* Addis Ababa, Ethiopia: Addis Ababa University: Unpublished.

Tomlinson, M. and R. Walker (2010). *Recurrent Poverty: The Impact of Family and Labour Market Changes.* York, UK: Joseph Rowntree Foundation.

UNDP (2015). *Human Development Report 2015.* New York: UNDP.

World Bank (2014). *Ethiopian Poverty Assessment.* Washington, DC: The World Bank.

Yonas, A. (2011). "The dynamics and persistence of urban poverty: Panel data evidence from Ethiopia", Technical Report, University of Gothenburg, Sweden.

Yonas, A. (2014). "Poverty persistence and intra-household heterogeneity in occupations: Evidence from urban Ethiopia", *World Development*, 40(1), 146–162.

11 Impact of gender wage differentials on poverty and inequalities in Cameroon[1]

Pierre M. Nguetse-Tegoum and Justin Bem

1. Introduction

Cameroon is a country in sub-Saharan Africa that experienced an unprecedented crisis due to a fall in its export revenues following the fall of oil prices and principal cash crops (cocoa, coffee) during 1985–94. The various cash constraints forced the government to implement several measures to improve the economy. With support from the Bretton Woods institutions, the country implemented several structural adjustment programs that directly and indirectly affected the poverty and employment situation in Cameroon. In fact, the liquidation and restructuring of numerous private and public companies, the freezing of recruitments for public service, retrenchment of some civil servants and a steep decline in private investments led to an explosion of under-employment and acceleration in the informalization of the economy. In 1996, more than 50 per cent of the Cameroonians were living below the poverty line and the rate of informalization was 85.9 per cent (INS, 1996).

Since 1994, the Cameroonian economy has resumed growth and in 2000 new programs with less constraints, such as the Initiative for Heavily Indebted Poor Countries (HIPC), have been negotiated with donors. However, despite this progress and reforms, the condition of living and of activity of Cameroonians remains alarming. In fact, the third Cameroonian Households Survey (ECAM 3) shows that the poverty headcount was steady at 40 per cent between 2001 and 2007; it also shows the strong significance of socioeconomic groups on the probability of a household being poor (INS, 2008). The same survey also reveals great wage differentials between men and women in the labor market; women were mostly engaged in unprotected jobs and earned on average two times less than men (INS, 2008). These facts corroborate the results of the Employment and the Informal Sector Survey (EESI) of 2005, which clearly established the existence of gender inequalities in the labor market in the Cameroonian economy (INS, 2005).

The current face of the labor market in Cameroon is as alarming as the poverty status of the country. Thus, the revision of the Poverty Reduction Strategy Paper (DRSP, 2003) has led to the Strategic Document for Growth and Employment (DSCE, 2009) in which development, the fight against poverty and social equity are based more on employment issues. For its implementation, this strategy needs to have reliable information and specific studies for a better understanding of the functioning of the labor market and its links with poverty, since these two phenomena are most often correlated in developing countries but they are rarely analyzed together (Gradín et al., 2006).

Moreover, in the context of globalization and trade liberalization, the issue of imperfect markets is arousing increasing interest. In particular, it is important to give special attention to the costs incurred by the inefficient use of labor; for example, in the case of gender wage differentials. This is because the functioning of the labor market has a great impact on economic growth and income distribution (Cambarnous, 1994). In addition, the 'classical' theoretical analysis based on the works of Arrow (1973) and Becker (1975) clearly show the implications of discrimination on profits, wages and efficiency in the allocation of work.

As highlighted by Nordman et al. (2009), gender and ethnic inequalities are likely to be greater in African countries where markets do not function efficiently and the states lack resources for introducing corrective policies. Also, understanding the roots of inequalities between the sexes and reducing the gender gap could help design poverty-reducing policies in these countries via corrective policies.

The objective of this paper is to analyze the distributional impact that gender wage differentials could have on poverty and income inequality in Cameroon. It assesses whether political actions aimed at establishing gender equality in the labor market, especially in the formal sector, can also contribute to significantly improving the welfare of beneficiary households. More specifically, the paper decomposes gender wage differentials in the formal sector (public and private formal), assesses poverty and inequalities as characterized by the labor market and, finally, assesses how a decrease in gender wage differentials can affect the standard of living of households.

The contribution of this study stems from at least two main advantages. First, despite the fact that we have some information on the gender income gap in Cameroon, so far no analysis has been done on the burden of gender discrimination on society. Second, the paper is a case study of a country in the Economic and Monetary Community of Central Africa States (Cameroon, Gabon, Equatorial Guinea, Chad and the Central African Republic), which is a region where there is a shortage of studies on gender gap issues.

This study is based on two key assumptions. The first is that the income gap between men and women can be totally explained by a number of observable variables. This means associating, certainly wrongly, the impact of unobservable factors such as absenteeism, skills and efforts of income differences to forms of discrimination. In some cases panel data can help overcome this weakness. However, such data does not exist in Cameroon. The second assumption is that the discrimination-free equilibrium wage coefficients are unbiased. This is unlikely since these coefficients are a weighted average of the men and women wage regression coefficients. However, this problem is inherent in models of the Oaxaca-Blinder type.

The rest of the document proceeds as follows. Section 2 discusses key literature while Section 3 deals with the methodology. Section 4 presents the data and some characteristics of the formal sector by gender. Section 5 gives the results of the study; the conclusions and socioeconomic policy implications are discussed in Section 6.

2. Literature review

Oaxaca (1973), in his pioneer study on income gap decomposition, defined the existence of wage differentials based on gender as a situation where the average income of men was higher than what they would have earned if males and females were paid according to the same criteria. Thus, gender-based wage differentials reflect the income gap between male and female workers with similar skills and certainly the same expected productivity.

In the same vein, Becker's (1964) human capital model predicts that earning differences arise from differences in the broad array of individual abilities and in educational investments. This implies that people are compensated in the workplace based on their abilities and skills (Borjas, 2000). According to Becker, the proclivity of individuals to invest in training and the acquisition of skills depends on the anticipated returns that they will receive as a consequence of the investment. Since women anticipate that they will get less returns on their skills as compared to their male counterparts, they are less likely to invest in education.

Economic literature distinguishes two major components in the income gap. The first is discrimination in the labor market, which expresses the fact that men and women with equal productive characteristics receive different incomes (Ehrenberg and Smith, 1994). The second is the gap due to the differences in productive characteristics such as educational levels, work experience, training and sometimes employment characteristics. To measure the income gap, we must first estimate the earning equations of men and women.

Costa and Silva (2008), using data from five Latin American countries (Argentina, Brazil, Salvador, Chile and Mexico), show that reducing gender inequalities can imply benefits not only for women but also for men, children and the elderly, and the poor. It can result in higher economic growth as well as in reducing poverty and inequalities. Gradín et al. (2006), working on European Union countries with data from the European Community Household Panel Survey conducted in 2001, show that gender discrimination increased poverty and income inequalities. According to these authors, an eradication of discrimination against women working in the private sector will result in a decrease in the number of people living under the poverty line; this drop may reach 10 per cent (as in Germany). The authors also reach the conclusion that the more an employed woman contributes to a household's income, the higher is the effect of discrimination on the poverty risk of individuals living in this household.

However, most studies conducted in Cameroon on the fight against poverty do not sufficiently take into account equity in the labor market or efficient allocation of human resources. This aspect of the problem is a central concern of our study.

The classical approach of measuring income gap was proposed separately by Blinder (1973) and Oaxaca (1973). It states that in the absence of gender wage differentials, the observable characteristics of individuals have an identical impact on the earnings of men and women. If the average income of men is W_h and that of women is W_f, then the decomposition of the income gap according to the remuneration structure of men is:

$$G = Ln(W_h) - Ln(W_f) = \bar{X}_f(\beta_h - \beta_f) + (\bar{X}_h - \bar{X}_f)\beta_h \tag{1}$$

where $\bar{X}_i$ is the vector of average characteristics of group i and β_i is the vector of coefficients ($i = m$ *or* f).

Eq. 1 can be rewritten in several ways according to what we consider the real non-discriminatory wage structure. Like Neuman and Oaxaca (2004), we estimate the gap as:

$$\begin{aligned} G = Ln(W_h) - Ln(W_f) &= \underbrace{\bar{X}_h(\beta_h - \beta_{nd})}_{A} + \underbrace{\bar{X}_f(\beta_{nd} - \beta_f)}_{B} \\ &\quad + \underbrace{(\bar{X}_h - \bar{X}_f)\beta_{nd}}_{C} + \underbrace{(\theta_h\lambda_h - \theta_f\lambda_f)}_{D} \end{aligned} \tag{2}$$

where β_{nd} is the vector of coefficients of the non-discriminatory structure.

The decomposition of income gap G as presented in Eq. 2 has four components. Component A is the men's advantage; some authors describe it as the share of the income gap resulting from the preference for men. Component B is a female's disadvantage. The sum of components A and B gives the income gap related to the gender of workers; it is income differentials resulting from 'pure' gender segregation. Component C captures the differential arising from differences in average productive characteristics between men and women. Component D expresses wage differentials resulting from the process of selectivity in the labor market. We introduced this component to capture the fact that the insertion process of formal sector workers in the labor market could not be random.

Gender wage gap cannot be fully captured by Eq. 2 for, despite the fact that the selection in labor has been included, the gap G cannot be measured accurately since the vector of productive characteristics (X) cannot be defined exhaustively. Factors such as skills and effort at work are unobservable. Their effects on income disparities between men and women are not taken into account and may therefore be wrongly confused with forms of discrimination. Panel data may in certain circumstances help resolve this problem of omitted or unobserved variables (Polachek and Kim, 1994).[2]

The other difficulty in the decomposition of the income gap is the choice of the non-discriminatory structure. This amounts to determining the vector β_{nd}. The choice of this vector is arbitrary. In general:

$$\beta_{nd} = \Omega\beta_h + (I - \Omega)\beta_f \tag{3}$$

where Ω is a weighting matrix.

In practice, we have the matrix of Oaxaca (1973), that of Reimers and the matrices of Cotton (1988), Oaxaca and Ransom (1994), and Neumark (1988). Taking into account the maximization of utility by employers, we propose the following weighting matrix $\Omega = (X'\,X)^{-1}\,(X'_h\,X_h)$, where X is the matrix of an individual's characteristics in the pooled sample (men and women) and X_h the matrix of the men's sample.

Eq. 3 is problematical since the coefficients of the non-discriminatory vector β_{nd} depend on earning equations. These coefficients are probably biased because it is unlikely that the coefficients of earning equations are unbiased. This is the main limitation of techniques based on the Oaxaca-Blinder model.

In our estimations we used the weighting matrices of Oaxaca, Cotton and Reimers[3] to appreciate how the choice of the weighting matrix could affect the results. This sensibility test is value added to the study done by Gradín et al. (2006), which was limited to Oaxaca's matrix.

Among the major studies related to poverty or the labor market, there is one by the World Bank (1995) that focuses on social basic needs (health, education and housing). Njinkeu et al. (1997) were interested in the dynamics of the labor market and Gbetnkom (1999) assessed the impact of trade liberalization on poverty. Fambon et al.'s papers (2005) are related to the impact of economic reforms on poverty and the dynamics of poverty in Cameroon. Foko et al. (2007) focused on multidimensional poverty while Nembot Ndeffo et al. (2007) highlighted the impact of equivalence scales on the spatial distribution of poverty in Cameroon. Yet, to our knowledge, no specific study has analyzed the potential impact of the wage gap between males and females on the welfare of households.

3. Methodology

To measure wage differentials and assess their impact on poverty and inequality, we must first estimate the earning equations for both men and women, define the living standard indicator and present poverty and inequality indices to be computed.

3.1 *Income equation*

As is the case in some African economies (Cote d'Ivoire, Mali, Senegal, Burkina Faso, Senegal and Chad), the Cameroon labor market too is segmented[4] into four segments: public, private formal, informal non-agricultural and subsistence agricultural (Adams, 1991; Schultz, 2004). However, given the difficulty of apprehending the mechanisms of remuneration in the informal sector, our study is limited to the workers in the formal sector. We, however, distinguish the public segment from the private segment. Government enterprises and services provide public goods and are generally subject to political objectives, while private formal companies in principle work for the maximization of their profits. Therefore, each sector has its own specificities with regard to the level of wages.

In each segment we estimated the earnings separately for men and women:

$$Ln(w_i) = \beta X_i + e_i \tag{4}$$

where w_i is the hourly income of activity; X_i is the vector of characteristics[5] and β is the vector of coefficients; and e_i is the vector of residuals distributed according to standard normal distribution $N(0, \sigma_e)$.

We know that the income of an individual is observed only if he is employed, so the estimate of vector β by Eq. 4 is potentially biased.

Yet, an individual participates in the labor market if:

$$\gamma Z_i + u_i > 0 \tag{5}$$

where, Z is the set of individual characteristics and u is the error term. There is a correlation ρ between the vectors u and e. The error terms e and u are distributed following a bivariate distribution.

To take into account the selectivity bias, we finally estimate the equation:

$$Ln(w_i) = \beta X_i + \theta_i \lambda_i + e_i \tag{6}$$

λ_i is the inverse Mills ratio; it is derived from Eq. 5 about labor market participation. This variable permits us to take into account the possible selectivity bias. Eq. 6 is estimated according to the two-stage procedure developed by Heckman (1979).

3.2 *Living standard indicator*

Our study focuses on monetary poverty and its assessment and passes through the estimation of a living standard indicator. Available data (the survey on employment and the informal sector) did not include information on households' final consumption expenditures. To overcome this problem, the standard of living indicator that we consider is the sum of jobs' earnings (main and secondary jobs) and out of employment incomes of all a household's members aged 15 years and above. Out of employment revenues include work pensions; other pensions; land and real state income; income from transferable securities; transfers received from other households; and scholarships and other incomes. In the second scenario, the standard of living indicator is simply the sum of earnings of a household.

Nevertheless, the choice of income rather than consumption as the standard of living indicator is likely to lead to results that diverge from those obtained in other studies on poverty done in Cameroon. Income does not turn directly into welfare and a modest income may be accompanied by a good quality of life, as noted by sociologist Reigen (1987). However, the purpose of this study is not to describe the extent of poverty in Cameroon but to assess the impact of an eradication of gender wage differentials on the income and standard of living of households.

To make incomes comparable between different regions in terms of real purchasing power, we use regional price deflators (see Table 11.A1 in Appendix A). This permits us to bring all the regions of Cameroon at the same price level. As only regional price indices for 2001 are available, we assumed that the relative prices between the different regions remained stable between 2001 and 2005. For the choice of consumption units, we consulted Nembot Ndeffo et al.'s (2007) study. These researchers computed an empirical scale of equivalence with the harmonized datasets of 1996 and 2001 household surveys (see Table 11.A2 in Appendix A).

3.3 *Poverty line and poverty indices*

Any study of monetary poverty necessitates the definition of a poverty threshold (z) for classifying individuals as poor or non-poor (Haugthon and Khandker, 2009). In studies based on a monetary indicator, views are divided between the choice of an absolute poverty line and a relative poverty line. We chose an absolute poverty line because this addresses our objectives better. Therefore, the threshold of USD 1 per consumption unit per day was adopted; this is about 15,000 cfaf per month. Therefore, household i is classified as poor if its income per adult equivalent is below the poverty line and a person is said to be poor if he lives in a poor household.

To assess the extent of poverty as prescribed by the labor market, we used the FGT indices (Foster et al., 1984). The general formula is:

$$P_\alpha = \frac{1}{n}\sum_{i=1}^{q}\left(\frac{z - y_i}{z}\right)^\alpha \tag{7}$$

where n is the size of the population in terms of total number of individuals, q is the number of poor individuals, z is the poverty line, y_i is income per adult equivalent of the household and α is a parameter measuring aversion to inequality between the poor; the higher α is, the more weight it gives to the situation of the poorest of the poor population.

For $\alpha = 0$, we have P_0, the rate or incidence of poverty;
For $\alpha = 1$, we have P_1, depth or gap of poverty; and
For $\alpha = 2$, we have P_2, the severity of poverty.

3.4. *Measuring living standard inequalities*

To measure income inequalities, we computed the Gini index; its general formula is:

$$I_\rho = 1 - \frac{\xi(\rho)}{\bar{y}}, \text{ with } \xi(\rho) = \sum_{i=1}^{n}\left[\frac{(\nu_i)^\rho - (\nu_{i+1})^\rho}{(\nu_1)^\rho}\right] y_i \text{ and } \nu_i = \sum_{k=i}^{n} w_k \tag{8}$$

$\bar{y}$ is the average income of the population, y_i and w_i are, respectively, the income and the weight of individual *i*. The parameter ρ indicates the level of aversion to inequality in society. In Eq. 8, individuals are ranked in ascending order of incomes. Two extreme situations arise. If the distribution is equal, then each individual receives the mean income $\bar{y}$, which signifies that a per cent of the population has a per cent share of the income.

3.5 Measuring the impact of gender wage differentials on poverty and inequality

An assessment of the impact of gender wage differentials on poverty and income inequalities uses the approach proposed by Gradín et al. (2006), which is a continuation of Jenkins's (1994) study. For these authors, gender wage discrimination is first an individual concern.

More specifically, let us denote w_i the hourly activity income of female worker *i* in the formal sector and w_i^{nd} her counterfactual non-discriminatory income. Then, the female worker *i* is affected by income gender segregation if her counterfactual income is superior to what she is actually earning, that is to say $w_i^{nd} > w_i$; in this case the individual wage gap (g_i) is positive. However, if the individual wage gap is null, then female worker *i* does not suffer from gender wage segregation.

$$\text{With}\begin{cases} w_i^{nd} = w_i + g_i \\ \text{where } g_i = Max\left(exp\left(\beta_{nd}X_i + \theta_f\lambda_i + \frac{\sigma_e^2}{2}\right) - exp\left(\beta_f X_i + \theta_f\lambda_i + \frac{\sigma_e^2}{2}\right); 0\right) \end{cases} \quad (9)$$

From the initial households' income distribution $Y = (y_1, y_2, \ldots, y_H)$, it is now possible to conjecture a counterfactual income distribution $Y^c = (y_1^c, y_2^c, \ldots, y_H^c)$; H is the total number of households. In the counterfactual distribution Y^c, the job income of all women working in the formal sector is replaced by their counterfactual incomes, which is what they would have earned if the labor market was functioning 'perfectly'.

We have:

$$Y^C = Y + Y^* \quad (10)$$

where $Y^* = (y_1^c - y_1, y_2^c - y_2, \ldots, y_H^c - y_H)$ is the vector of discrimination.

To measure the impact of discrimination on poverty, we computed the variations of poverty indices depending on whether we used the initial distribution Y or the counterfactual non-discriminatory distribution Y^c while maintaining the same poverty line, which is USD 1 per day per adult equivalent.

All things being equal, the impact is then given by:

$$\Delta P_\alpha(Y, Y^c, z) = P_\alpha(Y^c, z) - P_\alpha(Y, z) \ \text{ and } \ \Delta_r P_\alpha = \frac{\Delta P_\alpha(Y, Y^c, z)}{P_\alpha(Y, z)} * 100 \quad (11)$$

ΔP_α measures the absolute impact of gender income differentials on poverty; the relative impact is given by $\Delta_r P_\alpha$.

Similarly, we compared the Gini indices derived from the two distributions to see which one was more egalitarian:

$$\Delta I(Y,Y^c,z) = I(Y^c,z) - I(Y,z) \text{ and } \Delta_r I = \frac{\Delta I(Y,Y^c,z)}{I(Y,z)} * 100 \qquad (12)$$

The discrimination vector Y^* can be seen as a discriminatory tax. Thus, its impact will be neutral if it is distributed proportionally to initial income, that is, $\Delta I = 0$. This discriminatory tax will be said to be regressive if $\Delta I > 0$ and it is progressive if $\Delta I < 0$.

4. The data

4.1 Description of the survey results

The data at our disposal is that from the Employment and the Informal Sector Survey (EESI) carried out in 2005 by the National Institute of Statistics. This nationwide survey was the first exercise of its kind in Cameroon. It comprised two phases. The first phase was an employment survey that collected data on socio-demographic characteristics of individuals and on employment. The second phase did a survey of the 'enterprise' type carried out in non-agricultural informal units identified during the first phase. EESI was a variant of the 1-2-3 system of surveys for which Phase 3 on poverty has not been carried out.

Within the framework of this study, we use Phase 1. This phase relied on a random sample of 8,540 households. The sample design was stratified according to the 10 regions and areas of residence. The cities of Yaoundé and Douala were regarded as survey regions. The survey clearly identified the four segments of the labor market.

The sample consisted of individuals aged 15 years and above who were working in the formal sector. People still going to school were excluded from the sample so as not to bias the education variables. We therefore had 2,364 individuals (Table 11.A3 in Appendix A). Nevertheless, for estimating equations on sectoral participation in the labor market, we also referred to people who were seeking jobs.

The income variable used is the hourly income of the main activity. This income is the ratio between the monthly income of an individual and the number of hours devoted to work during this period. For an individual who had a job but had not normally worked within the reference month because of strike, sickness or holidays, the survey considered his usual number of working hours per month. The job income includes the salary, bonuses, profit sharing, end of year bonuses and benefits in kind.

4.2 *Some characteristics of Cameroon's formal sector by gender*

The formal sector in Cameroon is very narrow. It has only 10.7 per cent of the workers aged 15 years and above, with 5.4 per cent in the public sector and 5.3 per cent in the private sector. The majority of the workforce is male; in fact, whatever the segment, women represent less than 30 per cent of the workforce. Women are on average younger than men (37.8 years against 40.2 years in the public and 34.7 years against 36.2 years in the private sector).

Despite their low representation in formal jobs, the women in this sector are more educated than men. This difference is more pronounced in the private sector where the average number of years of study for a woman is 11 years against 9.7 years for a man. However, women's productive advantages concerning education do not seem to confer a favorable situation in their employment status and in their earnings, perhaps because they are less experienced, especially in the private sector where the difference in experience between women and men is 1.4 years. In the public sector, 51 per cent of the women are senior staff against 57.5 per cent men. It follows that the average income of a woman is 107,547 cfaf against 131,820 cfaf for a man, yet they both put in roughly the same time at work. In the private sector, the differences between male and female workers are less important. Socio-professional status is in favor of women, but the hourly income of a man is more than that of a woman (524 cfaf against 518 cfaf) (Table 11.1).

Table 11.1 Characteristics of workers in the formal sector, by gender

Variables		*Public sector*		*Private formal*	
		Males	*Females*	*Males*	*Females*
Percentage of persons working in the sector		70.4	29.6	81.1	18.9
Average age		40.2	37.8	36.2	34.7
Average number years of study		11.7	12.3	9.7	11.0
Level of education	No level/primary	15.2	2.5	28.8	16.9
	Secondary	50.8	68.1	52.2	60.7
	Higher	34.1	29.3	18.9	22.3
	Together	*100.0*	*100.0*	*100.0*	*100.0*
Semi-professional status	High rank officer/self-employed	57.5	51.0	25.3	33.1
	Skilled employee/laborer	31.9	40.9	48.1	46.9
	Laborer	10.6	8.1	26.7	20.0
	Together	100.0	100.0	100.0	100.0
Time devoted to the job per week (hours)		39.4	38.7	51.2	46.3
Average monthly income (cfaf)		131,820	107,547	103,809	97,935
Average hourly income (cfaf)		877	736	524	518
Average years of work experience		8.9	8.3	6.4	5.0

Source: Authors' computations using data of the survey on employment and informal sector of 2005

Note: Phase 1 = authors' estimations; weighted data

5. Results

5.1 Income equations: results from the equations

The results on income equations are presented in Tables 11.2 and 11.3. Implementation of the Chow test justifies the segmentation of the formal sector into two segments (public and private). Moreover, this test also reveals that whatever the segment, the structure of remuneration for men is different from that for women at the threshold of 5 per cent. In all equations, the variables are generally significant and explain at least 44 per cent of the dispersion of the hourly income. In addition, men and women working in the public sector do not constitute random samples of the active population since, in the two earning equations of this sector, the inverse Mills ratio is significant at the 10 per cent threshold. The negative sign of this variable expresses the fact that unobservable factors that encourage the participation of an individual in the labor market negatively affect his/her income once he/she has succeeded in entering public service. On the other hand, these factors have no effect if an individual goes to the private sector (Mills ratio is not significant).

The Mincer key variables (education and experience) are significant in all equations. We computed the returns to education from the Mincer 'extended' equation[6] because it allows the returns to education to vary with the volume of investment made in education (Angrist and Lavy, 1997).

Table 11.2 Equations of labor market participation

Variables	*Public sector*		*Private sector*	
	Males	*Females*	*Males*	*Females*
Douala	−0.687***	−0.643***	0.274***	0.493***
Yaoundé	−0.018	0.016	0.009	0.439***
Age	0.297***	0.360***	0.309***	0.286***
Age squared	−0.003***	−0.004***	−0.004***	−0.003***
Number of years of study	0.126***	0.255***	0.051***	0.155***
Be in union	1.134***	0.170*	1.019***	−0.316***
Percentage of inactive persons in the household	−1.551***	−1.317***	−1.942***	−1.484***
Constant	-6.907***	-10.306***	-5.818***	-7.496***
Statistics of the model				
Pseudo R^2 (%)	56.1	57.0	44.4	38.2
LR $\chi^2(13)$	1766.8	1220.9	1497.0	556.3
Observations	2443	2727	2554	2573

Source: EESI (2005)

Note: Phase 1 = authors' estimations. *= significant at 10%; **= significant at 5%; ***= significant at 1%

Table 11.3 Estimation of income equations

Dependent variable: logarithm of the hourly income					
Variables	*Modalities*	*Public*		*Private formal*	
		Males	*Females*	*Males*	*Females*
Years of studies successfully completed		0.081***	–0.008	–0.023*	–0.094*
Years of studies successfully completed squared		0.001	0.005**	0.007***	0.011***
Work experience		0.041***	0.047***	0.051***	0.098***
Work experience squared		–0.001***	–0.001*	–0.001***	–0.003**
Age (ref: less than 30 years)	*30–44 years*	0.174**	0.313**	0.210***	0.490***
	45 years and +	0.405***	0.432***	0.466***	0.440**
Region of residence (ref: other regions)	*Douala*	0.101***	0.048	0.261***	0.465***
	Yaoundé	0.250*	0.240***	0.203***	0.448***
Marital status	*In union*	0.102***	0.031	0.118**	–0.157
Migration status	*Migrant*	0.163***	0.156**	0.044	0,015
Constant		4.894***	4.720***	4.501***	4.121***
Selectivity test (***Mills***)		–0.198**	–0.070*	0.062	0.249
Statistics of the model					
Adjusted R^2 (in %)		52.4	44.6	56.6	52.1
Observations[(+)]		795	347	918	200
Chow test (χ^2 (12))		36,9		22,0	

Source: EESI (2005)

Note: Phase 1 = authors' estimations. *= significant at 10%; **= significant at 5%; ***= significant at 1%.[(+)]= The number of observations that are permitted to have the coefficients. Outliers were excluded using exploratory data analysis techniques; they help to have robust results.

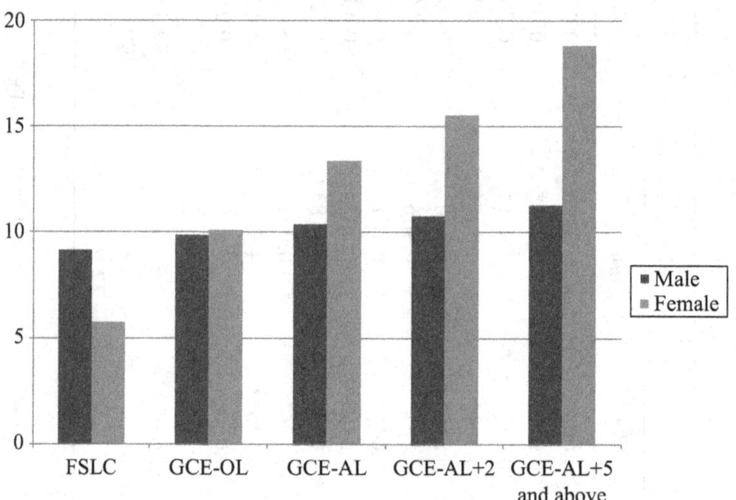

Figure 11.1 Marginal returns to education in the public sector with respect to the gender and certificate

Source: EESI (2005)

Note: Phase 1 = authors' estimations

The results (see Figures 11.1 and 11.2) show that education was more profitable in the formal private sector than in the public sector. The average marginal returns to education were around 10.2 per cent for men in the public sector and 12.6 per cent for women against 12 per cent and 15.5 per cent, respectively, in the formal private sector. Private companies operating in a competitive environment were guided by efficiency and maximization of profits, so they paid more attention to the backgrounds of the people who they recruited.

Additionally, whatever the segment, the marginal returns to education increased significantly with the level of education and they were very high in the private sector, reaching 31 per cent among women with a diploma at least equivalent to GCE-AL plus 5. Therefore, the completion of a level of education contributed to an increase in the hourly income of a worker. The returns to education in Cameroon's formal sector are thus convex. This result is contrary to the classical theory of human capital, which stipulates that there is a level at which the returns to education are constant or even decreasing. This convexity has also been observed in seven cities of the West African Economic and Monetary Union (WAEMU) (Abidjan, Bamako, Cotonou, Dakar, Lomé, Niamey and Ouagadougou) by Keupie et al. (2008) with the 1-2-3 surveys data.

The influence of work experience on hourly incomes has two phases. In the first phase an additional year of work contributes to an increase in the hourly income of a worker. In the public sector this phase corresponds to a period of about 28 years for women and 21 years for men. In the private sector, it

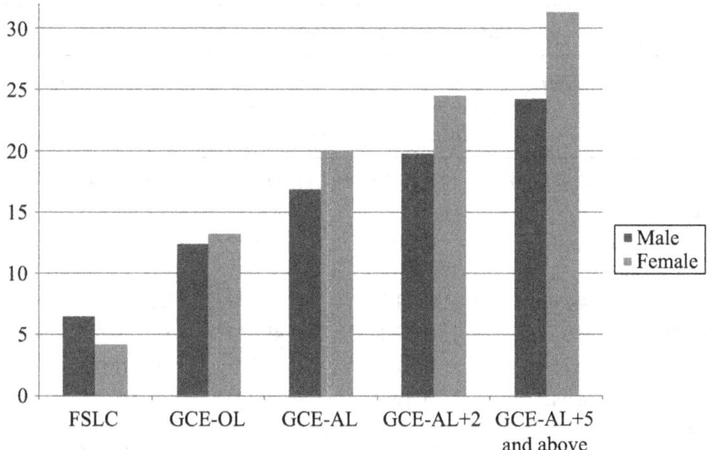

Figure 11.2 Marginal returns to education in the private formal sector with respect to gender and the certificate

Source: EESI (2005)

Note: Phase 1 = authors' estimations

is only 19 years for women against 26 years for men. In the second phase the marginal returns to professional experience become zero or decreasing. Other variables such as age and place of residence also significantly influence workers' incomes in the formal sector. Variables related to migration and marital status are less relevant in explaining workers' incomes.

Nevertheless, given the fact that the labor experience may not reflect the same reality for men and women mainly because of periods of childbearing, the earning equations were re-estimated excluding this variable. The results reveal that the coefficients of the remaining variables were not, in general, significantly different from those of earlier estimates (Table 11.4). With regard to education, for example, the same trends were observed: education was more profitable in the private than in the public sector; it was more beneficial for women as compared to men. The marginal returns increased and they were not significantly different from those obtained with the original equations, except perhaps for women in the formal private sector where there was a point variation in the average marginal returns. These findings led us to consider only the first estimates (those in Tables 11.2 and 11.3) in the rest of the study.

5.2 Income gap decomposition

Results on income gap decomposition are given in Table 11.5. We observe that in the public sector, the income gap was 0.163 and in the private sector, it was

Table 11.4 Estimation of Equation 6 (labor market experience variables excluded)

Dependent variable: logarithm of the hourly income					
Variables	*Modalities*	*Public*		*Private formal*	
		Males	*Females*	*Males*	*Females*
Years of studies successfully completed		0.073***	−0.102**	−0.035**	−0.065**
Years of studies successfully completed squared		0.001*	0.009***	0.008***	0.01***
Age (ref: less than 30 years)	*30–44 years*	0.210***	0.290**	0.308***	0,602***
	45 years and +	0.520***	0.494***	0.729***	0.542***
Region of residence (ref: other regions)	*Douala*	0.215***	0.165*	0.281***	0.492***
	Yaoundé	0.296***	0.282***	0.205***	0.501***
Marital status	*In union*	0.120*	0.001	0.173***	0.031
Migration status	*Migrant*	0.109**	0.097	0.073	−0.012
Constant		5,268***	6.224***	4.677***	4.407***
Selectivity test (Mills)		*−0.316****	*−0.187*	*0.029*	*0.119*
Statistics of the model					
Adjusted R^2 (in %)		48.9	39.9	53.2	48.7
Observations[(+)]		801	347	918	200

Source: EESI (2005)

Note: Phase 1 = authors' estimations. *= significant at 10%; **= significant at 5%; ***= significant at 1%. (+)= The number of observations that have coefficients. Outliers excluded using exploratory data analysis techniques; they help to have robust results.

0.089. These differences indicate that the average hourly income of a man was 17.7 per cent higher than that of a woman in the public sector and 9.3 per cent in the private sector.

In the public sector, whatever the non-discriminatory wage structure considered, the 'pure' gender wage differentials that incorporate a male's advantage and a female's disadvantage were very important; they were about twice the income gap. With Oaxaca's method, it was 0.313; it was 0.319 and 0.317, respectively, with Reimers and Cotton's matrices. According to the last approach, the income gap can be largely attributable to the disadvantages that women face in the labor market. This component represented up to 69.1 per cent of the total income gender segregation.

Conversely, in the absence of gender wage gaps in the public sector, women would be better paid. In fact, whatever the weighting matrix used, it is noted that the income gap between men and women would be negative (−0.016 to −0.009), signifying a situation in favor of women. Subsequently, the hourly income of a woman would have been around 2.7 per cent higher than that of a man. This is because the level of education of female workers was higher than that of male workers. In fact, women's education contributed to reducing the income gap by at least 27 per cent (see Table 11.A4 in Appendix A). In contrast, work experience was in favor of male workers. The sign of the selectivity component indicates that the process of entering the public sector was in favor of women and helped reduce nearly 44 per cent of gender wage differentials. This may be a result of the gradual incorporation of gender dimension in recruitments in Cameroon's civil service.

In the private sector we omitted the selectivity component since the referring variables were not significant (see Eq. 6). The findings were almost the same as in the public sector. The total gender wage differentials were very high and varied between 0.079 and 0.111 according to the technique used. The part in the gap in income attributable to a difference in average productive characteristics was negative in favor of women. It varied between -0.045 and -0.013. Thus, if the imperfections of the labor market were to be absorbed, women working in the private sector would be better paid than men thanks to their level of education as opposed to men's experience for the same working time and similar functions (see Table 11.A5 in Appendix A). Moreover, unlike the public sector and by referring to Reimers or Cotton's weighing matrices, it is not possible to say whether the gender income gap is mainly due to a male's advantage or to a female's disadvantage in the labor market.

Table 11.5 Decomposition of the total income gap

	Oaxaca $\Omega = I$	*Reimers* $\Omega = (0,5)I$	*Cotton* $\Omega = P_b I$
Public sector Gap = 0,163			
Selectivity	-0.141	-0.141	-0.141
Difference in productive characteristics	-0.009	-0.016	-0.013
Gender wage differentials	0.313	0.319	0.317
Male advantage (%)	0.0	51.1	30.9
Female disadvantage (%)	100.0	48.9	69.1
Private sector gap = 0,089			
Difference in productive characteristics	-0. 013	-0.045	-0.025
Gender wage differentials	0.079	0.111	0.091
Male advantage (%)	0.0	64.4	29.8
Female disadvantage (%)	100.0	35.6	70.2

Source: EESI (2005)

Note: Phase 1 = authors' estimations

5.3 *Monetary poverty and income inequality as prescribed by the labor market*

To estimate poverty as prescribed by the labor market, we considered the first standard of living indicator, which is the sum of activity incomes and out of employment incomes (Table 11.6). We considered all persons aged 15 years and above to take into consideration early entry into work activity, which is a reality in developing countries. It should be noted that activity incomes accounted for 86.3 per cent of the total revenue. Given that this data is on a monthly basis, we used the poverty line of 15,000 cfaf per month per adult equivalent; this amount is equal to 0.62 of the median income. This threshold is different from the one used by the National Institute of Statistics, which uses the final consumption as the living standard indicator.[7]

The results indicate that 45.1 per cent of Cameroonian households were poor and half of the Cameroonians (50.8 per cent) lived on less than 1 dollar per day. Poverty presented large spatial disparities; people living in rural areas were more affected than those living in cities (31.5 per cent against 60.8 per cent). In the rural area of North Cameroon, more than seven persons out of 10 were poor. Agricultural and pastoral activities in which a large majority of the rural people were engaged were not profitable because the climate is very rough and also because the families are large.

Regarding the characteristics of the household head, we see that poverty affected people living in female-headed households more than those living in male-headed households (see Table 11.A6 in Appendix A). This result is contrary to that of the National Statistics Institute (INS, 2008); it is, however,

Table 11.6 Spatial dimensions of poverty prescribed by the labor market

	Incidence of poverty	*Depth of poverty*	*Severity of poverty*	*Gini index*	*Income per adult equivalent (thousands of cfaf)*
Zone of residence					
Douala	23.6	9.1	5.2	0.462	40.0
Yaoundé	23.6	10.2	6.1	0.494	42.1
Other towns	41.6	18.4	10.8	0.477	27.1
Rural forest	40.7	19.1	11.7	0.432	23.4
Rural highlands	57.6	30.1	19.7	0.516	19.7
Rural savannah	73.4	35.9	22.4	0.464	14.1
Area of residence					
Urban	31.5	13.4	7.9	0.487	34.9
Rural	60.8	30.2	19.2	0.489	18.0
Cameroon	50.8	24.5	15.3	0.514	23.8

Source: EESI (2005)

Note: Phase 1 = authors' estimations

consistent with that of Nembot Ndeffo et al. (2007). Women in the formal sector were paid less than men and those working in the informal sector were often confined to congested or low productive activities.[8]

Table 11.A6 (in Appendix A) also shows that monetary poverty prescribed by the labor market increased with household size and decreased with the level of education of the household head as poverty was based on final consumption (INS, 2002a, 2008) and multidimensional poverty (Foko et al., 2007). Regarding the institutional sector of the household head, there seems to be a strong link between the sector of activity and poverty. People living in households whose heads were employed in the formal sector were least affected by poverty and its incidence was 8.4 per cent if the household head was employed in the public sector and 13.3 per cent if he was in the private sector. In contrast, the most affected were those living in households whose heads worked in the informal sector: the poverty rate was 45.2 per cent if he was in the non-agricultural segment and 68.2 per cent if he was engaged in agricultural activities. The incidence of poverty was 51.1 per cent among people living in households whose heads were unemployed or inactive.

5.4 *Impact of gender income differentials on poverty and inequality*

For this impact analysis we successively considered the two standard of living indicators and mostly focused on people living in households with at least one woman working in the informal sector. These potential beneficiaries accounted for 6 per cent of Cameroon's total population, or about 1,050,000 persons.[9]

The impact on poverty

The results presented in Table 11.7 are obtained using the first standard of living indicator; that is, the sum of job incomes and out of employment

Table 11.7 Impact of gender wage differentials on poverty on the group of potential beneficiaries

	Oaxaca	*Reimers*	*Cotton*
Absolute variation of the income per adult equivalent (in cfaf)	5179	2437	3692
Relative variation of the income per adult equivalent (in cfaf)	7.2	3.4	5.1
Absolute variation of poverty incidence ΔP_0	-2.4	-1.5	-1.6
Relative variation of poverty incidence $\Delta_r P_0$	-26.5	-16.9	-18.1
Absolute variation of poverty depth ΔP_1	-0.7	-0.5	-0.7
Relative variation of poverty depth $\Delta_r P_1$	-21.5	-13.7	-18.9
Absolute variation of poverty severity ΔP_2	-0.4	-0.3	-0.4
Relative variation of poverty severity $\Delta_r P_2$	-21.5	-13.3	-18.5

Source: EESI (2005)

Note: Phase 1 = authors' estimations

incomes. These results show that the elimination of gender wage differentials in the formal sector in Cameroon would advance the welfare of people living in households with at least one woman working in this sector. Such a situation will lead to an increase of 8,000 cfaf (Reimers approach) to 17,000 cfaf (Oaxaca's approach) in the average monthly income of a female worker in the public sector against 5,000 cfaf and 11,000 cfaf, respectively, for a woman in the formal private sector. The impact of this additional income would be an increase of 3.4 per cent to 7.2 per cent in the average income per adult equivalent of households, and therefore a decrease in indicators of poverty in the group of beneficiaries. The incidence of poverty would regress from 1.5 to 2.4 points, the depth of about 17 per cent and the severity of poverty of at least 13 per cent. The impact at the national level would consequently be a decrease of about 0.15 points of the proportion of people living on less than USD 1 per day.

An explanation of these results may arise from the fact that an increase in women's incomes consequential to the elimination of gender wage inequalities in the labor market will result, all things being equal, in an increase in the share of a woman's income in the total income of a household. This will lead to a better allocation of the household budget and thus improve the standard of living. In fact, Hoddinott and Haddad (1995) used the Côte d'Ivoire living standard survey data from 1986–87 to show that an increase in a woman's income share in the total income of a household increased the share of expenditure on food, reduced the share allocated to alcohol and tobacco and also reduced the share of expenditure on meals taken out of the household.

The impact on income inequality

To better illustrate the impact of the gender income gap on inequalities, we associated the Theil index to the Gini index. The results (Table 11.8) with the first standard of living indicator show that the eradication of income gap in the formal sector will actually lead to a decline in income inequalities

Table 11.8 Impact of gender wage differentials on inequalities: group of individuals living in households with at least one woman working in the formal sector

Index	*Weighting matrix*		
	Oaxaca	*Reimers*	*Cotton*
Absolute variation of Gini index	–0.005	–0.003	–0.004
Relative variation of Gini index (%)	-1.2	-0.6	-0.9
Absolute variation of Theil index	–0.009	–0.004	–0.007
Relative variation of Theil index (%)	-2.7	-1.5	-1.9

Source: EESI (2005)

Note: Phase 1 = authors' estimations

Table 11.9 Impact of gender income gap on inequalities (national level)

Index	*Weighting matrix*		
	Oaxaca	*Reimers*	*Cotton*
Absolute variation of Gini index	0.003	0.002	0.002
Relative variation of Gini index (%)	0.5	0.3	0.4
Absolute variation of Theil index	0.006	0.005	0.005
Relative variation of Theil index (%)	1.2	0.9	1.0

Source: EESI (2005)

Note: Phase 1 = authors' estimations

in a group of individuals living in households with at least one woman working in this sector. Whatever the weighting matrix used, there will be a decrease in the inequality indices. For example, with the Oaxaca matrix, the Gini index will go down from 0.434 to 0.429, a decrease of 1.2 per cent. With the Theil index, the differences between the initial situation and the counterfactual situation are more pronounced and illustrate a reduction of income inequalities of at least 1.5 per cent. So, within a group of beneficiaries, the non-discriminatory income that they would receive can be seen as a discriminatory progressive tax, which will benefit people belonging to low-income households more.

However, as shown in Table 11.9, the formal sector discrimination tax is progressive if we consider all of the Cameroonian population. The Gini index will increase by at least 0.4 per cent and the Theil index by about 1 per cent, all things been equal, indicating an increase in income inequalities. People living in households with at least one woman working in the formal sector were much less affected by poverty than the rest of the population (9.1 per cent against 53.5 per cent). Thus, increasing their incomes through the discrimination tax in the formal sector can only increase living standard inequalities and could even be a source of social tensions. However, this analysis is limited because it does not capture the impact of the discriminatory tax on the other sectors of activity and does not consider the relationship between economic agents.

6. Summary, conclusion and policy implications

The problems addressed by this study were gender wage differentials, poverty as characterized by the labor market and the impact of gender discrimination on income inequalities. The methodology used had three main points: Mincer's earning equations, an analysis of income gap using the classical approach developed by Oaxaca and Blinder and an analysis of the impact of the gender income gap on poverty based on the methodology proposed by Carlos Gradin. The data used was from the survey on employment and the informal sector conducted in 2005 by the National Institute of Statistics of Cameroon.

Regarding income gap, the earning functions confirmed the segmentation of the formal labor market into two sub-sectors: public sector and the private formal sector. We also noted that regardless of the segment, the earning function of women was different from that of men. The results indicated that the returns to education in the formal sector were convex; also, higher education was more profitable among female workers than among male workers. An analysis of the decomposition of the income gap showed that in the absence of discrimination in the formal labor market, women would be much better paid than men thanks to their the level of education. This factor contributed significantly to improving women's incomes, thus reducing the income gap. According to the segment it appears that gender discrimination was probably more severe in the public sector than in the formal private sector.

Poverty characterized by the labor market affected half the Cameroonians (50.8 per cent). People living in rural areas were more affected than those living in urban areas. Looking at the characteristics of the household head, it became clear that people living in households headed by women were poorer than those living in households headed by men. Monetary poverty characterized by the labor market declined when the level of education of the head of the household increased. Moreover, there seems to be a strong link between the employment sector of a household head and poverty; people living in households whose heads worked in rural agriculture were the most affected.

The impact of the gender wage gap on poverty shows that the eradication of gender wage differentials in the formal sector would help improve the living standard of people in households with at least one woman working in the formal sector. There should be an increase in women's incomes who were currently facing discrimination, particularly those with the lowest incomes; this would also result in reducing poverty indices and income inequalities in concerned households. At the national level, it would reduce the incidence of poverty, but at the same time income inequalities will also increase.

Regarding the impact of the suppression of gender wage discrimination on income inequalities, the study revealed a mixed picture. Within a group of households where there was at least one woman working in the formal sector, the non-discriminatory income that they received could be seen as a discriminatory progressive tax, which benefited low-income households more. But the formal sector discrimination tax was progressive if we considered all of the Cameroonian population. Households which had at least one woman working in the formal sector were less poor than the other households. Thus, increasing their incomes through a discrimination tax will increase income inequalities at the national level.

Policy recommendations

In terms of socioeconomic policy recommendations, the study suggests that the government:

- Develop a sustained social awareness strategy using the Convention on the Elimination of All Forms of Discrimination against Women (CEDAW), adopted by Cameroon in 1994, and gender discrimination evidence from data and research. This strategy can be used to: (1) help people understand the impact of gender bias; (2) promote gender equality at work and in the community; and (3) increase the public's understanding of the causes for the gender wage gap and why it is important to close the gap. Public and private enterprises, as well as civil society, should be part of this initiative.
- Apply a gender-based analysis (GBA) to the design, development, implementation and evaluation of all government policies and programs, including projects conducted with development partners. The implementation of this reform may require the development of a practical tool that will help ensure that GBA is applied from the beginning of any program or policy design process with a gender approach in civil service recruitments. This will help increase the impact of public investments in poverty reduction, especially for households headed by women.
- Improve women's negotiating powers through their better representation in senior positions in public institutions (the government, Parliament and public enterprises); a diverse representation of women on boards to a minimum of 30 per cent, with appropriate penalties for non-compliance and bonuses for public and private enterprises where gender equality is practiced.

To efficiently fight against gender discrimination and improve the living conditions of Cameroonians, the government should also facilitate women's access to productive resources such as micro-credit and land, as well as promote the transition of informal production units into SMEs/SMIs.

Appendix A

Table 11.A1 Regional price indices by area (base = Yaoundé)

Regions	*Urban areas*	*Rural areas*	*Together*
Douala	1.012		1.012
Yaoundé	1.000		1.000
Adamaoua	0.986	0.976	0.982
Centre	0.877	0.916	0.909
Est	0.880	0.924	0.914
Extrême Nord	0.940	0.759	0.787
Littoral	0.913	0.801	0.862
Nord	0.901	0.779	0.826
Nord Ouest	0.838	0.799	0.813
Ouest	0.895	0.815	0.841
Sud	0.934	0.940	0.939
Sud Ouest	0.836	0.871	0.855
Cameroon	0.946	0.916	0.933

Source: INS (2002b)

Table 11.A2 Coefficients of equivalence calculated on the basis of the harmonized ECAMI-ECAMII data

Age groups	*Coefficients of equivalence between the first adult and the other members of the household*
Head of household	1
Other adults	0.80
Boys aged 15 but less than 20 years	0.74
Girls aged 15 but less than 20 years	0.79
Boys aged 10 but less than 15 years	0.65
Girls aged 10 but less than 15 years	0.65
Boys aged 5 but less than 10 years	0.64
Girls aged 5 but less than 10 years	0.63
Boys aged 0 but less than 5 years	0.53
Girls aged 0 but less than 5 years	0.51

Source: Nembot Ndeffo et al. (2007)

Table 11.A3 Distribution of the sample of workers in the formal sector

	Public	*Private*	*Together*
Male	840	950	1,790
Female	364	210	574
Total	1,204	1,160	2,364

Source: EESI (2005)

Note: Phase 1 = authors' estimations

Table 11.A4 Contribution of variables to the components of income gap: case of the public sector

Technique	*Variables*	*Male advantage*	*Female disadvantage*	*Difference in productive characteristics*
Oaxaca	Education	0.000	0.229	–0.047
	Experience	0.000	–0.056	0.006
	Constant	0.000	0.174	0.000
Reimers	Education	0.108	0.114	–0.040
	Experience	–0.030	–0.028	0.008
	Constant	0.087	0.087	0.000
Cotton	Education	0.065	0.160	–0.043
	Experience	–0.018	–0.039	0.007
	Constant	0.052	0.122	0.000

Source: EESI (2005)

Note: Phase 1 = authors' estimations

Table 11.A5 Contribution of variables to the components of income gap: case of the private sector

Technique	*Variables*	*Male advantage*	*Female disadvantage*	*Difference in productive characteristics*
Oaxaca	Education	0.000	0.280	–0.080
	Experience	0.000	–0.150	0.033
	Constant	0.000	0.379	0.000
Reimers	Education	0.124	0.140	–0.064
	Experience	–0.073	–0.075	0.031
	Constant	0.190	0.190	0.000
Cotton	Education	0.047	0.227	–0.074
	Experience	–0.028	–0.122	0.032
	Constant	0.072	0.307	0.000

Source: EESI (2005)

Note: Phase 1 = authors' estimations

Table 11.A6 Distribution of monetary poverty as prescribed by labor according to some characteristics of the household head

Characteristics	*Incidence of poverty*	*Depth of poverty*	*Severity of poverty*	*Gini index*	*Income per adult equivalent (thousands of cfaf)*
Sex					
Male	48.6	22.2	13.3	0.502	24.8
Female	59.6	33.5	23.1	0.556	19.8
Level of education					
No level	72.5	36.8	23.8	0.456	13.4
Primary	56.3	27.5	17.1	0.459	18.4
Secondary 1st cycle	37.6	16.2	9.5	0.447	26.5
Secondary 2nd cycle	22.0	7.4	3.7	0.414	37.4
Higher education	7.5	3.8	2.7	0.438	71.9
Institutional Sector					
Public	8.4	2.8	1.3	0.393	51.2
Private formal	13.3	4.1	1.9	0.481	52.1
Informal non-agricultural	45.2	19.3	10.7	0.450	23.4
Informal agricultural	68.2	34.1	21.7	0.471	14.9
Inactive	51.1	29.3	21.3	0.485	21.3
Household's size					
1 person	31.1	17.1	12.1	0.555	42.9
2–3 persons	39.9	19.9	13.0	0.526	31.6
4–5 persons	50.1	24.0	14.9	0.507	23.5
More than 5 persons	55.3	26.4	16.3	0.490	20.6
Cameroon	50.8	24.5	15.3	0.514	23.8

Source: EESI (2005)

Note: Phase 1 = authors' estimations; weighted data

Notes

1 This study was conducted with a grant from the African Economic Research Consortium (AERC). We would like to express our thanks to all those who contributed directly or indirectly to its achievement. We would particularly like to thank Professors Eric Thorbecke, Jean Yves Duclos, David Sahn, John Strauss and Patrick Plane, and also anonymous commentators, for their contributions.

2 Supposing that unobserved factors have a constant effect over time, if at time 1, we note α_i the unobserved effect, then $y_{I1} = \beta x_{I1} + \alpha_i + \epsilon_{i1}$ and at time 2, $y_{I2} = \beta x_{I2} + \alpha_i + \epsilon_{i2}$, using the first differences, we have $y_{I2} - y_{I1} = \beta(x_{I2} - x_{11}) + \epsilon_{i2} - \epsilon_{i1})$. The estimation of the equation in first differences can in some cases solve the problem of unobserved or omitted factors.

3 Several authors of studies related to gender wage differentials have used these matrices. For example, François (1997) used Cotton's and Reimers's matrices. On the other hand, others, such as Pilar González et al. (2005), used the weightings of Oaxaca, Cotton and Neumark.

4 Labor market segmentation can be defined as a situation where workers with similar productive characteristics get different salaries. For example, these differences can be observed between rural and urban wages or between those in the formal and the informal sectors. They may also exist between employees engaged in various industries (Marouani, 2002).

5 The key variables are schooling and labor market experience. According to the human capital theory, both variables positively affect workers' incomes (Mincer, 1974). The square of these variable are expected to have a negative sign to illustrate the concavity of schooling and work experience.

6 Eq. 3 can also be written as: $Ln(w_i) = c + r_1 S + r_2 S^2 + aE + bE^2 + \theta_i \lambda_i + e_i$ Then, $\frac{\partial Ln(w_i)}{\partial S} = r_1 + 2r_2 S$ is the marginal rate of return to education.

7 The poverty line used by the National Institute of the Statistics of Cameroon in 2007 to measure monetary poverty was 22,454 cfaf per month and, in 2001, it was 19,378 cfaf per month.

8 While considering individuals aged 15 years and above, the monthly income of a woman working in the informal sector was about half that earned by a man: 19,400 cfaf against 36,000 cfaf in the non-agricultural sector and 8,900 cfaf against 17,300 cfaf in the agricultural sector (authors' calculations using EESI data).

9 The results of the Third General Housing and Population Census indicate that Cameroon's total population was 17,463,836 in 2005.

References

Adams, J. (1991). "The rural labour market in Zimbabwe", *Development and Change*, 22(2), 297–320.

Angrist, J. and V. Lavy (1997). "The effect of a change in language of instruction on the returns to schooling in Morocco", *Journal of Labour Economics*, 15(1), S48–S76.

Arrow, K. (1973). "The theory of discrimination", in O.A. Ashenfelter and A. Rees (eds), *Discrimination in Labor Markets*. Princeton, NJ: Princeton University Press, pp. 3–33.

Becker, G. (1964). "Human capital: A theoretical and empirical analysis, with special reference to education", in Gary Backer (ed.), *National Bureau of Economic Research* (1993 edition). New York : Columbia University Press for the National Bureau for Economic Research.

Becker, G. (1975). *The Economics of Discrimination* (2nd ed.). Chicago: The University of Chicago Press.

Blinder, A. (1973). "Wage discrimination: Reduced form and structural estimates", *Journal of Human Resources*, 8(4), 436–455.

Borjas, G. (2000). "The economic progress of immigrants", in Georges Borjas (ed.), *Issues in the Economics of Immigration*. Chicago: The University of Chicago Press, pp. 15–50.

Cambarnous, F. (1994). "Discrimination et le marché du travail: concept et coût", Centre d'économie de développement, Université Montesqieu-Bordeau IV-France.

Costa, J. and E. Silva (2008). "The burden of inequality for society", *International Poverty Centre*, 8–9.

Cotton, J. (1988). "On the decomposition of wage differentials", *Review of Economics and Statistics*, 70, 236–243.

Ministère de l'Économie, de la Planification de l'Aménagement du Territoire (DRSP) (2003). *Document de stratégie de réduction de la pauvreté*. République du Cameroun.

Ministère de l'Économie, de la Planification de l'Aménagement du Territoire (DSCE) (2009). *Document de stratégie pour la Croissance et l'Emploi*. République du Cameroun. Available at: www.minepat.gov.cm/index.php/fr/component/docman/doc_details/108-document-de-strategies-pour-la-croissance-et-l-emploi-dsce

EESI (2005) "Enquête sur l'Emploi et le Secteur Informal -EESI 1", République du Cameroun, Institut National de la Statistique. Available at: www.statistics-cameroon.org.

Ehrenberg, R. and R. Smith (1994). *Modern Labour Economics: Theory and Public Policy* (5th ed.). New York: Harper Collins College Publishers.

Fambon, S., Baye F. M., Tamba I., Noumba I. and Amin A. (2005). "Réformes Economiques et pauvreté au Cameroun durant les années 80 et 90", Recherche Collaborative sur la pauvreté/AERC Vol 2 rapport final.

Foko, T.B.A., F. Ndem and T. Rosine (2007). "Pauvreté et Inégalités des Conditions de vie au Cameroun: une approche Micro-Multidimensionnelle", Cahier de Recherche PMMA 2007-Réseau PEP.

Foster, J., G. Joel, and E. Thorbecke (1984). "A class of decomposable poverty measures", *Econometrica*, 52(3), 761–766.

Gbetnkom, D. (1999). "Libéralisation commerciale et pauvreté en Afrique Subsaharienne: l'examen du cas du Cameroun", *Revue Africaine des Sciences Economiques et Gestion*, 1(2), 107–135.

González, P., M.C. Santos and L.D. Santos (2005). "The gender wage gap in Portugal: Recent evolution and decomposition", CETE – Centro de Estudos de Economia Industrial, do Trabalho e da Empresa. Research Center on Industrial, Labour and Managerial Economics, DP 2005–05.

Gradín, C., C. Del Río, and O. Cantó (2006). "Poverty and women's labor market activity: The role of gender wage discrimination in the EU", Society for the Study of Economic Inequality (ECINEQ), Working Papers 2006–40.

Haugthon, J. and S. Khandker (2009). "Handbook on poverty and inequality", The International Bank for Reconstruction and Development, The World Bank.

Heckman, J. (1979). "Sample selection bias as a specification error", *Econometrica*, 47(1), 153.

Hoddinott, J. and L. Haddad (1995). "Does female income share influence household expenditures? Evidence from Cote d'Ivoire", *Oxford Bulletin of Economics and Statistics*, 57(1), 77–96.

INS (1997). *Conditions de vie des ménages au Cameroun en 1996, Enquête camerounaise auprès des ménages – Volume 2,* Institut National de la Statistique.

INS (2002a). "Conditions de vie des populations et profil de pauvreté au Cameroun en 2001. Deuxième Enquête Camerounaise auprès des ménages", Institut National de la Statistique, République du Cameroun.

INS (2002b). "Document de méthodologie: Calcul du seuil de pauvreté et de l'indicateur de niveau de vie. Deuxième Enquête Camerounaise auprès des ménages", Institut National de la Statistique, République du Cameroun.

INS (2005). "Phase 1: Enquête Emploi. Enquête sur l'Emploi et le Secteur Informel", Institut National de la Statistique, République du Cameroun.

INS (2008). "Tendances, profil et déterminants de la pauvreté au Cameroun entre 2001–2007. Troisième Enquête Camerounaise auprès des ménages", Institut National de la Statistique, République du Cameroun.

Jenkins, S.P. (1994). "Earnings discrimination measurement: A distributional approach", *Journal of Econometrics,* 61, 81–102.

Keupie, M., C. Nordman, and F. Roubeau (2008). "Education and earnings in urban West Africa", *Journal of Comparative Economics,* 37, 491–515.

Marouani, A.M. (2002). "Imperfections du marche du travail et modèles d'équilibre général calculables: une revue de littérature", DIAL – UR CIPRE de l'IRD et Université de Paris-Dauphine.

Mincer, J. (1974). *Schooling, Experience and Schooling.* New York: Columbia University Press.

Nembot Ndeffo, L., N. Ngwen, P. Joubert Nguetse Tegoum, and M. Makoudem (2007). "Impact des échelles d'équivalence sur la répartition spatiale de la pauvreté au Cameroun: une approche dynamique", PMMA Working Paper 2007–04, Réseau PEP.

Neuman, S. and R. Oaxaca (2004). "Wage differentials in the 1990s in Israel: Endowments, discrimination, and selectivity", IZA Discussion Paper Series 1362.

Neumark, D. (1988). "Employer's discriminatory behaviour and the estimation of wage discrimination", *Journal of Human Resources,* 23, 279–295.

Njinkeu, D., G. Kobou, and I. Noumba (1998). "Structural adjustment and poverty in Cameroon: A labour market analysis", ICEG of Development, Final report.

Nordman, C., A.S. Robilliard, and F. Roubau (2009). "Decomposing gender and ethnic earnings gaps in seven West African cities", Développement Institutions et Analyses à Long terme (DIAL), DT 2009/07.

Oaxaca, R. (1973). "Male-female wage differentials labor markets", *International Economic Review,* 14(3), 693–709.

Oaxaca, R. and M. Ransom (1994). "On discrimination and the decomposition of wage differentials", *Journal of Econometrics,* 61(1), 5–21.

Polachek, S.W. and M.K. Kim (1994). "Panel estimates of the gender earnings gap: Individual-specific intercept and individual-specific slope models", *Journal of Econometrics,* 61(1), 23–42.

Reigen, S. (1987). *The Possibility of Politics Study in Political Economy of Welfare State.* Oxford: Clarendon Press.

Schultz, T. (2004). "Evidence of returns to schooling in Africa from household surveys: Monitoring and restructuring the market for education", *Journal of African Economies,* 13, 95–148.

World Bank (1995). "Cameroon:Diversity, Growth, and Poverty Reduction". Report N°13167-CM. Washington, DC: The World Bank.

12 Econometric analysis of business start-ups in Rwanda

Joseph Ndagijimana, Tharcisse Nzasingizimana and Almas Heshmati

1. Introduction

Today there is extensive literature on various aspects of economic development and on aspects such as interest rate, inflation, exchange rate and taxation and their different combinations. Some econometric studies try and explain the link between the interest rate spread and the remaining factors and several other variables such as non-performing loans, reserve requirements, lending interest rate and financial taxation. Literature in each area is comprehensive and several reviews provide overviews of the research field. For instance, Bernanke (1990) studied stylized empirical results on firms' financial constraints and the effects that they had on firms. The author found that financial constraints hindered firms' abilities to carry out their optimal investment and growth trajectories. The severity of the constraints depended on institutional and firm-specific characteristics and the nature of investment projects. Balogun et al. (2016) provide a survey of financial liberalization in sub-Saharan Africa aimed at reversing the ill effects of financial repression. The authors find evidence of diverse and contrasting effects on savings, investments and economic growth. In another study Roache (2007) offers a systematic review of the importance of R&D investments in explaining economic growth and the effectiveness of public R&D policies in crowding-in private R&D investments. Vanacker and Deloof (2015) investigated the evolution of entrepreneurial firms' debt policies. A firm's debt policy was found stable over time and in determining its future debt policies.

Governments and other socioeconomic actors in different countries are very vigilant about the evolution of the spread of interest rates. Interest rate is both a facilitator and a constraint on investment opportunities in economic development. High indebtedness of states through increased interest rates and tax pressures have limited credit markets for private sector development. This shows that interest rates play a fundamental role in economic regulation with implications for economic growth and in the development of different industries and sectors in the economy (Berument et al., 2014).

Interest rates differ across banks and credit institutions; they also differ over time. Many factors affect the levels and variations, including investment risks and supply and demand. The interest rate spread variable is a pre-occupation of many economists in business, banking and government, mainly due to its link with the investment, savings and the repayment capacities of businesses in general. A large interest rate spread is harmful for development in general and for business start-ups in particular. Definitions of various determinants related to start-ups can be different depending on the type of economic activity (De Fiore and Tristani, 2011).

In this research, the determinants used are (though they are not necessarily limited to only these) (Jonas Costa Da Silva et al., 2015) interest rate spread, inflation, exchange rate and taxation. For example, for economists, interest rate is the price that allows bringing in an equilibrium between savings and investments and supply and demand for money in a market economy (Ceylan et al., 2015). Our study uses this general definition to investigate the interest rate spread and its evolution.

Our study contributes to literature in a number of ways. First, it empirically investigates the relationships between interest rate spread and its determinants in a dynamic development economic environment. Second, it studies the relationships in the context of business start-ups. And finally it provides insights into windows of policy opportunities to promote business start-ups.

The rest of this study is organized as follows. Section 2 reviews general literature about the Rwandan context and the importance of start-ups. Section 3 discusses business start-ups in Rwanda; it explains the current state, development over time, potential for further development, key components and the role of the government as an introduction to the sector. Section 4 presents the research methods and techniques while Section 5 details the data and models, as well as gives an analysis of the empirical results. The last section provides a conclusion and also gives important recommendations on effective use of the findings for promoting business start-ups in Rwanda.

2. Related literature

A number of reviews on start-ups and financial constraints, the evolution of debt and public finance policies and stability of firms' debt structures are mentioned in the Introduction. The reasons for an increase in interest rates in less-developed countries are almost the same; the only difference lies in the structure of the financial system in each country and in how money functions in that system (Ho and Lee, 1986).

2.1 General context

Barajas et al. (2000) conducted a study on this subject in Colombia. They indicate that during 1974–96, the interest rate spread in public banks was 24.6 per cent. They used both a model of a multiple linear regression equation and a simultaneous equations model to explain the factors behind the interest rate spreads. The explanatory variables that they used in their study are taxes and functions of variable costs, including wages and non-performing loans. This situation resulted in the reduction of reserve requirements and a shift in deposits away from demand deposits and towards savings.

Birchwood et al. (2016) covered eight countries of the Eastern Caribbean Currency Union (ECCU) and used income statements and consolidated balance sheets of commercial banks to determine interest rates using an accounting approach. The authors acknowledge that this descriptive approach did not clearly capture the behavior of start-ups. To overcome this shortcoming, the authors introduced a model based on competition between banks. The model introduced price elasticities of demand for loans and demand for deposits as key variables in determining the potential impact of any change in the determinants of interest rates.

Based on the existence of simultaneity in the formulation of supply and demand models, all the authors mentioned earlier used a system of simultaneous equations. Using 24 quarterly observations for each of the eight countries in the ECCU region over six years, the determinants of interest rate spreads were obtained by alternative least squares. The econometric results for these countries show that economic growth was negatively correlated with interest rates. An increase in deposits raised the interest rate spreads due to an increase in resources and administrative costs. A 1.2 per cent increase in the supply of lendable deposits led to an increase of 1 per cent in lending interest rates. A 1 per cent increase in lending interest rates was due to a decrease of 4.6 per cent in the demand for lendable funds.

Antwi and Antwi (2013) conducted a study in Ghana. They noted that their market share in the banking system explained the overall behavior of banks and found that there was a lack of perfect competition in starting a business due to the banking system in the country. In addition, high operating costs, largely dominated by wages as well as bank net profits, had a significant impact on the increase in interest rate spreads in the country. Their study also shows that cash banks, taxation and inflation exchange rate may also have a significant impact on the gap between interest rates even if their impact was smaller than that of operating costs.

A study by Yang et al. (2011) shows that Pacific island nations and the Caribbean have higher interest rates than Fiji islands, which have a relatively lower bank interest rate spread. Their study also shows that the main problems in starting a business were (in order of magnitude): bank net profits (65 per cent), operating costs (6 per cent), taxation (5 per cent), inflation (5 per cent), exchange rate (7 per cent) and non-performing loans (12 per cent). Further, the study notes that income other than interest (fees and commissions) was an important element in reducing the interest rate spreads, as it could compensate for any increase because of the variables mentioned earlier. The authors say: 'The Fijian oligopolistic market structure gives room to banks on the unfair basis and seems to be selective, accepting only a limited number of small enterprises that can be provided loans in order to maximize their profit.'

2.2 *The Rwandan context*

Like central banks in many countries, the National Bank of Rwanda (BNR) ensures the supervision of banks in the monetary and financial sectors. It introduces Rwanda's monetary policy using tools of control such as reserve requirements and issuing of treasury bills and bonds. BNR also intervenes in the creation of necessary liquidity or in the withdrawal of excess liquidity. The policy includes aspects of currency or exchange rate stabilization (Chen et al., 2002).

Regarding the management of liquidity, the banking system in Rwanda has been in a situation of permanent excess cash for many years. In order to adjust the banking liquidity to monetary measures, BNR has intervened by borrowing on the monetary market and by selling foreign currency in commercial banks in order to reduce the excess liquidity. This government borrowing system resulted in an increase of 16.2 per cent in the total domestic loans given by the central bank to commercial banks (Chen et al., 2002).

The lending interest rates charged by commercial banks were still at a high level, averaging at 18 per cent, while the deposit interest rate kept decreasing. In 2010, it was 7.1 per cent for a maturity period of three months. The large gap between lending and saving interest rates discouraged savings and starting new businesses (BNR, 2011, 2012).

2.3 *Importance of business start-ups in creating jobs and poverty reduction*

Introduction

The first objective of entering a new business is to have an occupation and reach a certain profit; this requires specific technical skills. Currently, the most common businesses include trading, construction, repairs and personal services such as hairdressing. Skills gained from training or apprenticeship are mainly provided by private rather than public institutions. Governments should recognize their importance in the household income sector and in poverty reduction and include them in their annual economic planning (OECD, 1996).

Creation of productive employment

There is evidence that start-ups contribute much to economic growth and in reducing poverty and they can provide better opportunities than other economic activities such as agriculture. The extent to which new businesses exist on the strategic radar screen in Rwanda shows that they are seen as entities ready to be transformed into formalized SMEs in order to access finance easily.

In Rwanda, many households are engaged in farm and non-farm activities at the same time. In urban areas, families start small enterprises and earn wage incomes, which is a pattern that is likely to increase over time (Fox and Sohnesen, 2012).

Even if their productivity is low, family enterprises provide earnings usually higher than anything their owners could acquire in the formal sector. Most of them have no employees and are self-employed. Some of them start a business in response to local business service opportunities (such as an increased demand for a certain service), whereas others are started because a household lacks alternative means of earning a living.

Such enterprises mainly sell services (hairdressing, repairs) and produce consumer goods (used clothing, household supplies, vegetables, eggs). They can also contribute to the industrial sector by transforming agriculture products or natural resources into charcoal, bricks, etc. Further, some also pursue artisanal activities such as woodworking, dressmaking and tailoring and construction. In urban areas, sometimes traders and hawkers sell in stores and shopping malls.

Despite their small scale, start-ups are an instrument for reducing poverty with the potential of becoming even more powerful. Households starting small enterprises are less likely to be poor and are clustered in the middle quintiles of the income distribution. The employment they provide, including employment for young people, comes from seizing a business opportunity and starting a new enterprise. Rural households gain a higher hourly income from family enterprises than from agricultural work. In urban areas, some start-up owners make more money than they would from a wage job (Filmer and Fox, 2014).

Government intervention

The Rwandan government has put in considerable efforts in coordinating its donors focusing on aid effectiveness. However, the ownership of its policies does not escape prominent related constraints. Rwanda is still a developing country that is highly aid dependent with development cooperation.

Since 2010 most of the donors are mainly engaged in traditional sectors of development coordination such as education and health, whereas sectors such as manufacturing, services, off-farm industry and ICT are apparently less popular among donors.

Such a situation should change because in developing countries young people pass many years idle or doing odd jobs while seeking salaried jobs in companies around the country (Grimm et al., 2010). Better monitoring and evaluation will help governments to identify which programs might be scaled up effectively. Related public policies should be put in place with a certain focus on two elements:

1 urban policies that provide adequate locations where new entrepreneurs can work and sell their products along with essential support services such as lighting, water, sanitation and security; and
2 financial sector policies and programs that encourage private providers to improve household access to financial services, including saving and credit cooperatives or some guarantee fund institutions (Fox and Sohnesen, 2012).

Most programs provide support to set up a business but sometimes participants need assistance even after a business is started.

Conclusion

Start-ups are growing as a share of the labor force not because of regulatory or economic growth failures, but because in low-income countries such as Rwanda, they are the best option for labor force participants who want to use their skills to create non-farm incomes for their families.

Thus, traders and personal services' providers need premises not outside the town (to stay near their customers), but in central business districts (on sidewalks), at bus stop and terminals, near major road intersections and other places that are convenient for people to shop in.

Repair shops and manufactures such as metalworking operations need to cluster to realize agglomeration efficiencies and for sharing technology. Industrial estates designed for large firms can include start-ups in planning and space location.

3. Business start-ups in Rwanda

Starting a business in Rwanda requires an entrepreneur to plan and take decisions on a number of important issues. These include decisions in relation to location, the size of the start-up, investments required, contact with supportive institutions and, if the firm does not want to remain in the informal sector, ensuring that it moves to the formal sector by registering with the Business Registration Office, Rwanda Development Board (www.rdb.rw; Rutayisire, 2010).

3.1 Current state

The government agency, the Rwanda Development Board (RDB), is responsible for promoting investments and facilitating market entry for investors in both the public and private sectors. It is often a good place to start when one is considering establishing a business in Rwanda. RDB offers a range of services to potential investors, including assistance in acquiring licenses, certificates, approvals, authorizations and permits required by law to set up and operate a business enterprise in Rwanda (The World Bank, 2006). These aspects may seem similar but together they provide all necessary documents characterizing a formal enterprise with legal protection, rights and obligations (The World Bank, 2006).

In Rwanda a business can be registered as an individual business with national, foreign or joint ownership. Registering a company in Rwanda is done online and it takes less than a week to obtain a Certificate of Incorporation. The registrar's office in RDB acts as a one-stop-shop which takes care of all formalities related to the registration of a start-up in the country. This process has rationalized complex procedures and helps in attracting foreign and national investors to establish companies in Rwanda (The World Bank, 2010).

3.2 Development over time

Figure 12.1 shows the development of entrepreneurship in Rwanda in 2000–15. It shows that a large number of new businesses were registered during this time. We can see that from 2011 there has been a steep upward trend. This is explained by the fact that in this year new businesses were encouraged to register using the online system.

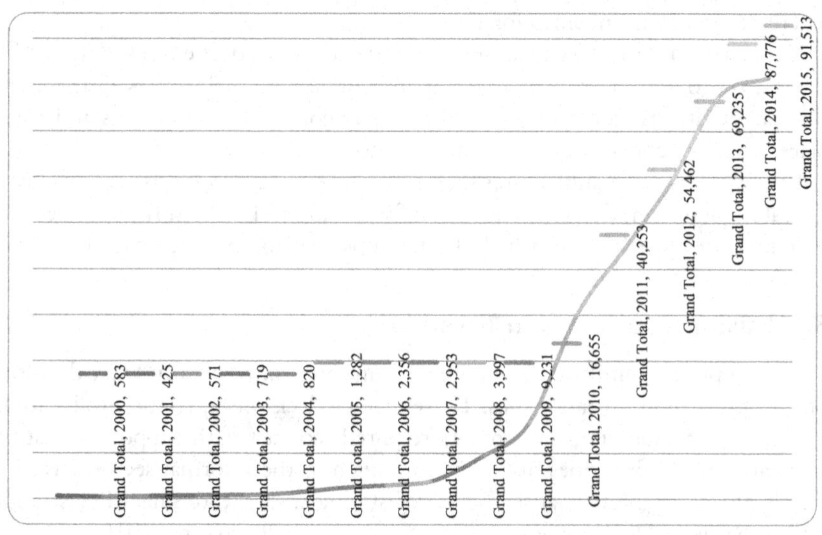

Figure 12.1 New businesses registration trend (2000–15)

Source: Calculations based on the Office of the Registrar General's (ORG's) data (The World Bank, 2013)

Annual data show that in 2015 the growth rate in registering new businesses reduced to 4 per cent (91,513) from 27 per cent in 2014 (87,776) and in 2013 (69,235). From 2015 most registered firms are start-ups; they are not transitions from informal to formal status. In addition to the success of online registration for firms, urbanization is also rapidly making progress, leading to high growth rates in new entrepreneurship (Behuria and Goodfellow, 2016).

3.3 *Potential for further development*

The Office of Registrar General (ORG) is committed to promoting Rwanda as a preferred investment destination. This commitment is practiced through the provision of world-class registration services and systems, provision of updated and quick information to all clients and improved business operations in the country. The aim is to achieve stated national goals through developing and ensuring compliance with a modern and internationally competitive corporate governance framework (Rahim, 2012).

3.4 *Key components and government rule*

Three steps are required for getting an investment certificate: an application for an investment registration, notice of acceptance or refusal and issuance of an investment registration certificate.

The application for investment registration involves the following steps:

A Application letter requesting investment registration;
B Submission of a business plan or a feasibility study;
C Shareholding structure sheet; and
D Certificate of the company's incorporation.

The investment application letter should clearly indicate the following: the name and address of the proposed business enterprise and its legal form; the nature of the proposed business activity and the level of planned capital investment; the estimated number of persons to be employed and the categories of jobs to be created; the nature and volume of waste that will be generated by the enterprise's operations and proposed methods for its management; and the nature of support and facilitation that the investor is seeking from RDB (African Development Bank Group, 2012).

The investment business plan or feasibility study should clearly indicate the state of the following 13 items:

1 Executive summary of the project;
2 Profile of the project promoter(s);
3 Project background;
4 Market study or market analysis;
5 Investment plan over a five-year period;
6 The level of loans and equity financing;
7 Projected statement of income and expenditure five years ahead;
8 Projected balance sheet (five years ahead);
9 Projected statement of cash flows (five years ahead);
10 Payback period, net present value (NPV) and investment return rate (IRR);
11 Loan amortization schedule for a bank loan (if any);
12 Project implementation plan/schedule; and
13 Notes on assumptions made in the business plan.

Once the application for investment registration is approved, an acceptance letter for the project is issued. Otherwise, a notice of refusal and the reason for the refusal is given. In case the documents are not in order or the information provided is inadequate, improvements are requested. Upon the receipt of proof of payment, an investment registration certificate is issued. The investment certificate allows access to investment incentives provided in the investment code. It takes two days to process the application and issue the certificate of investment registration if all documents are submitted and they are in order.

Finally, there are a number of criteria related to an investment project's evaluation, including level of investment, non-trading activity, creation of high skill and quality jobs, transfer of skills and technology, use of local raw materials, potential for export, potential to create backward and forward linkages, and innovation and creativity (Dahlman, 2007).

4. Methodology

All scientific research requires methods and techniques for collecting and analyzing data on the subject of the study. The following methods and techniques were used in this study.

Snape and Spencer (2003) define 'method' as all the intellectual operations by which a discipline seeks to achieve the truth it pursues, in showing and verifying it. We used three research methods. First, the comparative method allowed us to compare the influences that the various factors have on starting a business in Rwanda. Second, we also used the dialectical method that integrates inductive and deductive approaches. We combined empirical facts with reasoning to clarify various aspects of starting a business in Rwanda. Finally, the systems approach clarified the impact of various economic factors on starting a business (Bank, 2013).

The techniques used were rigorous operative procedures, which are well-defined and transmittable and which can be applied again under the same conditions adapted to similar problems and phenomena (Cassell and Symon, 2004). An attempt was also made to use quantitative techniques for an efficiency analysis (Greene, 2008). In general, the techniques employed in this study include: (1) the documentary technique which helped in consulting documents related to the subject such as books, magazines, papers, reports and the internet; (2) statistical technique for the data; and (3) EViews in an econometric analysis of the behavior of starting a business in Rwanda between 2006–15.

5. Data and econometric model

The purpose of this section is to empirically verify the validity of the theories developed over the years in economic practices in Rwanda. This was done through statistical techniques for collecting and analyzing data and using methods of estimating econometric models to identify the main determinants or factors, in particular in the interest rate spread, inflation, exchange rate and taxes that influence starting a business in Rwanda.

Our econometric analysis involved a study of the influence of interest rate spread (lending rate minus deposit rate), inflation rate, exchange rate (FRW/USD) and taxation (measured by the tax on goods and services) on starting a business in Rwanda. Starting a business in Rwanda is measured by the number of new entrants in business irrespective of economic sectors. Sectoral heterogeneity in response to changes in the factors mentioned earlier is controlled for.

Appendix A presents the data that was used in our regressing model. This data was provided by the National Institute of Statistics of Rwanda (NISR) in conjunction with the BNR. Other data was collected from the Rwanda Development Board (RDB). Availability of ready and workable data pushed us to use unique quarterly data from 2006 to 2015 for the econometric analysis.

The econometric model of starting a business as a function of its determinants is specified as:

$$BS = \alpha + \beta_1 \, IRS + \beta_2 \, INF + \beta_3 \, ER + \beta_4 \, TAX + \varepsilon \tag{1}$$

where the dependent variable is new business start-ups (*BS*), independent variables include interest rate spread (*IRS*), inflation (*INF*), exchange rate (*ER*) and taxation (*TAX*). The model is appended with a random error term (ε) to take into account the fact that the model is not supposed to fully represent the actual relationship between the independent variables and the dependent variable (*BS*).

5.1 *Model specification and testing*

Some time series models do not respect basic principles of stationarity and co-integration, which implies tests before any estimation. Therefore, we had to test stationarity and co-integration of our variables *BS*, *IRS*, *IFL*, *ER* and *TAX*.

The following three conditions must be fulfilled for a series to be stationary:

- either $E(Y_t) = E(Y_{t+m}) = \mu$, $\forall vt$ and $\forall vm$, the mean is independent of time.
- var $(Y_t) \neq \infty$, the variance is finite and independent of time.
- cov $(Y_t, Y_{t+k}) = E[(Y_t - \mu)(Y_{t+k} - \mu) = \gamma_k$, the covariance is independent of time.

where Y refers to business start-ups *BS*. In short, for a series to be stationary, it is necessary that its mean, its variance and its auto-covariance do not change over time. Note that a series that is not stationary in the sense defined here is called non-stationary. A chronological stationary series is important because if it is not stationary, we can study the behavior for a given period only. Therefore, it is not possible to make a generalization for other periods. Such non-stationary series will have no reliable practical value. Similarly, the student test (*t*-test) cannot be used. Therefore, as noted by Granger, a co-integration test can be thought to be a pre-test to avoid a fake regression situation (Granger, 1986).

The stationarity test was used to test the null hypothesis H_0: $\alpha - 1 = 0$ (non-stationary) and the alternative hypothesis H_1: $\alpha - 1 < 0$ (stationary) for the following models:

1 $\Delta Y_t = (\alpha - 1)Y_{t-1} + \nu_t$ Model with no intercept or trend
2 $\Delta Y_t = \beta_0 + (\alpha - 1)Y_{t-1} + \nu_t$ Model with intercept but without tendency
3 $\Delta Y_t = \beta_0 + \beta_{1t} + (\alpha - 1)Y_{t-1} + \nu_t$ Model with intercept and trend

where Y refers to business start-ups, *BS* in our model. We have a unit root if $\alpha = 1$ and the model is non-stationary. In this case the statistic τ (tau) replaces the student test. The Augmented Dickey-Fuller (ADF) test was used by adding more differentiated terms Y_t (that is, $\alpha_i \sum_{i=1} \Delta Y_{t-1}$) to correct errors in the auto-correlation model of *DF*. Thus, the properties of constant mean, variance and covariance and stationarity allow for the generalization of the result across time periods.

5.2 Model testing

Test of variables' stationarity

Tables 12.B1–12.B6 (Appendix B) helped us choose the optimum lag length to use for the Augmented Dicky-Fuller (*ADF*) test. After comparing the critical values in each table by identifying the minimum Akaike information criterion, the lag length for *BS* was 2; it was 1 for *INF*; while *IRS*, *ER* and *TAX* variables did not require any lag value for the stationarity test as their *P*, lag length, was equal to 0.

A1 ADF TEST FOR THE BS VARIABLE

Table 12.1 shows the results of the *ADF* test for new business start-ups (*BS*) variable and its first difference.

Table 12.1 shows that the *BS* variable is not stationary, as all test critical values for all levels (1 per cent, 5 per cent and 10 per cent) are less that their corresponding *ADF* test statistics. To make this variable stationary, we differentiated it and applied the *ADF* test to its first difference. The results are presented in the second half of Table 12.1, which shows that *BS* is integrated of order 1 as its first difference is stationary.

A2 ADF TEST FOR THE IRS VARIABLE

Table 12.2 shows the *ADF* test for interest rate spread (*IRS*) and its first difference.

Table 12.2 shows that the *IRS* variable is not stationary. Its first difference was tested and the results are presented in the second part of Table 12.2. Consequently, Table 12.2 shows that *IRS* is integrated of order 1. All its test critical values are greater than their corresponding *ADF* test statistics.

Table 12.1 Results of the *ADF* test for the *BS* variable and its first difference

Model	*ADF test statistic*	*Test critical values: 1 per cent*	*Test critical values: 5 per cent*	*Test critical values: 10 per cent*
BS variable:				
Trend and intercept	-2.0849	-4.2268	-3.5366	-3.2003
Intercept	1.3789	-3.6210	-2.9434	-2.6102
None	3.1570	-2.6289	-1.9501	-1.6113
BS first difference:				
Trend and intercept	-5.9021	-4.2268	-3.5366	-3.2003
Intercept	-5.3628	-3.6210	-2.9434	-2.6102
None	-3.8260	-2.6289	-1.9501	-1.6113

Source: Authors' computations.

Table 12.2 Results of the *ADF* test for the *IRS* variable and its first difference

Model	*ADF test statistic*	*Test critical values: 1 per cent*	*Test critical values: 5 per cent*	*Test critical values: 10 per cent*
IRS variable:				
Trend and intercept	-2.4553	-4.2118	-3.5297	-3.1964
Intercept	-2.4808	-3.6104	-2.9389	-2.6079
None	0.0839	-2.6256	-1.9496	-1.6115
IRS first difference:				
Trend and intercept	-5.7066	-4.2191	-3.5330	-3.1983
Intercept	-5.7687	-3.6155	-2.9411	-2.6090
None	-5.8272	-2.6272	-1.9498	-1.6114

Source: Authors' computations.

Table 12.3 Results of the *ADF* test for the *INF* variable and its first difference

Model	*ADF test statistic*	*Test critical values: 1 per cent*	*Test critical values: 5 per cent*	*Test critical values: 10 per cent*
Trend and intercept	-3.5971	-4.2191	-3.5330	-3.1983
Intercept	-2.4193	-3.6155	-2.9411	-2.6090
None	-1.7002	-2.6272	-1.9498	-1.6114

Source: Authors' computations.

A3 ADF TEST FOR THE INF VARIABLE

Table 12.3 shows the *ADF* test for the inflation rate (*INF*) variable and its first difference.

Table 12.3 shows that the *INF* variable is stationary: the test critical values are greater than the *ADF* test statistics at 5 per cent and 10 per cent with trend and intercept and also at 10 per cent without trend and intercept.

A4 ADF TEST FOR THE ER VARIABLE

Table 12.4 shows the *ADF* test results for the exchange rate (*ER*) variable and its first difference.

Table 12.4 shows that the *ER* variable is not stationary: the test critical values are less than their corresponding *ADF* test statistics at 1 per cent, 5 per cent and 10 per cent. To make the *ER* variable stationary, we differentiated it and applied the *ADF* test to its first difference, which resulted in the *ER* being integrated of order 1 as its first difference is stationary.

A5 ADF TEST FOR THE TAX VARIABLE

Table 12.5 shows the *ADF* test results for the tax rate variable (*TAX*) and its first difference.

Table 12.4 Results of the *ADF* test for the *ER* variable

Model	*ADF test statistic*	*Test critical values: 1 per cent*	*Test critical values: 5 per cent*	*Test critical values: 10 per cent*
ER variable:				
Trend and intercept	-0.6435	-4.2118	-3.5297	-3.1964
Intercept	4.4021	-3.6104	-2.9389	-2.6079
None	5.7040	-2.6256	-1.9496	-1.6115
ER first difference:				
Trend and intercept	-6.7146	-4.2191	-3.5330	-3.1983
Intercept	-4.2381	-3.6155	-2.9411	-2.6090
None	-2.7197	-2.6272	-1.9498	-1.6114

Source: Authors' computations.

Table 12.5 Results of the *ADF* test for the *TAX* variable and its first difference

Model	*ADF test statistic*	*Test critical values: 1 per cent*	*Test critical values: 5 per cent*	*Test critical values: 10 per cent*
TAX variable:				
Trend and intercept	-2.4190	-4.2118	-3.5297	-3.1964
Intercept	-0.5662	-3.6104	-2.9389	-2.6079
None	2.7993	-2.6256	-1.9496	-1.6115
TAX first difference:				
Trend and intercept	-5.4973	-4.2191	-3.5330	-3.1983
Intercept	-5.5720	-3.6155	-2.9411	-2.6090
None	-4.5462	-2.6272	-1.9498	-1.6114

Source: Authors' computations.

Table 12.5 shows that the *TAX* variable is not stationary. To make the *TAX* variable stationary, we differentiated it and applied the *ADF* test to its first difference. The results are presented in Table 12.5. In conclusion, the *ADF* test revealed that only the inflation rate (*INF*) variable was stationary while other variables were not stationary but that their first differences were stationary. This means that they were integrated of order 1.

Co-integration test

We first estimated the following model:

$$BS = \alpha + \beta_1 \, IRS + \beta_2 \, INF + \beta_3 \, ER + \beta_4 \, TAX + \varepsilon \tag{2}$$

After estimation we obtained:

$$BS = -42766.6 - 710.1 \, IRS + 28.2 \, INF + 79.7 \, ER + 0.1 \, TAX$$
$$t\text{-value } (-4.9494) \; (-2.6813) \; (0.3989) \; (4.9280) \; (4.5493)$$

Table 12.6 Results of the *ADF* test for residuals

Model	*ADF test statistic*	*Test critical values: 1 per cent*	*Test critical values: 5 per cent*	*Test critical values: 10 per cent*
Trend and intercept	-4.5105	-4.2191	-3.5330	-3.1983
Intercept	-4.6046	-3.6155	-2.9411	-2.6090
None	-4.6800	-2.6272	-1.9498	-1.6114

Source: Authors' computations.

Then, we carried out the stationarity test of residuals, which are presented in Table 12.6.

The test results in Table 12.6 show that all residuals are stationary since their ADF test statistics are less than their corresponding critical values, which implies that interest rate spread (*IRS*), inflation rate (*INF*), exchange rate (*ER*) and taxation (*TAX*) grow together in the long run when one starts a new business in Rwanda.

5.3 *Estimation of long-run and short-run models*

Long-run relation

The estimated model of a business start-up as a function of its key determinants is:

$$BS = \alpha + \beta_1\ IRS + \beta_2\ INF + \beta_3\ ER + \beta_4\ TAX + \varepsilon \qquad (3)$$

The ordinary least square (*OLS*) method gives the following results (see also Appendix C for detailed results):

$$b = -42766.6 - 710.1\ IRS + 28.2\ INF + 79.7\ ER + 0.1\ TAX$$
$$t\text{-value}\ (-4.9494)\ (-2.6813)\ (0.3989)\ (4.9280)\ (4.5493)$$

The results indicate that our model explains more than 95 per cent of the variations in the number of start-ups in Rwanda. The estimations show that all coefficients are statistically significant except for inflation (*INF*) and that multicollinearity is almost not present. This means that in the long run, the number of new businesses increases and grows with interest rate spread (*IRS*), FRW/USD exchange rate (*ER*) and taxes (*TAX*); and that inflation rate (*INF*) does not follow the increase in start-ups over time.

Note that we used 40 observations for each variable, which are quarterly data flows from 2006 to 2015 with some provisional data that has not yet been officially released for the last quarter of 2015.

In addition, the auto-correlation of errors and heteroscedasticity were absent according to the tests conducted, since all test probabilities were higher than the degree of significance of 5 per cent apart from the inflation rate with the test probability of 0.6923 (see Appendix C).

Short-run relation

Granger has postulated that if we have co-integration, we can estimate the short-run relation by using the error correction model. For our case the start-up model is:

$$\Delta\, BS_t = \alpha_0 + \alpha_1 \Delta\, IRS_t + \alpha_2 \Delta\, INF_t + \alpha_3 \Delta\, ER_t + \alpha_4 \Delta\, TAX_t + \alpha_5 U_{t-1} + \varepsilon_{1t} \tag{4}$$

The summary results after estimation are (also see Appendix D):

$$\Delta\, BS_t = 498.366 + 205.788\Delta IRS_t + 54.987\Delta INF_t + 12.821\Delta ER_t + 0.009\Delta TAX_t - 0.504\ U_{t-1}$$

t-value (1.658) (0.720) (0.756) (0.327) (0.158) (–3.525)

As the probability of the lagged residuals (Appendix D) is less than 5 per cent, we conclude that the coefficient α_5 is significant as the model specifies. It is worth mentioning that this coefficient must have a negative sign, as it is made of forces that drive to the long-run equilibrium while other coefficients are like shocks in each period towards the equilibrium.

From the results we can see that other things being equal, if the interest rate spread (*IRS*) increases by 1 per cent, then 206 new businesses (*BS*) follow; if the inflation rate (*INF*) rises by 1 per cent, then 55 new businesses are born; and if the FRW/USD exchange rate (*ER*) increases by 1 FRW, then 13 new businesses are started. The interest rate spread seems to have the strongest effect on start-ups in Rwanda while the exchange rate has the weakest effect.

Finally, 50.4 per cent of the shocks are eliminated every quarter by new businesses starting in Rwanda, thus requiring a year, 11 months and 24 days to reach the long-run equilibrium. Note that in the short-run our model explains 32 per cent of the variations in starting a new business in Rwanda.

6. Summary, conclusion and recommendations

The theoretical part of this study showed that the interest rate spread is the pre-occupation of many economic theories and models in business, banking and government, mainly due to its link with investments, savings and firms' repayment capacities. The various determinants related to starting new businesses were identified as the interest rate spread, inflation, exchange rate and taxation. In addition it was noted that income sources other than interest rate are important elements in reducing the interest rate spreads.

Based on empirical results, the following recommendations are made. First, commercial banks should review the cost of financial intermediation and analyze and track the sectors that they finance and the securities that they receive from borrowers in order to reduce the lending interest rate by hiring qualified staff and looking at how they can apply up-to-date information technology tools in both soft and hard forms. Second, in order to stimulate savings, commercial banks are advised to increase deposit interest rates to the optimum level. Third, the central bank is advised to set up a financial system that aims at reducing the interest rate spread by playing on the determinants of the reference rate of interest. Fourth, the central bank should increase its focus on price stability and a stable FRW/USD exchange rate, as well as pay greater attention to securing low-cost finance for investments. Fifth, concerned officials should also encourage the establishment of a financial market that is effective in addressing the lack of long-term investments. Thus, business start-ups and interest rate spread, inflation, exchange rate and taxation will grow in harmony. Finally, future researchers need to analyze the determinants of the reference rate of interest.

Appendix A

Table 12.A1 Data used in the analysis

Quarter	*New business (BS)*	*Interest rate spread (IRS)*	*Inflation rate (INF)*	*FRW/USD exchange rate (ER)*	*Tax on products, millions FRW(TAX)*
2006 Q1	544	7.4	8.6	553.4	28,085
2006 Q2	403	7.4	11.8	551.9	29,885
2006 Q3	701	7.9	11.8	551.7	32,519
2006 Q4	708	8.0	15.0	550.2	33,158
2007 Q1	690	8.1	15.3	548.2	34,286
2007 Q2	675	8.2	10.3	546.0	37,809
2007 Q3	848	8.5	10.4	548.4	37,356
2007 Q4	740	8.6	7.6	545.6	40,878
2008 Q1	889	10.2	5.7	543.6	43,243
2008 Q2	974	10.4	13.5	543.1	45,754
2008 Q3	1,026	10.1	19.8	547.5	53,770
2008 Q4	1,108	10.0	23.2	552.7	60,711
2009 Q1	2,332	10.2	16.6	563.6	58,818
2009 Q2	1,923	8.1	10.7	563.8	55,215
2009 Q3	2,464	8.4	6.8	564.6	53,990
2009 Q4	2,512	7.9	6.3	566.4	57,162
2010 Q1	3,524	9.5	2.7	583.1	57,527
2010 Q2	3,104	10.3	5.9	578.6	56,777
2010 Q3	4,371	10.8	1.7	589.0	63,929
2010 Q4	5,656	10.4	-0.1	592.4	70,305
2011 Q1	7,237	8.9	3.9	600.3	70,875
2011 Q2	9,235	8.5	5.1	599.3	75,667
2011 Q3	11,278	9.3	5.7	599.8	78,391
2011 Q4	12,503	9.0	8.3	601.8	79,365
2012 Q1	12,380	8.6	9.0	605.1	83,386
2012 Q2	14,036	8.2	6.8	608.6	85,116

Quarter	*New business (BS)*	*Interest rate spread (IRS)*	*Inflation rate (INF)*	*FRW/USD exchange rate (ER)*	*Tax on products, millions FRW(TAX)*
2012 Q3	14,333	8.3	6.8	613.6	94,409
2012 Q4	13,713	6.2	4.1	628.8	88,655
2013 Q1	14,722	6.5	3.2	633.2	89,136
2013 Q2	17,496	6.6	4.1	640.1	95,407
2013 Q3	18,270	8.2	5.7	649.0	103,106
2013 Q4	18,747	8.6	4.1	664.3	106,075
2014 Q1	20,765	8.8	3.8	674.6	111,160
2014 Q2	19,300	8.7	2.1	681.4	126,666
2014 Q3	23,441	9.1	-0.2	684.2	122,232
2014 Q4	24,270	9.5	2.2	690.3	116,756
2015 Q1	20,319	9.1	1.2	702.3	116,769
2015 Q2	19,014	9.0	2.8	712.1	116,769
2015 Q3	23,647	9.1	2.8	725.0	116,769
2015 Q4	28,533	9.2	2.8	739.0	116,769

Appendix B

Lag length choice for each variable and the equation's residuals

Table 12.B1 Table of Akaike and Schwarz criteria for *BS*

P	*Model 1: with intercept*		*Model 2: with trend and intercept*		*Model 3: without trend and intercept*	
	Akaike	*Schwarz*	*Akaike*	*Schwarz*	*Akaike*	*Schwarz*
5	17.5485	17.7227	17.4113	17.6290	17.5632	17.6938
4	17.5485	17.7227	17.4113	17.6290	17.5632	17.6938
3	17.5485	17.7227	17.4113	17.6290	17.5632	17.6938
2	17.5485	17.7227	17.4113	17.6290	17.5632	17.6938
1	17.6418	17.7271	17.5442	17.6722	17.6180	17.6606
0	17.6418	17.7271	17.5442	17.6722	17.6180	17.6606

Note: $P = 2$

Table 12.B2 Table of Akaike and Schwarz criteria for *IRS*

P	*Model 1: with intercept*		*Model 2: with trend and intercept*		*Model 3: without trend and intercept*	
	Akaike	*Schwarz*	*Akaike*	*Schwarz*	*Akaike*	*Schwarz*
5	2.2992	2.4734	2.3456	2.5633	2.3495	2.3921
4	2.2992	2.4734	2.3456	2.5633	2.3495	2.3921
3	2.2434	2.3287	2.3456	2.5633	2.3495	2.3921
2	2.2434	2.3287	2.2909	2.4189	2.3495	2.3921
1	2.2434	2.3287	2.2909	2.4189	2.3495	2.3921
0	2.2434	2.3287	2.2909	2.4189	2.3495	2.3921

Note: $P = 0$

Table 12.B3 Table of Akaike and Schwarz criteria for *INF*

P	*Model 1: with intercept*		*Model 2: with trend and intercept*		*Model 3: without trend and intercept*	
	Akaike	*Schwarz*	*Akaike*	*Schwarz*	*Akaike*	*Schwarz*
5	5.0285	5.1577	4.9130	5.0854	5.0578	5.1440
4	5.0285	5.1577	4.9130	5.0854	5.0578	5.1440
3	5.0285	5.1577	4.9130	5.0854	5.0578	5.1440
2	5.0285	5.1577	4.9130	5.0854	5.0578	5.1440
1	5.0285	5.1577	4.9130	5.0854	5.0578	5.1440
0	5.1065	5.1918	5.0462	5.1742	5.0942	5.1369

Note: $P = 1$

Table 12.B4 Table of Akaike and Schwarz criteria for *ER*

P	*Model 1: with intercept*		*Model 2: with trend and intercept*		*Model 3: without trend and intercept*	
	Akaike	*Schwarz*	*Akaike*	*Schwarz*	*Akaike*	*Schwarz*
5	5.9968	6.0821	5.9196	6.0476	6.1973	6.4195
4	5.9968	6.0821	5.9196	6.0476	6.1973	6.4195
3	5.9968	6.0821	5.9196	6.0476	6.2043	6.3349
2	5.9968	6.0821	5.9196	6.0476	6.2043	6.3349
1	5.9968	6.0821	5.9196	6.0476	6.2640	6.3502
0	5.9968	6.0821	5.9196	6.0476	6.2784	6.3211

Note: $P = 0$

Table 12.B5 Table of Akaike and Schwarz criteria for *TAX*

P	*Model 1: with intercept*		*Model 2: with trend and intercept*		*Model 3: without trend and intercept*	
	Akaike	*Schwarz*	*Akaike*	*Schwarz*	*Akaike*	*Schwarz*
5	19.5970	19.6823	19.5196	19.6920	19.6286	19.6713
4	19.5970	19.6823	19.5196	19.6920	19.6286	19.6713
3	19.5970	19.6823	19.5196	19.6920	19.6286	19.6713
2	19.5970	19.6823	19.5196	19.6920	19.6286	19.6713
1	19.5970	19.6823	19.5196	19.6920	19.6286	19.6713
0	19.5970	19.6823	19.5056	19.6336	19.6286	19.6713

Note: $P = 0$

Table 12.B6 Table of Akaike and Schwarz criteria for equation's residuals

P	*Model 1: with intercept*		*Model 2: with trend and intercept*		*Model 3: without trend and intercept*	
	Akaike	*Schwarz*	*Akaike*	*Schwarz*	*Akaike*	*Schwarz*
5	17.5993	17.7286	17.6503	17.8227	17.5467	17.6329
4	17.5993	17.7286	17.6503	17.8227	17.5467	17.6329
3	17.5993	17.7286	17.6503	17.8227	17.5467	17.6329
2	17.5993	17.7286	17.6503	17.8227	17.5467	17.6329
1	17.5993	17.7286	17.6503	17.8227	17.5467	17.6329
0	17.6513	17.7366	17.6999	17.8278	17.6002	17.6428

Note: $P = 1$

Appendix C

Dependent Variable: *N*
Method: Least Squares
Date: 04/12/16 Time: 02:15
Sample: 1 40
Included observations: 40

Table 12.C1 Estimation of the long-run model

Variable	*Coefficient*	*Std. Error*	*t-Statistic*	*Prob.*
C	-42766.56	8640.751	-4.949404	0.0000
IS	-710.0606	264.8132	-2.681364	0.0111
INF	28.22257	70.73529	0.398989	0.6923
E	79.69530	16.17169	4.928076	0.0000
TAX	0.135094	0.029695	4.549324	0.0001
R-squared	0.963284	Mean dependent var		9460.775
Adjusted R-squared	0.959088	S.D. dependent var		8748.631
S.E. of regression	1769.552	Akaike info criterion		17.91131
Sum squared resid	1.10E+08	Schwarz criterion		18.12242
Log likelihood	-353.2262	Hannan-Quinn criter.		17.98764
F-statistic	229.5687	Durbin-Watson stat		1.230562
Prob(F-statistic)	0.000000			

Appendix D

Dependent Variable: *DN*
Method: Least Squares
Date: 04/12/16 Time: 04:49
Sample: 1 38
Included observations: 38

Table 12.D1 Estimation of the short-run model

Variable	*Coefficient*	*Std. Error*	*t-Statistic*	*Prob.*
C	498.3664	300.5135	1.658383	0.1070
DIS	205.7875	285.8153	0.720002	0.4768
DINF	54.98687	72.78132	0.755508	0.4555
DE	12.82119	39.19752	0.327092	0.7457
DTAX	0.008585	0.054443	0.157679	0.8757
LAGRESID01	-0.504237	0.143035	-3.525262	0.0013
R-squared	0.318660	Mean dependent var		607.9737
Adjusted R-squared	0.212201	S.D.dependent var		1473.449
S.E. of regression	1307.804	Akaike info criterion		17.33403
Sum squared resid	54731242	Schwarz criterion		17.59259
Log likelihood	-323.3465	Hannan-Quinn criter.		17.42602
F-statistic	2.993260	Durbin-Watson stat		1.540215
Prob(F-statistic)	0.025071			

References

African Development Bank Group (2012). "Leveraging capital markets for small and medium enterprise financing Rwanda", African Development Bank Group, Tunis-Belvédère.

Antwi, G.O. and J. Antwi (2013). "Do financial sector reforms improve competition of banks? An application of Panzar and Rosse Model: The case of Ghanaian banks", *International Journal of Financial Research*, 4(3), 43–61.

Balogun, W.O., J.B. Dahalan, and S.B. Hassan (2016). "Interest rate liberalization, quality institutions and stock market development in selected Sub-Saharan African countries", *International Journal of Economics and Financial Issues*, 6(2), 786–792.

Bank, W. (2013). *Doing Business 2014: Understanding Regulations for Small and Medium-Size Enterprises. Doing Business 2014: Understanding Regulations for Small and Medium-Size Enterprises.* Available at: http://doi.org/10.1596/978-0-8213-9984-2.

Barajas, A., R. Steiner and N. Salazar (1999). "Interest Spreads in Banking in Colombia, 1974–96." IMF Staff Papers, 46(2), 196–224.

Behuria, P. and T. Goodfellow (2016). "Rwanda: Unpacking two decades of economic growth", ESID Working Paper No. 57.

Bernanke, B.S. (1990). "On the predictive power of interest rates and interest rate spreads", *New England Economic Review*, (November/December), 51–68.

Berument, M.H., N.B. Ceylan, and B. Dogan (2014). "An interest-rate-spread-based measure of Turkish monetary policy", *Applied Economics*, 46(15), 1804–1813.

Birchwood, A., M. Brei, and D. Noel (2016). "Interest margins and bank regulation in Central America and the Caribbean", Document de Travail Working Paper, (2016-33), 0–29.

BNR (2011). "Economic review", National Bank of Rwanda.

BNR (2012). "Economic review", National Bank of Rwanda.

Cassell, C. and G. Symon (2004). "Essential guide to qualitative methods in organizational research", Athenaeum Studi Periodici Di Letteratura E Storia Dell Antichita, 388. Available at: http://doi.org/Book.

Ceylan, N.B., B. Dogan, and M.H. Berument (2015). "Three-factor asset pricing model and portfolio holdings of foreign investors: Evidence from an emerging market – Borsa Istanbul", *Economic Research-Ekonomska Istraživanja*, 28(1), 467–486.

Chen, J., L. Fu, A.A. Ungar, and X. Zhao (2002). "Alternative fidelity measure between two states of an N-state quantum system", *Physical Review A*, 65(26). Available at: doi.org/10.1103/PhysRevA.65.054304.

Dahlman, C. (2007). "Technology, globalization, and international competitiveness: Challenges for developing countries", in D. O'Connor and M. Kjöllerström (eds), *Industrial Development for the 21st Century.* Hyderabad: Orient Longman, Zed Books and United Nations, pp. 29–83. Available at: http://doi.org/10.4016/12667.01.

De Fiore, F. and O. Tristani (2011). «Credit and the natural rate of interest", *Journal of Money, Credit and Banking*, 43(2–3), 407–440.

Filmer, D. and L. Fox (2014). *Youth Employment in Sub-Saharan Africa.* Available at: http://doi.org/10.1596/978-1-4648-0107-5.

Fox, L. and T.P. Sohnesen (2012). "Household enterprises in Sub-Saharan Africa: Why they matter for growth, jobs, and livelihoods", World Bank, Policy Research Working Paper WPS6184.

Granger, C.W.J. (1986). "Developments in the study of cointegrated economic variables", *Oxford Bulletin of Economics and Statistics*, 48(3), 213–228.

Greene, W.H. (2008). "The econometric approach to efficiency analysis", *The Measurement of Productive Efficiency and Productivity Change*, 92–250.

Grimm, S., H. Höß, K. Knappe, M. Siebold, J. Sperrfechter, and I. Vogler (2010). "Coordinating China and DAC development partners: Challenges to the aid architecture in Rwanda. Studies", Deutsches Institut für Entwicklungspolitik.

Ho, T.S.Y. and S.B. Lee (1986). "Term structure movements and pricing interest rate contingent claims", *The Journal of Finance*, 41(5), 1011–1029.

Jonas Costa Da Silva, G., L. Abrão, and S. Pirtouscheg (2015). "ScienceDirect basic interest rate, bank competition and bank spread in personal credit operations in Brazil: A theoretical and empirical analysis", *EconomiA*, 16, 32–45.

OECD (1996). *Small Businesses, Job Creation and Growth: Facts, Obstacles and Best Practices.* Available at: http://doi.org/10.1002/1098-240X(200006)23:3<246::AID-NUR9>3.0.CO;2-H.

Rahim, M.M. (2012). "Legal regulation of corporate social responsibility: Evidence from Bangladesh", *Common Law World Review*, 41, 97–133.

Roache, S.K. (2007). "Public Investment and Growth in the Eastern Carribean", *Money Affairs*, XX(2), 111–131.

Rutayisire, M.J. (2010). "Economic liberalization, monetary policy and money demand in Rwanda: 1980–2005", National Bank of Rwanda, AERC Research Paper 193.

Snape, D. and L. Spencer (2003). "The foundations of qualitative research", Qualitative Research Practice: A Guide for Social Science Students and Researchers, 2–10.

Vanacker, T. and M. Deloof (2015). "Credit availability, start-up financing, and survival: Evidence from the recent financial crisis", Unpublished Research Paper, Ghent University, Department of Accountancy and Corporate Finance.

World Bank (2006). "Doing Business-2006", www.Doingbusiness.org. Available at: www.doingbusiness.org/reports/global-reports/doing-business-2006.

World Bank (2010). *Investing Across Borders: Indicators of Foreign Direct Investment.* Available at: http://iab.worldbank.org.

World Bank (2013). *Doing Business 2013.* Available at: http://doi.org/10.1596/978-0-8213-9615-5.

Yang, Y., M. Davies, S. Wang, J. Dunn, and W. Wu (2011). "Monetary policy transmission mechanisms in Pacific Island countries", IMF Working Paper, 1–25. Available at: www.imf.org/external/pubs/ft/wp/2011/wp1196.pdf.

Part IV

Diversity, conflicts and hazardous factors

13 A within-country study of conflict and poverty in Nigeria

Chinasa I. Ikelu

1. Introduction

The nature and causes of the intensity of a conflict are a deeply explored field in political economy. The idea that data on conflict and other variables may not be comparable has found extensive empirical and theoretical support, especially in Blattman and Miguel's (2009) comprehensive work on civil war.

However, there are also a number of theoretical and empirical studies that have established a link between poverty and conflict. Proponents of the frustration–aggression theory suggest that individuals become aggressive when there are obstacles (perceived and real) to their success in life (Rupesinghe et al., 1996, cited in Draman, 2003). Some other studies suggest that social conflicts in developing countries are fuelled by greed and opportunities for looting the resources of the state rather than any grievance (Draman, 2003).

What has been a more recent research topic is a study of the duration of a conflict. Over several decades, researchers have been focusing on the question of whether poorer districts are the scene of more violence or is it the case that poorer districts are the first to be affected by civil conflict. A common answer to this question is that poorer areas are more likely to experience the onset of conflict (Cox, 1972; Do and Iyer, 2010).

Recent developments in the field include running several specifications to check the robustness of findings, including variables such as measures of geography and economic development indicators (Do and Iyer, 2010). These variables have been found to be economically important in determining or predicting the intensity of conflict over time. Other potential determinants, such as measures of social capital and political participation (Bohara et al., 2006) and ultra-left political activities (Acharya, 2007), are not found to robustly explain the incidence of civil conflict once the effects of geography and poverty have been accounted for (Do and Iyer, 2010). It is therefore important to examine whether insurgency attacks can help and better explain the intensity of conflict in Nigeria by carrying out a within-country analysis. Keeping this in mind, this paper follows previous literature to examine whether the risk factors of conflict identified in within-country studies can explain the variations in the intensity of conflicts in Nigeria. The paper also uses a better measure of conflict intensity based on the total number of deaths instead of using a dummy variable for whether an area experienced conflict or not. It also investigates events based on violence against civilians, remote violence, riots/protests and a battle on a change of territory.[1] Further, it also studies the areas most affected by conflict over time and investigates the relationships between the risk factors, poverty and intensity of conflict in these areas. Lastly, it provides evidence for this relationship by establishing causality using the difference-in-differences approach.

An econometric analysis of the determinants of conflict was done considering a range of relative and economic development factors such as poverty, educational levels and under-five mortality; social diversity factors such as ethnic, linguistic and religious fractionalization; and geographic factors such as latitude. For this, it used a combined dataset from the Demographic and Health Survey (DHS) and the Armed Conflict Location and Events Data (ACLED) to assess the mechanism through which conflict can arise; this is also used to further confirm other within-country studies on this subject.

The paper found that poverty determined the intensity of conflict in Plateau and Benue states. That is, poorer individuals residing in these states were more exposed and prone to conflict than their counterparts in other regions. This result is robust to the use of other measures of relative development such as literacy rates and under-five mortality rates. Estimates confirm that areas with higher illiteracy rates are more prone to conflict and areas with high infant mortality are also associated with high conflict intensity.

However, there could be different mechanisms to link poverty with conflict. For example, poorer people might harbor a high degree of grievances against the government, thereby leading to the likelihood of joining insurgent or aggrieved groups. As a way to address this, this paper looks at other potential determinants of grievances and conflict such as ethnic, linguistic and religious fractionalization. It finds that these measures affect conflict once economic backwardness is controlled. This correlation and result are analogous to cross-country literature, which finds a strong relationship between social diversity and the likelihood of civil war (Montalvo and Reynal-Querol, 2005).

The rest of this paper is organized as follows. Section 2 discusses conflict in Nigeria. Section 3 documents relevant theoretical and empirical literature. Section 4 looks at the empirical strategy and data that narrows the discussion to measuring conflict and poverty and model specifications. Section 5 explains the determinants of conflict and further robustness checks while Section 6 establishes the causal impact of poverty on conflict. Section 7 gives a conclusion and discusses the findings and policy implications.

2. Conflict in Nigeria

Conflict is a struggle between individuals over values or claims to status, power and scarce resources in which the aims of the conflicting parties are asserting their values or claims over those of others (Goodhand and Hulme, 1999). Women are the worst affected and they have also frequently become victims of rape, molestation, sexual abuse and physical torture (Kumar et al., 2011).

Nigeria is a country in West Africa bordering Benin in the west, Chad and Cameroon in the east and Niger in the north. With an estimated population of 182,202,000 and a gross domestic product (GDP) per capita of $2,640, 62 per cent of the population was extremely poor in 2011 (Ikelu and Onyukwu, 2016). Oil is the major source of revenue, contributing 40 per cent to GDP and 80 per cent to government revenues. Nigeria's democracy is considered an anocracy characterized by regimes featuring inherent qualities of political instability and ineffectiveness as well as an incoherent mix of democratic traits and practices.

The Jos crisis that unleashed massive killings and destruction turned worse in September 2001 with the 10-day riots leaving over 3,000 dead (Danfulani and Fwatshak, 2002). Similar riots erupted in November 2008 and January 2010, resulting in estimated deaths of 381 and 200 people, respectively (Obikili, 2015) (Figure 13.1).

The Boko Haram, popularly known as Jama'at Ahl as-Sunnah lid-da'wawal-Jihad is an Islamic sect based in the north-eastern part of Nigeria. The sect started its campaign against the Nigerian state and territory in 2009 with a prison break in Bauchi state. Since then, it has launched campaigns against the government of Nigeria in Borno, Yobe and Adamawa states (Obikili, 2015). The bulk of the sect's attacks have been in the north-eastern states of Borno and Yobe, though attacks have occurred across a large part of northern Nigeria, including a few attacks in the federal capital territory of Abuja (Adesoji, 2010). In the six years since the conflict with Boko Haram began in the region, as many as 7,000 Nigerian women and girls have been abducted and approximately 20,000 civilians have died. Countless communities and villages throughout the affected areas have

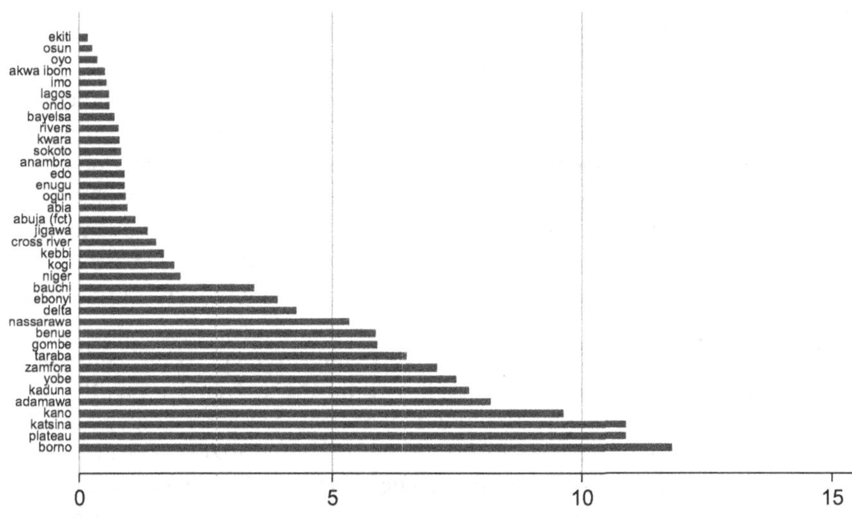

Figure 13.1 Highest levels of conflict-terrorism related fatalities 2004–14

been razed, resulting in the internal displacement of 2.2 million people, including approximately 461,000 women of reproductive age.

Conflicts in many areas of Nigeria began in 1999 when democracy was recognized in the country (Ginifer and Olawale, 2005). Lagos state accounted for at least 50 cases of conflict between 1999 and 2003 (Adebanwi, 2003). Since the return of democracy, various incidents of violence have marred the country. This paper focuses on the fatalities of the Jos crisis and the violence and attacks by Boko Haram in the northeast.

3. Relevant theoretical and empirical literature

Most of the studies (see Atwood, 2003; Draman, 2003; Goodhand, 2001; Hettne, 2003; Ikejiaku, 2009; Justino, 2006, 2009, 2010; Syed, 2007) that have examined the nexus between conflict and poverty have scrutinized it from the theoretical point of view. This paper builds on this theory and applies data to ascertain if poorer areas are exposed to conflict or otherwise. According to some studies, conflict is more likely to occur in poor countries and conflict-affected countries generally have higher levels of poverty and lower growth rates (Collier, 1999; Collier et al., 2003).

The link between violent conflicts and poverty broadly examines three types of inter-relationships (Goodhand, 2001):

- Conflict causes chronic poverty (costs of conflict analysis).
- Chronic poverty causes conflict (grievance-based analysis).
- Resource wealth, rather than poverty, causes conflict (greed-based analysis).

The current study focuses on the grievance-based analysis[2] to answer the research question. The grievance-based analysis is a scenario whereby low levels of development lead to grievances against the government and hence greater willingness to join anti-government forces (Collier and Hoeffler, 2004). The grievance-based analysis is also known as the 'opportunity cost' view as documented by Collier and Hoeffler (1998), who noted that insurgencies are concentrated in poorer areas where the cost of recruiting rebel forces is low, thereby inducing people to join the movement by paying lower wages to the recruits. The authors found no statistical relationship between grievances and violent conflict across samples of over 100 countries. Using district-level evidence from Indonesia, Barron et al. (2004) also did not find any statistical association between poverty and the onset of communal violence.

However, some literature has shown that improvement is an explanatory variable like poverty, which is often rolled within the grievance topic, that may contribute to decreasing the likelihood of violent conflict taking place. For instance, Collier and Hoeffler (2001) argue that prioritizing investments in education and health may signal a government's commitment to peace by keeping the population content. On the other hand, increases in equal opportunities in access to education by excluded groups may decrease social tensions. This ideology affirms the United States' action policies in the education sector (see Bush and Saltarelli, 2000). Some evidence also suggests that higher enrollment rates increase opportunity costs of recruiting militants by rebel groups (Do and Iyer, 2010; Thyne, 2005).

Kanbur (2007) in his paper found that theoretically it was true, on average and in a statistical sense, that violent conflict was a feature of poorer rather than richer societies. Additionally, a World Bank study on civil wars found that poverty was a significant statistical determinant of civil war on average but there were insufficient variations around this average to warrant careful country-specific analyses (see Collier et al., 2003).

In addition to the theoretical background, Addison et al. (2013) discuss how poverty may lead to conflict and explore some of the implications of large-scale violence for people in chronic poverty. They suggest two possible links of the exact mechanism by which poverty is particularly associated with conflict: chronic poverty can fuel social discontent, which in some cases leads to violence, and chronic poverty can make recruiting fighters easier. They conclude that these mechanisms are likely to interact with the final outcome being determined by a country's circumstances and history.

Pinstrup-Andersen and Shimokawa (2008) empirically employed the discrete-time hazard model to examine the effect of time-varying socioeconomic factors on conflict. They found that income poverty and poor health and nutritional status were more significantly associated with armed conflict than GDP per capita, annual GDP growth and the ratio of primary commodity exports over GDP. In their detailed analysis that tracked civil war casualties across space and time in Nepal, Do and Iyer (2010) found that conflict-related deaths were significantly higher in poorer districts of Nepal and in geographical locations that favored insurgents, such as mountains and forests. They also found that poorer districts were likely to be drawn into insurgency earlier using a proportional hazard duration model. In their systematic analysis of the drivers of conflict in Nigeria using quantitative data, Babatunde and Cali (2015) found that the effect of price shocks, particularly affecting consumption goods and oil, on conflict increased in election years.

In addition, using state-level empirical evidence for India, Justino (2004) found that public expenditure on social services and improvements in education enrollments were effective means of reducing civil unrest, as they directly affected important causes of social conflict, notably poverty. Using household-level data for Uganda during 1999–2000, Deininger (2003) found that higher levels of education decreased an individual's propensity to engage in civil strife at a declining rate up to an absolute minimum between 8.1 and 5.9 years of schooling per household depending on the specification. Malapit et al. (2003) show empirically that provinces with lower Human Development Index (HDI) outcomes in the Mindanao region of the Philippines experienced higher levels of conflict. Otu et al. (2010), in their study of poverty being a potential conflict escalator in Nigeria's Niger Delta, found that poverty was a major cause of conflict in the region.

4. Data and empirical strategy

4.1 Data

A quantitative approach was adopted to analyze the data with the help of Quantum Geographic and Information System (QGIS) and Stata.[3] Using the generated data,[4] the ACLED dataset was merged by using an identifier for the variable. This was done at the individual level, which is the unit of analysis in this paper. Data used for this study was obtained from DHS and ACLED. Unlike DHS, the Living Standard Measurement Survey (LSMS) did not account for the location of a respondent until recently. Economic status is defined in terms of wealth as measured through an index based on responses to a series of household asset questions contained in the DHS survey instrument. ACLED is the most comprehensive public collection of political violence and protest data for developing countries from 1997 to the present time. This data and analysis project produces information on specific dates and locations of political violence and protests, the type of event, the groups involved, fatalities and changes in territorial control. Information is recorded on the battles, killings, riots and recruitment activities of rebels, governments, militias, armed groups, protesters and civilians (Raleigh et al., 2010).

Further, the DHS program collects and disseminates accurate, nationally representative data on topics such as fertility, family planning, maternal and child health, gender, HIV/AIDS, malaria, nutrition and environmental health. The DHS program implements DHS and other surveys to meet the needs of her partner organizations and the people.

4.2 Measuring conflict and poverty

Conflict was measured by the total number of deaths in an area. Other measures of conflict can include injuries, forced conscriptions (involuntary labor), abductions, forced migrations, protest marches and disruptions to economic activities caused by strikes (Do and Iyer, 2010). This measure is based on the data provided by ACLED. A drawback of using data from a non-governmental organization instead of academic data arises because the former does not use systematic definitions, which can create inconsistencies in counting conflicts.

Poverty was measured by the wealth index as provided by the DHS data. The poorest were coded 1 while the richest were coded 5.

Table 13.1 summarizes the variables used for the study. About 26 per cent of the deaths were caused by violence against civilians, 3 per cent by remote violence and 34 per cent by riots and protests. Eighteen per cent of the population was regarded as poorer in Nigeria in the analysis period and 22 were considered richest. Also, 22 per cent had primary education, 32 per cent had secondary education and only 6 per cent had higher education (tertiary education).

Table 13.1 Summary statistics

		Obs	*Mean*	*s.d*	*Min*	*Max*
Measures of conflict intensity						
Deaths caused by violence against civilians		7620	0.26	0.44	0	1
Deaths caused by remote violence		7620	0.03	0.17	0	1
Deaths caused by riots and protests		7620	0.34	0.47	0	1
Geography						
Latitude		7620	8.68	2.51	4.79	13.05
Relative development indicators						
Poverty rate (measured by the wealth index)	Poorest	7620	0.18	0.39	0	1
	Middle	7620	0.2	0.4	0	1
	Richer	7620	0.2	0.4	0	1
	Richest	7620	0.22	0.42	0	1
Literacy rate (primary)		7620	0.22	0.42	0	1
Literacy rate (secondary)		7620	0.32	0.47	0	1
Literacy rate (tertiary)		7620	0.06	0.06	0	1
Under-five mortality rate		2341	2	1.39	1	10
Ethnic language and religious fractionalization						
Ethnic fractionalization		7620	0.68	0.55	0	3.86
Linguistic fractionalization		7620	0.62	0.7	0	3.93
Religious fractionalization		7620	0.39	0.28	-0.26	0.92

4.3 *Model*

The methodology used in assessing the correlates of conflict in Nigeria is the multiple regression analysis. This analysis is of the form:

$$y_i = \beta + \beta_1 X_{1i} + \beta_2 X_2 i + \beta_3 X_{3i} + \cdots + \beta_n X_{ni} + \varepsilon_i \tag{1}$$

where y_i is the measure of the intensity of conflict in area i, β is the constant term, X_i's are the set of economic and relative development factors and ε captures the error.

The multiple regression analysis – which is a special type of structural equation modeling – can be helpful in attenuating measurement errors and understanding the conceptual framework of the question being studied. This model allows us to assess the impact of multiple factors on conflict simultaneously. The multiple regression analysis also allows one to estimate the association with poverty after controlling for the impact of other factors. The interpretation is that all other factors being equal, a unit increase in the poverty measure will increase the intensity of conflict by a certain unit.[5]

We set up a multiple regression model because we believe the explanatory variable influences the dependent variable. If we are to confirm this belief, we need to examine whether or not it is supported by data. That is, we need to ask whether the data provides any evidence to suggest that the dependent variable is related to each of the explanatory variables. If a given explanatory variable, say X_n has no bearing on the dependent variable, y then $\beta_n = 0$. Testing this null hypothesis is called a test of significance for the explanatory variable X_n. Therefore, to find whether the data contains any evidence suggesting y is related to x_n, we test the null hypothesis:

H_0: *There is no relationship between conflict intensity and poverty*

against the alternative hypothesis:

H_1: *There is no relationship between conflict intensity and poverty*

For this, the test statistic proposed by Hill et al. (2011) is used:

$$t = \frac{b_n - \beta_n}{se(b_n)} \sim t_{(N-n)} \qquad (2)$$

Decision rule: for a test with level of significance α, we reject the null hypothesis if the probability value is less than the significance level and accept if otherwise.

5. Determinants of conflict

5.1 Poverty: a significant predictor of conflict

We find that poorer areas are more exposed and prone to conflict-related deaths using Eq. 2. The estimate for this specification can be found in Table 13.2, column 1. The coefficient of poverty is significant. To have a better understanding of the extent of this significance, it is clear that for a 1 per cent increase in wealth, conflict decreases by 0.38 per cent. Alternatively, a doubling of the size of the wealth index brings about a 38 per cent decrease in conflict.

In addition, the relationship between conflict and poverty is clear from the maps in Figures 13.2 and 13.3. Figure 13.2 shows the conflict intensity across states of Nigeria while Figure 13.3 shows the incidence of poverty. Comparing the two maps, we can see that states which have high poverty also tend to have high levels of conflict. That is, poorer areas are exposed to more conflicts.

Table 13.2 Ordinary least squares analysis of the determinants of conflict intensity

DV = Conflict	*(1)*	*(2)*	*(3)*	*(4)*	*(5)*	*(6)*
	Poverty	*Ethnic diversity*	*VAC*	*Remote violence*	*Riots and protests*	*BNCT*
Poverty	–0.38***	–0.36***	0.37***	0.14***	–0.48***	–0.14***
	(0.02)	(0.02)	(0.07)	(0.02)	(0.03)	(0.05)
Ethnic fractionalization		1.22***				
		(0.12)				
Observations	6,671	6,671	1,987	249	2,566	2,818
R-squared	0.028	0.040	0.013	0.176	0.069	0.003

Note: Robust standard errors in parentheses. ***= $p < 0.01$, **= $p < 0.05$, *= $p < 0.1$. Regressions based on individual-level data.

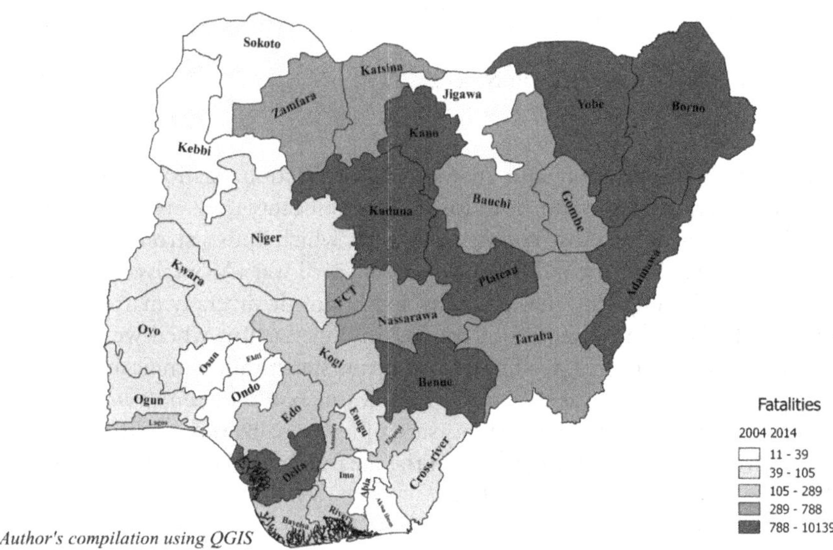

Author's compilation using QGIS

Figure 13.2 Total number of fatalities across Nigeria from 2004 to 2014

Other potential determinants suggested in within-country literature or proposed by other scholars were found to robustly explain the incidence of conflict once the effects of poverty had been accounted for. An example of one of these explanatory variables is ethnic fractionalization. Fearon and Laitin (2003) found that neither ethnic fractionalization nor religious fractionalization had any statistically significant effect on the probability of civil wars. Also, ethnic polarization initiated by Esteban and Ray (1994) and Wolfson (1994) was not found to affect the level of violence in the Nepalese civil war (Do and

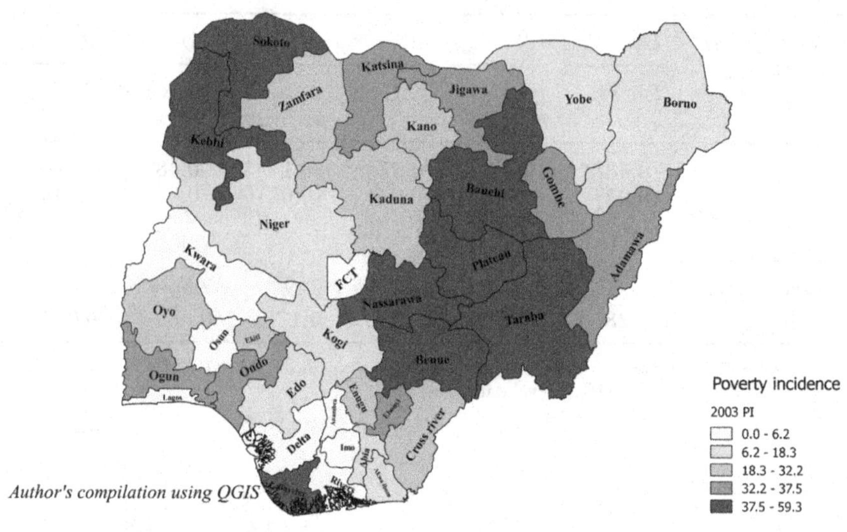

Author's compilation using QGIS

Figure 13.3 Poverty incidence in Nigeria (2003)

Iyer, 2010). In our study and analysis, ethnic fractionalization and linguistic fractionalization happen to be statistically significant; they are similar to the results of some of the cross-country literature, which finds a strong relationship between social diversity and the likelihood of civil war (Montalvo and Reynal-Querol, 2005), implying that ethnicity and linguistic diversity matter and help explain the level and intensity of conflict in Nigeria. But when we use ethnic polarization as a control, we find that it is not statistically significant although linguistic polarization was statistically significant (*results available on request*). A reason for this might be that the measure of fractionalization traditionally used in literature performs a bit better than the measure of polarization proposed by Montalvo and Reynal-Querol (2005).

5.2 *Robustness check of the association between conflict and poverty*

Re-running the specification given earlier with the level of education (a measure of relative development) instead of poverty, we obtained results that confirmed that areas with higher illiteracy rates were more prone to conflict. That is, areas with higher literacy rates were less exposed to conflict. Do and Iyer (2010) obtained similar results in their within-country study. They also found that the presence of roads – a measure of infrastructure – was associated with lower conflicts.

Table 13.3 tests the robustness of the relationship between economic backwardness and conflict using a different measure of relative development – the

Table 13.3 Robustness of the relationship between conflict and poverty

DV = Conflict	*(1)*	*(2)*	*(3)*	*(4)*
	Literacy	*Under-five mortality*	*Clustered at state level*	*Probit*
Literacy	−1.02*** (0.04)		−1.02*** (0.29)	
Under-five		0.27*** (0.05)		
Poverty				−0.02* (0.01)
Observations	7,620	2,341	7,620	7,620
R-squared	0.071	0.010	0.071	

Note: Robust standard errors in parentheses. ***= $p < 0.01$, **= $p < 0.05$, *= $p < 0.1$.

under-five mortality rate (children who have died before their fifth birthday). Although Do and Iyer (2010) used the infant mortality rate as their alternative measure of relative development, they provided this alternative using children who had died before their first birthday. Our result remains robust when we include under-five infant mortality. Areas with high infant mortality are associated with high conflict intensity.

The estimates reported in Table 13.3 are lower than the ones obtained earlier, implying that unobserved factors such as economic backwardness better drive this inverse relationship. Additionally, once we controlled for geographic variables such as latitude, poverty became statistically insignificant (*results available on request*). This is because regressions that include latitude and ethnic fractionalization in the same specification run the risk of multi-collinearity due to the highly correlated nature of both variables (Alesina et al., 2003).

Finally, we used the probabilistic model to capture the intensity of conflict by disaggregation using dummies to assign a region 1 if it suffered more than 50 fatalities and zero otherwise. We again found that poorer areas were more exposed to a higher number of fatalities or simply put that poorer areas were more likely to suffer a higher number of conflict-related deaths. This is evident in Table 13.3, column 4.

6. Establishing causality: does poverty cause conflict?

6.1 Additional controls and difference-in-differences approach

The specification given earlier explains that poverty remains a significant predictor of conflict after adding several controls of social diversity, relative development and geography. Next, we investigate the reasons why poorer areas are more exposed to conflict since there is an assumption that conflict may be causing poverty. Therefore a research design and possible natural experiment was used that could be exploited to illustrate this causality. One way is to control for potential confounders by running additional regressions with a range of characteristics to see if the main results remained robust to the inclusion of these additional variables. Another way is to carry out a difference-in-differences design by comparing groups given a certain exogenous shock that took place in the country. To control partially for confounders,[6] we ran an additional regression by controlling for more characteristics such as religious fractionalization[7] to see if the main results remained robust to the inclusion of these variables. The results remained robust with the inclusion of religious fractionalization. A unit decrease of poverty by 4 per cent reduced conflict by the same percentage at the 1 per cent level of significance.

In addition to this hypothesis and using sufficient variations such as a drop in oil prices as an exogenous shock, the within-country analysis was carefully studied to see if cities that depended on the government for employment experienced more conflicts than rural areas that depended less on the government. If this scenario and argument are true, then we should see differential changes in the levels of conflict after the drop in the price of oil. To test this hypothesis empirically, the difference-in-differences approach[8] with fixed effects was employed, which compares the levels of conflict measured by the number of fatalities before and after the drop in oil prices. Explicitly, we estimated the regression:

$$y_{it} = \beta_i + \gamma_t + (Poverty_i \times Time_t)\,\sigma + \chi'_{it}\varphi + \varepsilon_{it} \qquad (3)$$

where y_{it} is the level of conflict as measured by the number of fatalities for individual i in year t; β_i are state fixed effects that control for both observable and unobservable time-invariant characteristics of an individual; γ_t are year fixed effects that capture the exogenous shock common to the country; $Poverty_i \times Time_t$ interacts the wealth index indicator with time during which the price of oil dropped sharply; χ'_{it} is a vector of time-varying controls; and ε_{it} is the error term.

The coefficient of interest is sigma, which captures the differential change in conflict levels in poor areas versus the cities that rely on the government for employment during a drop in oil prices. We estimated Eq. 3 using the ordinary least square (OLS). The DID results are reported in Table 13.4 and Table 13.5. On average, the poorest regions became –1.56 more exposed to conflicts as compared to their richest counterparts during the decline in oil prices, every other thing remaining constant. Table 13.4, column 1 gives the estimates of the effect of poverty on conflict, controlling for geographic characteristics of the states that interacted with the post-2008 indicator. Column 2 integrates more controls interacted with at the time of the exogenous shock. Compared to the results without the interaction, the estimated effect of poverty on conflict was smaller in magnitude but remained statistically significant.

Table 13.4 DID estimates: conflict and poverty

DV = Conflict	*(1)*	*(2)*
	Conflict	*Conflict*
Post-2008	1.306***	
	(0.161)	
Poverty	1.487***	
	(0.341)	
Poverty x post-2008	-1.561***	-2.748***
	(0.357)	(0.119)
Latitude x post-2008		0.713***
		(0.01)
Poverty x post-2008		-0.831***
		(0.03)
Constant	2.881***	1.266***
	(0.153)	(0.13)
Observations	7,620	7,620

Note: Estimates are based on OLS regressions. Geographic and other controls interacted with a post-2008 indicator reported in column 2. Robust standard errors in parentheses. ***= $p < 0.01$, **= $p < 0.05$, *= $p < 0.1$.

Table 13.5 Additional controls: poverty, literacy, under-five mortality, ethnic, linguistic and religious fractionalization

DV = Conflict	*Controls*	*Controls*	*Controls*
Poverty	-0.0486*		
	(0.0268)		
Linguistic fractionalization	-8.065***	-7.889***	-8.987***
	(0.268)	(0.257)	(0.460)
Ethnic fractionalization	5.683***	5.332***	4.636***
	(0.120)	(0.124)	(0.250)
Religious fractionalization	-3.649***	-3.026***	-2.865***
	(0.134)	(0.137)	(0.238)
Literacy		-0.544***	
		(0.0425)	
Under-five mortality			0.162***
			(0.0509)
Constant	4.917***	5.227***	5.401***
	(0.125)	(0.113)	(0.223)
Observations	7,620	7,620	2,341
R-squared	0.241	0.258	0.192

Note: Estimates are based on OLS regressions. Literacy and under-five mortality as additional controls reported in columns 2 and 3, respectively. Robust standard errors in parentheses. *** = $p < 0.01$, ** = $p < 0.05$, * = $p < 0.1$

7. Conclusion

This paper did an econometric analysis of a within-country study of conflict intensity and poverty in Nigeria. It was found that conflict intensity was higher in places that were exposed to greater poverty. This study supports the grievance-based analysis of poverty and conflict whereby high levels of poverty lead to a greater level of grievances against the government, thereby leading to conflicts in these areas. The study also found strong evidence that ethnic, linguistic and religious diversity were correlated with the intensity of civil conflict in Nigeria. Reducing poverty, infant mortality rates and increasing the level of education among the population may help in ensuring that conflicts are reduced in areas that are prone to conflicts. For these reasons, the findings of the study have critical policy implications in explaining the level of conflicts in Nigeria.

In addition to the gaps identified and the studies done, researchers can study the role of social protection in conflict-afflicted areas, which can lead to questions such as: To what extent does social protection contribute towards keeping social cohesion before the onset of conflict? What is the role of social protection policies during a conflict?

Cross-country studies can also be conducted to examine the predictors of conflict in each country. A similar econometric analysis can be carried out for single countries such as Rwanda and the Democratic Republic of Congo so as to understand the dynamics of conflict and poverty in these regions. This is necessary and critical at this time, as the world is battling terrorism, conflict and internally displaced persons. The methodology used in this paper is far from perfect and these imperfections can be helpful in designing further research.

Finally, the other angle of causal impacts of conflicts on the economic performance of countries can be studied to assess the policy implications of such findings on the country of study and the economics of conflict in general.

Notes

1 Detailed explanation and examples of event type can be found on the Armed Conflict Location and Events Data (ACLED) website.
2 The grievance concept refers to historical injustices, poverty and inter-group inequalities. This concept is also known as relative deprivation – the perception by one or more parties that they are being unjustly treated (Syed, 2007).
3 See www.qgis.com and www.stata.com.
4 The DHS is available on the United States Agency for International Development (USAID) website. Data was averaged over states so that there were enough observations per individual. By averaging data over states, the sample size bias that arises due to the small size of the states was eliminated.
5 Refer to Wooldridge (2003) for a thorough analysis of the multiple regression models.
6 A factor in econometric analysis that causes the effects of two different processes to be indistinguishable (same).
7 Little's study utilizes religious fractionalization as an additional control. Religious fractionalization was calculated along the lines of ethnic and linguistic fractionalization.
8 This trails the line taken by Wantchekon and Garcia-Ponce (2014)

References

Acharya, A. (2007). "The causes of insurgency in Nepal", Working Paper.

Addison, T., K. Back, T. Braunholtz-Speight (2013). "Violent conflict and chronic poverty" in A. Shepherd and J. Brunt (eds), *Chronic Poverty*. Basingstoke: Palgrave Macmillan.

Adebanwi, W. (2003). "The politics of inclusion and exclusion: Integrating the dilemmas of citizenship in Nigeria", Unpublished Mimeo.

Adesoji, A. (2010). "The Boko Haram uprising and Islamic revivalism in Nigeria/ Die Boko-Haram-Unruhen und die Wiederbelebung des Islam in Nigeria", *Africa Spectrum*, 45(2), 95–108.

Alesina, A., A. Devleeschauwer, W. Easterly, S. Kurlat, and R. Wacziarg (2003). "Fractionalization", *Journal of Economic Growth*, 8, 155–194.

Atwood, J.B. (2003). "The link between poverty and violent conflict", *New England Journal of Public Policy*, 19(1), Article 10.

Babatunde, A. and M. Cali (2015). "Income shocks and conflict: Evidence from Nigeria", Policy Research Working Paper 7213, The World Bank Group.

Barron, P.K., K. Kaiser and M. Pradhan (2004). "Local conflict in Indonesia: Measuring incidence and identifying patterns", World Bank Policy Research Working Paper 3384. Washington, DC: The World Bank.

Hettne, B. (2003). *Breeding Inequality-Reaping Violence: Exploring Linkages and Causality in Colombia and Beyond*. Uppsala: Collegium for Development Studies.

Blattman, C. and E. Miguel (2009). "Civil War", National Bureau of Economic Research, NBER Working Paper 14801.

Bohara, A., M. Neil, and N. Mani (2006). "Opportunity, democracy and the exchange of political violence: A sub-national analysis of conflict in Nepal", *Journal of Conflict Resolution*, 50(1), 108–128.

Bush, K.D. and D. Saltarelli (2000). "Two faces of education in the ethnic conflict towards a peacebuilding education for children", Technical Report, UNICEF. Innocenti Insight.

Collier, P. (1999). "On the economic consequences of Civil War", *Oxford Economic Papers*, 51(1), 168–183.

Collier, P., L. Elliot, H. Hegre, A. Hoeffler, M. Reynal-Querol, and N. Sambanis (2003). *Breaking the Conflict Trap: Civil War and Development Policy*. Oxford: The World Bank, Oxford University Press.

Collier, P. and A. Hoeffler (1998). "On the economic causes of Civil War", Oxford Economic Papers, 50, 563–573.

Collier, P. and A. Hoeffler (2001). *Greed and Grievance in Civil War*. Washington, DC: The World Bank.

Collier, P. and A. Hoeffler (2004). *Murder by Numbers: Socio-Economic Determinants of Homicide and Civil War*. Oxford: Centre for the Study of African Economies.

Cox, D.R. (1972). "Regression models and life tables (with discussion)", *Journal of the Royal Statistical Society*, 34, 187–220.

Danfulani, U.H.D. and S.U. Fwatshak (2002). "Briefing: The September 2001 events in Jos, Nigeria", *African Affairs*, 101(403), 243–255.

Deininger, K. (2003). "Causes and consequences of civil strife: Micro-level evidence from Uganda", *Oxford Economic Papers*, 55, 579–606.

Do, Q.T. and L. Iyer (2010). "Geography, poverty and conflict in Nepal", *Journal of Peace Research*, 47(6), 735–748.

Draman, R. (2003). "Poverty and conflict in Africa: Explaining a complex relationship", Expert Group meeting on Africa-Canada Parliamentary Strengthening Program, Addis Ababa, 19–23 May. Available at: www.parlcent.ca/povertyreduction/seminar1_e.pdf.

Esteban, J. and D. Ray (1994). "On the measurement of polarization", *Econometrica*, 62(4), 819–851.

Fearon, J.D. and D.D. Laitin (2003). "Ethnicity, insurgency and Civil War", *American Political Science Review*, 97(1), 75–90.

Ginifer, J. and I. Olawale (2005). *Armed Violence and Poverty in Nigeria*. Bradford, UK: Centre for International Co-operation and Security, Department of Peace Studies, University of Bradford.

Goodhand, J. (2001). "Violent conflict, poverty and chronic poverty", CPRC Working Paper 6.

Goodhand, J. and D. Hulme (1999). "From wars to complex political emergencies: Understanding conflict and peace-building in the new world disorder", *Third World Quarterly*, 20(1), 13–26.

Hill, R.C., W.E. Griffiths, and M.A. Lim (2011). *Principles of Econometrics* (4th ed.). West Sussex, UK: John Wiley and Sons Inc.

Ikejiaku, B.V. (2009). "The Relationship between poverty, conflict and development", *Journal of Sustainable Development*, 2(1), 15–28.

Ikelu, C. and E. Onyukwu (2016). "Dynamics and determinants of poverty in Nigeria: Evidence from panel survey", in A. Heshmati (ed), *Poverty and Well-Being in East Africa: A Multi-Faceted Economic Approach*. Switzerland: Springer International Publishing, pp. 89–116.

Justino, P. (2004). "Redistribution, inequality and political conflict", PRUS Working Paper No. 18, Department of Economics, the University of Sussex, UK.

Justino, P. (2006). "On the links between violent conflict and chronic poverty: How much do we really know?", CPRC Working Paper 61, Institute of Development Studies at the University of Sussex.

Justino, P. (2009). "Poverty and violent conflict: A micro-level perspective on the causes and duration of warfare", MICROCON Research Working Paper 6, Institute of Development Studies at the University of Sussex.

Justino, P. (2010). "War and poverty", MICROCON Research Working Paper 32. Brighton: MICROCON.

Kanbur, R. (2007). "Poverty inequality and conflict", Cornell University Working Paper 2007-01.

Kumar, A., K. Aphun, H. Thangjam, and K.B. Singh (2011). "Situating conflict and poverty in Manipur", CPRC-IIPA Working Paper No. 37.

Malapit, H.J., T. Clemente, and C. Yunzal (7–9 April 2003). "Does violent conflict make chronic poverty more likely? The mindanao experience", Paper presented at the conference 'Staying Poor: Chronic Poverty and Development Policy', Manchester.

Montalvo, J.G. and M. Reynal-Querol (2005). "Ethnic polarization, potential conflict and civil wars", *American Economic Review*, 95(3), 796–816.

Syed, M.M. (2007) "The Conflict-Growth Nexus and the Poverty of Nations." DESA Working Paper No. 43.

Obikili, N. (2015). "An examination of sub national growth in Nigeria: 1999–2012", *South African Journal of Economics*, 83(3), 335–356.

Otu, A.E., A.S. Ukommi and E.O. Agha (2010). "Poverty: A potential conflict escalator in Nigeria's Niger delta", *Bangladesh e-Journal of Sociology*, 7(1), 33–41.

Pinstrup-Andersen, P. and S. Shimokawa (2008). "Do poverty and poor health and nutrition increase the risk of armed conflict onset?", *Food Policy*, 33, 513–520.

Raleigh, C., A. Linke, H. Hegre, and J. Karlsen (2010). "Introducing ACLED-armed conflict and event data", *Journal of Peace Research*, 47(5), 651–660.

Rupesinghe, K., P. Sciarone, and L. van de Goor (eds.) (1996). *Between Development and Destruction: An Enquiry Into the Causes of Conflict in Post-Colonial States.* The Hague: The Netherlands Ministry of Foreign Affairs.

Thyne, C.L. (2005). *ABC's, 123's and the Golden Rule: The Pacifying Effect of Education on Civil Conflict, 1980–1999.* Available at: http://myweb.uiowa.edu/cthyne/research.htm.

Wantchekon, L. and O. Garcia-Ponce (2014). "Critical junctures: Independence movements and democracy in Africa", Unpublished Article.

Wolfson, M.C. (1994). "When inequalities diverge", *American Economic Review*, 84(2), 353–358.

Wooldridge, J.R. (2003). *Introductory Econometrics: A Modern Approach.* Cincinnati, OH: South-Western College Publishing.

14 The cost of commercial motorcycle accidents in Uganda

Richard Sebaggala, Fred Matovu, Dan Ayebale, Vincent Kisenyi, and Messarck Katusiimeh

1. Introduction

Road traffic accidents (RTAs) are among the leading causes of death and injuries globally. Globally about 1.25 million people die each year as a result of RTAs, which means that a road user dies every 30 seconds or 3,400 people die daily. It is estimated that between 20 and 50 million people also suffer non-fatal injuries, with many incurring permanent disabilities as result of injuries from RTAs (World Health Organization, 2015). In Africa, RTAs constitute 25 per cent of all injury-related deaths which claim the most economically productive population (15–59 years) (African Development Bank, 2013). Mortality and morbidity rates are higher for men than for women in Africa. This means that the impact on the economic survival of African families and societies is substantial. The World Health Organization's Global Status Report on Road Safety (2013) named Uganda among countries with alarmingly high road accident rates. It is also argued that if traffic accidents continue to increase at this trend, the health losses from traffic injuries may be ranked as second to HIV/AIDS by 2020. The death toll and injuries from road accidents have health repercussions, particularly in a country where the healthcare system is already overburdened and social protection for those surviving with life-changing injuries is lacking.

Injuries due to motorcycle accidents represent a major but often-neglected emerging public health problem in developing countries which contribute significantly to overall road traffic injuries (Kobusingye et al., 2001, 2002; Peden, 2004). Available evidence from annual crime reports shows that road safety in Uganda is poor and has deteriorated over the last 20 years. The increase in the rate of road accidents is mainly due to the growing number of vehicles and lack of appropriate road safety interventions. The number of people who died due to road traffic accidents grew from 660 in 1991 to 2,954 in 2010.

The growth of hired/commercial motorcycles (commonly known as *boda boda* in Uganda) as a mode of transportation has increased road safety challenges (Uganda Police, 2011). Statistics show that Kampala city alone had between 50,000–80,000 *boda boda* cyclists and that on average two patients died every week as a result of *boda boda* accidents. The national referral hospital (Mulago) alone receives between 10 and 20 victims of *boda boda* accidents daily. The *boda*

boda business is a money-making activity involving many players; and given the rate of unemployment in Uganda, the number of *boda boda* motorcyclists is expected to increase. This will also lead to an increase in motorcycle accidents. Evidence shows that as the number of motorcycles increases, the number of accidents, especially those involving motorcycle riders, will also increase (Umar et al., 1995; Widyastuti, 2012). Empirical evidence from elsewhere shows that the probability of a motorcyclist being injured in an accident is higher than that for a car user (Widyastuti and Bird, 2004). The pain, grief, suffering and loss of life as well as the economic consequences of *boda boda* accidents can be huge for individual victims, their families and the country. However, these have not been estimated empirically.

Notwithstanding this, the continued increase in the number of *boda boda* accidents has created a demand for necessary road safety improvements. Information and evidence on the costs of *boda boda* accidents such as immediate hospitalization and rehabilitation and indirect costs to society (for example, opportunity costs in terms of lost labor and output, lost financial support to the families and relatives of the victims, and costs in terms of disabilities and death of victims) have not been fully examined. This partly explains why interventions to prevent the problem are very few and largely ad-hoc in Uganda. There has been little effort to estimate the costs of *boda boda* accidents in the country. A recent study conducted by Makerere University College of Health Sciences and the Department of Orthopedics is the only available study on costs of *boda boda* accidents. The study reveals that at least 62.5 per cent of the budget allocated to the Directorate of Surgery at Mulago hospital was spent on victims of accidents involving *boda boda*s and that the average cost of treating a *boda boda* victim with head injuries or broken limbs was about Ugx 700,359 (or USD 280).[1] However, this study does not provide the full scale and magnitude of the cost of *boda boda* accidents because it focuses on costs borne by the health system (Kigera et al., 2010). Government and other stakeholders need accurate information and evidence, particularly on how much savings can be gained by implementing road safety improvements to address *boda boda* casualties. Anecdotal information and reporting of accidents by the media and the police traffic department limit our understanding of the extent of traffic safety problem so as to design appropriate policy action. Interventions for effective road injury prevention need to be based on data and objective information, not on anecdotal evidence. Therefore, there is a need for a comprehensive research study which estimates both direct and indirect costs of *boda boda* accidents in Uganda.

Our study is the first of its kind which provides a comprehensive estimate of the costs of *boda boda* accidents using the widely used traditional human capital method, the willingness-to-pay method and a qualitative evaluation of the pain, grief and suffering of *boda boda* accident victims. The main aim of the study is to build evidence about the cost of motorcycle accidents in Uganda and provide the rationale for investing in national road safety programs.

The rest of the paper is organized as follows. Section 2 presents a detailed review of literature on the methods that are commonly used to estimate economic costs of accidents. Section 3 presents the methodology for the study. Section 4 presents the findings obtained from multiple data sources used in the study. First, it presents the socioeconomic characteristics of the motorcycle riders who were interviewed; this is followed by estimates of the incidence of motorcycle accidents and the costs associated with the accidents. This section also gives estimates of the riders' willingness to pay for interventions to avoid fatal accidents. Section 5 discusses the results and gives the conclusions and policy recommendations.

2. Literature review

The debilitating effects of road accidents on victims, their families and society are discussed extensively in road safety literature. In addition to lost output, productivity and money spent on care and treatment, road accidents also cause considerable pain, grief and suffering, and it is the poor households that are hit the hardest when they experience a loss of an economically productive family member, or by disabilities if the accident is not fatal (African Development Bank, 2013) Overall, the adverse effects of road accidents on households, health facilities and the macro-economy in general can be substantial (Ajibola, 2015). Therefore, death and disabilities from road accidents are not only a public health problem but also a developmental problem.

Interventions for improving road safety require information on the benefits of improved safety based on imputed values or valuation of human life. There are various techniques available for valuing road casualties, including the gross output method (human capital approach), the net output method, the life insurance approach, the court awards approach (the amounts awarded by courts for compensation to survivors or surviving dependents in the case of a fatality), the implicit public sector valuation approach, the friction-cost approach (valuing the cost involved in replacing the killed or injured person to restore the previous production level) and the willingness-to-pay approach.

The traditional method of valuation is the human capital method. This method involves estimating an ex-post sum of various identifiable costs such as loss of work income and medical expenses minus the pain and suffering (Abelson, 2008). However, since the fundamental premise of welfare economics is that public policy decisions should reflect the preference of those who will be affected by them, the willingness-to-pay approach has conceptually become a more satisfactory way of measuring the costs of accidents (Abelson, 2008; Maier et al., 1989). According to Widyastuti et al. (2005), only using the human capital approach to estimate the cost of accidents is inappropriate. They recommend a combination of the human capital approach and the individual willingness-to-pay approach. A study by the Transport Research Laboratory (1995) concluded that the human capital approach should be supplemented with some human element which is subjective. It values the subjective costs using the WTP method. WTP measures how much the concerned individuals are *ready* to pay in order to improve their safety and thus provide information on the extent of the need to promote an effective intervention for the affected community.

Economic reasoning suggests that the missing price information associated with safety issues can only be substituted by the amount that the people are willing to pay for the 'product'. The method evaluates how individuals value safety, rather than reacting to how much an accident might have cost them (Widyastuti, 2012). The WTP method is considered appropriate where there is a need to pursue social welfare as a result of a reduction in accidents (Jacobs et al., 2000), it provides a practical understanding of the value that individuals or a community places on road safety (Sakashita et al., 2012) and it is a conceptually more satisfactory way of addressing the issue of accident losses (Maier et al., 1989).

2.1 *The human capital approach for cost estimation*

The human capital approach/gross output method has been widely used to classify and estimate the cost of road accidents. Table 14.1 gives the costs, data requirements, data sources and estimation procedures when applying this approach.

Table 14.1 Components of the human capital approach

Component of costs	*Data requirements*	*Data sources*	*Estimation*
Hospital/ medical costs	Hospitalization days (serious and slight injuries); daily hospital costs for serious and slight casualties; and general practitioner costs for serious and slight casualties	Hospital medical records; Survey data	$MC_i = (DST_i * HC_i) + GP_i$ Where: MC_i is medical cost of a serious or slight injury causality; DST_i is duration of stay (days of hospitalization) for injury causality; HC_i is daily hospital cost for injury causality; and GP_i is general practitioner costs for injury causality
Lost output/ productivity	*Fatal* casualties *and permanent disabilities* Average age of fatal cases; Average age of retirement; Average income (monthly earnings)	Hospital and medical records from health facilities; Police traffic data on injuries and fatalities; Survey data	Lost labor output of fatalities and permanent disabilities were computed over the rest of their expected productive working life and discounted to an equivalent present value
	Serious and slight causality Time lost due to serious and slight injury causality		Calculated as the average daily wage rate of each person involved in the crash, multiplied by the number of days off work and summing up for all the people involved in the crash
Motorcycle damage	Motorcycle damage costs	Survey data	Calculated as the average cost of motorcycle repairs multiplied by the number of motorcycles involved in the accidents

2.2 The willingness-to-pay (WTP) method

The value of an individual life reflects what people would be willing to pay (or sacrifice) to obtain benefits or to avoid costs (Jones-Lee, 1989). This ex-ante approach involves some assessment of individuals' risk and the willingness to commit resources in exchange for reducing the risk to an acceptable level. This trade-off between risk and economic resources, measured in terms of the marginal rate of substitution of wealth for risk of death or injury, accords well with the fundamental principle of the social cost-benefit analysis that public sector allocative decisions should be based on the preferences of those who will be affected by the concerned decisions.

The WTP method is used to estimate the value that individuals will pay to avoid intangible costs that result from injury or death in a motorcycle accident. The implementation of the WTP approach is through a survey questionnaire and there are two methods of collecting data in order to estimate how much an individual would be willing to pay for reducing the risk of an accident: 'revealed preferences' and 'stated preferences'. The stated preference approach is more appropriately used when the WTP information cannot be verified from the market. It is considered superior because it is possible to ask questions directly about the trade-off between risk and money and it is also possible to consider a wider and more systematic range of trade-offs than is available in the revealed preference approach (Widyastuti, 2012).

3. Methodology

Two approaches were adopted to establish the medical and repair costs and lost output as a result of *boda boda* accidents and what the individuals were willing to pay for reduced risk of injuries or death due to *boda boda* accidents: the human capital approach and the WTP approach. Estimating the cost of *boda boda* accidents using the combination of the two methods provides better value and offers policy recommendations that justify interventions for reducing road accidents in general and *boda boda* accidents in particular.

However, given that a majority of *boda boda* riders come from poor backgrounds, the direct financial and opportunity costs of accidents are the tip of the iceberg in comparison to the pain, grief and suffering of those involved in the accidents. In most of the studies using the human capital approach, a fixed percentage of the direct costs and loss of productivity is added to represent the pain, grief and suffering.

However, when implementing the stated preference approach in estimating WTP, researchers have commonly used the contingent valuation (CV) approach (Chaturabong et al., 2010). Our study also adopts this approach. Our questionnaire was designed to determine the amount of money that each *boda boda* motorcyclist would pay to reduce the risk of loss of life in an accident. The data gathered on the number of accidents, number of severities of motorcyclists per each severity type (fatal, slight and serious) and demographic information about motorcycle deaths and injuries obtained from police reports were used to get a picture of the probability of casualty involved in the accident. The questionnaire had questions related to: (1) socioeconomic and household characteristics of motorcyclists; (2) the riding and risk-taking behavior of motorcycle users such as size of engine, helmet use, experience of being involved in an accident; and (3) valuation questions which were designed to ask the respondents to provide estimates of the relevant rates that they were willing to pay for a reduction in the probability of fatalities and injuries due to *boda boda* accidents.

In the design of the CV questions, three scenarios were used to elicit respondents' willingness to pay. In each scenario both open-ended and closed-ended questions were used. The first scenario evaluated the WTP of respondents for their own risk of death; the second scenario evaluated the WTP for reducing the risk of severe injuries; and the third scenario evaluated the WTP of respondents to participate in proposed interventions by the Kampala city authority to streamline the *boda boda* industry and reduce accidents. According to Chaturabong et al. (2010), for the closed-ended questions (also referred to as 'dichotomous choice' or 'referendum' questions), a respondent was asked whether he or she was willing to pay a specified amount of money presented as the value of the risk reduction. The respondent was expected to answer 'yes' or 'no'. For opened-ended questions, a respondent was asked to state the maximum amount that he or she was willing to pay for the good that was being valued (in this case, accident risk reduction).

First scenario: risk of fatality. In the first scenario, the respondents were told that it was estimated that in Uganda on average 10 out of 100,000 people died as a result of road accidents in a year. In the closed-ended question, the respondents were asked: 'Are you willing to pay a certain amount of money to reduce fatality risks from 10 to five deaths in every 100,000 people or a 50 per cent reduction in fatality risks?' The respondent then answered 'yes' or 'no'. In the open-ended questions, the respondents were simply asked: 'How much are you willing to pay to reduce fatality risks from 10 to five deaths in every 100,000 people or a 50 per cent reduction in fatality risks?'

Second scenario: risk of severe injury. In the second scenario, the respondents were asked to imagine that they had to wear helmets while riding motorcycles. The average cost of a helmet is 50,000[2] Uganda shillings per helmet and the probability of having severe injury due to a motorcycle accident was 10/100,000 each year. In the closed-ended question, the respondents were asked: 'Are you willing to pay 50,000 Ugandan shillings to buy a helmet which can reduce the risk of severe injury from 10 to three severe injured people in every 100,000 people or reduction in the risks of severe injury by 70 per cent?' The respondent then answered 'yes' or 'no'. The second question asked if respondents were willing to pay for the helmet if its price was increased – over a range of prices up to the average maximum price of Ugx 140,000 derived from the pilot.

Third scenario: *boda boda* streamlining program by Kampala Capital City Authority (KCCA). As pointed out earlier, KCCA has plans of streamlining the *boda boda* industry through a number of efforts, including registration of *boda boda* riders in the city, training the riders, issuing operational permits, supplying reflector jackets and helmets, gazzetting stages and introduction of wardens, among others. Out of these proposed interventions, we considered two options: (1) supply of reflector jackets and helmets, and (2) training because these interventions are directly related to reducing accidents. The closed-ended question was: 'If the cost of getting a reflector jacket and helmet (or training) was 100,000 Uganda shillings[3] (and higher price ranges) would you be willing to pay this amount to reduce the number of motorcycle accidents and injuries by half each year in Kampala?' The second question was: 'What is the maximum amount of money that you will pay to get a reflector jacket and helmet (or training) to reduce the number of *boda boda* accidents and injuries by half each year in Kampala?'[4]

According to Krupnick et al. (2002), many contingent valuation (CV) studies fail to pass the test of internal and external validity because of three problems: (1) respondents may not understand the risk changes they are being asked to value; (2) respondents may not believe that the risk changes apply to them; and (3) respondents may lack experience in trading money for quantitative risk changes or lack the realization that they engage in this activity. These pitfalls are challenging because of the low levels of education of the respondents. Our approach in dealing with the problem was to explain to the respondents using real examples about probabilities and risk reductions during the contingent valuation survey. Evidence shows that a brief training of the respondents in the survey regarding probability, risk and risk changes enabled them to process risk information better and hence give more elaborate reasons about their preferences for risk reduction (Mahmud, 2005). This fact was established during a pre-test of the survey instruments and was emphasized during the course of the study.

In the CV questionnaire, we exposed the concepts of probability of different events occurring, risks and implications of risk changes, such as flipping a coin, to determine which team started a football match and buying a lottery ticket as examples to introduce the concept of probabilities to the respondents. Mortality risks were discussed using the example of risk of dying in a traffic accident. The respondents were asked test questions after each example. If the respondents got the answers right, then the enumerator proceeded to WTP questions, otherwise the process was repeated until the respondents got it right.

3.1 Sample size and sampling

Our study's participants were selected from two divisions within Kampala district: central and Kawempe (randomly selected from the four divisions on the outskirts of Kampala). The rationale for this is that besides the central division, the other divisions are largely homogenous in a number of aspects such as traffic flow. We expected the central division to have comparatively unique characteristics because of higher risks associated with high concentrations of traffic. Therefore, using the fish *bowl* sampling *technique,* Kawempe division was randomly selected out of the four divisions on the outskirts (Nakawa, Makindye, Lubaga and Kawempe).

Based on Muhumuza's (2012) study, Kampala central and Kawempe divisions had 550 and 350 stages of *boda boda* riders, respectively, in 2012.

To ensure that the *boda boda* stages selected were representative of the *boda boda* population in the selected divisions of Kampala city, we used the following formulation to determine the appropriate sample size of *boda boda* stages in the study:

$$n = \frac{Nz^2}{(E^2)*(N-1)+z^2} \tag{1}$$

where n = sample size, N = total population (900 stages), Z = z-table value (1.96) and E = sampling error value (0.05).

Using this formula, 400 *boda boda* stages were selected and covered in both Kampala central and Kawempe divisions. The number of *boda boda* stages in each division that participated in the study was determined by probability proportionate to size (PPS) of the *boda boda* stage in each division (Table 14.2).

We selected four *boda boda* riders randomly from each stage using a list of riders at each stage with the help of the chairperson of the respective *boda boda* stage. A total of 1,600 respondents were interviewed in the study.

3.2 Data processing and analysis

To ensure a sound statistical analysis, reliable data sources and fully evidenced conclusions, we did the following at the design, data collection and analysis stages: the design of the data included templates and survey questionnaires to ensure that useful and robust data was collected. Secondary data from hospital records, national aggregates and traffic police reports was obtained for the human capital approach. In estimates of the costs of accidents (direct and indirect) using the human capital method, secondary and survey data was used to provide a complete picture of motorcycle accident costs at individual and national levels.

For the contingent evaluation survey that was used to elicit *boda bodas*' willingness to pay to reduce motorcycle accidents, we controlled for response biases such as yeah-saying and non-responses by providing relevant information before eliciting the participants' willingness to pay; a pilot study was also done to identify any shortcomings. We used the payment card (PC) as the elicitation method to determine WTP. Respondents were asked to choose the maximum values that they were willing to pay using both closed- and open-ended questions.

Table 14.2 Number of motorcycle stages selected for the survey

Division	*Existing number of motorcycle stages*	*Number of motorcycle stages selected*
Kampala central	550	(550/900 × 400) = 244
Kawempe	350	(350/900 × 400) = 156
Total	900	400

Computation of value of statistical life

The aim of using the WTP approach was to estimate *boda boda* riders' marginal rate of substitution (*MRS*) between money and reducing the risk of being killed in a *boda boda* accident. Therefore, to compute the value of statistical life (VOSL) and its covariates, we applied an approach which is similar to what was used by (Maier et al., 1989). If we denote the *i-th* *boda boda* rider's marginal rate of substitution by MRS_i,

$$\text{then the estimate for } MRS_i = \frac{b_i}{5/100{,}000} = \frac{b_i^{100{,}000}}{5} \tag{2}$$

For example, in our study, *boda boda* riders were asked about their willingness to pay to reduce fatality risks from 10 to five deaths in every 100,000 people or a 50 per cent reduction in fatality risks. If the answer was b_i, then the marginal rate of substitution could be estimated. In a population of *N boda boda* riders, the average of MRS ($\sum_i MRS_i \frac{1}{N}$) was interpreted as the willingness to pay for a risk reduction which reduced the expected number of the deaths by 1(5). This is referred to as the value of statistical life (VOSL) or the marginal value of safety (MVS). Based on individual evaluations, we examined the influence of a rider's socioeconomic characteristics and different attributes (age, education, experience, marital status, monthly income, motorcycle ownership, number of dependents and ever experienced an accident). In estimating the regression model, we adopted a log-linear model (where MVS is in the logs) specification over linear specification with the help of the Box-cox test.[5]

Computation of lost output/productivity

Lost output/productivity refers to the losses suffered by a country as a result of the loss of productive capacity of the people affected by motorcycle accidents. The total average lost output for a fatal motorcycle accident is the sum of each future year's lost output, which was estimated based on the following formula adopted from Anh et al. (2005):

$$\text{Lost output (fatality)} = \sum_{i=1}^{N} \frac{W(1+g)i}{(1+r)i} \tag{3}$$

where W = average yearly per capita gross domestic product, r = discount rate, g = growth rate of the economy and i = average number of years of lost output per fatal accident.

In our study we included both the average and median age of victims of fatal accidents for better information; this was estimated at 35 and 28 years, respectively.[6] The average loss of productive years was computed based on a retirement age of 60 years. Hence, the average number of years foregone by a fatal motorcycle accident were 25 and 32, respectively. The average GDP per capita was 1.4 m Uganda shillings ($558) in 2013. The average growth rate of the economy for the last 10 years was 7 per cent. Therefore, the g considered in this study is 7 per cent.

The discount rate (r) considered is 12 per cent based on *prime interest rates* in Uganda (the Central Bank rate). N is 571, based on the number of motorcyclists who were reported dead by the police in 2011–12 (Uganda Police, 2011).

4. Findings

4.1 Socioeconomic characteristics of respondents

A total of 1,600 respondents from 400 *boda boda* stages in Kampala were interviewed. The respondents were hired/commercial motorcycle users who worked in the central and Kawempe divisions in Kampala. The socioeconomic and demographic information collected included age, education, marital status, experience, occupation in other economic activities and previous employment, daily and weekly earnings, number of dependents, type of motorcycle and ownership of motorcycle. Tables 14.3 and 14.4 give the socioeconomic characteristics of *boda boda* motorcyclists.

Table 14.3 Socioeconomic characteristics of *boda boda* motorcyclists

Characteristics	*Frequency (n = 1,600)*	*Per cent*
Education		
No education	83	5.2
Primary education	712	44.5
Secondary education	763	47.7
Post-secondary	42	2.6
Marital status		
Single	251	15.7
Married	1,334	83.4
Divorced/separated	15	0.9
Previous employment status		
Employed	1,265	79.1
Additional sources of income		
Nothing else	1,004	62.8
Farming	214	13.4
Salaried employment	27	1.7
Other	282	17.6
Casual workers (building/driving)	73	4.6
Motorcycle ownership		
Self fully paid	839	52.4
Self on loan	328	20.5
Contracted	426	26.6
Others	7	0.44

Source: Survey data

Table 14.4 Descriptive statistics

Variable	*Obs*	*Mean*	*Std. Dev.*	*Min*	*Max*
Daily income	1,600	22,236.9	7,701	5,000	60,000
Weekly income	1,600	131,573.8	47,047	10,000	420,000
Age (years)	1,600	30.3	6.1	17	65
Number of dependents	1,549	5.5	3.2	1	30
Rider's experience	1,600	5.8	3.7	0.08	24

Source: Survey data

Many people view the *boda boda* business as an extremely odd job, implying that only the less educated and less significant sections of the people are engaged in it. However, our survey results reveal that more than 50 per cent of the *boda boda* riders had received secondary and higher education, 83 per cent were married, 79.1 per cent were previously employed, 62.8 per cent relied on the *boda boda* business and nothing else, and 73 per cent owned the motorcycles.

Table 14.4 shows that *boda boda* riders on average earned more than the average monthly income of a Ugandan from all sources standing at Ugx 303,700 according to the Uganda Bureau of Statistics Household Survey (2009–10). For instance, the average daily and weekly incomes of *boda boda* cyclists in Kampala varied in the interval 22 and 574 Uganda shillings, respectively. According to estimates of a 2012 statistical abstract based on household consumption expenditure data of the Uganda Bureau of Statistics, about 50 per cent of the richest households in Kampala spent at least 475,500 shillings per month on consumption as of financial year 2009–10 (at 2005–06 constant prices). Therefore, putting these figures into perspective vis-à-vis a *boda boda* rider's income per month, this implies that *boda boda* riders were among the richest income earners in Uganda. What is not clear is whether the *boda boda* riders knew this fact because it has a bearing on their spending behavior in particular and attitude to road safety in general.

Table 14.4 also shows that the average age of *boda boda* riders was 30 years. This implies that a majority of the *boda boda* riders were from the young population. With respect to the number of dependents and experience in the *boda boda* business, it is evident from Table 14.4 that the average number of dependents per cyclist was 5.5 and a rider had experience of 5.8 years. One can infer from the riders' experience and the fact that a majority of riders had been previously employed (79 per cent) and focused on the *boda boda* business alone (63 per cent) that *boda boda* riders were not in the *boda boda* occupation because of economic hardships and high rates of unemployment but out of choice like other people are in their occupations. This implies that *boda boda* riders did appreciate and love their occupation and for purposes of safety they would be willing to accept any changes that improve their work and welfare.

Table 14.5 Involvement in motorcycle accidents

Category	*N*	*Percentage (%)*
Reported having been involved in motorcycle accidents	1600	55.1
Reported having been involved in motorcycle accidents once	882	65.8
Reported having been involved in motorcycle accidents more than once	882	34.2
Know a friend/associate who has been involved in an accident	1600	96.6

Source: Survey data

4.2 *Incidence of motorcycle accidents*

Out of the 1,600 motorcycle riders who participated in the survey, 55.1 per cent riders had experienced at least one accident. Table 14.5 shows that 34.2 per cent of the riders had experienced more than one accident in their lifetime as *boda boda* riders. The respondents were also asked whether they had any friends or associates who had been involved in a motorcycle accident that resulted in an injury. More than 96 per cent of the respondents answered in the affirmative. These figures indicate that a majority of the *boda boda* riders had been involved in motorcycle accidents that resulted in injuries.

4.3 *Cost components of motorcycle accidents in Uganda*

The cost components are estimated in two groups: tangible and intangible. Tangible costs include cost of treatment (medical expenses) and repair costs. Intangible costs include lost output, pain, grief and suffering based on the WTP approach.

Medical costs of motorcycle accidents

Although medical costs constitute only a small proportion of the total costs of motorcycle accidents, they are the first and most tangible economic burden experienced by a victim and his immediate family and friends. Table 14.6 shows the total medical costs based on data estimates from the survey and Mulago hospital. The results show that medical costs for a cyclist who was seriously injured translated into 7,977,135 Uganda shillings. If we consider the data from the Uganda police department between January–December 2012 when 3,043 motorcyclists were reported to have been seriously injured as a result of motorcycle accidents, this translates into 24,274,423,022 Uganda shillings or approximately 24 billion Uganda shillings.

Even when we consider slightly lower estimates for better results from the Mulago hospital study by Kigera et al. (2010) of 56,740 Uganda shillings and 8.3 days as the average cost of a patient in a ward and hospitalization days, respectively, medical costs for motorcycle accidents both to the individual and the country as a whole are substantial (Table 14.7).

Table 14.6 Medical costs of *boda boda* accidents

Components	*Description*	*Amounts/ days*	*Total medical cost (DST*HS) + GP in Uganda shillings per cyclist*
DST	Duration of days away from work as a result of injury/days of hospitalization (obtained from the survey)	46.6	
HS	Hospital costs for injury causality (average treatment cost of injury obtained from survey)	156,154	
GP	General practitioner costs for injury causality (obtained from the Mulago study; represents the average cost for a *boda boda* patient)	700,359	
Total			7,977,135.40
	If we consider the total number of persons who were seriously injured as a result of motorcycle accidents between January–December 2012 based on the Traffic Police Report data		24,274,423,022

Source: Survey data, the Police Traffic Department and Mulago's study

Table 14.7 Medical costs of *boda boda* accidents

Components	*Description*	*Amounts/ days*	*Total medical cost (DST*HS) + GP in Uganda shillings per cyclist*
DST	Days of hospitalization	8.3	
HS	Average cost of maintaining a patient in a ward	56,740	
GP	General practitioner costs for injury causality (obtained from the Mulago study; represents the average cost for a *boda boda* patient)	700,359	
Total			1,171,301
	If we consider the total number of persons who were seriously injured as a result of motorcycle accidents between January–December 2012 based on Traffic Police data		3,534,268,943

Source: Survey data, the Police Traffic Department and the Mulago study

Lost output/productivity

An analysis of the survey data reveals that an estimated 389 *boda boda* riders were away from work due to serious injuries involving motorcycle accidents, amounting to an average of 46.6 lost days of work (Table 14.8). Valuing this missed time for the workers' actual daily incomes, an estimated 403 million Uganda shillings of economic output was lost due to time off from productive activities. Using police data from 2012 which reported 3,043 motorcycle accidents with serious injuries and based on the average number of days away from work and average daily income from the survey, it is evident that over 3 billion Uganda shillings of economic output was lost in 2012.

In addition, computation of the lost output due to premature deaths in motorcycle accidents was Uganda shillings 446,963 per cyclist, translating into 255,216,071 Uganda shillings in 2012 if we consider the number of persons

Table 14.8 Lost output due to serious motorcycle accidents and fatalities

Lost productivity due to serious motorcycle injuries				
	Number of days away from work due to serious injuries in accidents (average)	Average daily income	Number of people involved	Total cost (Uganda shillings)
Study sample	46.6	22,237	389	403,098,994
Estimates based on 3,043 motorcycle accidents in 2012 (as reported by the police)	46.6	22,237	3,043	3,153,291,101
Lost productivity due to fatal motorcycle accidents				
	average GDP per capita (W)	$(1+g)^i$	$(1+r)^i$	Total cost (Uganda shillings) $W((1+g)^I/(1+r)^i)$
Average age	1,400,000	(1 + 0.07)^25	(1 + 0.12)^25	446,963
Median age	1,400,000	(1 + 0.07)^32	(1 + 0.12)^32	324,663
Based on police data (2012) when 571 persons died as a result of motorcycle accidents = N				
Average age	Lost output =			255,216,071
Median age				185,382,316

Source: Survey data, the Police Traffic Department, Mulago hospital and the Ministry of Finance, Planning and Economic Development

killed as a result of motorcycle accidents in January–December 2012 and average age at death at 35. The computation of economic loss based on a median age of 28 years still presents a huge economic loss to the nation amounting to 185,382,316 Uganda shillings. These findings imply that prevention of fatalities in motorcycle accidents and disabilities from severe injuries could have significant economic pay-offs.

Repair costs

In our survey we established the cost of repairs for those respondents who had motorcycle accidents. The results in Table 14.9 show that, on average, ***boda boda*** riders spent three times their daily incomes on motorcycle repairs (79,524 Uganda shillings). However, the average costs for severe injuries were higher (115,098 Uganda shillings), implying that the costs of motorcycle repairs increase with the severity of the accident. Therefore, 70 and 44 million Uganda shillings on average were spent on repairs by all accident victims and those who reported severe physical injuries, respectively. Estimating the repairs costs based on 3,043 severe motorcycle accidents reported in the police data in 2012, the country lost approximately 350 million Uganda shillings.

4.4 *Willingness to pay for reducing fatalities*

In any attempt at valuing the impact of any policy on society, researchers measure people's strength of preference for safety initiatives using the WTP approach and compute VOSL. VOSL is a convenient way to summarize the value of small reductions in mortality risks. This is what economists refer to as the monetary value of reducing mortality risks, commonly called 'value of life' (a reduced form of the value of statistical life (VOSL)). Alternative terms for VOSL are ***value per statistical life***, ***value per life saved*** and ***value of prevented fatality***. VSL does not measure what an individual is willing to pay to avoid death with certainty. It measures the willingness to pay for a very small change in risk.

To understand the VOSL concept and our computations, we now demonstrate the concept and how we arrived at the figures presented in Table 14.9 with an example: suppose that in a city composed of 100,000 identical individuals (in this case motorcycle riders in Kampala), there is an investment project that will make the city's roads safer. However, based on police data, it is known

Table 14.9 Expenditure on repairs due to motorcycle accidents

Variable	*Mean*	*Std. Deviation*	*Total cost (Ugx)*	*Total costs (USD)*
All accidents (n = 882)	79,524	129,744.70	70,140,168	28056
Severe injuries (n = 389)	115097.7	161329.3	44,773,005	17909

Source: Survey data (1 USD = 2,500 Ugx)

that on average 10 motorcyclists die every year on these roads and the project is expected to reduce the number of expected fatalities from 10 to five per year. This implies that the annual risk of dying due to a motorcycle accident is 10 for 100,000 people and the anticipated project or intervention will reduce this number from 10 to five. In a statistical sense, this means that the project or any safety intervention will reduce the annual risk of dying in a motorcycle accident by 0.0005 (5/100,000). In a population of 100,000, in a statistical sense any safety intervention is expected to result in five fewer deaths from motorcycle accidents each year. Suppose now that each member of the city (in this case a *boda boda* rider) is willing to pay 222,550 Ugx (average amount obtained from the survey) annually to reduce the risk of dying in a motorcycle accident from 10 to five in 100,000 people (half the number of fatalities in 100,000 people). Therefore, the value of preventing one fatality in one accident is defined as the aggregate amount that all affected individuals in society are willing to pay for these small risk reductions. The corresponding VOSL will be Ugx 222,550/(5/100,000) = (222,550*100,000)/5 = Ugx 4,450,000,000 (or USD 1,780,000). This represents the estimated value of life.

In our study out of the 1,600 *boda boda* riders, over 96 per cent were willing to pay for a risk reduction which lowered the expected number of deaths from 10 to five in 100,000 people. This implies that *boda boda* riders in Kampala are willing to pay the price for reducing the risk of fatal motorcycle accidents. Figure 14.1 gives the distribution of the willingness-to-pay values. It is evident from the figure that *boda boda* riders are willing to pay between 3,000 and 5 million Uganda shillings to reduce the number of deaths in motorcycle accidents from 10 to five in 100,000 people. However, a majority are willing to pay less than 100,000 Uganda shillings and between 100,000–500,000 Uganda shillings (49.3 per cent). The average amount that the riders are willing to pay is 222,550 Uganda shillings per year or they are willing to forfeit 222,550 Uganda shillings a year to

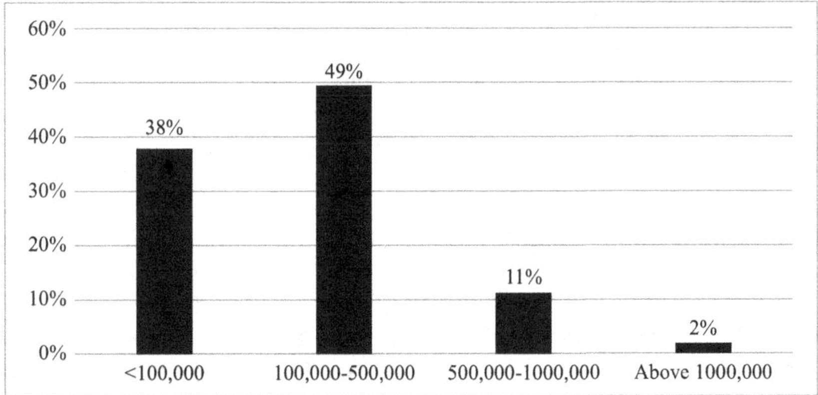

Figure 14.1 WTP values

Table 14.10 Estimated VOSL

Description		Average MRS for all
Marginal rate of substitution (MRSi)	Income change due to a unit change in a risk given by: $\frac{b_i}{5/100{,}000} = \frac{b_i^{100{,}000}}{5}$ *b_i represent the average amount the* boda boda *riders were willing to pay, which is equivalent to Ugx* 222,550	respondents gives the WTP for a risk reduction which reduces expected deaths by 1(5)
Total WTP	This value is referred to as the value of saving a statistical life or marginal value of safety	4,450,000,000 ($1,780,000)

reduce the risk of dying in motorcycle accidents from 10 in 100,000 people to five in 100,000 people.

Table 14.10 gives the value of statistical life for Uganda by using the contingent valuation. Our results on willingness to pay to reduce fatalities in motorcycle accidents indicate that *boda boda* riders were prepared to pay, on average, Ugx 222,550 for a risk reduction of five in 100,000. Therefore, the 'value of an average life' in this instance would be (Ugx 222,550 × 100,000)/5 = Ugx 4.45 billion. This is defined as the total amount that *boda boda* riders selected in Kampala will pay per year to save five statistical lives in motorcycle accidents.

3.5 Economic burden of motorcycle accidents

To estimate the economic burden of motorcycle accidents in Uganda, we combined the medical costs of accidents, lost output due to severe injuries and fatalities, and repair and human costs (pain, grief and suffering). The computation of lost output is based on 2012 police data that reported the number of persons killed and injured in motorcycle accidents. In 2012, there were 3,043 officially reported severe motorcycle accidents in which 571 people died. These figures exclude the number of persons who had minor injuries. In estimating medical expenses, the computations are based on results obtained from a study by Mulago hospital on the cost of treating a *boda boda* patient. Pain, grief and suffering are calculated as a percentage of lost labor output due to injuries and fatality. The percentages considered are based on the Asian Development Bank's estimates of 28 per cent and 50 per cent of the total cost of a fatal and injury accident, respectively. Table 14.11 shows the estimated economic burden of motorcycle accidents in Uganda to be Ugx 8,902,482,162 (approximately USD 3.6 million). Although these figures do not take into account the administrative and funeral costs of motorcycle accident victims, they reveal that the current level of motorcycle accidents is associated with a reduction in the country's growth prospects of

Table 14.11 Estimates of the economic burden of motorcycle accidents at the national level

Variable	*Total cost (Ugx)*	*Total cost (USD)*	*Per cent contribution*
Medical expenses	3,534,268,943	1,413,708	39.7
Lost output due to a severe injury	3,153,291,101	1,261,316	35.4
Lost output due to a fatality	225,216,071	90,086	2.5
Repair costs	350,000,000	140,000	3.9
Human costs (pain, grief and suffering)	1,639,706,050	655,882	18.4
Total	8,902,482,165	3,560,993	100.0

about USD 3.6 million annually. Medical expenses and lost output due to severe injuries are the biggest component of motorcycle costs, contributing 40 per cent and 35 per cent, respectively.

3.6 Factors influencing WTP values

The relationship between WTP values (rider's marginal value of safety) and the underlying influence of socioeconomic factors was investigated by means of a regression analysis. The log-linear regression model was applied to analyze the significant factors influencing respondents' willingness to pay. The independent variables considered in the analysis included the age in complete years, motorcycle riding experience, education dummies, marital status, motorcycle ownership status and a dummy if ever experienced an accident. The results of the regression analysis are given in Table 14.12.

The results in Table 14.12 show that only three variables were statistically significant: income, marital status and motorcycle ownership. From an economic point of view, the positive significant effect of income concurs with many studies that have found that higher incomes are associated with higher WTP values. As expected, riders who owned motorcycles significantly and positively influenced WTP values. Surprisingly, however, being married was associated with less WTP values as compared to unmarried motorcycle riders. In many studies, age has proved to be an important factor in explaining willingness to pay for safety. However, in our study age was not statistically significant, although it had the right sign. The other factors that were insignificant were education, number of dependents, riding experience and accident experience. The negative coefficient of education and riding experience suggest that these variables were not only unimportant in a rider's risk evaluation, but they were also associated with lower MVS.

Table 14.12 Regression analysis results

LnMVS	*Coef.*	*p-value*
Age	0.007	0.282
Monthly income	0.000	0.023*
Riding experience	-0.005	0.649
Primary	-0.190	0.182
Secondary	-0.159	0.264
Married	-0.150	0.076**
Number of-dependents	0.001	0.936
Ever_Had_Accident	-0.049	0.436
Own motorcycle	0.217	0.002*
Constant	21.289	0.000
Number of Observations = 1,541		
R-squared = 0.02		

Note: *= statistically significant at 5%, **= statistically significant at 10%

5. Conclusion and policy recommendations

The descriptive analysis of our study shows that the incidence and risk of motorcycle accidents is high and *boda boda* riders are largely to blame in most of the accidents that they are involved in. Therefore, safety initiatives should mostly address the behavior of motorcycle riders alongside other road users. For instance, public awareness campaigns are needed to change the behavior of motorcycle riders and also for enforcing legislative traffic regulations and measures. It is perhaps true that most *boda boda* riders do not understand the health and economic implications associated with their reckless behavior. Our study's results provide rich information that will be helpful for fact-based advocacy to change the behavior of *boda boda* riders. Information on the costs of accidents to an individual and to society as a whole can be used by *boda boda* associations, local administrations, authorities and civil society organizations to influence behavior change among *boda boda* riders. Awareness campaigns by these stakeholders should communicate the health and economic consequences of undesirable traffic behavior and associated motorcycle accidents to the riders. The police should intensify the use of a combination of enforcement and penalties to prevent the violation of traffic regulations, thus increasing road safety.

This study highlighted the direct and indirect costs of motorcycle accidents in Uganda using a multi-method approach. Quantitative estimates and descriptions from qualitative interviews provide both tangible and intangible costs of motorcycle accidents (both for fatalities and severe injuries). The estimates were found to be huge for a poor developing country. This information should help provide a momentum for improving the safety of the motorcycle industry in Kampala and the rest of the country.

The study provides estimates of intangible costs (such as medical expenses, lost output/productivity due to injuries and death and repair costs). The estimates show that motorcycle accidents are associated with huge burdens that are borne by accident victims and their families and friends, as well as by society as a whole. The estimation and presentation of these costs highlights the need for every member of society to recognize and be aware of the importance of road safety. The results also show that it cost approximately 7 million Uganda shillings to treat a *boda boda* accident victim who was severely injured and more than 3 billion Uganda shillings were lost due to days away from productive work as a result of severe injuries and death. Motorcycle repair costs were 350 million Uganda shillings based on 2012 police data on motorcycle accidents.

The study also provides estimates of the value of preventing motorcycle accidents based on the willingness-to-pay method using a contingent evaluation. The estimates show that on average *boda boda* riders are willing to pay Ugx 222,550 a year for reducing mortality risks associated with motorcycle accidents; this translates into 4.45 billion Uganda shillings ($1,1,780,000), the value of statistical life (VOSL). This implies that *boda boda* riders are willing to spend 4.45 billion Uganda shillings per year for risk reduction, which reduces the expected number of motorcycle fatalities from 10 to five in 100,000 people. This represents the monetary value of increased safety and shows that *boda boda* riders are concerned about traffic safety and are also willing to pay a sizeable amount of money for improved safety. The estimates are comparable to those from other developing countries. A regression analysis of the factors influencing marginal value of safety (MVS) revealed that income, marital status and ownership of motorcycles significantly influenced a rider's evaluation of safety. The results on the effects of motorcycle ownership on MVS should be of interest to the government and *boda boda* associations in their efforts to streamline the industry. Attempts that enable riders to own the motorcycles seem to affect safety evaluations.

The economic burden of motorcycle costs were approximately USD 3.6 million. Although these figures do not take into account the administrative and funeral costs of motorcycle accidents, the estimates reveal that if motorcycle accidents continue, the country's growth prospects will fall by USD 3.6 million annually. Medical expenses and lost output due to severe injuries formed the biggest component of motorcycle costs, contributing 40 per cent and 35 per cent, respectively. The fact that current initiatives and the level of investments are inadequate in stopping or reversing increasing motorcycle fatalities and injuries, political will and funding levels in the sector should be commensurate with the scale of accidents and associated economic costs.

The results of our study demonstrate that the economic costs of motorcycle accidents to the economy are huge in terms of output losses due to mortality and disabilities. The costs associated with motorcycle accidents such as lost output due to death and injuries, medical expenses for treatment and repair costs are poverty-inducing problems. At a macro-level, Uganda's economy loses about USD 3.6 million annually due to motorcycle accidents. These resources can be used for poverty-reducing interventions. At the individual level, reducing motorcycle accidents can contribute significantly to savings in healthcare, repair costs and income losses, which can be put into consumption or investment for improving household welfare.

More specifically, the paper presented the monetary value of increased safety from motorcycle accidents in Uganda and presented social and economic rationale for safety investments and interventions for improving road traffic safety for motorcyclists. The key policy implication of the study is that reducing motorcycle casualties and fatalities by promoting the use of helmets, reflector jackets, awareness campaigns and training on road safety and regulations will reduce the social and economic sufferings of victims, unlock growth and free resources for more productive use. The findings provide a cost-benefit analysis of investments in areas that will promote the prevention, treatment, care and management of motorcycle accidents in Uganda.

Notes

1 The average exchange rate at the time of the study was USD 1 = Ugx 2,500.
2 The average cost of a helmet of different types and from a range of market outlets within the capital city.
3 The range of actual costs was established from the market and by using KCCA records.
4 The results for scenarios 2 and 3 are not presented in this paper, but they show that the willingness to pay for a helmet reduced more significantly as we varied the cost of helmet from Ugx 20,000 to Ugx 140,000 shillings. With respect to the interventions that KCCA proposes to implement in an effort to streamline the *boda boda* industry in Kampala, the results show that 54 per cent of the riders interviewed were not willing to pay for these activities and therefore KCCA will face some challenges in changing the face of the *boda boda* industry in Kampala.
5 Box Cox = $N/2*\log(RSS_{largest}/RSS_{smallest}) \sim \chi 2$. If the estimated value exceeds the critical value (from tables Chi-squared at the 5 per cent level with 1 degree of freedom is 3.84), then *reject* the null hypothesis that the models are the same (that is, there is a significant difference in terms of goodness of fit).
6 These figures were obtained from the Mulago hospital database of people who had died as a result of *boda boda* accidents.

References

Abelson, P. (2008). "Establishing a monetary value for lives saved: Issues and controversies", Working Papers in Cost-Benefit Analysis, WP 2008-02. Applied Economics and Department of Economics, Sydney University.

African Development Bank (2013). *Mortality in Africa: The Share of Road Traffic Fatalities.* Tunis: ADB.

Ajibola, M.A. (2015). "Impact assessment of road traffic accidents on Nigerian economy", *Journal of Research in Humanities and Social Science*, 3(12), 8–16.

Anh, T.T., N.X. Dao, and T.T. Anh (2005). "The cost of road traffic accident in Vietnam", *Eastern Asia Society for Transportation Studies.* Kampala: Uganda Police, 1923–1933.

Chaturabong, P., K. Kanitpong, and P. Jiwattanakulpaisarn (2010). "Analysis of motorcycle accident costs in Thailand by willingness to pay method", *Transportation Research Board*, 1(4), 1–17.

Jacobs, G., A.A. Thomas, and A. Astrop (2000). *Estimating Global Road Fatalities.* London: DFID, Department for International Development.

Jones-Lee, M.W. (1989). *The Economic of Safety and Physical Risk.* London: Blackwell.

Kigera, J., L. Nguku, and E.K. Naddumba (2010). "Magnitude and impact on clinical services of injuries attributable to Bodaboda accidents as seen at Mulago hospital", *East and Central African Journal of Surgery*, 15(1), 57–61.

Kobusingye, O., D. Guwatudde, and R. Lett (2001). "Injury patterns in rural and urban Uganda", *International Society for Child and Adolescent Injury Prevention Journal*, 7(1), 46–50.

Kobusingye, O.C., D. Guwatudde, G. Owor, and R.R. Lett (2002). "Citywide trauma experience in Kampala, Uganda: A call for intervention", *International Society for Child and Adolescent Injury Prevention Journal*, 8(2), 133–136.

Krupnick, A., A. Alberini, N. Simon, B. O'Brien, R. Goeree, and M. Heintzelman (2002). "Age, health and the willingness to pay for mortality risk reductions: A contingent valuation survey of Ontario residents", *Risk and Uncertainty Journal*, 24(2), 1010–1023.

Mahmud, M. (2005). "Contingent valuation of mortality risk reductions in developing countries: A mission impossible?", Working Paper in Economics, 2005–169, Gothenburg University.

Maier, G., S. Gerking, and P. Weiss (1989). "The economics of traffic accidents on Austrian roads: Risk lovers or policy deficit?", *Empirica Journal*, 16(2), 177–192.

Muhumuza, S. (2012). *Evaluation Report for the Helmet Use Project Among Commercial Boda Boda Operators in Kampala Under the Uganda Helmet Vaccine Initiative.* Kampala, Uganda: Uganda Helmet Vaccine Initiative.

Peden, M. (2004). "Safety, commentary World Health Day. World Health Organization dedicates World Health Day to road safety", *Injury Prevention Journal*, 10(2), 1110–1136.

Sakashita, C., S. Jan, and R. Ivers (2012, October 4). "The application of contingent valuation surveys to obtain willingness to pay data in road safety research: Methodological review and recommendations." A paper presented at the Australasian Road Safety Research, Policing and Education Conference 2012, Australia, Sydney. Available at: http://acrs.org.au/files/arsrpe/Sakashita%20et%20al%20%20The%20application%20of%20contingent%20valuation%20surveys.pdf.

Transport and Road Research Laboratory (1995). *Costing Road Accidents in Developing Countries (10).* London: Transport and Road Research Laboratory.

Uganda Police (2011). *Annual Crime and Traffic Road Safety Report.* Kampala: Uganda Police.

Umar, R.S., M.G. Mackay, and B.L. Hills (1995). "Preliminary analysis of exclusive motorcycle lanes along the Federal Highway F02, Shah Alam, Malaysia", *IATSS Research*, 19(2), 93–98.

Widyastuti, H. (2012). *Valuing Motorcycle Casualties in Developing Countries Using Willingness to Pay Method: Discrete Choice Modelling Approach School of Civil Engineering and by Stated Preference.* Newcastle, UK: University of Newcastle.

Widyastuti, H. and R.N. Bird (2004). "Assessing the social cost of motorcycle casualties in developing countries", *Universities Transport Study Group*, 1(7), 1–20.
Widyastuti, H., C. Mulley, and D. Dissanayake (2005). "Binary choices model to value motorcyclists slight injury cost in Surabaya", *Eastern Asia Society for Transportation Studies Journal*, *7*(1997), 2674–2685.
World Health Organization (2015). "World Health Statistics", *Journal of Chemical Information and Modeling*, 53(1). Geneva: World Health Organization.

Index of authors

Index of subjects

Printed in the United States
By Bookmasters